A FIELD GUIDE TO
EASTERN
BUTTERFLIES

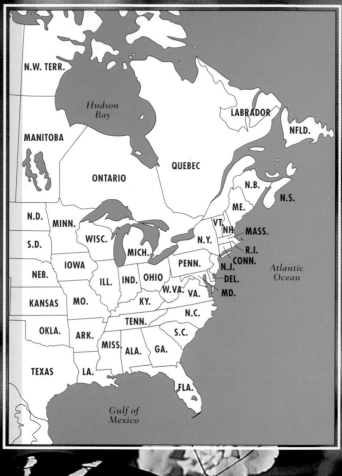

N.W. TERR.

Hudson Bay

LABRADOR

MANITOBA

NFLD.

ONTARIO

QUEBEC

N.B.

N.S.

N.D.

MINN.

ME.

VT.

NH

MASS.

WISC.

N.Y.

R.I.

S.D.

MICH.

CONN.

IOWA

ILL.

IND.

OHIO

PENN.

N.J.

DEL.

Atlantic Ocean

NEB.

W.VA.

VA.

MD.

KANSAS

MO.

KY.

OKLA.

ARK.

TENN.

N.C.

S.C.

MISS.

ALA.

GA.

TEXAS

LA.

FLA.

Gulf of Mexico

A FIELD GUIDE TO

EASTERN
BUTTERFLIES

PAUL OPLER

Illustrated by
VICHAI MALIKUL

SPONSORED BY THE NATIONAL AUDUBON SOCIETY,
THE NATIONAL WILDLIFE FEDERATION, AND
THE ROGER TORY PETERSON INSTITUTE

HOUGHTON MIFFLIN COMPANY
BOSTON   NEW YORK

PETERSON FIELD GUIDES and PETERSON FIELD GUIDE SERIES
are registered trademarks of Houghton Mifflin Company.

LIBRARY OF CONGRESS CATALOGING-IN-PUBLICATION DATA

Opler, Paul A.
A field guide to eastern butterflies : Paul Opler ;
illustrated by Vichai Malikul.
p. cm. — (The Peterson field guide series)
"Sponsored by the National Audubon Society, the National Wildlife
Federation, and the Roger Tory Peterson Institute."
Includes bibliographic references (p.   ) and index.
ISBN 0-395-90453-6
1. Butterflies—East (U.S.) 2. Butterflies—Canada—Eastern.
3. Butterflies—Greenland. I. Title. II. Series.
QL551.E16065 1998
595.78'9'0974 — dc21   98-13623

Book design by Anne Chalmers
Typeface: Linotype-Hell Fairfield; Futura Condensed (Adobe)

PRINTED IN THE UNITED STATES OF AMERICA
RMT 10 9 8 7 6 5 4 3 2

We dedicate this book to the late

ALEXANDER BARRETT "BILL" KLOTS,

who wrote the original version of this Field Guide.
He first published his book in 1951 and
forever changed the ways that we
think about and study our
butterfly fauna.

Editor's Note

As a young man growing up in upstate New York, I became interested in the natural world at an early age. I have always had a great interest and concern for butterflies and their natural history. I can remember a time when Pipevine Swallowtails invaded our area. This butterfly does not normally occur in upstate New York, but I was able to find their caterpillars and raise them to beautiful adult butterflies.

In my youth, there was no Field Guide for the identification of butterflies; the standard handbook was W. J. Holland's cumbersome *Butterfly Book*, first published in 1897. After I began my Field Guide series with the first two bird guides, the *Field Guide to the Butterflies*, by Alexander (Bill) Klots, first published in 1951, was one of the first guides. Bill Klots's book was the first modern identification guide to our butterflies. It opened up the application of ecology to butterflies and was the first to express concern about the conservation of butterfly populations.

Through the years my interests in butterflies have continued undiminished. I am very concerned with the conservation of butterflies and moths. Almost from its founding by Robert Michael Pyle, I have been a counselor to the Xerces Society, an international invertebrate conservation group. I have been especially concerned with the decline and virtual disappearance of the large silk moths (Family Saturniidae) from much of the East.

Both my wife, Virginia, and I engage in butterfly photography at home and on most of our trips — except of course on Antarctica, where penguins thrive rather than butterflies. I commend photography as one way to develop a collection without actually killing the objects of our interest. Virginia has cultivated a butterfly garden outside my studio in Connecticut, and butterflies are in view much of the year.

The Klots guide upholds a standard of quality to which many

other butterfly books have aspired but seldom met. Now, more than 40 years later, I am proud to present this new Field Guide by Paul Opler, with marvelous illustrations by Vichai Malikul. This new work covers the more than 500 species now known from our territory.

The species accounts are up to date and are nicely complemented by the illustrations and range maps. Whether you live in eastern Canada, Ohio, or south Texas, you will find this guide equally useful. The introductory chapters give a good grounding in many topics of concern to natural historians. They explain butterfly structure and biology, their distribution and conservation, and gardening for butterflies.

Paul Opler and Vichai Malikul have provided you with this wonderful new butterfly book. I urge you to take it with you on all of your trips afield. You might wish to study it on long winter nights, to dream of surprises you will find in spring, when the days grow longer and warmer and the first butterflies appear.

ROGER TORY PETERSON

ACKNOWLEDGMENTS

The following reviewed portions of the species treatments for errors of omission or commission: C. D. Ferris, D. Harvey, R. O. Kendall, R. C. Lederhouse, C. D. MacNeill, E. M. Pike, R. K. Robbins, R. E. Stanford, and S. R. Steinhauser. M. C. Nielsen and G. Tudor read and critiqued the entire species accounts section.

The interlibrary loan section of Colorado State University's Morgan Library assisted in obtaining those hard-to-locate references that helped make the treatment as complete as possible.

R. A. Layberry provided extensive data on Canadian butterflies, including a summary of the holdings of the Canadian National Collection at Ottawa.

The following provided technical advice, data, or other assistance, much of it extensive: T. J. Allen, G. T. Austin, H. D. Baggett, R. A. Bailowitz, G. J. Balogh, A. F. Beck, W. F. Boscoe, J. P. Brock, F. M. Brown, V. R. Brownell, J. M. Burns, J. V. Calhoun, S. J. Cary, C. V. Covell, Jr., N. Dankert, K. Davenport, J. M. DeWind (deceased), J. F. Doyle, R. L. Edwards, F. C. Elia, C. A. Ely, J. H. Fales, F. D. Fee, C. D. Ferris, L. A. Ferge, H. A. Freeman, T. P. Friedlander, L. F. Gall, G. B. Gier, J. Glassberg, P. C. Hammond, C. E. Harp, D. Harvey, J. R. Heitzman, D. F. Hess, A. M. Holmes, D. C. Iftner, B. S. Jackson, F. H. Karpuleon (deceased), R. O. Kendall, A. B. Klots (deceased), E. C. Knudson, B. C. Kondratieff, G. O. Krizek, J. D. Lafontaine, R. A. Layberry, C. W. Leahy, W. W. McGuire, G. M. Marrone, J. R. Maudsley, E. H. Metzler, D. G. Miller, J. Y. Miller, L. D. Miller, M. C. Minno, R. Mitz, J. M. Nelson, Jr., M. C. Nielsen, C. G. Oliver, K. S. Pado, H. Pavulaan, J. P. Pelham, J. R. Powers, W. B. Preston, R. M. Pyle, E. L. Quinter, J. E. Riddlebarger, J. and N. Riggenbach, R. K. Robbins, R. C. Rosche, R. A. Royer, P. J. Savage, J. A. Scott, D. Schlicht, J. H. Shepard, J. A. Shuey, A. C. Smith, M. J. Smith, R.

E. Stanford, A. B. Swengel, J. W. Tilden (deceased), G. Tudor, C. Tufts, T. W. Turner, W. H. Wagner Jr., R. K. Walton, S. Williams, and D. M. Wright.

For graciously lending specimens under their care: M. D. Bowers (Museum of Comparative Zoology), J. M. Burns (Smithsonian Institution), C. V. Covell, Jr. (University of Louisville), C. Darling (Royal Ontario Museum), G. Godfrey (Illinois Natural History Survey), K. C. Kim (Pennsylvania State University), B. C. Kondratieff (Colorado State University), J. D. Lafontaine (Canadian National Collection), J. A. Powell (California Insect Survey), F. H. Rindge (American Museum of Natural History), R. K. Robbins (Smithsonian Institution), C. A. Triplehorn (Ohio State University), M. J. Weissmann (University of Colorado).

Studies in Texas's Lower Rio Grande Valley were facilitated by R. Farmer, Audubon Society Sabal Palm Grove Sanctuary; D. E. Prichard, Manager, Santa Ana National Wildlife Refuge; and D. Riskind, Texas Parks and Wildlife. R. O. Kendall, M. C. Minno, J. Struttmann, A. D. Warren, and W. D. Winter kindly provided analyses of errors and inconsistencies that are corrected in this reprinting.

H. Foster, S. Kunhardt, and L. White of Houghton Mifflin Co. provided many suggestions that improved the design and quality of the manuscript, while R. T. and V. Peterson hosted the author and provided advice and materials. D. Carlson, BioGraphics, Fort Collins, Colo., executed the black and white illustrations, while C. M. Lemos, also of Fort Collins, labeled the color plates.

Photographs are by Paul Opler, except where noted. For provision of some color slides, we are indebted to George O. Krizek (Plate 2, figures 1, 2, and 7; Plate 4, figures 2, 6, and 7; and pages 135, 239, 264, and 267), Jim Ebner (page 190), and to John R. Riggenbach (page 278).

Finally, the author lovingly remembers his late wife Sandra, who died just before publication of this guide, and the artist thanks his wife Nit fondly for her love and patience.

Paul A. Opler
Vichai Malikul

PREFACE

My interest in butterflies was kindled in 1948 when my friend Peter Robinson and I admired the butterflies enameled onto the lid of his mother's jewelry box. We set out with nets made of discarded nylon stockings (with runs) and wire coat hangers. Our only book was a small nature guide with crude paintings of 20 or so butterfly species — primarily eastern. Since we lived in California, of course almost none of the butterflies we encountered were in this book. Later I acquired William Holland's *Butterfly Book*, first published in 1898, and Comstock's 1927 *Butterflies of California*. Then came Alexander Klots's *Field Guide to the Butterflies* in 1951. What a breath of fresh air to read a book that treated butterflies as living organisms to be understood, not merely as specimens to be acquired. His discussions of ecology, biology, and distribution spurred my growing interest in biology, distribution, and host plants.

My interest in butterflies and the field of entomology was further encouraged by my parents and teachers. My fifth grade teacher, Mrs. McKeon, arranged for my friend and me to tour the entomology collection at the University of California at Berkeley. Similar kinds of encouragement continued through grammar school and high school, so that by the time I entered college, U.C. Berkeley—of course!—my course was already set.

Although I grew up with western butterflies and now live in Colorado, I have had extensive experience with eastern butterflies. My introduction to them came when I was a nature counselor in a summer camp near Bear Mountain, New York, in 1960, and my knowledge of eastern habitats and species grew during 1962 and 1963 when I was a newly married army enlistee in New York City. During that time I was able to travel throughout much of New England. Later, beginning in 1974, my first permanent position in the U.S. Fish and Wildlife Service was in Washington,

D.C. From there I was able to travel throughout much of the Southeast and Appalachians, and was able to study eastern butterflies in the extensive Smithsonian Institution collections.

I studied eastern butterflies and their natural history in the field and through photography. George Krizek and I wrote an encyclopedic book on eastern U.S. butterflies that was published in 1984, and at the end of this process I had become an "authority" on eastern species—only to find my governmental position transferred to Colorado.

In developing this book I extended my range west to the 100th meridian and north of the U.S. border to include all of eastern Canada. I carefully reviewed the available literature and gathered detailed distribution records so as to be sure to include all species that occur or have occurred within the book's area. Roy Kendall of San Antonio, Texas, and Ross Layberry of Ottawa, Ontario, played major roles in providing extensive distributional information on Texas and Canadian butterflies, respectively.

I have included all species documented to occur in the East, and have tried to provide the most important kinds of information for each species: What are the identifying marks? Where is its range and habitat? When does it fly?

Chapters on butterfly biology, butterfly study, butterfly gardening, and butterfly conservation should make this book especially useful to the growing army of butterfly observers and photographers. Collectors will find it useful as well, but though collection is necessary to identify some difficult skipper species, most butterflies can be identified without killing them. The collection of specimens is still important in some instances, but I feel strongly that collected individuals should be useful and should not merely be stockpiled.

Perhaps the book's most attractive feature are the excellent plates painted in acrylic and watercolors by Vichai Malikul. These are without doubt the most complete and accurate portrayals of eastern butterfly species. Mr. Malikul, who was born in Bangkok, Thailand, is a self-taught illustrator who enjoyed drawing portraits and scenery from an early age. After graduating from high school in 1962, Vichai was hired as a biological illustrator in the medical laboratory of the Southeast Asia Treaty Organization in Bangkok, Thailand. When he came to the United States in 1967 to further his art education, Mr. Malikul joined the Smithsonian Institution as a scientific illustrator in the Southeast Asia Mosquito Project. Sixteen years later, Vichai transferred to the Smithsonian's Department of Entomology, where he has been illustrating small Lepidoptera for Dr. D. R. Davis. Mr. Malikul studied advertising art at the National Art Academy in Washington, D.C.

and graduated in illustration and photography from Montgomery College. He has illustrated many scientific monographs on mosquitoes, and his art has been hung in the Smithsonian and has graced the covers of national scientific journals. His illustrations in this guide are his first extensive experience in butterfly illustration. Mr. Malikul is justly proud of these color paintings, which required thousands of hours of painstaking detailed work. He considers these illustrations to be the culmination of his dreams, and hopes that they will be appreciated by the users of this guide for several decades.

Vichai Malikul is active in the Guild of Natural Science Illustrators and is a leader in the U.S. Thai community, in 1991 becoming Executive Vice President of the Asian Pacific American Heritage Council. He and his wife, Phaungthong (Nit), and their two daughters live in Maryland.

CONTENTS

LIST OF ILLUSTRATIONS

Range maps and photographs distributed throughout the book

LIST OF PLATES (grouped after page 43)

A FIELD GUIDE TO

EASTERN BUTTERFLIES

How to Use This Book

This book replaces Alexander Klots's 1951 *Field Guide to the Butterflies*. The first field guide on butterflies in the Peterson series may have been the most widely sold and used book on North American insects. Klots's book stimulated a revolution in the way we look at and think about butterflies, just as the first bird guide by Roger Tory Peterson revolutionized bird study in North America. Now, more than 40 years after its first publication, discovery of additional butterfly species, many changes in nomenclature, expanded knowledge of species' life histories, and extensive new information on butterfly distribution necessitated the preparation of this completely new Field Guide.

The sequence of species follows the 1981 Miller and Brown checklist and catalogue of North American butterflies, except that the true butterflies (Superfamily Papilionoidea) appear before the skippers (Superfamily Hesperioidea). The choice of generic and species names is conservative and generally follows those that appear in Opler and Krizek's 1984 treatment of eastern butterfly life histories. English names follow the list published by the North American Butterfly Association (Glassberg 1995).

Identification

SPECIES INCLUDED: The number of butterflies east of the 100th meridian is greater than that to the west of it. Although only 422 species were reported by Klots in his original field guide to the butterflies, there are now known to be 524 species in the East. This is due to new colonists from the south being found in Florida and southern Texas, the ranges of western and arctic butterflies now known to extend east of the 100th meridian, and newly discovered butterfly species.

AREA COVERED: The area of North America to the east of the 100th meridian and north of the Mexico-U.S. boundary and the Caribbean including the eastern United States, eastern Canada including the Canadian arctic archipelago, and Greenland (see map opposite title page).

ILLUSTRATIONS: Most species are illustrated by color paintings executed by Vichai Malikul. All species resident in the area covered, as well as nonresidents with five or more occurrences, are illustrated. A few distinctive species with fewer than five occurrences are also illustrated. We have selected the most diagnostic views to illustrate the species. The upperside is indicated by the portrayal of the left-hand wings and the body, the underside by wings pointed to the right without the body. We have tried to show that portion of the butterfly that can be used for identification without capture. For example, most hairstreaks perch with the wings closed above the body. In some instances, however, the critical characteristics are on portions of the butterfly that can be seen only if the insect is netted.

Photographs of caterpillars and chrysalids on Plates 2–4 show typical examples of these life stages. Since the color paintings (Plates 5–39) show butterflies with their wings spread, the photographs throughout the text are intended to give an idea of how free-living adult butterflies appear in nature.

MEASUREMENTS: Size of each butterfly is given in both inches and millimeters, the latter in parentheses. In most cases these are based on actual measurements. These are intended to give the normal expanse of the butterfly from one wing-tip to the other. For many butterflies one sex is normally larger than the other. These differences are not mentioned in the species accounts unless they are extreme, but general tendencies are mentioned in the family or generic statements.

EARLY STAGES: Only the last instar of the caterpillars (larvae) is described, and that only in very general terms, since the book is intended as an identification guide to adult butterflies. The plants used as food by the caterpillars are listed. Common names are given in the text for most familiar species, and scientific names may be found in the index to plants. Scientific names are given in the text only for unfamiliar or rare plants. The flight dates for the adult insects are given, and if the species ranges widely in the East, some indication of flight period differences in several areas is given. For butterflies found rarely in southern Texas, the months of occurrence are given, but the dates when the butterflies are known in their permanent range to the south in Latin America is also given. This will give a better idea of when the butterfly might be expected north of the Mexican border. When the number of distinct adult flights (broods) is known, this is given in parentheses following the flight period.

RANGE: The entire range of the butterfly is given with greatest emphasis on its occurrence in eastern North America. If the butterfly also occurs in Eurasia, this fact is indicated by the word *Holarctic*. The occurrence in the West and the range in Latin America, including the butterfly's southern limit, is given in general terms. In addition to the text description, range maps are included for most species. These are usually on the same page with the species account. Many private collections, museums, and the literature were exhaustively combed for distributional information to construct the range statements and maps. Major contributors and state compilers are listed in the acknowledgments. The maps were originally executed by Mark Foerster of Fort Collins, Colorado, under the guidance of BioGraphics, Inc. The maps were re-created in color by Larry Rosche. On the maps, pink indicates the region where each butterfly is resident, while blue indicates places that the butterfly might appear as a stray or may colonize and become a temporary resident. Yellow dots indicate the extralimital appearance of strays where the species is not expected to appear on a regular basis.

HABITAT: The key to finding butterflies in nature oftens depends on a knowledge of their habitats. This knowledge also is an important aid to identification. For example, the very similar Eyed Brown and Appalachian Brown occur in very different habitats—the former in open marshes, the latter along wooded streams or at the edges of wooded swamps. Knowledge of the habitats of tropical butterflies is often scanty, but I have made a good attempt to describe the habitats of these extralimital species. Strays often may be found in habitats not typical of their resident territory.

ABOUT BUTTERFLIES

WHAT ARE BUTTERFLIES?

Whenever I give a talk on butterflies, I am invariably asked, "What is the difference between butterflies and moths?" This question once had the facile answer: "Butterflies fly in the day, are brightly colored, have clubbed antennae, and lack the wing coupling mechanism, the frenulum, possessed by most moths." Recently, a group of tropical American "moths" has been shown to possess the detailed structure of butterflies rather than that of geometrid moths to which they had been assigned. These butterflies, then, are the Hedyliidae, and are most closely related to the true butterflies (Superfamily Papilionoidea). They are nocturnal and lack the clubbed antennae of most other butterflies.

Now when I am asked the butterfly vs. moth question, I respond that "butterflies" are a related group of the Order Lepidoptera. They *tend* to be primarily diurnal, and have clubbed antennae; but butterflies are really just part of the vast evolutionary variation in the order. Butterflies have become popular partly because they are conspicuous and because there are neither too few nor too many species to pique our interest.

STRUCTURE

Butterflies share many traits with other related insects. The adults have compound eyes, antennae, three main body divisions (head, thorax, and abdomen), three pairs of legs, and a hard, chitonous exoskeleton (Fig. 1). They share with other higher Lepidoptera their two pairs of scale-covered wings, suctorial tubelike proboscis, and long filamentous antennae.

HEAD: Looking in greater detail, we find the antennae are made up of separate segments. The underside of the terminal club is the

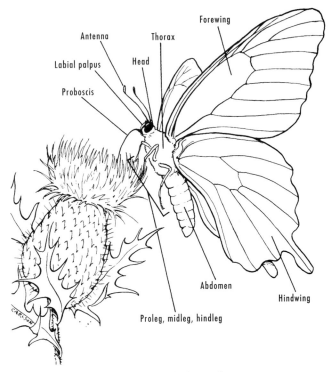

Antenna

Labial palpus

Head

Proboscis

Thorax

Forewing

Proleg, midleg, hindleg

Abdomen

Hindwing

Figure 1. Parts of the butterfly

nudum. The antennal clubs of true butterflies are rounded, but in most skippers there is an extension, the *apiculus.* The adult's compound eyes are composed of a variable number of separate visual elements, the *ommatidia.* It has been shown that most insects, including butterflies, can see better in the ultraviolet wavelengths, including those not detectable by human sight. On the underside of the head, the coiled *proboscis* lies between the two three-segmented *labial palpi.* The antennae contain sensory organs and cells to help with balance, motion, and smell. The proboscis is used to take in fluids such as moisture from wet sand or mud, nectar from flowers, and fluids from ripe fruit, sap flows, carrion, or dung. The length of the proboscis is a good indication of the adult food habits. It is relatively long in nectar-feeding species, especially skippers, and is relatively short in butterflies that feed on sap flows or rotting fruit. The palpi serve as "bookends" for the proboscis. They may be long and directed forward as in the Snout Butterfly or curved upward as in most gossamer wings.

THORAX: The thorax is composed of three segments—the *prothorax, mesothorax,* and *metathorax.* A pair of legs is attached to each thoracic segment, and the wings are attached to the mesothorax and metathorax. Each leg consists of several segments. Beginning at the leg's origin next to the body, these segments are the *coxa, trochanter, femur, tibia,* and five-segmented *tarsus.* At the end of each leg is a *tarsal claw* surrounded by a pad or *pulvillus.* The front legs *(prolegs)* of butterflies in some families are strongly reduced and are not used for walking. The best known of these are the brushfoots or Nymphalidae, but snouts, metalmarks, and gossamer wings have reduced front legs in at least one sex. Internally, the thorax is largely muscular, containing the muscles that move the wings and legs. The thoracic muscles in some butterflies may aid in warming the body through shivering.

ABDOMEN: The elongated abdomen contains the majority of the digestive, excretory, and reproductive organs. It also contains the most important energy storage structures, the *fat body.* At the end of the abdomen are the external genitalia. These structures have been shown to be of importance in the separation of butterfly

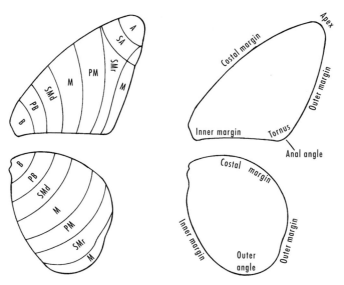

Figure 2. Parts of butterfly wing areas and margins

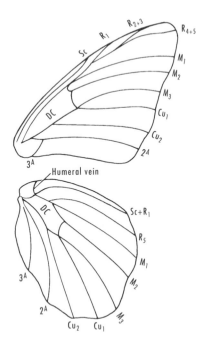

Figure 3. Butterfly wing veins

species by taxonomists. Some species, especially certain tropical skippers, can be identified with certainty only by killing them and dissecting their genitalia. These species are mentioned in the book, but the associated genitalia features are not described.

WINGS: Adult butterflies have two pairs of wings, the *forewings* and the *hindwings*. The wings are used by butterflies not only for flight; they also play an important role in courtship, regulating body temperature, and avoiding predators. The colors and patterns on both surfaces of the wings are among the most obvious features of these insects, and they play an important role in the identification of species.

Each wing is made of two chitonous sheets that are pressed together and enclose a system of lengthwise veins, with a few strengthening cross structures. Both surfaces of the wings are covered with overlapping rows of tiny scales. The scales are usually finely ribbed and may be pigmented. *Androconia* are scales that appear modified to be dispensers of sex attractants—the *phero-mones*. Androconia or modifed sex scales occur on the wings, legs, or bodies of adults, usually males. On the wings they may be scattered or appear in specialized patches or "brands." The scales may be in folds of the forewings (some skippers) or hindwings (some swallowtails). Identifying field marks are usually located by referring to specific areas of the wings or specific veins or *cells,* or spaces enclosed by specific veins. Each of these areas, veins, and cells has a name; all are labeled in Figs. 2 and 3.

The areas and margins of the wings are shown on Fig. 3. Proceeding from the base toward the outer edge, these areas are: *basal, postbasal, submedian, median, postmedian, submarginal,* and *marginal.* The margins are the *costal* for the leading margin, the *outer* for the outer edge, and the *inner* for the trailing edge. The tip of the forewing is termed the *apex,* while just in from the apex are the *apical* and *subapical* areas. The junction of the hindwing's outer and inner margins is the *tornus.*

The veins have had both letter and number systems devised by different workers. Current specialists prefer the letter system (Fig. 3). In a clockwise sequence (on righthand wings) these veins or vein systems are lettered *Sc* (subcostal), *R* (radial), *M* (medial), *Cu* (cubital), *A* (anal). All but the subcostal have more than one branch, and these are numbered with subscripts proceeding from the most forward branch, e.g. R_1, R_2, R_5. As mentioned above, the areas between veins are the cells, and the most basal of these is termed either the *cell* or *discal cell.* The other cells are named for the vein or vein branch in front of it.

LIFE HISTORY

The life cycle of butterflies is termed complete, because there are four different stages—the *egg, larva* (caterpillar), *pupa* (chrysalis), and *adult* (Fig. 4). The complete life cycle is shared by other advanced insects such as beetles, flies, caddisflies, and wasps (*Holometabola*), but less advanced groups such as grasshoppers and true bugs (*Hemimetabola*) have only three stages—the egg, nymph, and adult. In butterflies, each life stage may proceed directly through its development. If there is no resting stage, the entire life cycle, from deposition of the egg to emergence of the adult, requires about a month for most butterflies. The egg hatches in about five days; the caterpillar stage, which involves four or five instars with a molt after each one, takes about 15 days; the adult emerges about 10 days after formation of the chrysalis. The summer generations of butterflies with more than one flight period each year develop directly in the manner described above.

Most species of butterflies have a resting stage at one or two points in their life cycle. If the rest is merely a slowdown of metabolism due to cold temperature, it is termed *hibernation,* but if it is a physiological arrest, usually triggered by a seasonal change in day length, it is called *diapause.* Diapause is a way that insects have evolved to space out their stages so that the adults emerge when weather is likely to be favorable and caterpillars hatch when there is food to eat. Hibernation or diapause occurs at distinctive times in the cycle of different species or higher groups. Some species, usually those of arid western habitats, can spend several years in diapause, usually in the pupal stage.

EGGS: Females lay eggs singly or in groups. They are usually laid directly on the host plant, but in some species, such as fritillaries *(Speyeria),* they may be dropped on the ground near dried violets, or they may be attached to other plants or objects next to the host. The female detects the proper host plant by sensory cells on her prolegs or antennae. Inside the egg, the development of the insect embryo takes place. If development proceeds directly, the egg will hatch in a period ranging from a few days to about a week.

LARVAE: The young caterpillar's first solid food may be its eggshell. The caterpillar begins to eat immediately after hatching, or it may enter diapause, as do most fritillaries *(Speyeria).* Young caterpillars usually eat more tender materials (young leaves or flower buds) than they do in their later instars. Since the skin of the caterpillar does not grow or stretch, it must be exchanged for a new one several times during larval development. As the caterpillar grows, the new skin is developing underneath the old one. When its skin becomes relatively taut, molting is stimulated; the old skin splits, and the larva emerges with a new skin and head capsule. Caterpillars usually pass through four or five instars, and the color patterns and sizes and distribution of setae (the "hairs" of the caterpillar) usually differ with each instar. Some species may undergo diapause or hibernation in the caterpillar stage. Caterpillars of Cabbage Whites *(Pieris rapae)* and sulphurs *(Colias)* usually hibernate, while those of many satyrs (Subfamily Satyrinae) often undergo diapause.

Most caterpillars live solitarily, but those of several species, usually those whose eggs are laid in groups, feed communally, at least for the first few instars. Examples of such species are frequent in the brushfoots, for example, checkerspots, patches, crescents, tortoiseshells (including the Mourning Cloak), and emperors. In other families, communal feeding is rare; among our resident gossamer wings it is found in the Atala *(Eumaeus atala),* and the Gold-banded Skipper *(Autochton cellus)* is the only North American skipper with such behavior.

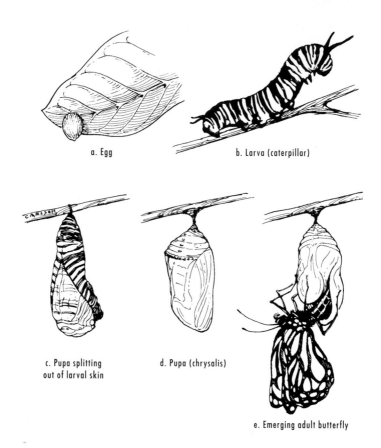

a. Egg

b. Larva (caterpillar)

c. Pupa splitting out of larval skin

d. Pupa (chrysalis)

e. Emerging adult butterfly

Figure 4. The four life stages of the Monarch butterfly

Relatively few butterflies have caterpillars that feed in the open during broad daylight. Most live in folded or bunched leaf shelters or hide during the day under loose bark or in leaf litter. Caterpillars found feeding in the open are either distasteful or possess physical deterrents, such as spines, that discourage would-be predators. The searching ability of insect parasites, usually tiny wasps or flies, is so highly developed that they usually discover and parasitize most butterfly eggs and caterpillars. Remember that, on average, only two of the hundreds of eggs laid by each female butterfly must complete their development and reproduce to ensure the next generation.

CHRYSALIDS: When the caterpillar completes its feeding, it usually leaves the host plant and wanders to find a sheltered spot where it will form its chrysalis. The chrysalis is an immobile (except for giant-skippers), nutritious object that would make a welcome meal for many predators. Different species pupate in different sorts of situations. For example, many gossamer wings form their pupae in leaf litter or loose soil under their host plant, while swallowtails often pupate on tree trunks. The caterpillars of most butterflies make a silk mat into which the cremaster, a hook at the distal end of the chrysalis, is set. This is done in one deft movement as the skin of the last caterpillar instar is discarded. Inside the chrysalis, the structures of the caterpillar are broken down and the adult structures are formed.

ADULTS: Upon emergence from the chrysalis, the adult butterfly must expand its wings by pumping its body fluid (called hemolymph — insects do not have blood in the usual sense) through its still-soft veins. After expanding, the adult usually rests for an hour or more before the wings can support flight.

Each butterfly species has a different adult life span, and different generations of the same species may have very different life expectancies. Some butterflies have a life expectancy of only a few days upon emergence. The Barred Yellow (*Eurema daira*) and several blues are examples of such short-lived species. In most situations a life span of a week or two is normal, and much longer life spans are exceptional. Butterflies that have delayed egg development, such as some fritillaries (*Speyeria*) and wood-nymphs (*Cercyonis*), or that overwinter as adults may have much longer life spans. The winter (dry season) generation of many tropical butterflies, such as are found in southern Florida and southern Texas, must survive for at least three or four months to lay eggs at the beginning of the next growing season. The generation of the Monarch (*Danaus plexippus*) that migrates south for the winter lives six or seven months, whereas the adults of the summer generations live only a few weeks. Female Zebras (*Heliconius charithonius*) develop their eggs slowly and may lay only one or two eggs a day over a period of several months. The northern butterflies that overwinter as adults, tortoiseshells (*Nymphalis milberti* and *N. vau-album*) and anglewings (*Polygonia*), may live for six months. The Mourning Cloak (*Nymphalis antiopa*), which usually has only a single generation each year, is the butterfly longevity champion at 10 to 11 months. You can determine the life span of butterflies near where you live by capturing them, putting distinctive marks on their wings with square-tipped marking pens, and then watching for them later.

FINDING A MATE: The adult butterfly spends its time searching for mates, mating, laying eggs, and in maintenance activity (feeding and resting). Each butterfly species has one of two primary mate-locating strategies. The males of *patrolling* species fly through likely habitats in search of receptive females, while the males of *perching* species select a perch on top of a leaf, twig, or rock, and fly out to investigate passing insects in hopes they may be receptive females. If the passing insect is a receptive female, the male forces her to the ground and the steps leading to mating take place. If the passing insect is another male, who might also have a nearby perch, the two will often engage in an upwards spiraling flight, after which one male, usually the resident, will return to his perch or another one nearby. If the passing insect is another species (or if the butterfly encounters an inanimate object) the male will almost immediately return to his perch after only a perfunctory investigation. This behavior of perching males has been termed territoriality by some and aggressiveness by others. But only in a few butterflies does it seem that the males actually *defend* an established territory, although the spiral flight of interacting males does seem to spread the males through the environment. In mountainous areas, especially in the west of our area, perching males will select hilltops as their perching sites, and unmated females will orient toward hilltops. The perching mate-location method seems to work best for species that are relatively rare in the environment.

FEEDING: Adults have only a suctorial proboscis and cannot chew solid foods. As a result they feed on sugar-rich or proteinaceous fluids to renew their energy reserves. Many butterflies feed on the nectar of flowers, and many others, especially brushfoots, feed on sap flows, rotting fruit, bird droppings, or dung. Freshly emerged butterflies, usually males of patrolling species, gather in groups on wet sand or mud to imbibe water rich in salts. It is thought that this salt intake may have a role in temperature regulation, especially cooling.

KEEPING WARM: Butterflies are cold-blooded; that is, they have no internal mechanism that keeps their body temperature at a constant level. In order to become active and engage in flight and other daily activities, butterflies must warm their bodies to a certain level. This is usually done by basking in full sun. Some butterflies are *lateral baskers*; these species sit with their wings closed, holding them perpendicular to the sun. These species may have black or otherwise darkened scales under their wings, especially where they overlap the abdomen. *Dorsal baskers* perch with their wings opened to take full advantage of the sun. In cool or cloudy weather, butterflies may not fly at all, or they may have to alight frequently to bask.

An adult butterfly has a schedule that it adheres to each day. Flight usually does not begin until after eight o'clock (daylight-saving time), although some tropical skippers may become active before sunrise! During the day, males may restrict their courtship activities to particular hours or may seek mates all day. In any event, mating pairs are usually seen only during a characteristic part of the day, and egg laying (oviposition) is usually limited to a few hours. For example, sulphurs (*Colias*) usually lay eggs only around midday.

ROOSTING: Each species of butterfly has a characteristic roosting posture and location that it assumes during inclement weather or overnight. Most butterflies perch with their wings closed, with their head directly downward, and their antennae straight ahead. Many tropical butterflies that roost under large leaves do so with their wings open, and duskywings roost with their wings wrapped around a small twig. Some species roost under leaves, some on tree trunks, and some in low, dense vegetation. A few tropical species roost in caves or under cliff overhangs. Most butterflies roost alone, but some form communal roosts. Most notable are the roosts that heliconians, including the Zebra, return to night after night.

How to Study Butterflies

Butterfly awareness and appreciation among the public has increased appreciably in recent years. The fact that large animals are not readily accessible to city-dwellers and suburbanites has increased interest in bird watching and appreciation of invertebrates. Another element in the growing army of butterfly aficionados are birders who seek new challenges. Most people who use this book will probably be those interested in observing and photographing butterflies, while those interested in starting or continuing a collection will be in the minority. Concern about conservation and the need to prevent inhumane treatment to all animals are in part behind these trends.

BUTTERFLY WATCHING

Butterfly watching can be carried out casually, with little or no equipment. On the other hand, you may get involved in scientific study through observation, or you may wish to take trips to remote locations to see butterflies not found near your normal haunts.

WHAT TO TAKE: Obviously, you should have a copy of this Field Guide. Binoculars or opera glasses are very helpful. The binoculars should be capable of focusing at close distances (five or six feet). They should have low magnification (6–8X) and have good light-gathering capability. Bring a small pocket notebook to record your observations. Write down the date and time of each observation. If you wish to capture specimens that are difficult to identify or so that a small group may observe a common species more closely, you should have an insect net. You should have a pair of forceps; the tongs used for handling postage stamps are excellent. Handle any butterfly gently by the forewing costal margin. You may want small glassine envelopes or small transparent containers in which to hold butterflies briefly so that they can be passed around in a small group and then released.

WHEN TO WATCH: In southern Florida and south Texas, adult butterflies may be observed throughout the year on any day warm enough for butterfly activity—generally above 60°F (15°C). As you move northward or to higher elevations, the butterfly season will be increasingly brief. In the tundra or above the timberline, the butterfly season lasts about two months, mid-June to mid-August. At middle latitudes in the East, look for butterflies beginning in April. You may expect to find them until there have been nights with temperatures below freezing.

The best conditions are found on clear, calm, warm days. Normally butterflies begin their daily activity about nine o'clock and continue until about four o'clock, but in midsummer when it is warmest, some butterflies become active shortly after sunrise, and some are still active until after six o'clock. If you're interested in photographing butterflies, go out early when they are just becoming active or on overcast days when they're not fully active.

You should look for butterflies at different times during the season, as different species have different flight periods. Some have just a single flight in the spring; some have a single flight in the summer or fall; many have two or more flights during the year.

In early spring, as buds are just beginning to open, over much of the East you can find Falcate Orangetips, the first whites, Spring Azures, Silvery Blues, elfins, duskywings, overwintered adults of Mourning Cloaks, tortoiseshells, and anglewings. Most swallowtails, brushfoots, and true skippers don't begin their flights until late spring or early summer, while mid- to late summer is a time when you should expect hairstreaks, fritillaries, some skippers, and immigrants from further south. Go out at different times during the year and keep detailed notes so that you can make your own local butterfly calendar. In the North, on the Great Plains, and in the Deep South, the timing may be different. In the arctic and subarctic regions, you can find almost all of the species over a period of several weeks; on the plains, the butterfly fauna is limited, and the early spring species may be absent; while in the most southern areas, the best seasons may vary. In southern Florida and the Keys, April and May seem best, while in Texas's lower Rio Grande Valley, most residents and butterfly colonists from Mexico are present during October and November.

WHERE TO FIND BUTTERFLIES: Butterflies can be found in any habitat where suitable plants are found, even in cities and suburbs. Many habitats have species found only there, and many species are limited geographically. To find all of the butterflies near your home you will have to visit each habitat. After becoming familiar with all of the local butterflies, you may wish to travel to more exotic hunting grounds.

To find the different habitats in your area, carefully study the chapter on butterfly distribution and decide which habitats are likely to be found in your vicinity. We have many butterfly habitats in the area covered by this book, but most can be broadly characterized as forests, grasslands, or wetlands. There are many forms of each type, especially when you consider latitude, soil type, and topography. Investigate all of the possible local habitat types that are found on land with public access. There are many well-known sites in the East where special butterflies may be found. You can get an idea about some of these from the localities listed for each species on the plate legends.

BUTTERFLY PHOTOGRAPHY

Photographing butterflies is an excellent way to build a collection of the common species in your area, or to document rare species or different kinds of behavior. (Remember that some butterflies, especially skippers, cannot be identified without dissection.) Photographing a butterfly is much more difficult than catching one in a net.

EQUIPMENT: You should have a good 35mm single lens reflex camera (SLR) with a lens that can focus at close range and provide a relatively large image of the butterfly on film. A macro lens is best, but extension rings on a normal portrait lens is a less expensive and workable, albeit awkward, substitute. The focusing distance is indicated by the length of the lens. I use a 105mm macro lens, and find it much better than a 55mm macro. Others use telephoto macro lenses, with or without zoom capability. You may find that you have focusing problems with a telephoto lens. You probably do not want a camera with autofocusing or autoflash capabilities.

I use electronic flash for my photography, because it gives reliable lighting and provides greater depth of field that translates into sharper, better lit photos. You should obtain an electronic flash unit that is capable of adjusting its strength based on the distance from the camera to the subject. Some people use ring light flashes or two flashes mounted on brackets to either side of the camera.

If you choose not to use a flash, or if you specialize in photographing the life stages of butterflies, you should use a tripod. A tripod will provide better pictures whenever it is feasible to use one. If you specialize in taking photos of free-living butterflies, you will probably find a tripod impractical. You may also want a bellows that lets you take closeups of tiny objects such as butterfly eggs and caterpillars.

HOW TO PHOTOGRAPH: You should first be familiar with your camera. I usually have my camera set on the smallest aperture possible, f16, f22, or f32, and on the automatic flash timing $\frac{1}{60}$ sec. or $\frac{1}{25}$ sec. Use the film with the slowest speed possible for your setup. Take a trial roll or two at various settings duplicating the conditions you expect to encounter.

Butterflies in nature should be approached slowly. Keep as low as possible, and avoid letting your shadow fall on your subject. Be patient, as you may need to approach a butterfly several times before you can take a picture. Often you may have to inch forward on your knees, kneel on hard rocky surfaces (knee pads may help), or even lie flat on the ground. You may have to wade in water or kneel in mud if you want your photo badly enough. When you do find a cooperative subject, you should take several pictures at different exposures and poses. I usually take pictures at several f-stops, and take vertical as well as horizontal frames.

WHEN TO PHOTOGRAPH: Early in the morning or late in the afternoon are good times to find butterflies that are not too active. Partly cloudy days with somewhat lower than seasonal temperatures will provide good subject cooperation. Learn to recognize the situations where butterflies are more likely to be successfully approached. Don't try to photograph butterflies in midair! Butterflies taking nectar at flowers or imbibing fluids are usually approachable, as are mating pairs. Basking butterflies and perching males can be photographed with relative ease. Females that are ovipositing or courting pairs usually move too often to be photographed.

MAKING A COLLECTION

Keeping a butterfly collection is an excellent way to study the structure and variation of butterflies, but before you begin a collection, decide whether you are willing to make the commitment to take care of your collection.

COLLECTING: Butterflies may be obtained in several ways: by netting them, by trapping them, by searching for road kills, and by raising them.

Netting is the most direct way to catch butterflies, whether you want to observe them more closely and then release them or add them to your collection. Butterfly nets may be purchased from the supply companies listed in the Appendixes. If you wish, you can make your own net. Use a dowel or rounded mop or broom handle, a piece of flexible yet heavy wire, a four-inch piece of aluminum pipe, and netting (Fig. 5). The net handle should be at

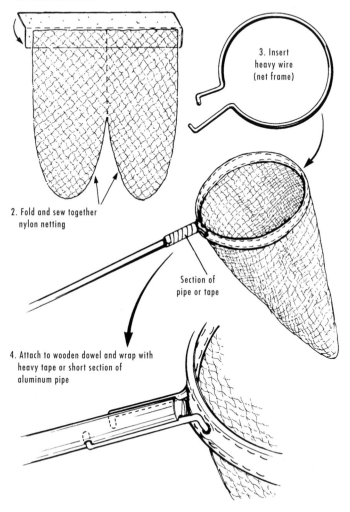

1. Heavy cloth (canvas or muslin) Fold over netting and sew to form a hollow tube

3. Insert heavy wire (net frame)

2. Fold and sew together nylon netting

Section of pipe or tape

4. Attach to wooden dowel and wrap with heavy tape or short section of aluminum pipe

Figure 5. Making a butterfly net

least 3½ feet long, but may be as long as 5 feet. Some collectors use nets with handle extensions to collect species such as hairstreaks that perch high in trees. The diameter of the net hoop should be at least 18 inches, but no more than 36 inches. The length of the net bag should be twice its diameter. Use a translucent yet tough curtain material such as nylon or bobbinet. A ring of muslin or canvas is sewed at the opening of the net bag to protect it from fraying. Some prefer to dye their net bags dark green, since they feel green bags are less likely to alarm their quarry.

As with butterflies you want to photograph, approach butterflies you are trying to net slowly, while keeping your shadow from falling on them. Net butterflies while they rest on vegetation, flowers, or twigs with a deliberate but not violent side swing, flipping over the net bag once the butterfly is inside. For butterflies perched on the ground or rocks, drop the net over them with a little leverage so that the net makes a *thwap* as it hits the ground. Quickly kneel and hold the tip of the net in the air so that the insect will fly or crawl up—not escape under the edge. Butterflies perched on tree trunks are difficult to capture. Try slowly moving the net up from below, then quickly clamping the net over the butterfly. Swing at butterflies in flight only if you feel they won't stop, and use a following swing from behind. Never run after a butterfly. Rarely does a chase result in capture; more often it frightens a butterfly that might have perched, and it sometimes results in injury to the collector.

Bait traps are the best way to collect forest nymphalids, such as Mourning Cloaks, anglewings, tortoiseshells, and satyrs, that rarely or never visit flowers. Hang traps in the shade or in the forest canopy. Use a bait made with overripe fruit (such as bananas, peaches, or pears), beer, and molasses or brown sugar. The butterflies will squeeze into the trap, then fly up into the net.

If you want to collect but don't wish to kill butterflies yourself, you may purchase specimens from dealers, or you might try searching for road kills. One gentleman in New Jersey found most of that state's butterflies by riding a bicycle slowly along country roads while scanning the road edges for butterflies that had been struck by passing vehicles.

Butterflies may also be obtained by raising them from eggs, caterpillars, or pupae (see below).

Once you have netted a butterfly, it should be killed as quickly and as humanely as possible. This may be done by introducing the insect into a jar containing poison gas or by placing it in a glassine envelope, then putting it in your freezer. Poison jars may be purchased from a dealer, or you may use a wide-mouth jar with tissue soaked in ethyl acetate. Do not let young children handle

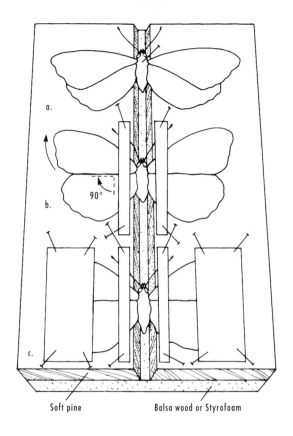

a.

b.

90°

c.

Soft pine   Balsa wood or Styrofoam

Figure 6. Mounting a butterfly

poisons if they do not realize that such substances are also poisonous to people. Until they are ready for mounting, butterflies should be kept in glassine envelopes in a tight container, such as a sandwich box, in the freezer.

Some authors suggest that butterflies may be "pinched" on the thorax with both wings up, but this method makes them difficult to mount properly. And butterflies are immobilized by being pinched, but they do not always die immediately. You may immobilize a butterfly by lightly pinching it, then quickly place it in an envelope in a poison jar. But never pinch skippers or small gossamer wings.

Note: All butterfly populations within national parks, state parks, wildlife refuges, and nature preserves are protected. Collecting specimens in these places is usually prohibited unless permits for study or research are issued by the respective land management agency or conservation group. Permits are usually not granted for the purpose of adding to a private collection. Never enter private land without first obtaining permission from the land owner.

MOUNTING: Butterflies should be mounted on insect pins with their wings spread at right angles to their bodies. To do this properly, the butterflies should be relaxed after being taken from the freezer. Specimens that had been allowed to dry should be rehydrated in a "relaxing" container. I place butterflies between layers of wet paper towels in a tight plastic container for two days. If you keep them longer under conditions of high humidity they will mold. Be sure each envelope is labeled with waterproof ink. The wings of properly relaxed butterflies can be moved up and down easily.

When ready for mounting, place the insect pin (size #2 or #3) in the center of the thorax and push it through so that about ⅓ of the pin remains above the insect's body. Push the pin into the soft wood in the center of the mounting board (Fig. 6). Use a narrow strip of thick paper to hold the wings flat on the board. Use fine pins or needles to tease the wings into the proper position, then place strips of paper over the positioned wings and pin them down without putting pins through the wings themselves. Use pins to brace the antennae and abdomen.

A mounted butterfly should be kept on the board for at least two weeks, until the insect is completely dry. After removing the specimen from the board, label it properly.

LABELING: A proper label for a pinned specimen is made with indelible ink on stiff, high quality paper. The label information should include *at least* state or province, county, locality, date, and collector's name. If collected in mountainous terrain, you should include the elevation. You may wish to add labels with biological information such as the names of nectar plants, or the plant on which you found the caterpillar that was raised for the adult specimen.

Labels should be small, preferably no larger than 1 in. by ½ in. The label should be pinned through the center and positioned below the insect's body so that it may be read easily.

STORING: Butterflies should be kept in boxes or cases with suitable pinning bottoms and tight-fitting lids. These can be purchased from supply houses. You may make your own boxes, but homemade insect boxes often are not sufficiently tight fitting to exclude other insects, such as carpet beetles and book lice, that can destroy your specimens. Advanced collectors will probably want to use cases with glass-topped museum drawers. Commonly used drawers are named after the major collections that adopt them. Two of these are the "California Academy" and "Cornell" drawers. Each has custom-sized pinning trays that allow one to expand the arrangement in a drawer by moving the pinning trays instead of moving each pinned specimen individually.

Within the boxes, you may want to arrange the insects in rows or columns in accordance with the list beginning on p. 409. Above the specimens for each species, add labels that give the name of the family and subfamily, and the scientific name. Or you may wish to arrange your collection according to habitat, or by the nectar plants that each species uses.

You must be vigilant to be sure that insects do not destroy your collection. Fumigants such as napthalene may be kept in each box or case to insure that pests do not survive. Some fumigants, such as paradichlorobenzene (PDB), can cause health problems, so be careful to use fumigants that are not toxic to humans. Instead of using fumigants, some collection managers may merely examine each box at least twice a year for pest damage and then treat each box with heat or cold. Keeping the box overnight at subfreezing temperatures or placing it in a slow, drying oven can kill any pests inside without using chemical poisons.

RAISING BUTTERFLIES

Raising butterflies is an excellent way to obtain photographs of all the different life stages of a butterfly, and it is also the best way to obtain perfect specimens for your collection.

You can raise butterflies either by obtaining eggs or by searching for caterpillars. The former ensures that you observe the entire life cycle, but it involves a much greater effort than if you start with partly grown caterpillars.

Butterfly eggs may be obtained either by following egg-laying female butterflies or by caging mated females. To find butterfly eggs, watch for females engaged in their characteristic egg-laying behavior. Such a female will be found fluttering slowly near plants, periodically touching down and "tasting" plants with the tarsi on her front legs. If the plant is the correct species and is acceptable, the female will deposit one or more eggs, depending on whether she belongs to a species that lays its eggs in batches, and then flutter off in search of the next spot to place an egg. You may follow along behind and collect the number of eggs that you need. Collect each egg on a small piece of the host plant to which it is attached.

Familiarity with the host plants of local butterflies and the time of day that each prefers to lay eggs will make your egg-gathering efforts easier.

Since the females of many species are difficult to follow in nature, you may want to try to obtain eggs from captive females. Different butterflies require different approaches. The best method for most species is to confine females in fine wire mesh cages; these should be large enough so that the butterflies can flutter around freely. You should provide fresh bouquets for larval food and nectar sources. Several bright lamps should be focused on the cage so that the female butterflies cannot find dark corners; if they do so they will not lay eggs. Search the larval host plant each day for eggs and remove them for special handling.

Some butterflies will lay eggs only under special conditions. For example, the best way to obtain eggs from fritillaries (Genus *Speyeria*) is to confine gravid females in inflated paper bags.

Keep the eggs in small vials or Petri dishes with small pieces of damp paper toweling or filter paper. When the caterpillars hatch out, place them in separate small containers with small amounts of fresh food plant. Never place too many caterpillars in a single container, as overcrowding will often result in disease or cannibalism. Keep damp paper toweling or filter paper in the container. Do not let the insides of the containers become either too wet or too dry.

You may also find caterpillars in nature by searching their host plants at the proper season. You should know what part of the plants the caterpillars feed on, and you should be aware that many species construct shelters within which they hide during rest periods — usually during the day.

Remember that butterfly eggs, caterpillars, or chrysalids collected in nature are likely to already have been found by tiny parasitic wasps and flies, and that often half or more of the caterpillars that you find will produce adult parasites instead of adult butterflies.

Whenever you collect caterpillars, make sure that you have an adequate fresh food plant growing nearby or a supply kept in a refrigerator. Growing a variety of local caterpillar plants in your yard is a good idea if you plan to do much rearing. Remember not to use pesticides on or near plants you plan to feed to your "livestock."

You may use a variety of containers to raise your caterpillars. Plastic sandwich boxes or Tupperware may work for small caterpillars, but caterpillars that will eventually produce chrysalids that need to hang should be kept in containers such as small cages or large wide-mouthed jars. Control the moisture in your rearing containers carefully and provide clean paper toweling every day or so. Remove the caterpillar droppings (frass) if they become too messy or moldy.

As the caterpillars near full size, make sure that they have suitable sites on which to hang or form their chrysalids. Provide sticks or pieces of bark. The chrysalids, once formed, may be kept in a drier environment than that of the caterpillars. The chrysalids of single-brooded species may need to overwinter before they will hatch. You may keep chrysalids of such species in sandwich boxes or tight plastic containers in your refrigerator until the following spring.

The chrysalids of some swallowtails, orangetips, and marbles may enter a state of physiological arrest (diapause) and not produce adult butterflies for two or three years. The chrysalids of these species should be kept under natural light and temperature conditions. Sometimes placing water droplets on swallowtail chrysalids each day will help them hatch more readily.

Watch your rearing containers at least daily for signs that the chrysalids are getting ready to produce an adult. Such chrysalids will usually turn dark, and within 24 hours of emergence, you will be able to see the adult's wing pattern (in miniature) through the now transparent shell of the chrysalid. When the adult butterflies hatch make sure that they have enough room to hang and let their wings spread, expand, and dry. After their wings have hardened, you may photograph them in your garden and then release them, or you may want to keep them for your collection.

BUTTERFLY GARDENING

Planting butterfly nectar plants and caterpillar food plants is an excellent way to increase the number and variety of butterflies in your yard. Whether you live in a garden apartment, in a separate residence, or on a farm, there are ways to increase your enjoyment of butterflies.

Today, we have a better understanding of how caterpillars and adult butterflies use food resources, and this understanding has considerably improved our ability to attract butterflies and fulfill their needs.

When you plan your butterfly garden, you should be aware of several principles. First, of course, you should be familiar with general gardening techniques. You should also know the common butterfly species in your vicinity and include both their adult nectar plants and caterpillar food plants to the extent that this is practical. If your yard lacks caterpillar food plants, you will attract only a few butterflies that happen to wander by. Similarly, if your yard lacks nectar plants, the butterflies that your yard produces will fly elsewhere in search of "greener pastures."

Place your nectar plants in patches, and include a variety of species that flower in different seasons so that your garden will be continually attractive from spring through fall. Patches of plants that flower at the same time are much more attractive to butterflies than a single plant with only a few flowers.

If you live on a farm that already has flowery fields or meadows, you may not need to plant a separate garden. If you have limited space, you can still plant a few attractive plants in flower boxes or other containers.

If you have the space, a separate garden planted especially for butterflies will be most successful. Gardening principles may dictate that trees, shrubs, and some other perennials be planted to the garden's back or sides. Remember that most butterflies love sun and shun shade, so plan the garden's exposures accordingly. If your garden is too shady, open it up by severely pruning or cutting back selected trees or tall shrubs.

You can vary the diversity of your garden by adding large rocks, small hills, and different soils. Take advantage of your yard's special features. For example, if you have a hilltop or a small stream, you might plan your garden to blend with these natural features.

Butterflies are encouraged by "weediness." If you can leave a few weeds and let your lawn include some dandelions and clovers, you will see more butterflies. Avoid or minimize the use of pesticides, either insecticides or herbicides, on your property. Plan your vegetable garden so that you include sufficient cabbage family plants (cabbage, turnips, broccoli, kale, etc.) and carrot family plants (carrots, dill, parsley) to account for the needs of both your family and butterflies.

Which plants to include in your butterfly garden will depend on your location as well as the kinds of butterflies found in your region. Some plants that do very well in one site may be failures in others. I have listed nectar plants that will do well in much of our area together with others that do best in a few regions in Table 1. There are many other kinds of flowers visited by butter-

COMMON NAME	LATIN NAME	REGIONS
Bee Balm	*Monarda didyma*	Northeast
Bougainvillea	*Bougainvillea* species	South
Butterfly Bush	*Buddleia* species	All
Butterfly Milkweed	*Asclepias tuberosa*	All; sandy soil
Common Lilac	*Syringa vulgaris*	All
Dame's-rocket	*Hesperis matronalis*	Midwest, Northeast
Firewheel, Indian Blanket	*Gaillardia pulchella*	Midwest
French Lavender	*Lavandula dentata*	All
French Marigold	*Tagetes patula*	All
Hibiscus	*Hibiscus*	South
Lantana	*Lantana camara*	South
New England Aster	*Aster novi-belgii*	All
Phlox	*Phlox* species	All
Purple Coneflower	*Echinacea angustifolia*	All
Verbena	*Verbena* species	All
Zinnia	*Zinnia* species	All

Table 1. Nectar plants for eastern butterfly gardens

flies. You can find out which ones are most successful in your area by visiting other yards, gardens, or nearby fields.

There is a greater variety of caterpillar food plants than nectar plants. This information is included in the species accounts. A few caterpillar plants that are successful over much of the East are listed in Table 2.

Caterpillar food plants may also include shrubs and trees in your yard as well as grasses in your lawn. I have already mentioned your vegetable garden, and you may encourage a few weeds such as mallows (*Malva*), asters, and Lamb's Quarters (*Chenopodium album*). If you live in a rural area, you should ask your county extension agent whether the culture of some plants such as thistles or milkweeds is prohibited.

Some butterflies do not visit flowers, and you may wish to enhance your property for these species as well. Most anglewings, leafwings, emperors, and wood nymphs seldom visit flowers, but feed on rotting fruit, sap flows, dung, bird droppings, or carrion instead. Although you will probably not wish to scatter carcasses or fresh dung about your yard, you can place overripe fruit or sugar mixtures in shady areas where these forest dwellers might find them.

Male butterflies, primarily species that "patrol" for mates, visit moist sand or mud where they imbibe fluids rich in salts. The

COMMON NAME	LATIN NAME	REGIONS
Alfalfa	*Medicago sativa*	Midwest
Bermuda Grass	*Cynodon dactylon*	South
Cabbage, Broccoli	*Brassica* species	All
Carrot, Dill, Parsley	Apiaceae	All
Cassias	*Cassia* species	South
Citrus	*Citrus* species	South
Hackberry	*Celtis* species	South
Hollyhock	*Alcea rosea*	All
Passion-vines	*Passiflora* species	South
Pipe Vine	*Aristolochia* species	South
Sassafras	*Sassafras albidum*	All
Tulip-tree	*Liriodendron tulipifera*	South, Midwest
Willows	*Salix* species	All
Wisteria	*Wisteria* species	All

Table 2. Caterpillar host plants for eastern butterfly gardens

explanation for this behavior is not completely understood, but you might experiment by keeping a wet sand patch or wet sand barrel in a sunny spot in or adjacent to your garden.

Over time you may want to adjust the composition of your garden by adding or substituting different varieties and species. Remember that you should not remove native plants from the wild. You can obtain plants or seeds of native species from specialty nurseries. Seeds or plants of weedy exotics may be removed from vacant lots or fields, but you should first seek permission from the land owner.

CONSERVATION OF BUTTERFLIES

Butterflies, as well as other insects, have finally begun to be considered "wildlife," living organisms worthy of conservation attention and concern. The United States Endangered Species Act of 1973, as well as many state and provincial laws, provide the means to recognize, protect, and manage declining butterfly populations. Moreover, private conservation organizations and local jurisdictions may also take actions to protect habitats of endangered species.

Since at least the arrival of European colonists, habitat change and loss due to residential, agricultural, and commercial development has resulted in profound changes in the composition of eastern butterfly communities. Some species have become rarer, others have become more abundant and widespread, and exotic species from Europe and tropical America have been introduced here. A new host of European weeds has formed a plant community in disturbed areas to which many of our native butterflies have adapted.

Declining species may require intervention at several levels. At the first, local populations may decline or disappear, while at the second, a species may decline throughout much of its range. In the first instance, local citizens should call these changes to the attention of community leaders and conservation groups; while range-wide changes should be of national, state, or provincial concern. Species or subspecies with naturally small ranges or narrow habitat preferences should be watched especially closely.

Although the only eastern butterfly protected by federal law is the endangered Schaus' Swallowtail *(Papilio aristodemus ponceanus),* a number of other species and subspecies are recognized as endangered or threatened by several states and provinces. Many other butterflies are classified as "of special concern" or "status undetermined." A discussion of several threatened eastern habitats or ecosystems, rather than a species-by-species discussion, will provide a better understanding of our butterfly conservation problems.

FLORIDA KEYS

South Florida and south Texas are the only eastern ecosystems where you may see resident tropical butterflies. On the Florida Keys, housing development and associated mosquito control efforts have threatened the butterflies of two habitat types: *hardwood hammocks* and *pine scrub*. Most of the butterflies in these two habitats are geographic subspecies of more widespread West Indian species.

The endangered Schaus' Swallowtail is limited to hardwood hammocks. Much of its habitat near Miami and on Key Largo and Matecumbe Key was destroyed by housing development, but small populations survive on North Key Largo and on the keys of Biscayne National Park. The Bahaman Swallowtail (*Papilio andraemon bonhotei*) is found in small numbers only in Biscayne National Park. At the time of this writing, the Miami Blue (*Hemiargus thomasi bethunebakeri*) and the Large Purplewing (*Eunica tatila tatilista*) have declined and are found only in a few hardwood hammocks on the keys. The Florida Leafwing (*Anaea floridalis*) and Bartram's Scrub-Hairstreak (*Strymon acis bartrami*) have their major populations limited to pine scrub on Big Pine Key, where their host plant woolly croton (*Croton*) is limited. Much of Big Pine Key is included in the Key Deer National Wildlife Refuge.

LOWER RIO GRANDE VALLEY

A number of endangered habitats occur along the lower Rio Grande Valley in Cameron, Hidalgo, and Starr counties of south Texas. Collectively, these habitats are referred to as *Tamaulipan brushland*. More butterfly species, more than 300, have been found in this small area than in all the rest of eastern North America! The U.S. range of many butterflies is limited to the valley, but most of the species are widespread in Mexico. Only a few thousand acres of original habitat remain, in places such as Bentsen-Rio Grande Valley State Park, Santa Ana National Wildlife Refuge, and the Rio Grande National Wildlife Refuge Complex. The vast majority of the original habitat has been cleared for agriculture and housing. Although most of the Tamaulipan brushland ecosystem occurs in adjacent Mexico, it is also being cleared there for agriculture.

A string of hardwood swamps and associated moist bottomlands lies along the Atlantic Coastal Plain, Gulf Coast, and Mississippi River Valley from southern Delaware and southern Illinois. Originally these once vast swamps were the domain of Carolina Parakeets, Ivory-billed Woodpeckers, and Bachman's Warblers. Now, after draining and clearing for logging, agriculture, and conversion to even-aged pine plantations, only small remnants of these forests remain. Although no butterflies endemic to such swamps have become extinct or are considered endangered, many of the species are very limited in their occurrence. The Creole Pearlyeye (*Enodia creola*), Yehl Skipper (*Poanes yehl*), and the roadsideskippers (*Amblyscirtes aesculapius, A. carolina,* and *A. reversa*) are the species of most concern.

PINE-OAK BARRENS

Sand barrens in a strip extending discontinuously from southern New England across the Great Lakes region to central Wisconsin have been subject to development and suppression of natural ecological processes. Historically, periodic fires would burn these habitats and return the plant communities to an early succession. Lupine (*Lupinus perennis*) thrives in the openings created by such fires, but it is much rarer where fires are suppressed. Three butterflies, the Frosted Elfin (*Callophrys irus*), the Karner Blue (*Lycaeides melissa samuelis*), and Persius Duskywing (*Erynnis persius*) feed only on lupine in these areas. The Karner Blue was the first threatened United States butterfly to receive legal protection. It is listed as endangered by New York.

Acquisition and management of remaining barrens habitats is under study and will provide ways to perpetuate these species in local parks and preserves.

FRESHWATER WETLANDS

The northern states and southern Canada are rich in wetlands — bogs, marshes, fens, and swamps. But clearing and filling of these wetlands over much of the East has caused a number of butterflies to become rare at the state or local level, although they are not close to being of concern at the national level. Species found mainly in freshwater marshes and wet meadows that have declined in several areas are the Bronze Copper (*Lycaena hyllus*), Harris Checkerspot (*Chlosyne harrisii*), Mitchell's Satyr (*Neonympha mitchellii*), and the Black Dash (*Euphyes conspicuus*).

Over the past several decades, the Bronze Copper has disappeared from most of New England, and Mitchell's Satyr is extirpated in Ohio and most likely in New Jersey as well. Conservationists are now concerned about the condition of the habitats of Mitchell's Satyr in its Michigan stronghold.

The Bog Elfin (*Callophrys lanoraieensis*) and Bog Copper (*Lycaena epixanthe*) are limited to acid bogs, the former species only in northern New England and southern Quebec. Although these habitats are widespread, mining for peat moss and clearing have destroyed several, and there is some concern about their butterfly communities.

TALL-GRASS PRAIRIES

Extending west from the edge of the formerly vast deciduous forests, the prairies once stretched to the base of the Rocky Mountains. The tall-grass prairies were limited to the eastern part, where rainfall was highest and soils were deepest. Further west, the tall-grass prairies met the mid-grass prairies, which gradually merged with the dry short-grass prairies of the high plains. As the pioneers moved west, they plowed the prairies and converted them into the richest agricultural area in the world. Probably more than 90 percent of the tall-grass prairie has been lost, and some states such as Iowa have lost as much as 99 percent of this habitat.

Two butterflies, the Poweshiek Skipperling (*Oarisma poweshiek*) and the Dakota Skipper (*Hesperia dacotae*), are limited in their occurrence to unplowed tall-grass prairie, mainly in preserves. Populations of both species should be preserved wherever found. The Regal Fritillary (*Speyeria idalia*) has its metropolis in the tall-grass prairie and mid-grass prairie region, but it also occurs in wet meadows in other areas. This species, one of our most striking butterflies, has disappeared from most of its former haunts east of the Appalachians, and it is considered a rare find anywhere east of the Mississippi. Only in a few areas west of the Mississippi, primarily in Nebraska and South Dakota, is it found in significant numbers. This significant species merits a national effort at protection and habitat recovery.

FUTURE OF CONSERVATION

Those of us who collect and study butterflies should treat our rich heritage with care and responsibility. We should not collect specimens from small local colonies that are threatened with extinction, and we should not collect huge numbers from any population for whimsical purposes. The Lepidopterists' Society has formulated a policy with regard to collections of specimens, and this has been adopted by several other organizations. This policy is given in the Appendixes, and anyone who collects these insects should study its provisions and recommendations.

6

BUTTERFLY HABITATS

The distribution of butterflies is dynamic and ever-changing, even without the influence of man's effects on the biosphere. Each species has a unique distribution that changes from year to year, as some populations contract or die out while others expand or are formed anew by colonists and migrants.

The distribution of butterflies that are found in weedy habitats changes at the greatest rate, while that of species found in forests and other relatively stable, predictable habitats changes most slowly.

Ecologists and biogeographers have devised many schemes that help us understand the general, broad-scale patterns of animal and plant distributions. These schemes include life zones, eco-regions, and biotic provinces.

LIFE ZONES

Perhaps the most useful scheme for describing butterfly distributions is that of the life zones, devised by C. H. Merriam. The seven life zones are based on elevational and latitudinal changes in plant communities that reflect the physiological tolerance of different plants to changes in seasonal temperatures and length of growing season (Fig. 7).

In the tropics, temperatures almost never fall below freezing, and there is a year-round growing season. As one travels further north or higher in elevation the average temperature decreases and the growing season, the number of days between the last killing spring frost and the first fall or winter killing frost, shortens.

Following are brief descriptions of the seven life zones beginning with the most permissive, the Tropical, and ending with the harshest, the Arctic.

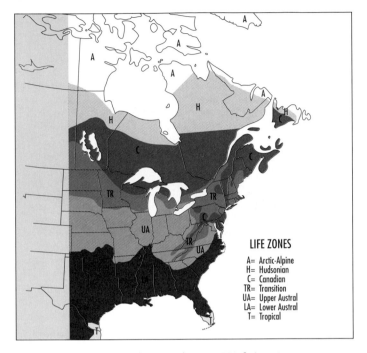

Figure 7. Life zones of eastern North America

TROPICAL LIFE ZONE: Found at the tip of peninsular Florida and the keys, and in the lower Rio Grande Valley of south Texas, the Tropical Life Zone has an essentially year-round frost-free growing season, and the average temperature of every month is greater than 65°F (18°C). This zone extends through the lowlands of the West Indies, Mexico, Central America, and South America south to northern Argentina and northern Chile.

Here we find resident butterflies that cannot withstand freezing in any life stage. This is the richest zone for butterflies, and most of the species covered in this book are found within its limits.

Butterflies found entirely or primarily in the Tropical Life Zone include the Polydamas Swallowtail (*Battus polydamas*), Ornythion Swallowtail (*Papilio ornythion*), Tropical White (*Appias drusilla*), Orange-barred Sulphur (*Phoebis philea*), Bartam's Scrub-Hairstreak (*Strymon acis bartrami*), Julia (*Dryas iulia*), Zebra

(Heliconius charithonius), Mangrove Skipper *(Phocides pigmalion)*, and Tropical Checkered-Skipper *(Pyrgus oileus)*.

LOWER AUSTRAL LIFE ZONE: This life zone has somewhat harsher winters than those of the Tropical Life Zone. There are at least a few freezing nights each winter, and average summer high temperatures are 79°F (26°C) or more. In our area, this zone covers the region known as the Deep South, where cotton and peanuts may be grown successfully and where Spanish moss, canebrakes, and baldcypress may be seen, but extends west to south-central Texas where mesquite thickets dominate.

Some typical lower austral butterflies include the Southern Pearly-eye *(Enodia portlandia)*, Gemmed Satyr *(Cyllopsis gemma)*, Great Purple Hairstreak *(Atlides halesus)*, King's Hairstreak *(Satyrium kingi)*, Little Metalmark *(Calephelis virginiensis)*, Palamedes Swallowtail *(Papilio palamedes)*, Confused Cloudywing *(Thorybes confusis)*, Zarucco Duskywing *(Erynnis zarucco)*, Whirlabout *(Polites vibex)*, Yehl Skipper *(Poanes yehl)*, and Carolina Roadside-Skipper *(Amblyscirtes carolina)*.

UPPER AUSTRAL LIFE ZONE: This zone has winters with two or three months of freezing temperatures, and average high temperatures during summer range from 71° to 79°F (22–26°C). This zone occurs in a belt stretching from the central Atlantic coast west through the central Midwest and includes a bit of extreme southern Ontario.

The few butterflies found primarily in this life zone include the Regal Fritillary *(Speyeria idalia)*, Northern Metalmark *(Calephelis borealis)*, and the Dusky Azure *(Celastrina ebenina)*.

TRANSITION LIFE ZONE: This zone has winters with four to five months of freezing temperatures, and average summer high temperatures ranging from 65° to 71°F (18–22°C). It lies between the upper austral zone to the south and the Canadian to the north (or upslope). It comprises a broad swath extending from the New England coast west across the Great Lakes states, southern Ontario, and Quebec, most of Minnesota, North Dakota, and southwestern Manitoba. It also extends south in the Appalachians to northern Georgia and northeastern Alabama.

Quite a few butterflies fly primarily within this zone. These include the West Virginia White *(Pieris virginiensis)*, Bog Copper *(Lycaena epixanthe)*, Acadian Hairstreak *(Satyrium acadicum)*, Melissa Blue *(Lycaeides melissa)*, Aphrodite Fritillary *(Speyeria aphrodite)*, Harris' Checkerspot *(Chlosyne harrisii)*, Tawny Crescent *(Phyciodes batesii)*, Dreamy Duskywing *(Erynnis icelus)*, Indian Skipper *(Hesperia sassacus)*, and Long Dash *(Polites mystic)*.

CANADIAN LIFE ZONE: This is the least harsh of the truly boreal life zones, often dominated by conifers. Winters have six or more months of freezing temperatures, and average summer high temperatures range from 57° to 65 °F (14–18°C).

Most of the butterflies found in this zone are transcontinental or Holarctic (occurring in both North America and Eurasia). Only "islands" of this life zone occur in the Appalachians south to West Virginia. Elsewhere the zone extends west from northern New England and the Maritimes across southern Canada and the very northern portions of the Great Lakes states to central Manitoba.

Some typical butterflies in the Canadian Life Zone include the Pink-edged Sulphur (*Colias interior*), Hoary Elfin (*Callophrys polios*), Greenish Blue (*Plebejus saepiolus*), Atlantis Fritillary (*Speyeria atlantis*), Titania Fritillary (*Boloria titania*), Green Comma (*Polygonia faunus*), and Macoun's Arctic (*Oeneis macounii*).

HUDSONIAN LIFE ZONE: This is viewed by some biologists as a tension zone between the Arctic and Canadian life zones. The winter and summer temperatures are intermediate between those of the above zones. It occurs in the United States only as a narrow belt just below the alpine habitats on Mt. Washington, New Hampshire, and Mt. Katahdin, Maine. In Canada, it comprises the broad taiga belt that extends from the Labrador coast across the northern portion of the Canadian prairie provinces, and the southern Northwest Territories.

The Hudsonian Life Zone is not rich in butterflies, but some typical species include the Old World Swallowtail (*Papilio machaon*), Compton Tortoiseshell (*Nymphalis vau-album*), and the Grizzled Skipper (*Pyrgus centaureae*).

ARCTIC LIFE ZONE: This is the northernmost or highest elevation life zone. Within its limits, winters last 10 or more months, and maximum daily summer temperatures are usually below 61 °F (16°C). In our territory, the Arctic Life Zone is found only sparingly below northern Quebec, where it occurs on the tops of a few alpine peaks, including Mt. Washington, New Hampshire; Mt. Katahdin, Maine; and Mt. Albert, Quebec. The tundra and other barren habitats of the northernmost part of our territory include species adapted for the briefest of summers. Several require two years to complete their development. Typical species include the Labrador Sulphur (*Colias nastes*), Ross's Alpine (*Erebia rossii*), and Melissa Arctic (*Oeneis melissa*).

HABITATS

A butterfly species will be found where there are the correct climate and habitat, the proper caterpillar hosts, adult food sources, and historical opportunity for colonization. Other factors include competition between species and the presence of parasites and predators. In eastern North America, our disruption of natural environments and the creation of habitats dominated by crops, ornamental plants, and introduced weeds have obviously altered the abundance and distribution of the original butterfly communities—whatever they may have been.

The actual ecological communities found in any region are not only determined by which life zone they are in, but by the amount of precipitation in the area, soil, topography, susceptibility to fire, and history of human disturbance. There are a vast number of ecological communities in eastern North America.

The area covered by this book reaches from the tropical forests of south Texas and southern Florida north to the tundra of Greenland and the Canadian Archipelago and from the salt marshes of the Atlantic coast west to the short-grass prairies of the high plains. Within this vast area there are numberless landforms and vegetation. Since the caterpillars of most butterflies feed on only a few plants, knowing where to look for the plants will increase your ability to find butterflies.

Habitats where butterflies are found can be defined by the dominant plant type and by their relative wetness. I find the most convenient categories are forests, treeless regions, and wetlands. Within these major habitat divisions one may subdivide as finely as one wishes.

FORESTS: There is a wide variety of forests in our territory, but most can be described as classes of broadleaf deciduous forest or coniferous evergreen forest. Mixed deciduous forest is a mixture of these two types. The thorn forests of central and south Texas are composed of small-leafed thorny trees with tropical origins.

Throughout most of the eastern United States and southern Canada, the broadleaf deciduous forests are composed of oaks, hickories, and maples. The variety of plants increases to the south, and the southern Appalachians have the richest variety. Some typical widespread Eastern butterflies found mostly in or adjacent to broadleaf deciduous forests include the Eastern Tiger Swallowtail (*Papilio glaucus*), Spicebush Swallowtail (*Papilio troilus*), Banded Hairstreak (*Satyrium calanus*), Red-spotted Purple (*Limenitis arthemis astyanax*), Little Wood-Satyr (*Megisto cymela*), Northern Pearly-eye (*Enodia anthedon*), and Juvenal's Duskywing (*Erynnis juvenalis*).

Mixed conifer forests cover much of the Canadian Life Zone and are dominated by pines, hemlock, spruce, birches, poplars, and a few oaks. Typical butterflies include the White Admiral (*Limenitis arthemis arthemis*), Green Comma (*Polygonia faunus*), Persius Duskywing (*Erynnis persius*), and Arctic Skipper (*Carterocephalus palaemon*).

Two tropical forest types are found in our territory. In southern Florida and the upper keys one finds hardwood hammocks dominated by a mixture of tropical hardwoods. In these forests and associated small openings the lucky butterfly student may find the Schaus' Swallowtail *(Papilio aristodemus ponceanus)*. This species may be observed but not harassed or collected, as it is on the federal list of endangered species. Also in this habitat one may expect to glimpse the Tropical White *(Appias drusilla)*, Zebra *(Heliconius charithonius)*, and the Large Purplewing *(Eunica tatila)*. The thorn scrub of south Texas is dominated by Mesquite, but in the vicinity of the Rio Grande River contains a strong mixture of other tropical American shrubs and trees. Some typical butterflies include the Giant Swallowtail *(Papilio cresphontes)*, many pierids, Red-bordered Metalmark *(Caria ino)*, White Peacock *(Anartia jatrophae)*, Empress Leilia *(Asterocampa leilia)*, and many skippers of tropical affinities.

TREELESS REGIONS: Habitats normally devoid of trees include grasslands (prairie or tundra), dunes, barrens, rockfields, old fields, and vacant lots. Since most butterflies thrive in sunny conditions, several of these habitats can be quite rich, particularly if they harbor a wide variety of plants.

Our prairies now occur primarily in the Great Plains west of the Mississippi River, but remnants of the formerly extensive prairie "peninsula" are still found in eastern states such as Illinois and Ohio. As one proceeds westward and annual precipitation gradually decreases, the prairies become drier, and the typical grasses become shorter. The tall-grass prairies of the eastern Great Plains grade into the mid-grass prairies, and these in turn give way to the short-grass prairies. The short-grass prairies occur primarily to the west of this guide's territory, but some may be found near its western limits.

The rich tall-grass and mid-grass prairies have no endemic swallowtails or pierids, but they are the primary stronghold for the Regal Fritillary *(Speyeria idalia)* and several skippers including the Poweshiek Skipperling *(Oarisma poweshiek)*, Byssus Skipper *(Problema byssus)*, and the Dakota Skipper *(Hesperia dacotae)*. Short-grass prairie butterflies that barely enter our area are the Ridings' Satyr *(Neominois ridingsii)* and the Uncas Skipper *(Hesperia uncas)*.

Dunes are wind-formed sand hills found along the ocean's margins or lake shores. Old dune ranges may also form extensive vegetated sand hills at inland locations such as in the Carolinas, Michigan, Nebraska, and New Jersey. No species is entirely limited to such habitats, but these formations may be the best butterfly habitats in our region. For example, most of the colonies of the

Karner Blue *(Lycaeides melissa samuelis)* are found in pine barrens, well-vegetated sand hills dominated by pines and oaks. Other butterflies that thrive in these habitats include the Frosted Elfin *(Callophrys irus)*, Hoary Elfin *(Callophrys polios)*, Dusted Skipper *(Atrytonopsis hianna)*, and Yucca Giant-Skipper *(Megathymus yuccae)*. Shale barrens scattered along the Appalachians have vegetation similar to that found in many sand barrens, but the butterfly communities are somewhat different. Butterflies typical of these barrens include the Northern Hairstreak *(Satyrium ontario)*, Northern Metalmark *(Calephelis borealis)*, and the Grizzled Skipper *(Pyrgus centaureae)*.

Rockfields, including rock slides, are open rocky habitats usually above the timberline. In the East, only a few butterflies, notably the Melissa Arctic and Polixenes Arctic, abound in this habitat. The air temperature is higher over this habitat than in the surrounding tundra, allowing the butterflies to fly for longer periods in this generally inhospitable environment.

Two kinds of manmade habitats that are successfully colonized by butterflies are old fields and vacant lots. Old fields are areas that were previously cultivated and heavily grazed but subsequently abandoned and allowed to revert to natural vegetation, although a variable portion of the plants may be introduced European weeds. Eventually these meadowlike habitats will revert to young forests, as woody plants become established and grow to maturity. Many butterflies abound in such situations, including the Black Swallowtail *(Papilio polyxenes)*, American Copper *(Lycaena phlaeas)*, Eastern Tailed-Blue *(Everes comyntas)*, Regal Fritillary *(Speyeria idalia)*, Silver-bordered Fritillary *(Boloria selene)*, Pearl Crescent *(Phyciodes tharos)*, and Southern Cloudywing *(Thorybes bathyllus)*. Vacant lots in cities or suburbs are usually smaller than old fields and may be dominated by trash. A higher proportion of European weeds is usually present, and fewer butterflies are present. Those likely to occur include the Cabbage White *(Pieris rapae)*, Orange Sulphur *(Colias eurytheme)*, Dainty Sulphur *(Nathalis iole)*, Gray Hairstreak *(Strymon melinus)*, Painted Lady *(Vanessa cardui)*, Silver-spotted Skipper *(Epargyreus clarus)*, and the Sachem *(Atalopedes campestris)*.

WETLANDS: There are many kinds of wetlands, but not all are rich in butterflies. Common wetlands that do have special kinds of butterflies include fresh- and saltwater marshes, bogs, swamps, and sawgrass prairies.

Marshes are open areas often with standing water. Most have a slightly alkaline or neutral pH and standing herbaceous vegetation. Freshwater marshes, particularly those dominated by sedges, rushes, and a few shrubby plants, can be very rich for butterflies, especially checkerspots, satyrs, and skippers. The upper margins of salt marshes along the coast are home to a few skippers and other butterflies found in no other habitats. Restricted to such marshes are Aaron's Skipper (*Poanes aaroni*) and the Salt Marsh Skipper (*Panoquina panoquin*). The Eastern Pygmy-Blue (*Brephidium isophthalma*) may be found along the upper borders of southern salt marshes. The Rare Skipper (*Problema bulenta*) is found only in tidal freshwater or brackish marshes near the mouths of large rivers.

Bogs are open, acidic habitats, often surrounded by forests. They may be dominated by thick mats of sphagnum moss. Some sulphurs (*Colias*), the Bog Copper (*Lycaena epixanthe*), Bog Elfin (*Callophrys lanoraieensis*), Bog Fritillary (*Boloria eunomia*), and Black Dash (*Euphyes conspicuus*) are found there.

Swamps are usually wooded, with standing water and shrubs or herbaceous plants in their shallows. Northeastern swamps have relatively few kinds of butterflies, but the Appalachian Brown (*Satyrodes appalachia*) is one that is often found there. In the Southeast, wooded swamps may be rich in butterfly numbers and variety. Near the coast the Palamedes Swallowtail (*Papilio palamedes*) often abounds and is joined by other species including the Southern Pearly-eye (*Enodia portlandia*), the Creole Pearly-eye (*Enodia creola*), and many skippers including the Yehl Skipper (*Poanes yehl*), Duke's Skipper (*Euphyes dukesi*), and several road-side-skippers (*Amblyscirtes species*).

In the Everglades and other coastal areas of the South as far north as North Carolina, one may find prairies dominated by Sawgrass (*Cladium jamaicensis*), a large grasslike sedge. These extensive marshes dominated by a single plant are poor in butterflies, but they are the only habitat where one may find the Palatka Skipper (*Euphyes pilatka*).

The plates feature Vichai Malikul's paintings of adult butterflies. All butterflies believed to be resident in the area covered by this Field Guide or, if strays, found five or more times in our territory, are shown on the plates. Some distinctive strays found on fewer than five occasions are also illustrated. The plates are arranged in the same general order as the species accounts found in the text. Views most important to identification of each species are shown. Uppersides are shown by wings pointed left that are attached to the body. Wings pointed right, unaccompanied by attached bodies, represent the undersides. Where known, the sex of the specimens illustrated is indicated by the appropriate symbol, male (♂) or female (♀).

The illustrations use the Peterson Identification System. Arrows on the plates point to important field marks that are mentioned in the plate legends. The accompanying text is referenced by a page number on the plate legend. The relative size of the butterflies illustrated is indicated on the upper right corner of each legend page.

To identify a butterfly, match your specimen or photograph with the butterfly on the plates that most closely resembles it. Be sure that the field marks are in agreement. Then check the text and the accompanying maps to verify that the butterfly occurs in your area, was found in the proper habitat, and could be in flight at that time. Read the Similar Species section to eliminate any butterflies with which it might be confused.

The specimens are located in the National Museum of Natural History, Washington, D.C. The location where each specimen was collected is indicated on the plate legends.

PLATES

PLATE 1

FLOWERS FOR BUTTERFLY GARDENS

1. **COMMON ZINNIA** *Zinnia elegans*

2. **FRENCH MARIGOLD** *Tagetes patula*

3. **BEE BALM** *Monarda didyma*

4. **LANTANA** *Lantana camara*

5. Butterfly garden dominated by French Marigolds

6. Butterfly garden with a wide variety of flowers

7. **RED VALERIAN, JUPITER'S-BEARD** *Centranthus ruber*

8. **HIBISCUS** *Hibiscus* sp.

9. **VINCA, PERIWINKLE** *Vinca* sp.

1. COMMON ZINNIA

2. FRENCH MARIGOLD

3. BEE BALM

4. LANTANA

5. BUTTERFLY GARDEN: MARIGOLDS

6. VARIED BUTTERFLY GARDEN

7. RED VALERIAN

8. HIBISCUS

9. VINCA

PLATE 2

BUTTERFLY LARVAE (CATERPILLARS)

1. **SPICEBUSH SWALLOWTAIL** *Papilio troilus* **P.140**
Third instar

2. **SPICEBUSH SWALLOWTAIL** *Papilio troilus* **P. 140**
Last instar

3. **BLACK SWALLOWTAIL** *Papilio polyxenes* **P. 130**
Second instar

4. **BLACK SWALLOWTAIL** *Papilio polyxenes* **P. 130**
Last instar

5. **EASTERN TIGER SWALLOWTAIL** *Papilio glaucus* **P. 137**
Fourth instar

6. **EASTERN TIGER SWALLOWTAIL** *Papilio glaucus* **P. 137**
Last instar

7. **GIANT SWALLOWTAIL** *Papilio cresphontes* **P. 133**
Last instar

8. **CABBAGE WHITE** *Pieris rapae* **P. 149**
Last instar

9. **ORANGE SULPHUR** *Colias eurytheme* **P. 155**
Last instar

PLATE 3

BUTTERFLY LARVAE (CATERPILLARS)

1. **OLYMPIA MARBLE** *Euchloe olympia* P. 152
   Last instar

2. **GRAY COPPER** *Lycaena dione* P. 179
   Last instar

3. **GRAY HAIRSTREAK** *Strymon melinus* P. 207
   Last instar

4. **VARIEGATED FRITILLARY** *Euptoieta claudia* P. 235
   Last instar

5. **PAINTED LADY** *Vanessa cardui* P. 271
   Last instar

6. **VICEROY** *Limenitis archippus* P. 279
   Last instar

7. **MONARCH** *Danaus plexippus* P. 313
   Last instar

8. **SILVER-SPOTTED SKIPPER** *Epargyreus clarus* P. 319
   Last instar

9. **HAYHURST'S SCALLOPWING** *Staphylus hayhurstii* P. 338
   Last instar

PLATE 4

BUTTERFLY EARLY STAGES: EGGS AND PUPAE (CHRYSALIDS)

1. **BLACK SWALLOWTAIL** *Papilio polyxenes* **P. 130**
Chrysalid, brown form

2. **GIANT SWALLOWTAIL** *Papilio cresphontes* **P. 133**
Chrysalid, brown form

3. **CABBAGE WHITE** *Pieris rapae* **P. 149**
Egg on broccoli leaf

4. **CABBAGE WHITE** *Pieris rapae* **P. 149**
Chrysalid

5. **MUSTARD WHITE** *Pieris napi* **P. 147**
Chrysalid

6. **QUESTION MARK** *Polygonia interrogationis* **P. 261**
Chrysalid

7. **MILBERT'S TORTOISESHELL** *Nymphalis milberti* **P. 268**
Chrysalid with fully developed butterfly about to emerge

8. **MONARCH** *Danaus plexippus* **P. 313**
Chrysalid

9. **MONARCH** *Danaus plexippus* **P. 313**
Adult emerging from chrysalid

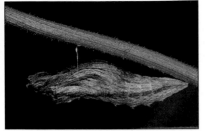

1. BLACK SWALLOWTAIL

2. GIANT SWALLOWTAIL

3. CABBAGE WHITE

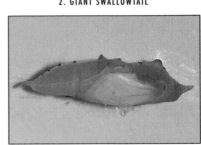

4. CABBAGE WHITE

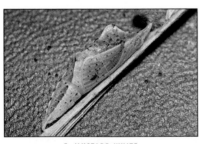

5. MUSTARD WHITE

6. QUESTION MARK

7. MILBERT'S TORTOISESHELL

8. MONARCH

9. MONARCH

PLATE 5   × ½

SWALLOWTAILS

POLYDAMAS SWALLOWTAIL *Battus polydamas,* female   **P. 128**
Winter Park, Fla. Lacks tails, black with yellow band.

RUBY-SPOTTED SWALLOWTAIL *Papilio anchisiades,* male   **P. 141**
Veracruz, Mexico. Lacks tails, black with pink patch on hindwing.

ZEBRA SWALLOWTAIL *Eurytides marcellus,* male   **P. 128**
Orange Co., Fla. Pale green-white with black stripes and long
tails.

PIPEVINE SWALLOWTAIL *Battus philenor,* male   **P. 126**
Hawkins Co., Tenn. Above black with iridescent blue-green hindwing; below hindwing has submarginal row of red-orange spots.

BLACK SWALLOWTAIL *Papilio polyxenes,* female   **P. 130**
Johnsonburg, N. J. Black with iridescent blue on hindwing.

BLACK SWALLOWTAIL *Papilio polyxenes,* male   **P. 130**
Fairfax Co., Va. Black with yellow band.

OZARK SWALLOWTAIL *Papilio joanae,* male   **P. 131**
Benton Co., Mo. Apical spot in yellow band short, pupil of eyespot touches edge of wing.

OZARK SWALLOWTAIL *Papilio joanae,* female   **P. 131**
Benton Co., Mo. Pupil of eyespot touches edge of wing.

SHORT-TAILED SWALLOWTAIL *Papilio brevicauda,* female   **P. 131**
Inverness Co., Nova Scotia. Short tails, orange in yellow band.

SPICEBUSH SWALLOWTAIL *Papilio troilus,* male   **P. 140**
Loudoun Co., Va. Iridescent blue-green patch and pale green
marginal spots on hindwing.

SPICEBUSH SWALLOWTAIL *Papilio troilus,* female   **P. 140**
Sciota, Pa. Blue iridescent patch on hindwing, tails spoon-
shaped.

EASTERN TIGER SWALLOWTAIL *Papilio glaucus,* female, black form   **P. 137**
Labette Co., Kans. Black with orange marginal spot on hindwing,
shadow of tiger stripes.

PLATE 5

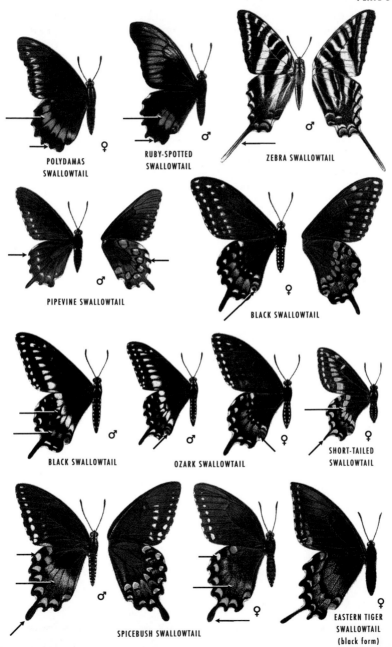

POLYDAMAS
SWALLOWTAIL ♀

RUBY-SPOTTED
SWALLOWTAIL ♂

ZEBRA SWALLOWTAIL ♂

PIPEVINE SWALLOWTAIL ♂

BLACK SWALLOWTAIL ♀

BLACK SWALLOWTAIL ♂

OZARK SWALLOWTAIL ♂

♀

SHORT-TAILED
SWALLOWTAIL ♀

SPICEBUSH SWALLOWTAIL ♂   ♀

EASTERN TIGER
SWALLOWTAIL
(black form) ♀

PLATE 6   × ½

SWALLOWTAILS

OLD WORLD SWALLOWTAIL *Papilio machaon,* male   **P. 132**
Riding Mts., Man. Hindwing eyespot is red-orange edged with black.

ANDROGEUS SWALLOWTAIL *Papilio androgeus,* female   **P. 137**
Tehuantepec, Mexico. Black with iridescent blue patch and pointed tails.

GIANT SWALLOWTAIL *Papilio cresphontes,* male   **P. 133**
Orange Co., Fla. Black with irregular diagonal yellow band.

BAHAMAN SWALLOWTAIL *Papilio andraemon,* male   **P. 135**
Dade Co., Fla. Forewing with yellow bar at end of cell; long, yellow-centered tails.

BROAD-BANDED SWALLOWTAIL *Papilio astyalus,* female   **P. 136**
Sinaloa, Mexico. Blue and gray-green band on hindwing; tails short.

THOAS SWALLOWTAIL *Papilio thoas,* male   **P. 134**
Cameron Co., Texas. Black with relatively even pale yellow diagonal band.

BROAD-BANDED SWALLOWTAIL *Papilio astyalus,* male   **P. 136**
Guanacaste, Costa Rica. Yellow bands very broad; tails narrow, all black.

ORNYTHION SWALLOWTAIL *Papilio ornythion,* male   **P. 136**
Kerr Co., Texas. Tails all black; diagonal band yellow-white.

ANDROGEUS SWALLOWTAIL *Papilio androgeus,* male   **P. 137**
Veracruz, Mexico. Extensive yellow, tails pointed.

SCHAUS' SWALLOWTAIL *Papilio aristodemus,* male   **P. 135**
Lower Matecumbe Key, Fla. Above yellow diagonal band is narrow; tails all black. Below hindwing has broad median chestnut band. *Endangered.*

PLATE 6

OLD WORLD
SWALLOWTAIL

ANDROGEUS
SWALLOWTAIL

GIANT SWALLOWTAIL

BAHAMAN
SWALLOWTAIL

BROAD-BANDED
SWALLOWTAIL

THOAS SWALLOWTAIL

BROAD-BANDED SWALLOWTAIL

ORNYTHION SWALLOWTAIL

ANDROGEUS SWALLOWTAIL

SCHAUS' SWALLOWTAIL

PLATE 7 × ½

SWALLOWTAILS AND WHITES

EASTERN TIGER SWALLOWTAIL *Papilio glaucus,* male   **P. 137**
Bullitt Co., Ky. Yellow with tiger stripes.

EASTERN TIGER SWALLOWTAIL *Papilio glaucus,* female   **P. 137**
Yellow form, Hawkins Co., Tenn. Yellow with tiger stripes; iridescent blue on hindwing.

TWO-TAILED SWALLOWTAIL *Papilio multicaudatus,* male   **P. 139**
Bexar Co., Texas. Large, two tails on each hindwing.

CANADIAN TIGER SWALLOWTAIL *Papilio canadensis,* male   **P. 138**
Windham Co., Vt. Small, black stripes broad, orange overscaling below.

CANADIAN TIGER SWALLOWTAIL *Papilio canadensis,* female   **P. 138**
Marathon Co., Wis. Small, black stripes broad, black along anal vein.

PALAMEDES SWALLOWTAIL *Papilio palamedes,* male   **P. 141**
Ga. Yellow postmedian band; tails filled with yellow. (× 1)

TROPICAL WHITE *Appias drusilla,* female   **P. 145**
Matheson Hammock, Fla. Above with black outer margin and costa; hindwing with yellow-orange; below hindwing satiny white.

TROPICAL WHITE *Appias drusilla,* male   **P. 145**
Matheson Hammock, Fla. Forewing elongate; white except for narrow black edging of forewing.

PINE WHITE *Neophasia menapia,* male   **P. 144**
Ferry Co., Wash. Forewing costa black from base to cell; apex black.

CABBAGE WHITE *Pieris rapae,* female   **P. 149**
Fairfax Co., Va. Above white with one or two white spots on forewing; apex black; underside of hindwing greenish yellow.

CHECKERED WHITE *Pontia protodice,* female   **P. 146**
Mildred, Ks. White with black checkered pattern.

WESTERN WHITE *Pontia occidentalis,* male   **P. 147**
Yakima Co., Wash. Forewing with marginal chevrons lighter than partial submarginal band.

WESTERN WHITE *Pontia occidentalis,* female   **P. 147**
Modoc Co., Calif. More strongly marked than male; below apex and hindwing marked with gray-green.

CHECKERED WHITE *Pontia protodice,* male   **P. 146**
Dallas Co., Texas. White with black marks on outer half of forewing.

PLATE 7

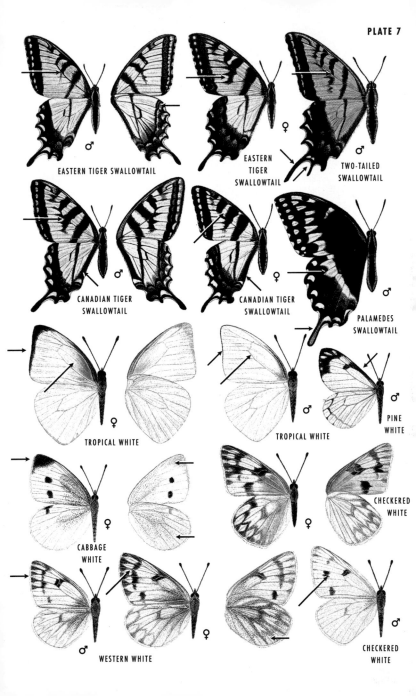

EASTERN TIGER SWALLOWTAIL

EASTERN TIGER SWALLOWTAIL

TWO-TAILED SWALLOWTAIL

CANADIAN TIGER SWALLOWTAIL

CANADIAN TIGER SWALLOWTAIL

PALAMEDES SWALLOWTAIL

TROPICAL WHITE

TROPICAL WHITE

PINE WHITE

CABBAGE WHITE

CHECKERED WHITE

WESTERN WHITE

CHECKERED WHITE

PLATE 8   × ¾

WHITES

MUSTARD WHITE *Pieris napi,* male   **P. 147**
Marathon Co., Wis. Usually lacks black spot on forewing above; hindwing veins outlined with green below.

MUSTARD WHITE *Pieris napi* (Arctic form), male   **P. 147**
White above, lacks black spots.

WEST VIRGINIA WHITE *Pieris virginiensis,* male   **P. 148**
New Brighton, Pa. White above, forewing apex rounded.

GREAT SOUTHERN WHITE *Ascia monuste,* male   **P. 150**
Volusia Co., Fla. White with zigzag black outer margin.

GREAT SOUTHERN WHITE *Ascia monuste,* female, light form   **P. 150**
Volusia Co., Fla. Gray with small black spot in forewing cell.

GREAT SOUTHERN WHITE *Ascia monuste,* female, dark form   **P. 150**
Volusia Co., Fla. Clouded black with small black spot in forewing cell.

WEST VIRGINIA WHITE *Pieris virginiensis,* male   **P. 148**
New Brighton, Pa. Hindwing veins diffusely lined with gray or brown.

FALCATE ORANGETIP *Anthocharis midea,* male   **P. 153**
Sullivan Co., Tenn. Upperside has tip of forewing orange; hindwing is marbled dark green.

FALCATE ORANGETIP *Anthocharis midea,* female   **P. 153**
Carter Co., Tenn. Lacks orange tip; has round black spot in cell.

GIANT WHITE *Ganyra josephina,* male   **P. 151**
Hidalgo Co., Texas. Very large, white with small black spot in cell.

OLYMPIA MARBLE *Euchloe olympia,* male   **P. 152**
Lake Co., Ill. Black bar in cell with gray apex above; open yellow-green marbling on hindwing below.

LARGE MARBLE *Euchloe ausonides,* male   **P. 152**
Riding Mts., Man. Small black mark in forewing cell; dense green marbling on hindwing below.

LYSIDE SULPHUR *Kricogonia lyside,* male   **P. 167**
Cameron Co., Texas. Apex squared off; hindwing with black bar.

LYSIDE SULPHUR *Kricogonia lyside,* female, white form   **P. 167**
Tamaulipas, Mexico. White with yellow at base of wings.

LYSIDE SULPHUR *Kricogonia lyside,* female, yellow form   **P. 167**
Cameron Co., Texas. Both wings pale yellow, darker at base.

GIANT WHITE *Ganyra josephina,* female   **P. 151**
Cameron Co., Texas. White with blurred black marks; black spot at end of forewing cell.

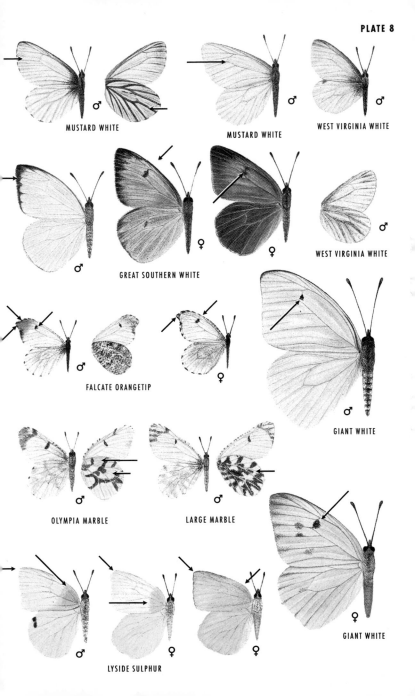

PLATE 8

MUSTARD WHITE

MUSTARD WHITE

WEST VIRGINIA WHITE

GREAT SOUTHERN WHITE

WEST VIRGINIA WHITE

FALCATE ORANGETIP

GIANT WHITE

OLYMPIA MARBLE

LARGE MARBLE

LYSIDE SULPHUR

GIANT WHITE

PLATE 9 × ³⁄₄

SULPHURS

ORANGE SULPHUR *Colias eurytheme,* male, spring form   **P. 155**
Dallas Co., Texas. Small, black margin, orange patch on forewing.

ORANGE SULPHUR *Colias eurytheme,* male, summer form   **P. 155**
Dallas Co., Texas. Large, orange extensive above; silver cell spot on hindwing below usually double; small black submarginal dots on underside of forewing.

ORANGE SULPHUR *Colias eurytheme,* yellow female   **P. 155**
Summer form, Ames, Iowa. Black outer margin irregular with included yellow spots.

ORANGE SULPHUR *Colias eurytheme,* white female   **P. 155**
Summer form, Dallas Co., Texas. Similar to yellow form except for greenish-white ground color.

CLOUDED SULPHUR *Colias philodice,* male   **P. 154**
Decatur, Ind. Regular black outer margin, clear yellow above; underside has double silver cell spot and black dusting on hindwing; forewing has submarginal series of tiny black marks.

CLOUDED SULPHUR *Colias philodice,* female   **P. 154**
Chaffeys Lock, Ont. Similar to male except for included yellow spots in black outer margins.

PINK-EDGED SULPHUR *Colias interior,* male   **P. 159**
Spruce Knob Lake, W. Va. Prominent pink fringes. Tiny black mark in forewing cell above. On underside hindwing is clear yellow with single silver cell spot outlined in pink.

PINK-EDGED SULPHUR *Colias interior,* female   **P. 159**
Spruce Knob Lake, W. Va. Forewing with diffuse black; hindwing lacks black on outer margin.

PALAENO SULPHUR *Colias palaeno,* male   **P. 160**
Fort Churchill, Man. Above wide black margin; underside of hindwing is dusky green with white cell spot not rimmed in pink.

PELIDNE SULPHUR *Colias pelidne,* male   **P. 158**
Nain, Labrador. Cell spots ringed heavily with dark pink; hindwing with heavy black scaling.

GIANT SULPHUR *Colias gigantea,* male   **P. 158**
Nelson River, Man. Lacks submarginal black spots on forewing; cell spot on hindwing may be double.

WESTERN SULPHUR *Colias occidentalis,* male   **P. 156**
Fort Calgary, B.C. Cell spot on hindwing usually single.

HECLA SULPHUR *Colias hecla,* male   **P. 156**
Baker Lake, N.W. Terr. Upperside deep orange; underside dusky green with elongate pink cell spot.

BOOTH'S SULPHUR *Colias hecla × nastes,* male   **P. 157**
Fort Churchill, Man. Intermediate in color and pattern between Hecla and Labrador sulphurs.

LABRADOR SULPHUR *Colias nastes,* male   **P. 157**
Fort Churchill, Man. Dingy white or green-yellow; black borders with enclosed white or green-yellow spots.

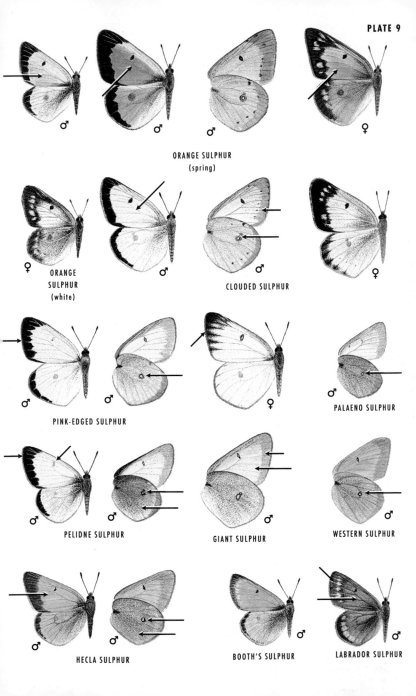

PLATE 9

ORANGE SULPHUR
(spring)

ORANGE
SULPHUR
(white)

CLOUDED SULPHUR

PINK-EDGED SULPHUR

PALAENO SULPHUR

PELIDNE SULPHUR

GIANT SULPHUR

WESTERN SULPHUR

HECLA SULPHUR

BOOTH'S SULPHUR

LABRADOR SULPHUR

PLATE 10   × ¾

SULPHURS

SOUTHERN DOGFACE *Colias cesonia,* male, St. Louis Co., Mo.   **P. 160**
  Yellow dog's head mark on forewing outlined in black.

SOUTHERN DOGFACE *Colias cesonia,* female   **P. 160**
  Brazoria Co., Texas. Forewing apex pointed; dog's head mark more diffuse.

CLOUDLESS SULPHUR *Phoebis sennae,* female   **P. 163**
  Harris Co., Texas. Hollow round black spot in cell; irregular black edging.

CLOUDLESS SULPHUR *Phoebis sennae,* male   **P. 163**
  Jackson Co., Texas. Clear lemon yellow.

STATIRA SULPHUR *Phoebis statira,* male, Dade Co., Fla.   **P. 166**
  Two-toned, inner half lemon yellow, outer half yellow-cream.

STATIRA SULPHUR *Phoebis statira,* female   **P. 166**
  Dade Co., Fla. Solid black cell spot; costal and outer margins evenly edged in black.

LARGE ORANGE SULPHUR *Phoebis agarithe,* male   **P. 164**
  Volusia Co., Fla. Bright orange above; below yellow-orange with straight submarginal line.

LARGE ORANGE SULPHUR *Phoebis agarithe,* female   **P. 164**
  Dallas Co., Texas. Pinkish-white with straight submarginal line on underside of forewing.

ORANGE-BARRED SULPHUR *Phoebis philea,* female   **P. 164**
  Volusia Co., Fla. Forewing with solid black cell spot and offset series of black marks; hindwing with outer half orange.

ORANGE-BARRED SULPHUR *Phoebis philea,* male   **P. 164**
  Volusia Co., Fla. Deep yellow with red-orange bar on forewing and broad red-orange margin on hindwing.

WHITE-ANGLED SULPHUR *Anteos clorinde,* male   **P. 161**
  Cochise Co., Ariz. Large. White or green-white with hooked apex and orange bar on forewing costa. Small cell spot on each wing.

YELLOW-ANGLED SULPHUR *Anteos maerula,* male   **P. 162**
  Tamaulipas, Mexico. Large. Hooked forewing apex. Yellow with small spot in cell.

DAINTY SULPHUR *Nathalis iole,* male, summer form   **P. 174**
  Dallas Co., Texas. Small. Apex black, black bar along inner margin of forewing. Hindwing greenish yellow.

DAINTY SULPHUR *Nathalis iole,* female, summer form   **P. 174**
  Dallas Co., Texas. Hindwing heavily marked with black.

DAINTY SULPHUR *Nathalis iole,* female, winter form   **P. 174**
  Willard, Mo. Black more extensive; underside of hindwing dark green.

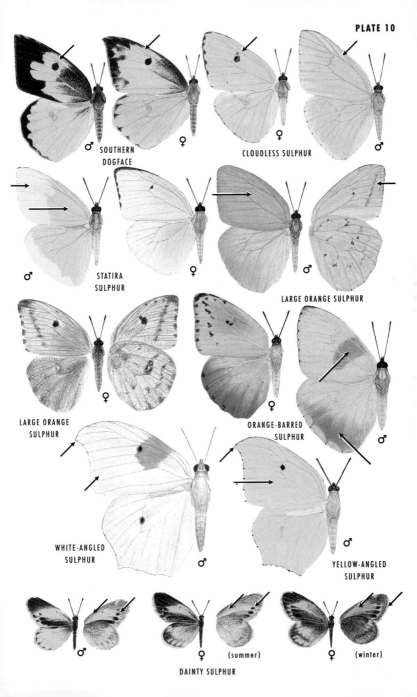

PLATE 10

♂ SOUTHERN
DOGFACE ♀

CLOUDLESS SULPHUR ♀ ♂

STATIRA
SULPHUR ♂ ♀

LARGE ORANGE SULPHUR ♂

LARGE ORANGE
SULPHUR ♀

ORANGE-BARRED
SULPHUR ♀ ♂

WHITE-ANGLED
SULPHUR ♂

YELLOW-ANGLED
SULPHUR ♂

DAINTY SULPHUR ♂ ♀ (summer) ♀ (winter)

PLATE 11   × ¾

SULPHURS

BARRED YELLOW *Eurema daira,* male, summer form   **P. 168**
  Highlands Co., Fla. Forewing apex black, black bar along inner edge
  of forewing.

BARRED YELLOW *Eurema daira,* female, summer form   **P. 168**
  Dade Co., Fla. Forewing apex black, hindwing with irregular black
  marginal patch.

BARRED YELLOW *Eurema daira,* male, winter form   **P. 168**
  Forewing apex and hindwing red-brown with 2 small black spots in
  cell.

BARRED YELLOW *Eurema daira,* male, summer form   **P. 168**
  Underside of hindwing satiny cream-white, lacks black spots.

BOISDUVAL'S YELLOW *Eurema boisduvalianum,* male   **P. 168**
  Tamaulipas, Mexico. Rare. Pale yellow. Irregular black margin with
  suggestion of dog's head on forewing. Stubby tail.

BOISDUVAL'S YELLOW *Eurema boisduvalianum,* female   **P. 168**
  Tamaulipas, Mexico. Pale yellow. Irregular black forewing apex. Suggestion of stubby tail.

ME×ICAN YELLOW *Eurema mexicanum,* male   **P. 169**
  St. Louis Co., Mo. Cream-white with poodle-head mark on forewing;
  suggestion of stubby tail.

TAILED ORANGE *Eurema proterpia,* male, summer form   **P. 169**
  Chiapas, Mexico. Orange with black costal bar on forewing. Veins
  outlined in black.

SLEEPY ORANGE *Eurema nicippe,* male, Dade Co., Fla.   **P. 172**
  Orange with irregular black margins on both wings. Small black spot
  in forewing cell. Underside of hindwing mottled orange-yellow.

SLEEPY ORANGE *Eurema nicippe,* female   **P. 172**
  Dade Co., Fla. Black margin broader than on male.

TAILED ORANGE *Eurema proterpia,* male, winter form   **P. 169**
  Tamaulipas, Mexico. Orange with black costal bar on forewing.
  Pointed tail on hindwing.

LITTLE YELLOW *Eurema lisa,* male   **P. 171**
  Dade Co., Fla. Yellow with black outer margins and small black cell
  spot on forewing.

LITTLE YELLOW *Eurema lisa, female,* Charleston Co., S.C.   **P. 171**
  Yellow with black margins and small black forewing cell spot.

DINA YELLOW *Eurema dina,* male   **P. 172**
  Dade Co., Fla. Orange-yellow with very narrow black edging on
  forewing costa and outer margin.

MIMOSA YELLOW *Eurema nise,* male, Hidalgo Co., Texas   **P. 171**
  Yellow with narrow black outer forewing margin.

MIMOSA YELLOW *Eurema nise,* female   **P. 171**
  Hidalgo Co., Texas. Yellow with narrow black outer margin.

DINA YELLOW *Eurema dina,* female, Dade Co., Fla.   **P. 172**
  Orange-yellow with diffuse black on forewing apex.

PLATE 11

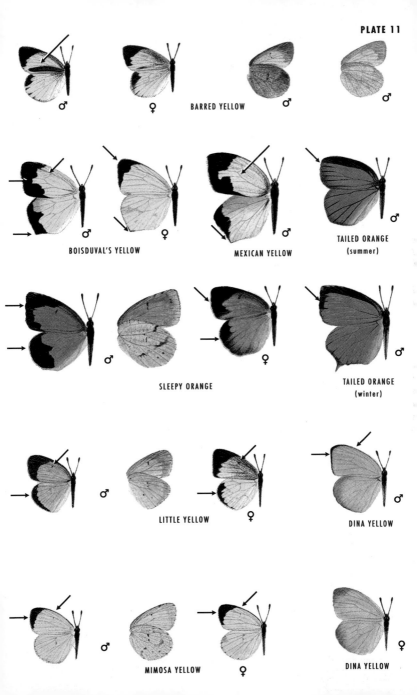

BARRED YELLOW

BOISDUVAL'S YELLOW

MEXICAN YELLOW

TAILED ORANGE
(summer)

SLEEPY ORANGE

TAILED ORANGE
(winter)

LITTLE YELLOW

DINA YELLOW

MIMOSA YELLOW

DINA YELLOW

PLATE 12   × 1

HARVESTER, COPPERS, HAIRSTREAKS

HARVESTER *Feniseca tarquinius*, female   **P. 177**
Kings Co., N.Y. Upperside orange with black areas and spots; underside of hindwing orange-brown with faint white scrawls.

AMERICAN COPPER *Lycaena phlaeas*, female   **P. 178**
Andover, N.J. Forewing iridescent fiery red-orange with black spots; hindwing gray with red-orange border. Underside of hindwing gray with marginal red-orange line.

PURPLISH COPPER *Lycaena helloides*, male   **P. 182**
Pinkney, Mich. Iridescent purple-brown; zigzag orange outer margin on hindwing.

PURPLISH COPPER *Lycaena helloides*, female   **P. 182**
Riding Mts., Man. Orange with black spots and black outer margin on forewing. Hindwing has zigzag orange outer margin on hindwing.

DORCAS COPPER *Lycaena dorcas*, female   **P. 181**
Penobscot Co., Me. Brown with limited light areas; hindwing with limited red-orange border near anal angle.

DORCAS COPPER *Lycaena dorcas*, male   **P. 181**
Penobscot Co., Me. Iridescent purple-brown; hindwing has only a few red-orange spots near anal angle.

BOG COPPER *Lycaena epixanthe*, male   **P. 180**
Halifax Co., N.S. Small, purple-brown above; off-white underneath with a thin zigzag red submarginal line on outer margin of hindwing.

RUDDY COPPER *Lycaena rubidus*, male   **P. 180**
Yakima Co., Wash. Fiery red-orange on both wings above.

BOG COPPER *Lycaena epixanthe*, female   **P. 180**
Lakehurst, N. J. Brown or gray-brown above; tan or brown below with thin red submarginal line on outer margin of hindwing.

GRAY COPPER *Lycaena dione*, male   **P. 179**
Cook Co., Ill. Gray above with one or two orange spots at anal angle of hindwing. Below gray-white with small black spots and zigzag red marginal line on outer margin of hindwing.

BRONZE COPPER *Lycaena hyllus*, male   **P. 179**
Caroline Co., Md. Above iridescent purple-brown with orange band along margin of hindwing. Below forewing orange with tiny black spots, hindwing off-white with tiny black spots and orange marginal band.

ATALA *Eumaeus atala*, male   **P. 183**
Dade Co., Fla. Abdomen red. Lacks tails. Iridescent blue-green above on velvet black, iridescent yellow-green on outer margin of hindwing; below black with 3 series of iridescent yellow-green marks.

GREAT PURPLE HAIRSTREAK *Atlides halesus*, male   **P. 185**
Horry Co., S.C. Underside of abdomen red. Above iridescent blue with black patch on forewing; iridescent gold marks near anal angle of hindwing. Black beneath with gold marks near anal angle of hindwing.

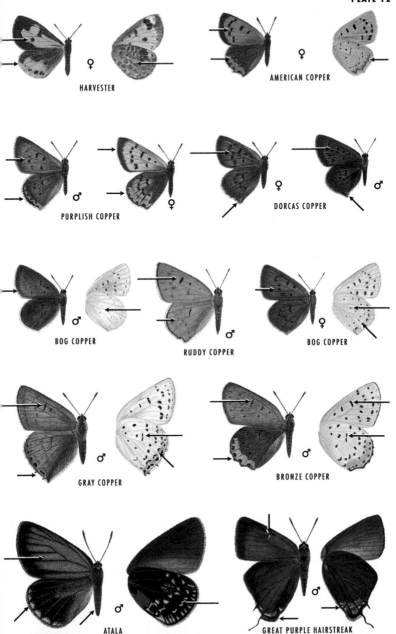

PLATE 12

HARVESTER ♀

AMERICAN COPPER ♀

PURPLISH COPPER ♂ ♀

DORCAS COPPER ♀ ♂

BOG COPPER ♂

RUDDY COPPER ♂

BOG COPPER ♀

GRAY COPPER ♂

BRONZE COPPER ♂

ATALA ♂

GREAT PURPLE HAIRSTREAK ♂

PLATE 13 × 1

HAIRSTREAKS

AMETHYST HAIRSTREAK *Chlorostrymon maesites,* male   **P. 186**
Dade Co., Fla. Yellow-green with thin postmedian line.

SILVER-BANDED HAIRSTREAK *Chlorostrymon simaethis,* female   **P. 186**
North Key Largo, Fla. Green with silver-white postmedian band.

CLENCH'S GREENSTREAK *Cyanophrys miserabilis,* male   **P. 194**
Cameron Co., Texas. Yellow-green with red-brown submarginal spots.

GOODSON'S GREENSTREAK *Cyanophrys goodsoni,* male   **P. 194**
Guanacaste, Costa Rica. Lacks tails. Green with single red-brown spot at anal angle.

JUNIPER HAIRSTREAK *Callophrys gryneus siva,* male   **P. 196**
Pennington Co., S.D. Yellow-green. White postmedian spot band aligned.

JUNIPER HAIRSTREAK *Callophrys gryneus gryneus,* male   **P. 195**
Freestone Co., Texas. Apple-green. White line continuous.

JUNIPER HAIRSTREAK *Callophrys gryneus sweadneri*   **P. 196**
Male, Volusia Co., Fla.

HESSEL'S HAIRSTREAK *Callophrys hesseli,* male   **P. 196**
Hoke Co., N.C. Blue-green. White line on hindwing broken.

XAMI HAIRSTREAK *Callophrys xami,* male   **P. 197**
Cameron Co., Texas. Yellow-green. White W near tails.

TROPICAL GREENSTREAK *Cyanophrys herodotus*   **P. 195**
Male, Guanacaste, Costa Rica. Single red-brown spot near tail.

ECHION HAIRSTREAK *Tmolus echion,* male   **P. 202**
Tamaulipas, Mexico. Irregular orange spot rows.

AZIA HAIRSTREAK *Ministrymon azia,* female   **P. 202**
Kerr Co., Texas. Narrow orange white-edged line.

RED-BANDED HAIRSTREAK *Calycopis cecrops,* male   **P. 204**
Dare Co., N.C. Postmedian line edged with red-orange.

DUSKY-BLUE GROUNDSTREAK *Calycopis isobeon,* male   **P. 204**
Hidalgo Co., Texas. Eyespot with orange equal to black.

FULVOUS HAIRSTREAK *Electrostrymon angelia,* male   **P. 206**
San Juan, Puerto Rico. Large eyespot; white-edged black line.

RUDDY HAIRSTREAK *Electrostrymon sangala,* male   **P. 205**
Sinaloa, Mexico. Postmedian line very thin.

NORTHERN HAIRSTREAK *Satyrium favonius ontario,* male   **P. 194**
Above gray-brown with orange spot on outer margin. Below narrow orange cap on blue tail spot; white-edged black W near anal margin.

SOUTHERN HAIRSTREAK *Satyrium favonius favonius*   **P. 193**
Female, Samsula, Fla. Two long tails. Orange extensive on hindwing.

PLATE 13

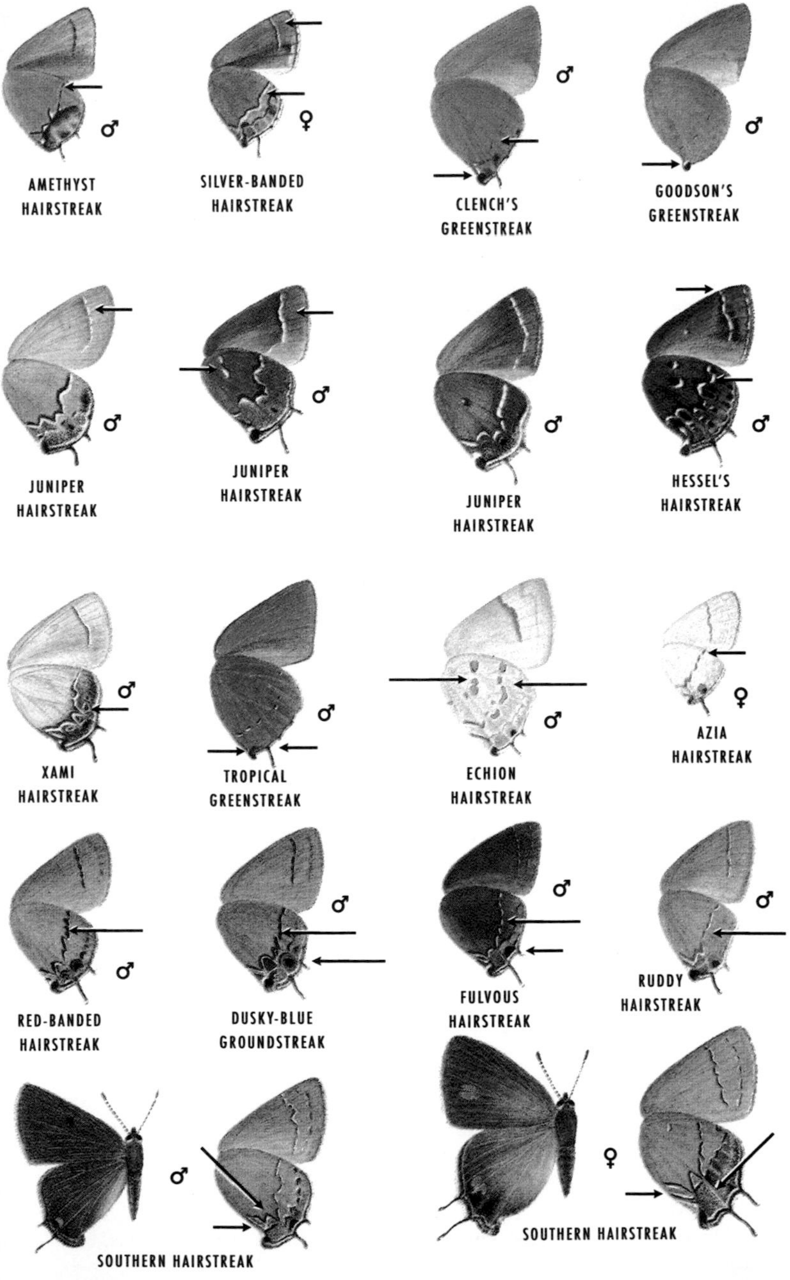

AMETHYST
HAIRSTREAK ♂

SILVER-BANDED
HAIRSTREAK ♀

CLENCH'S
GREENSTREAK ♂

GOODSON'S
GREENSTREAK ♂

JUNIPER
HAIRSTREAK ♂

JUNIPER
HAIRSTREAK ♂

JUNIPER
HAIRSTREAK ♂

HESSEL'S
HAIRSTREAK ♂

XAMI
HAIRSTREAK ♂

TROPICAL
GREENSTREAK ♂

ECHION
HAIRSTREAK ♂

AZIA
HAIRSTREAK ♀

RED-BANDED
HAIRSTREAK ♂

DUSKY-BLUE
GROUNDSTREAK ♂

FULVOUS
HAIRSTREAK ♂

RUDDY
HAIRSTREAK ♂

SOUTHERN HAIRSTREAK ♂

SOUTHERN HAIRSTREAK ♀

PLATE 14   × 1

HAIRSTREAKS

SOAPBERRY HAIRSTREAK *Phaeostrymon alcestis,* female   **P. 187**
Dallas Co., Texas. Discal cells with narrow black-edged white bars.

CORAL HAIRSTREAK *Satyrium titus,* male   **P. 188**
Washington, D.C. Lacks tails. Row of coral red spots on hindwing.

ACADIAN HAIRSTREAK *Satyrium acadicum,* male   **P. 189**
Walworth Co., Wis. Row of round black spots; blue tail-spot capped
with orange.

EDWARDS' HAIRSTREAK *Satyrium edwardsii,* female   **P. 190**
Sussex Co., N.J. Row of oval dark brown spots. Tail-spot lacks orange.

BANDED HAIRSTREAK *Satyrium calanus,* female   **P. 191**
Burlington Co., N.J. Band of dark, white-edged dashes.

HICKORY HAIRSTREAK *Satyrium caryaevorum,* female   **P. 191**
Sussex Co., N.J. Offset band of broad dark dashes. Thin black cap on
orange eyespot.

KING'S HAIRSTREAK *Satyrium kingi,* male   **P. 192**
Mt. Pleasant, S.C. Hindwing outer margin indented above tail. Blue
tail spot capped with orange.

STRIPED HAIRSTREAK *Satyrium liparops,* male   **P. 192**
Chester Co., N.J. Both wings striped with 3 thin white lines.

BROWN ELFIN *Callophrys augustinus,* female   **P. 197**
Frederick, Md. Lobed anal angle of hindwing. Brown or red-brown.

HOARY ELFIN *Callophrys polios,* male   **P. 197**
Chatsworth, N.J. Irregular white line on forewing. Outer half of hindwing frosted light gray.

FROSTED ELFIN *Callophrys irus,* male   **P. 198**
Holland, Ohio. Stubby tail. Above forewing with stigma. Irregular
white line below. Black spot above tail.

EASTERN PINE ELFIN *Callophrys niphon,* male   **P. 200**
Montgomery Co., Md. Hindwing with submarginal gray band outside
black inverted crescents.

WESTERN PINE ELFIN *Callophrys eryphon,* male   **P. 200**
Jefferson Co., Colo. Jagged submarginal dark bands.

HENRY'S ELFIN *Callophrys henrici,* male   **P. 199**
Forewing lacks stigma. Below postmedian line relatively straight.

BOG ELFIN *Callophrys lanoraieensis,* female   **P. 200**
Penobscot Co., Me. Small. Pattern reduced. Outer margin frosted
gray.

CLYTIE HAIRSTREAK *Ministrymon clytie,* female   **P. 203**
Guanacaste, Costa Rica. Forewing with orange median dash. Hindwing with orange lines.

MALLOW SCRUB-HAIRSTREAK *Strymon istapa,* male   **P. 209**
Dade Co., Fla. Short tail. Single, round basal spot on hindwing.

DISGUISED SCRUB-HAIRSTREAK *Strymon limenia,* male   **P. 210**
Runaway Bay, Jamaica. Tail long. Two round basal hindwing spots.

PLATE 14

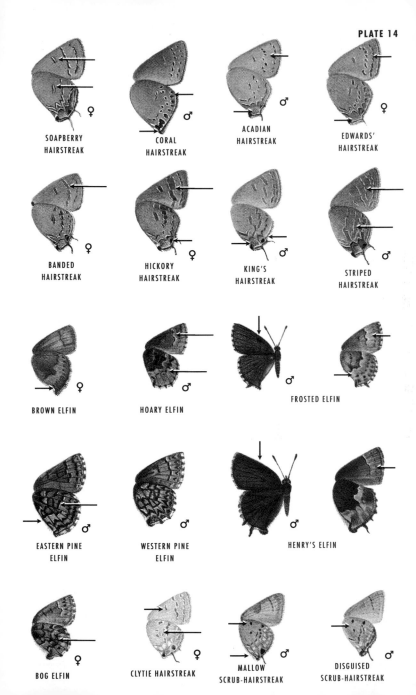

SOAPBERRY
HAIRSTREAK
♀

CORAL
HAIRSTREAK
♂

ACADIAN
HAIRSTREAK
♂

EDWARDS'
HAIRSTREAK
♀

BANDED
HAIRSTREAK
♀

HICKORY
HAIRSTREAK
♀

KING'S
HAIRSTREAK
♂

STRIPED
HAIRSTREAK
♂

BROWN ELFIN
♀

HOARY ELFIN
♂

FROSTED ELFIN
♂

EASTERN PINE
ELFIN
♂

WESTERN PINE
ELFIN
♂

HENRY'S ELFIN
♂

BOG ELFIN
♀

CLYTIE HAIRSTREAK
♀

MALLOW
SCRUB-HAIRSTREAK
♂

DISGUISED
SCRUB-HAIRSTREAK
♂

PLATE 15   × 1

HAIRSTREAKS AND BLUES

WHITE M HAIRSTREAK *Parrhasius m-album,* male   **P. 201**
Hernando Co., Fla. Iridescent blue above. Below hindwing with basal white spot on costa; white M near anal angle.

MARTIAL SCRUB-HAIRSTREAK *Strymon martialis,* male   **P. 208**
Dade Co., Fla. Above black with limited steel blue. Underside has strong black and white line; large, blurred eyespot on outer margin.

RED-CRESCENT SCRUB-HAIRSTREAK *Strymon rufofusca,* male   **P. 207**
Guanacaste, Costa Rica. Reddish orange line of short dashes on hindwing.

RED-LINED SCRUB-HAIRSTREAK *Strymon bebrycia,* male   **P. 208**
Guanacaste, Costa Rica. Hindwing with red-orange line, edged outwardly with white.

YOJOA SCRUB-HAIRSTREAK *Strymon yojoa,* male   **P. 208**
Veracruz, Mexico. Submarginal gray-white bands on both wings.

WHITE SCRUB-HAIRSTREAK *Strymon albata,* male   **P. 209**
Tamaulipas, Mexico. Extensive white patches. Eyespot with orange.

GRAY HAIRSTREAK *Strymon melinus,* male   **P. 207**
Labette Co., Kans. Gray with postmedian line relatively straight.

BARTRAM'S SCRUB-HAIRSTREAK *Strymon acis,* male   **P. 209**
Big Pine Key, Fla. Bold white line, large orange eyespot, and 2 white basal spots.

LACEY'S SCRUB-HAIRSTREAK *Strymon alea,* male   **P. 209**
Veracruz, Mexico. Complex pattern of blotches, lines, and spots.

TAILLESS SCRUB-HAIRSTREAK *Strymon cestri,* male   **P. 210**
Alajuela, Costa Rica. Lacks tails. Hindwing marbled gray and white.

LANTANA SCRUB-HAIRSTREAK *Strymon bazochii,* male   **P. 210**
Tamaulipas, Mexico. Lacks tails. Prominent costal spot on hindwing.

WESTERN PYGMY-BLUE *Brephidium exile,* female   **P. 211**
Cameron Co., Texas. Hindwing white basally. Fringe mainly white.

EASTERN PYGMY-BLUE *Brephidium isophthalma,* female   **P. 211**
Volusia Co., Fla. Hindwing and fringes dark brown.

EARLY HAIRSTREAK *Erora laetus,* female   **P. 213**
Buncombe Co., N.C. Lacks tails. Hindwing jade green or gray green. Orange postmedian line, submarginal row of orange spots.

CYNA BLUE *Zizula cyna,* male   **P. 213**
Brewster Co., Texas. Hindwing pale gray with minute black dots.

MIAMI BLUE *Hemiargus thomasi,* female   **P. 213**
Key Largo, Fla. Orange spot at anal angle. White hindwing band.

CERAUNUS BLUE *Hemiargus ceraunus,* female   **P. 213**
Dade Co., Fla. Postmedian row of dark dashes on both wings.

REAKIRT'S BLUE *Hemiargus isola,* female   **P. 214**
Douglas Co., Kans. Forewing apex squared off; row of 5 prominent round, black spots under forewing.

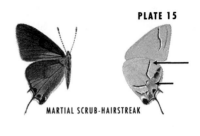

PLATE 15

WHITE M HAIRSTREAK

MARTIAL SCRUB-HAIRSTREAK

RED-CRESCENT SCRUB-HAIRSTREAK

RED-LINED SCRUB-HAIRSTREAK

YOJOA SCRUB-HAIRSTREAK

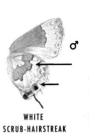

WHITE SCRUB-HAIRSTREAK

GRAY HAIRSTREAK

BARTRAM'S SCRUB-HAIRSTREAK

LACEY'S SCRUB-HAIRSTREAK

TAILLESS SCRUB-HAIRSTREAK

LANTANA SCRUB-HAIRSTREAK

WESTERN PYGMY-BLUE

EASTERN PYGMY-BLUE

EARLY HAIRSTREAK

CYNA BLUE

MIAMI BLUE

CERAUNUS BLUE

REAKIRT'S BLUE

PLATE 16 ✕ 1¼

BLUES

CASSIUS BLUE *Leptotes cassius,* female, Palm Beach Co., Fla. **P. 212**
Broken pale lines; blank areas along inner margin.

MARINE BLUE *Leptotes marina,* female **P. 212**
Grant Co., N. Mex. Continuous pale brown lines on both wings.

SILVERY BLUE *Glaucopsyche lygdamus,* male **P. 218**
Arostook Co., Me. Submarginal row of round, black, white-rimmed spots.

GREENISH BLUE *Plebejus saepiolus,* male **P. 220**
Crystal, Me. Gray white with irregular black dots.

EASTERN TAILED-BLUE *Everes comyntas,* male **P. 214**
Montgomery Co., Md. Tailed. Blue above. Distinct pattern underneath with black bar at end of cell; 2 large orange spots on outer margin.

EASTERN TAILED-BLUE *Everes comyntas,* female **P. 214**
Douglas Co., Kan. Brown above. Spring individuals with blue basally.

WESTERN TAILED-BLUE *Everes amyntula,* male **P. 215**
Kelwood, Man. Tailed. Black pattern lacking or indistinct. Single small orange spot near tail.

SPRING AZURE *Celastrina argiolus,* male **P. 216**
Sussex Co., Del. Blue above.

SPRING AZURE *Celastrina argiolus,* female, form *marginata* **P. 216**
Sussex Co., Del. Blue above with black costa and outer margin on forewing. Hindwing gray-white with small black spots.

SPRING AZURE *Celastrina argiolus,* female, summer form **P. 216**
Franklin Co., Kan. More extensive black and white patch on hindwing.

APPALACHIAN AZURE *Celastrina neglectamajor,* male **P. 217**
Pendleton Co., W. Va. Large. Chalk white submarginal row reduced to 1–3 clear-cut black spots.

SPRING AZURE *Celastrina argiolus lucia,* male **P. 216**
Stratton, Me. Small, dark.

DUSKY AZURE *Celastrina ebenina,* male **P. 217**
Bullitt Co., Ky. Uniformly black-gray.

DUSKY AZURE *Celastrina ebenina,* female **P. 217**
Menifee Co., Ky. Dark with restricted areas of blue-gray.

MELISSA BLUE *Lycaeides melissa,* male **P. 219**
Larimer Co., Colo. Blue above; below distinct black spot pattern; orange border extends to forewing.

KARNER BLUE *Lycaeides melissa samuelis,* female **P. 219**
Sullivan Co., N.Y. Blackish with blue basally.

NORTHERN BLUE *Lycaeides idas,* male **P. 219**
Picton, N.S. Submarginal orange spots reduced. Black spots at vein endings.

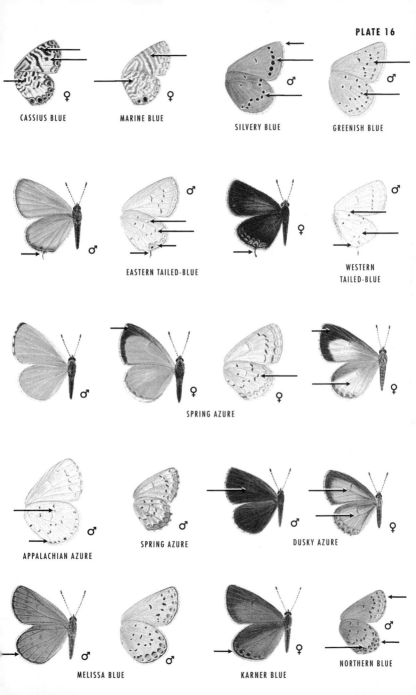

PLATE 16

CASSIUS BLUE

MARINE BLUE

SILVERY BLUE

GREENISH BLUE

EASTERN TAILED-BLUE

WESTERN TAILED-BLUE

SPRING AZURE

APPALACHIAN AZURE

SPRING AZURE

DUSKY AZURE

MELISSA BLUE

KARNER BLUE

NORTHERN BLUE

PLATE 17   × 1⅓

BLUES AND METALMARKS

LITTLE METALMARK *Calephelis virginiensis,* male   **P. 223**
Key Largo, Fla. Small. Fringes dark not checkered.

ARCTIC BLUE *Agriades glandon,* male   **P. 221**
Aweme, Man. Hindwing has black spots obsolete or surrounded by white patches.

CRANBERRY BLUE *Vacciniina optilete,* male   **P. 221**
Bilby, Alta. Two strong spot rows. One black-edged orange spot at anal angle.

RED-BORDERED METALMARK *Caria ino,* male   **P. 226**
Cameron Co., Texas. Base of forewing costa arched. Dark with reddish border.

NORTHERN METALMARK *Calephelis borealis,* male   **P. 224**
Sussex Co., N. J. Forewing rounded. Dark median band.

SWAMP METALMARK *Calephelis mutica,* male   **P. 225**
Berrien Co., Mich. Forewing relatively pointed. Brightly colored.

FATAL METALMARK *Calephelis nemesis,* male   **P. 224**
Hidalgo Co., Texas. Fringes checkered. Forewing pointed. Dark median band.

ROUNDED METALMARK *Calephelis nilus,* female   **P. 225**
Cameron Co., Texas. Indistinctly checkered fringe.

RAWSON'S METALMARK *Calephelis rawsoni,* female   **P. 225**
Brewster Co., Texas. Median band weak. Fringes checkered.

WALKER'S METALMARK *Apodemia walkeri,* female   **P. 228**
Ocotlan, Mexico. Gray with smeared white band and checks.

CURVE-WINGED METALMARK *Emesis emesia,* male   **P. 227**
Escuintla, Guatemala. Forewing costa curved with translucent white dash.

RED-BORDERED PIXIE *Melanis pixe,* female   **P. 226**
Veracruz, Mexico. Black. Forewing apex yellow-orange; red basal spot.

NARROW-WINGED METALMARK *Apodemia multiplaga*   **P. 227**
Male, Cameron Co., Texas. Outer margin of forewing concave. Dark brown with white spots and checks.

BLUE METALMARK *Lasaia sula,* male   **P. 226**
Hidalgo Co., Texas. Iridescent blue-green.

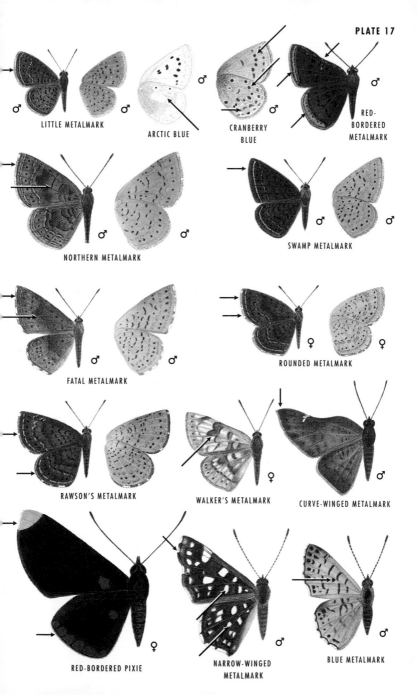

PLATE 17

LITTLE METALMARK

ARCTIC BLUE

CRANBERRY BLUE

RED-BORDERED METALMARK

NORTHERN METALMARK

SWAMP METALMARK

FATAL METALMARK

ROUNDED METALMARK

RAWSON'S METALMARK

WALKER'S METALMARK

CURVE-WINGED METALMARK

RED-BORDERED PIXIE

NARROW-WINGED METALMARK

BLUE METALMARK

PLATE 18 ⨯ 1

SNOUTS AND BRUSHFOOTS

AMERICAN SNOUT *Libytheana carinenta bachmanii*, male   **P. 230**
    Hidalgo Co., Texas. Beaklike snout; squared off apex.

SILVER-BORDERED FRITILLARY *Boloria selene*, male   **P. 243**
    Andover, N. J. Hindwing has metallic silver pattern.

AMERICAN SNOUT *Libytheana carinenta carinenta*, female   **P. 230**
    Harris Co., Texas. Beaklike snout. Restricted orange marks.

AMERICAN SNOUT *Libytheana carinenta motya*, male   **P. 230**
    Cuba. Beaklike snout. Blurred pattern.

BOG FRITILLARY *Boloria eunomia*, male   **P. 242**
    Nelson River, Man. White non-metallic pattern; round white sub-marginal spots.

MOUNTAIN FRITILLARY *Boloria napaea*, male   **P. 242**
    Shelf Lake, N.W. Terr. Pointed forewing and angled hindwing. Subtle pattern.

MEADOW FRITILLARY *Boloria bellona*, male   **P. 243**
    Greenwood Lake, Mich. Squared-off forewing apex; lacks off-white basal patch on hindwing below.

FRIGGA FRITILLARY *Boloria frigga*, male   **P. 244**
    Manitoba. Forewing apex pointed — not squared off; basal off-white patch on hindwing.

DINGY FRITILLARY *Boloria improba*, male   **P. 244**
    Shelf Lake, N.W. Terr. Pattern indistinct; outer half of hindwing is grayish.

POLARIS FRITILLARY *Boloria polaris*, male   **P. 245**
    Shepperville, Que. Hindwing with frosted white appearance; post-median black spots surrounded with white. High arctic.

FREIJA FRITILLARY *Boloria freija*, male   **P. 245**
    Hopedale, Labrador. Black zigzag line on hindwing; arrowhead-shaped white discal and costal spots.

TITANIA FRITILLARY *Boloria titania*, male   **P. 245**
    Mt. Washington, N.H. Hindwing with thin marginal white spots capped inwardly with brown.

ARCTIC FRITILLARY *Boloria chariclea*, male   **P. 246**
    Barnard Harbor, N.W. Terr. Marginal row of thin white streaks on hindwing. Arctic tundra only.

DOTTED CHECKERSPOT *Poladryas minuta*, male   **P. 247**
    Kerr Co., Texas. Hindwing has double row of marginal white spots and median double row of black dots.

TINY CHECKERSPOT *Dymasia dymas*, male   **P. 253**
    Texas. Hindwing has terminal black line and marginal white spots.

ELADA CHECKERSPOT *Texola elada*, female   **P. 254**
    Bexar Co., Texas. Small. Hindwing with red-orange marginal band.

SAGEBRUSH CHECKERSPOT *Chlosyne acastus*, male   **P. 252**
    Iron Co., Utah. Hindwing checkered pattern of off-white spots has pearly sheen. Western part of our area only.

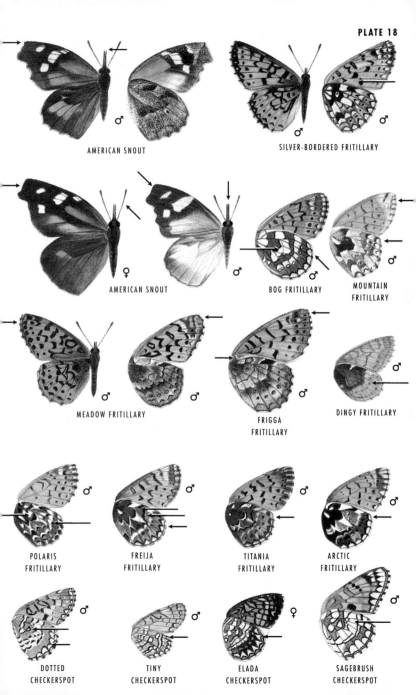

PLATE 18

AMERICAN SNOUT

SILVER-BORDERED FRITILLARY

AMERICAN SNOUT

BOG FRITILLARY

MOUNTAIN FRITILLARY

MEADOW FRITILLARY

FRIGGA FRITILLARY

DINGY FRITILLARY

POLARIS FRITILLARY

FREIJA FRITILLARY

TITANIA FRITILLARY

ARCTIC FRITILLARY

DOTTED CHECKERSPOT

TINY CHECKERSPOT

ELADA CHECKERSPOT

SAGEBRUSH CHECKERSPOT

PLATE 19 × ¾

BRUSHFOOTS AND ACMON BLUE

SILVERY CHECKERSPOT *Chlosyne nycteis*, male   **P. 251**
Green Oak, Mich. Upperside of hindwing has some white-centered submarginal spots. Underside of hindwing is pale with marginal crescent.

HARRIS' CHECKERSPOT *Chlosyne harrisii*, male   **P. 252**
Slippery Rock, Pa. Underside of hindwing has checkered pattern.

GORGONE CHECKERSPOT *Chlosyne gorgone*, male   **P. 251**
Dallas Co., Texas. Underside of hindwing has zigzag pattern of bars and scallops.

THEONA CHECKERSPOT *Thessalia theona*, female   **P. 247**
Llano Co., Texas. Has complex pattern on underside of hindwing.

FULVIA CHECKERSPOT *Thessalia fulvia*, female   **P. 248**
S. Ariz. Hindwing underside has black-lined veins on cream background; black submarginal band with included cream dots.

ACMON BLUE *Plebejus acmon*, male   **P. 221**
Underside of hindwing has submarginal row of orange spots, each containing metallic scales.

GULF FRITILLARY *Agraulis vanillae*, male   **P. 231**
Ottawa, Kan. Orange above. Underside of hindwing has pattern of elongate, metallic silver spots.

ZEBRA *Heliconius charithonius*, male   **P. 233**
Isla Morada, Fla. Black with narrow yellow stripes.

MEXICAN SILVERSPOT *Dione moneta*, male   **P. 232**
Tamaulipas, Mexico. Dark brown above. Underside of hindwing with silver spots; veins black-lined.

BANDED ORANGE HELICONIAN *Dryadula phaetusa*, male   **P. 232**
Oaxaca, Mexico. Orange and black tiger pattern above and below.

ERATO HELICONIAN *Heliconius erato*, male   **P. 234**
Jalisco, Mexico. Black with pink patch on forewing and thin yellow stripe on hindwing.

JULIA *Dryas iulia*, male   **P. 232**
Key Largo, Fla. Orange with narrow black border on outer margin.

PLATE 19

SILVERY CHECKERSPOT

HARRIS' CHECKERSPOT

GORGONE CHECKERSPOT

THEONA
CHECKERSPOT

FULVIA
CHECKERSPOT

ACMON BLUE

GULF FRITILLARY

ZEBRA

MEXICAN
SILVERSPOT

BANDED ORANGE
HELICONIAN

ERATO HELICONIAN

JULIA

PLATE 20   × ⅔

BRUSHFOOTS

VARIEGATED FRITILLARY *Euptoieta claudia,* male   **P. 235**
   Brinkley, Va. Forewing pointed; hindwing angled. Underside of
   hindwing mottled without silver spots.

MEXICAN FRITILLARY *Euptoieta hegesia,* male   **P. 235**
   Harris Co., Texas. Hindwing without strong angles. Basal half of
   hindwing below plain orange without pattern.

ISABELLA'S HELICONIAN *Eueides isabella,* male   **P. 233**
   Tamaulipas, Mexico. Forewing black with yellow patches on
   outer half; hindwing orange with 2 black stripes.

DIANA *Speyeria diana,* female   **P. 236**
   Carter Co., Tenn. Black with blue on outer half of hindwing.

GREAT SPANGLED FRITILLARY *Speyeria cybele,* male   **P. 237**
   Fairfax Co., Va. Forewing with black scaling on veins. Underside
   of hindwing has broad, pale submarginal band.

CALLIPPE FRITILLARY *Speyeria callippe,* male   **P. 240**
   Slope Co., N.D. Hindwing with metallic silver spots on bright
   blue-green background.

DIANA *Speyeria diana,* male   **P. 236**
   Fannin Co., Ga. Orange with black basally.

ATLANTIS FRITILLARY *Speyeria atlantis,* male   **P. 240**
   Oliverea, N.Y. Forewing has black outer margin; underside of
   hindwing has dark disk and narrow, pale submarginal band.

EDWARDS' FRITILLARY *Speyeria edwardsii,* female   **P. 239**
   Albany Co., Wyo. Hindwing gray-green with metallic silver spots.

REGAL FRITILLARY *Speyeria idalia,* male   **P. 239**
   Montgomery Co., Va. Upperside of forewing red-orange with or-
   nate black spots; hindwing black with postmedian row of white
   spots. Underside of hindwing black with silver-white spot pattern.

APHRODITE FRITILLARY *Speyeria aphrodite,* male   **P. 238**
   Lost River S.P., W. Va. Forewing with small black spot below cell;
   underside of hindwing has submarginal band narrow or lacking.

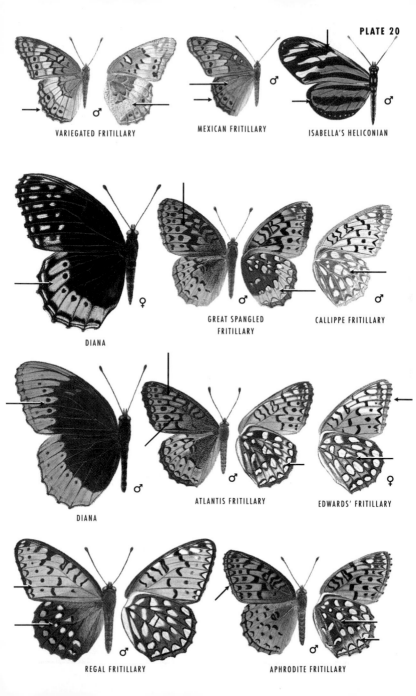

PLATE 20

VARIEGATED FRITILLARY ♂

MEXICAN FRITILLARY ♂

ISABELLA'S HELICONIAN ♂

DIANA ♀

GREAT SPANGLED FRITILLARY ♂

CALLIPPE FRITILLARY ♂

DIANA ♂

ATLANTIS FRITILLARY ♂

EDWARDS' FRITILLARY ♀

REGAL FRITILLARY ♂

APHRODITE FRITILLARY ♂

PLATE 21   × 1

BRUSHFOOTS

BORDERED PATCH *Chlosyne lacinia,* male, Bexar Co., Texas   **P. 248**
   Broad transverse orange band across hindwing above; repeated below
   in cream. White dots in black submarginal band.

MORMON FRITILLARY *Speyeria mormonia,* male   **P. 241**
   Pennington Co., S.D. Forewing rounded. Metallic silver spots small
   and round. Hindwing disk greenish.

CORONIS FRITILLARY *Speyeria coronis,* male, Albany Co., Wyo.   **P. 240**
   Hindwing with marginal silver spots rounded inwardly.

CRIMSON PATCH *Chlosyne janais,* male, Harris Co., Texas   **P. 249**
   Black with large red-orange patch on basal half of hindwing. On underside patch is cream-yellow subtended by red-orange margin.

BANDED PATCH *Chlosyne endeis,* female   **P. 249**
   Edwards Co., Texas. Larger than Definite Patch. Rare in s. Texas.

DEFINITE PATCH *Chlosyne definita,* female   **P. 249**
   Nueces Co., Texas. Orange submarginal band on hindwing has one
   included white spot.

TEXAN CRESCENT *Phyciodes texana,* female   **P. 254**
   Cameron Co., Texas. Outer margin of forewing concave. Brown with
   some red-brown scaling near base.

TEXAN CRESCENT *Phyciodes texana seminole,* male   **P. 254**
   Alachua Co., Fla. Larger spots and broader cream band on hindwing.

RED-SPOTTED PATCH *Chlosyne marina,* female   **P. 251**
   Tehuacan, Mexico. Forewing pointed. Black and white forewing.
   Hindwing has irregular yellow patch and red submarginal band.

ROSITA PATCH *Chlosyne rosita,* male   **P. 250**
   Chiapas, Mexico. A smaller version of Crimson Patch. Hindwing
   patch has some yellow basally.

ELF *Microtia elva,* male   **P. 253**
   Valles, Mexico. Small. Black with yellow-orange patches. Rare.

CUBAN CRESCENT *Phyciodes frisia,* male   **P. 255**
   Chokoloskee, Fla. Black and orange with orange-yellow band across
   hindwing. Southern Florida and keys.

TULCIS CRESCENT *Phyciodes frisia tulcis,* female   **P. 255**
   Nueces Co., Texas. Forewing outer margin slightly indented. Black
   and cream-yellow. Local in Lower Rio Grande Valley.

BLACK CRESCENT *Phyciodes ptolyca,* male   **P. 255**
   Veracruz, Mexico. Rare vagrant to s. Texas.

PHAON CRESCENT *Phyciodes phaon,* female   **P. 256**
   Dallas Co., Texas. Forewing with pale cream median band. Black
   markings extensive.

VESTA CRESCENT *Phyciodes vesta,* female   **P. 255**
   Cameron Co., Texas. Finely marked with black lines. Underside of
   forewing with irregular orange circles on darker background.

PAINTED CRESCENT *Phyciodes pictus,* female   **P. 259**
   Pima Co., Ariz. Western plains. Forewing apex and hindwing clear
   yellow cream.

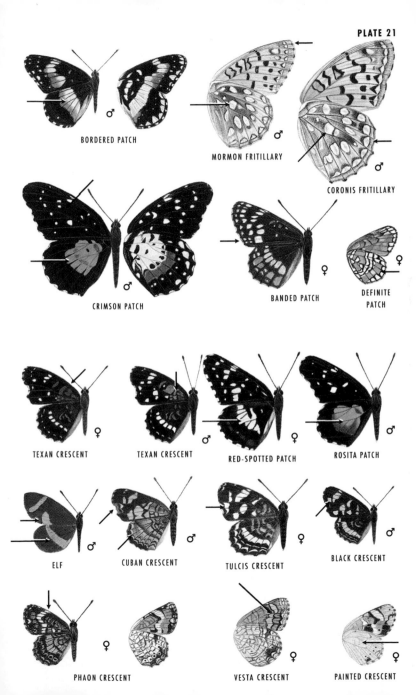

PLATE 21

BORDERED PATCH ♂

MORMON FRITILLARY ♂

CORONIS FRITILLARY ♂

CRIMSON PATCH ♂

BANDED PATCH ♀

DEFINITE PATCH ♀

TEXAN CRESCENT ♀

TEXAN CRESCENT ♂

RED-SPOTTED PATCH ♀

ROSITA PATCH ♂

ELF ♂

CUBAN CRESCENT ♂

TULCIS CRESCENT ♀

BLACK CRESCENT ♂

PHAON CRESCENT ♀

VESTA CRESCENT ♀

PAINTED CRESCENT ♀

PLATE 22   × ³⁄₄

BRUSHFOOTS

PEARL CRESCENT *Phyciodes tharos,* male, summer form   **P. 257**
Kerr Co., Texas. Black antennal clubs in East. Upperside with orange
areas on hindwing broken by fine black marks. Underside of hindwing with crescent in dark marginal patch.

NORTHERN CRESCENT *Phyciodes cocyta,* male   **P. 257**
Ottawa Co., Que. Orange antennal clubs. Orange areas on hindwing
relatively open. Underside of hindwing with pale tan crescent patch
on outer margin.

PEARL CRESCENT *Phyciodes tharos,* female, spring form   **P. 257**
Ice Mountain, W. Va. Same characters as for species, but seasonal
form also has pale yellow marginal line on hindwing. Underside has
more checkered pattern.

TAWNY CRESCENT *Phyciodes batesii,* male   **P. 258**
Ottawa Co., Que. Underside of forewing has black patch on inner
margin larger than that on costa. Hindwing is clear yellow-tan.

BALTIMORE CHECKERSPOT *Euphydryas phaeton,* female   **P. 260**
Hampshire Co., W. Va. Black on inner half. Several rows of cream
white spots and orange-red marginal crescents.

SATYR COMMA *Polygonia satyrus,* male   **P. 263**
Hymers, Ont. Narrow orange border on hindwing; black spot in center. Rare in East.

QUESTION MARK *Polygonia interrogationis,* female   **P. 261**
Summer form. Muskegon, Mich. Large. Hindwing black with pale-
tipped tail.

QUESTION MARK *Polygonia interrogationis,* female   **P. 261**
Winter form, Sussex Co., N. J. Silver-white question mark in center
of hindwing. Winter form has extensive orange on hindwing.

EASTERN COMMA *Polygonia comma,* female   **P. 262**
Summer form, Whitetop Mountain, Va. Short tail. Summer form
with hindwing almost entirely black.

EASTERN COMMA *Polygonia comma,* male, winter form   **P. 262**
Franklin Co., Kan. Stubby hindwing tails. Silver-white comma in
center of hindwing below. Winter form has extensive orange on hindwing above.

GRAY COMMA *Polygonia progne,* male   **P. 265**
Quincy, Ill. Upperside of hindwing black enclosing yellow-orange
submarginal dots. Below both wings with fine gray-brown striations.

GREEN COMMA *Polygonia faunus,* male   **P. 264**
Tobyhanna, Pa. Highly irregular wing shape. Black costal spots on
upperside of forewing fused or barely double. Underside of hindwing
has outer half lighter with submarginal green spots.

PLATE 22

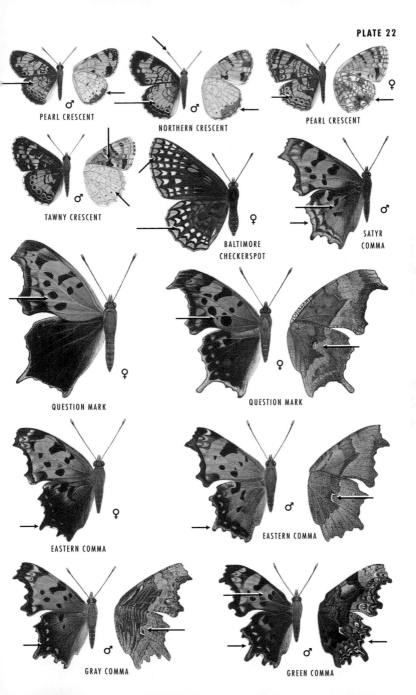

PEARL CRESCENT ♂

NORTHERN CRESCENT ♂

PEARL CRESCENT ♀

TAWNY CRESCENT ♂

BALTIMORE CHECKERSPOT ♀

SATYR COMMA ♂

QUESTION MARK ♀

QUESTION MARK ♀

EASTERN COMMA ♀

EASTERN COMMA ♂

GRAY COMMA ♂

GREEN COMMA ♂

PLATE 23   × ⅔

BRUSHFOOTS

HOARY COMMA *Polygonia gracilis,* male   **P. 264**
Carr Pond, Me. Outer half of hindwing distinctly pale. Comma mark
abruptly curved as in a fish-hook. Rare in East.

MILBERT'S TORTOISESHELL *Nymphalis milberti,* male   **P. 268**
Athens, Wis. Outer third of wings orange, bordered inwardly by yellow. Pale blue marks in black hindwing border. Squared-off forewing
apex; stubby hindwing tail.

CALIFORNIA TORTOISESHELL *Nymphalis californica,* male   **P. 267**
Okanogan Co., Wash. Irregular wings outline. Orange with black
marks and black outer margin. Rare strays appear in East after mass
migrations.

COMPTON TORTOISESHELL *Nymphalis vau-album,* male   **P. 266**
Sullivan Co., N.Y. Irregular wing outline with squared-off forewing
apex and tail on outer margin of hindwing. Single white spots on both
forewing and hindwing costal margins.

MOURNING CLOAK *Nymphalis antiopa,* male (× ⅓)   **P. 267**
Marathon Co., Wis. Irregular outline. Yellow border (fading to white
with age) with iridescent blue dots in purple-black background.

RED ADMIRAL *Vanessa atalanta,* female   **P. 270**
Hancock Co., Me. Black with red-orange bands across forewing and
outer margin of hindwing.

WEST COAST LADY *Vanessa annabella,* female   **P. 272**
Ventura Co., Calif. Squared-off apex. Hindwing has submarginal row
of blue black-edged spots in orange background.

PAINTED LADY *Vanessa cardui,* male   **P. 271**
Jamesburg, N.J. Migratory. Orange-pink and black with white spots in
forewing apical area. Hindwing has 4 small black submarginal spots.

AMERICAN LADY *Vanessa virginiensis,* female   **P. 270**
Willard, Mo. At least some blue in one or more submarginal spots on
hindwing. Two large, submarginal eyespots on underside of hindwing.

COMMON BUCKEYE *Junonia coenia,* male   **P. 273**
Long Island, N.Y. Brown with submarginal eyespots. White subapical
bar internal to large eyespot on forewing.

TROPICAL BUCKEYE *Junonia genoveva,* male   **P. 275**
Volusia Co., Fla. Forewing band wide, white diffused with orange or
brown; large eyespot edged with brown internally.

MANGROVE BUCKEYE *Junonia evarete,* male   **P. 274**
Key Largo, Fla. Forewing band narrow. Large eyespot ringed with orange — never brown.

DARK BUCKEYE *Junonia genoveva nigrosuffusa,* male   **P. 275**
Pima Co., Ariz. Individuals of this subspecies may be found in s.
Texas.

PLATE 23

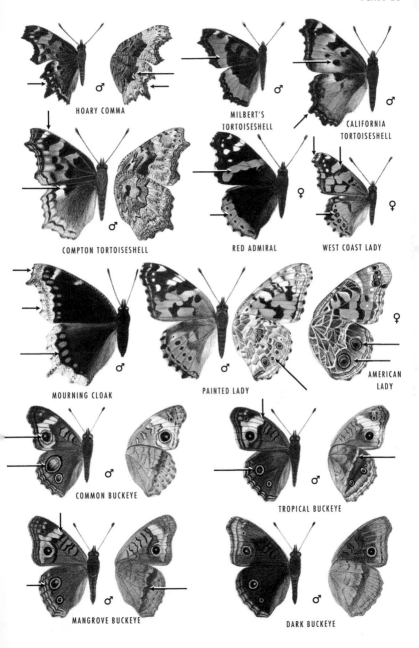

HOARY COMMA ♂

MILBERT'S
TORTOISESHELL ♂

CALIFORNIA
TORTOISESHELL ♂

COMPTON TORTOISESHELL ♂

RED ADMIRAL ♀

WEST COAST LADY ♀

MOURNING CLOAK ♂

PAINTED LADY ♂

AMERICAN
LADY ♀

COMMON BUCKEYE ♂

TROPICAL BUCKEYE ♂

MANGROVE BUCKEYE ♂

DARK BUCKEYE ♂

PLATE 24 × ⅔

BRUSHFOOTS

CALIFORNIA SISTER *Adelpha bredowii*, male **P. 281**
 Brewster Co., Texas. Orange patch on costa near apex. Median white band. Western stray to central Texas.

BAND-CELLED SISTER *Adelpha fessonia*, male **P. 281**
 Tamaulipas, Mexico. Orange patch near apex; white band. Regular stray to Lower Rio Grande Valley.

PAVON EMPEROR *Doxocopa pavon*, male **P. 294**
 Hidalgo Co., Texas. Squared-off forewing apex. Iridescent blue-purple with small orange apical patch.

SILVER EMPEROR *Doxocopa laure*, male **P. 294**
 Tamaulipas, Mexico. Note wing outline. Squared-off forewing apex. White median band on both wings invaded by orange on forewing.

BANDED PEACOCK *Anartia fatima*, male **P. 276**
 Hidalgo Co., Texas. Brown with white or cream-yellow band and broken red median band on hindwing. Rare stray.

CARIBBEAN PEACOCK *Anartia chrysopelea*, male **P. 276**
 Guantanamo, Cuba. Brown with white patches. Rare stray.

WHITE ADMIRAL *Limenitis arthemis arthemis*, male **P. 278**
 Miniota, Man. Black with white postmedian band and submarginal blue.

BANDED PURPLE *Limenitis "proserpina,"* male **P. 279**
 Monroe Co., Pa. One of several intermediates between White Admiral and Red-spotted Purple.

MEXICAN BLUEWING *Myscelia ethusa*, male **P. 282**
 Hidalgo Co., Texas. Blunt forewing apex. Black with iridescent blue lines and stripes.

RED-SPOTTED PURPLE *Limenitis a. astyanax*, male **P. 278**
 Long Island, N.Y. Blue-black with iridescent blue on hindwing. Underside has submarginal series of red-orange spots.

WEIDEMEYER'S ADMIRAL *Limenitis weidemeyerii*, male **P. 280**
 San Miguel Co., Colo. Black with postmedian white band and marginal white points.

WHITE PEACOCK *Anartia jatrophae*, male **P. 275**
 Dade Co., Fla. White with black postmedian points and orange margin.

VICEROY *Limenitis archippus floridensis*, male **P. 279**
 Oveido, Fla. Mimic of Queen (Pl. 27). Black postmedian line on hindwing and single row of marginal dashes in black border.

VICEROY *Limenitis archippus*, male **P. 279**
 Fairfax Co., Va. Mimics Monarch (Pl. 27). Postmedian black line on hindwing and single row of white dashes in black border. Hindwing paler on underside.

PLATE 24

CALIFORNIA SISTER

BAND-CELLED SISTER

PAVON EMPEROR

SILVER EMPEROR

BANDED PEACOCK

CARIBBEAN PEACOCK

WHITE ADMIRAL

BANDED PURPLE

MEXICAN BLUEWING

RED-SPOTTED PURPLE

WEIDEMEYER'S ADMIRAL

WHITE PEACOCK

VICEROY

VICEROY

PLATE 25   × 2/3

BRUSHFOOTS

PALE-SPOTTED LEAFWING *Anaea pithyusa,* male, Costa Rica   **P. 291**
Irregular outline, pointed tail. Blue and black pattern. Rare stray.

FLORIDA LEAFWING *Anaea floridalis,* female   **P. 289**
Big Pine Key, Fla. Hooked forewing apex and pointed tail on hind-wing. Red above with limited black markings.

ANGLED LEAFWING *Anaea glycerium,* male   **P. 290**
Veracruz, Mexico. Forewing outer margin irregular; hindwing outer margin concave between veins with short tail. Pattern black and orange. Rare stray.

GOATWEED LEAFWING *Anaea andria,* male   **P. 290**
Dallas Co., Texas. Hooked forewing apex and tail on hindwing outer margin. Red-orange above with limited black markings.

TROPICAL LEAFWING *Anaea aidea,* male   **P. 289**
Hidalgo Co., Texas. Hooked forewing apex, and irregular hindwing outer margin with tail. Faint yellow marginal points on hindwing.

CHESTNUT LEAFWING *Anaea echemus,* male, Cuba   **P. 291**
Chestnut brown. Hindwing with 2 or more oval black, white-tipped spots near tail. Rare stray.

COMMON MESTRA *Mestra amymone,* male, Tiger Hill, Texas   **P. 283**
Hindwing with median row of white spots and orange outer band.

MANY-BANDED DAGGERWING *Marpesia chiron,* male   **P. 288**
Veracruz, Mexico. Long pointed tail. Dark brown with 3 paler stripes and 3 faint white dots near forewing apex. Stray.

ANTILLEAN DAGGERWING *Marpesia eleuchea,* female, Cuba   **P. 288**
Squared-off forewing apex. Pointed tail shorter than that of Ruddy Daggerwing. Median black line on forewing sharply bent.

RUDDY DAGGERWING *Marpesia petreus,* male, Dade Co., Fla.   **P. 288**
Forewing highly produced. Long tail. Orange with thin black lines.

WAITER DAGGERWING *Marpesia zerynthia,* male, Harris Co., Texas   **P. 287**
Long tail on hindwing. Brown-black.

LARGE PURPLEWING *Eunica tatila,* male, Dade Co., Fla.   **P. 283**
Forewing margin irregular at apex. White spots on outer half of forewing. Both wings with violet-blue iridescence.

DINGY PURPLEWING *Eunica monima,* male, Dade Co., Fla.   **P. 282**
Smeared white spots on outer third of forewing. Wings brown-black with slight purplish gloss.

BLUE-EYED SAILOR *Dynamine dyonis,* male   **P. 283**
Bexar Co., Texas. Upperside bronze-green. Underside pattern of 2 round, blue submarginal spots shows through.

CRAMER'S EIGHTY-EIGHT *Diaethria clymena,* male, Ecuador   **P. 283**
Underside of forewing red. Hindwing with black outlined 88 or 89.

MEXICAN EIGHTY-EIGHT *Diaethria asteria,* male   **P. 283**
Mexico. Costal white bar on forewing. Thin 88 on hindwing.

RED RIM *Biblis hyperia,* male, Tamaulipas, Mexico   **P. 284**
Hindwing with lobed outer margin and red-pink submarginal band.

COMMON BANNER *Epiphile adrasta,* male   **P. 277**
Veracruz, Mexico. Squared-off apex. Brown with pale median band.

PLATE 25

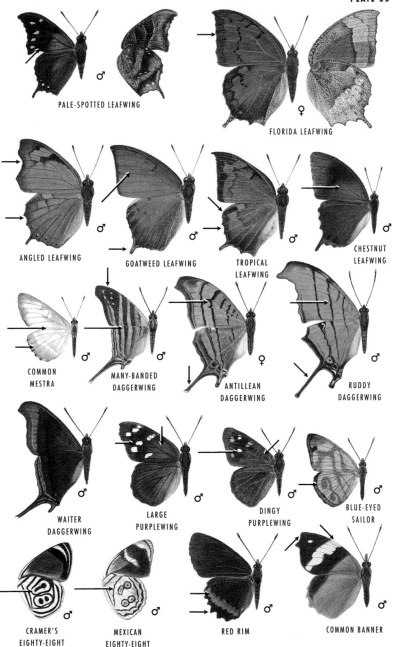

PALE-SPOTTED LEAFWING ♂

FLORIDA LEAFWING ♀

ANGLED LEAFWING ♂

GOATWEED LEAFWING ♂

TROPICAL LEAFWING ♂

CHESTNUT LEAFWING ♂

COMMON MESTRA

MANY-BANDED DAGGERWING ♂

ANTILLEAN DAGGERWING ♀

RUDDY DAGGERWING ♂

WAITER DAGGERWING ♂

LARGE PURPLEWING ♂

DINGY PURPLEWING ♂

BLUE-EYED SAILOR ♂

CRAMER'S EIGHTY-EIGHT ♂

MEXICAN EIGHTY-EIGHT ♂

RED RIM ♂

COMMON BANNER ♂

PLATE 26   × ⅔

BRUSHFOOTS

TAWNY EMPEROR *Asterocampa clyton,* male   **P. 293**
    Kent Co., Mich. Forewing has no black submarginal spot. Costa
    has 2 prominent discal bars.

HACKBERRY EMPEROR *Asterocampa celtis,* male   **P. 292**
    Cape May Co., N.J. Forewing has 1 prominent black submarginal
    spot. Costa has 1 black discal bar and 2 black spots instead of
    second bar.

EMPRESS LEILIA *Asterocampa leilia,* male   **P. 292**
    Live Oak Co., Texas. Forewing has 2 prominent submarginal
    black spots and 2 solid brown discal bars on costa. S. Texas and
    west.

TAWNY EMPEROR *Asterocampa clyton flora,* male   **P. 293**
    Volusia Co., Fla. One of more prominent geographic populations.
    Lacks submarginal black spot on forewing. Two bars on forewing
    costa.

PALE CRACKER *Hamadryas amphichloe,* male   **P. 286**
    Santiago, Cuba. Forewing with red discal bar; outer half of wings
    whitish. Only cracker likely to be found in Florida.

BLOMFILD'S BEAUTY *Smyrna blomfildia,* male   **P. 287**
    Veracruz, Mexico. Hindwing with wavy swirls and submarginal
    eyespots.

MALACHITE *Siproeta stelenes,* male   **P. 276**
    Dade Co., Fla. Translucent whitish green or yellow-green spots
    and patches on background of dark brown.

VARIABLE CRACKER *Hamadryas feronia,* male   **P. 285**
    Oaxaca, Mexico. Dull red bar in forewing discal cell. Hindwing
    eyespots have a blue ring surrounding a white-centered black
    spot.

GRAY CRACKER *Hamadryas februa,* female   **P. 285**
    Sinaloa, Mexico. Forewing discal bar with some red. Hindwing
    eyespots have orange scales before orange crescent.

BROWNISH CRACKER *Hamadryas iphthime,* male   **P. 286**
    Veracruz, Mexico. Red lacking in forewing discal bar. Hindwing
    eyespots each with a blue ring, followed inwardly by narrow
    brown ring, light blue ring, then thin black center with a white
    crescent.

RED CRACKER *Hamadryas amphinome,* male   **P. 285**
    Oaxaca, Mexico. Hindwing brick red with eyespots largely ob-
    scured.

GUATEMALAN CRACKER *Hamadryas guatemalena,* male   **P. 286**
    Mepastepec, Mexico. Forewing with red discal bar. Eyespots on
    hindwing each with a blue ring, followed inwardly by wide black
    ring, a blue ring, then a mottled brown and white center.

PLATE 26

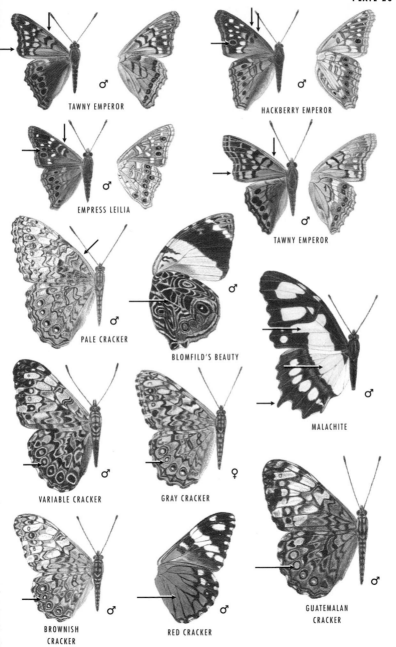

TAWNY EMPEROR ♂

HACKBERRY EMPEROR ♂

EMPRESS LEILIA ♂

TAWNY EMPEROR ♂

PALE CRACKER ♂

BLOMFILD'S BEAUTY ♂

MALACHITE ♂

VARIABLE CRACKER ♂

GRAY CRACKER ♀

BROWNISH CRACKER ♂

RED CRACKER ♂

GUATEMALAN CRACKER ♂

PLATE 27 × ²⁄₃

MILKWEED BUTTERFLIES, SATYRS

MONARCH *Danaus plexippus,* male **P. 313**
  Marathon Co., Wis. Bright orange with black along veins (note black scent patch along cubital vein Cu2) and black border containing 2 rows of white dots. Highly migratory.

QUEEN *Danaus gilippus,* male, Bell Co., Texas **P. 314**
   Chestnut brown with scattered white spots. Black veining on hindwing; double row of white spots in black border on outer margin.

KLUG'S CLEARWING *Dircenna klugii,* male **P. 316**
  Texas. Wings translucent pale orange. Rare stray.

MONARCH *Danaus plexippus,* female **P. 313**
  Essex Co., Va. Smokier than male; lacks scent patch.

MIMIC *Hypolimnas misippus,* male **P. 273**
  Layou, Dominica. Black with purple highlights and large white patch in each wing.

TIGER MIMIC-QUEEN *Lycorea cleobaea,* male **P. 315**
  Fla. Orange with tiger stripes. Hindwing stripes meet.

SOLDIER *Danaus eresimus,* male **P. 315**
  Castroville, Texas. Chocolate brown with black veining above.

MIMIC *Hypolimnas misippus,* female **P. 273**
  Layou, Dominica. Brown with black forewing apical area holding white bar.

VIOLA'S WOOD-SATYR *Megisto viola,* female **P. 302**
  Volusia Co., Fla. Strongly marked with large eyespots; postmedian line strongly bowed.

RED SATYR *Megisto rubricata,* female, Cameron Co., Texas **P. 303**
  Single eyespot and red-orange patch on each wing. Southwestern.

CREOLE PEARLY-EYE *Enodia creola,* male **P. 297**
  Sussex Co., Va. Forewing pointed with raised scent patches. Underside of forewing with straight submarginal row of 5 eyespots.

EYED BROWN *Satyrodes eurydice,* male **P. 298**
  Monroe Co., N.Y. Forewing with submarginal eyespots roughly equal, touching. Postmedian line on hindwing distinctly zigzag.

APPALACHIAN BROWN *Satyrodes appalachia,* male **P. 299**
  Burke's Garden, Va. Forewing with submarginal eyespots not equal. Postmedian line on hindwing gently sinuous.

SMOKY EYED BROWN *Satyrodes eurydice fumosa,* male **P. 298**
  Omaha, Neb. Large. Intermediate in appearance. Marshes on prairies.

LITTLE WOOD-SATYR *Megisto cymela,* male **P. 302**
  Waterloo, N.J. Two eyespots on forewing. Submarginal lines not strongly bowed.

NORTHERN PEARLY-EYE *Enodia anthedon,* male **P. 296**
  Florence Co., Wis. Forewing has straight submarginal row of 4 eyespots. Postmedian dark line gently sinuous.

SOUTHERN PEARLY-EYE *Enodia portlandia,* male **P. 295**
  Charleston Co., S.C. Forewing with curved submarginal row of 4 eyespots. Postmedian dark line bent or zigzag.

PLATE 27

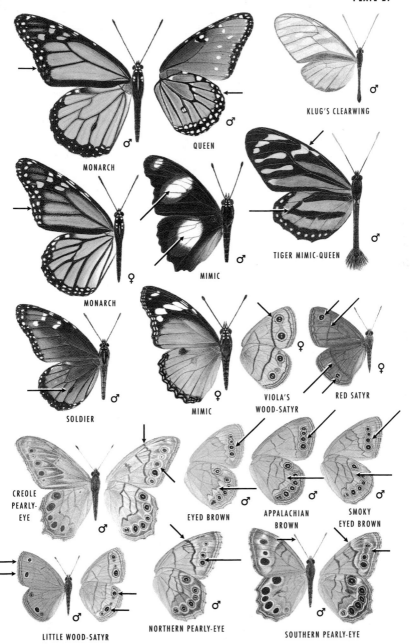

KLUG'S CLEARWING ♂

MONARCH ♂

QUEEN ♂

MONARCH ♀

MIMIC ♂

TIGER MIMIC-QUEEN ♂

SOLDIER ♂

MIMIC ♀

VIOLA'S WOOD-SATYR ♀

RED SATYR ♀

CREOLE PEARLY-EYE ♂

EYED BROWN ♂

APPALACHIAN BROWN ♂

SMOKY EYED BROWN ♂

LITTLE WOOD-SATYR ♂

NORTHERN PEARLY-EYE ♂

SOUTHERN PEARLY-EYE ♂

PLATE 28   × 1

SATYRS

CAROLINA SATYR *Hermeuptychia sosybius,* male   **P. 300**
Currituck Sound, N.C. Dark brown above, without eyespots. Many
small submarginal eyespots on both wings.

GEMMED SATYR *Cyllopsis gemma,* male   **P. 299**
Pickens Co., S.C. Oval patch on outer margin of hindwing containing
row of highly reflective scales.

COMMON RINGLET *Coenonympha tullia,* male   **P. 303**
Bemidji, Minn. Forewing with small black eyespot near apex. Hindwing with sinuous median line. Expanding range in Northeast.

RIDINGS' SATYR *Neominois ridingsii,* male   **P. 307**
Chinook, Mont. Gray with 2 black eyespots and cream patches on
forewing. Short-grass prairies.

GEORGIA SATYR *Neonympha areolata,* male   **P. 300**
Samsula, Fla. Hindwing with elongate submarginal eyespots and red-
orange lines. Pinewoods.

MITCHELL'S SATYR *Neonympha mitchellii,* male   **P. 301**
Cass Co., Mich. Wings translucent. Sumarginal rows of round, black,
yellow-rimmed eyespots. Marshes. Endangered.

THEANO ALPINE *Erebia theano,* female   **P. 306**
Fort Churchill, Man. Forewing with band of red-orange dashes; hindwing with band of yellow-cream spots.

COMMON ALPINE *Erebia epipsodea,* male   **P. 307**
Harlan, Sask. White-centered black eyespots in yellow-orange fields
on both wings.

ROSS'S ALPINE *Erebia rossii,* male   **P. 305**
Fort Churchill, Man. Forewing with 1–3 subapical black white-centered eyespots in red-orange ring. Underside of hindwing with pale
postmedian band.

RED-DISKED ALPINE *Erebia discoidalis,* male   **P. 306**
Oneida Co., Wis. Lacks eyespots. Large chestnut red patch on forewing. Underside of hindwing gray-brown.

DISA ALPINE *Erebia disa,* male   **P. 305**
Hymers, Ont. Forewing reddish. Hindwing gray-brown with conspicuous white spot beyond cell.

BANDED ALPINE *Erebia fasciata,* male   **P. 306**
Barnard Harbor, N.W. Terr. Lacks eyespots. Pale gray basal and postmedian bands.

COMMON WOOD-NYMPH *Cercyonis pegala,* male   **P. 304**
Currituck Sound, N.C. Large. Forewing with 2 submarginal yellow-
rimmed eyespots. Coastal plain populations have eyespots in large
yellow band.

COMMON WOOD-NYMPH *Cercyonis pegala nephele,* male   **P. 304**
Enfield, Me. Two large yellow-rimmed eyespots. Inland and northern
populations lack yellow band.

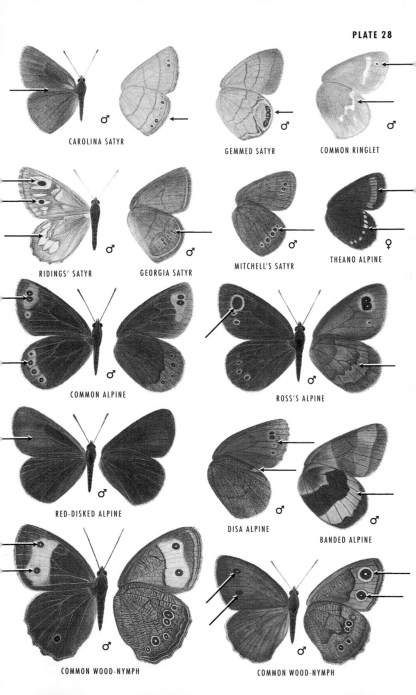

PLATE 28

CAROLINA SATYR ♂

GEMMED SATYR ♂

COMMON RINGLET ♂

RIDINGS' SATYR ♂

GEORGIA SATYR ♂

MITCHELL'S SATYR ♂

THEANO ALPINE ♀

COMMON ALPINE ♂

ROSS'S ALPINE ♂

RED-DISKED ALPINE ♂

DISA ALPINE ♂

BANDED ALPINE ♂

COMMON WOOD-NYMPH ♂

COMMON WOOD-NYMPH ♂

PLATE 29   × 1

ARCTICS

MACOUN'S ARCTIC *Oeneis macounii,* male   **P. 308**
Victoria Beach, Man. Large. Forewing with 2 submarginal eye-spots. Underside of hindwing cloudy gray-brown with median band.

CHRYXUS ARCTIC *Oeneis chryxus,* male   **P. 309**
Crawford Co., Mich. Forewing of male with dark band of special-ized scales on forewing. Underside of hindwing with fine black and white striations. Veins scaled white. Dark median band.

JUTTA ARCTIC *Oeneis jutta,* male   **P. 310**
Penobscot Co., Me. Gray-brown with yellow-orange submarginal band. Variable number of tiny eyespots. Bogs or wet tundra.

UHLER'S ARCTIC *Oeneis uhleri,* male   **P. 309**
Miniota, Man. Dull orange-brown. Underside of both wings with more than one, usually many, small submarginal eyespots.

WHITE-VEINED ARCTIC *Oeneis taygete,* male   **P. 310**
Mt. Albert, Que. Gray-brown without eyespots. Underside of hindwing with strong dark median band outlined with white. Veins often lined with white scales. Tundra.

ALBERTA ARCTIC *Oeneis alberta,* male   **P. 310**
Miniota, Man. Small. Yellow-gray. Underside of forewing with sharply bent postmedian line. Hindwing with distinctly outlined dark median band. Virgin prairies.

MELISSA ARCTIC *Oeneis melissa,* male   **P. 311**
Coos Co., N.H. Gray-brown with eyespots. Underside of hind-wing mottled black and white. Median band absent or weak.

POLIXENES ARCTIC *Oeneis polixenes,* male   **P. 311**
Mt. Katahdin, Me. Wings somewhat translucent. Tiny apical eye-spot. Median band on underside of hindwing pronounced.

PLATE 29

MACOUN'S ARCTIC

CHRYXUS ARCTIC

JUTTA ARCTIC

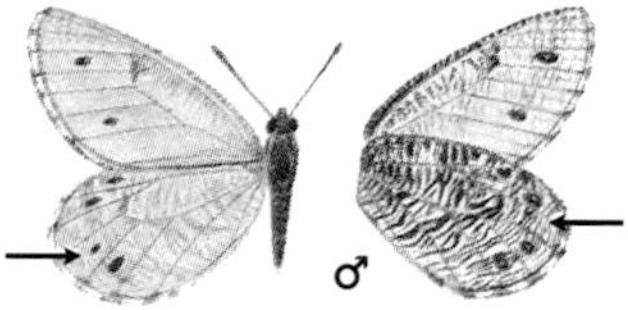

UHLER'S ARCTIC

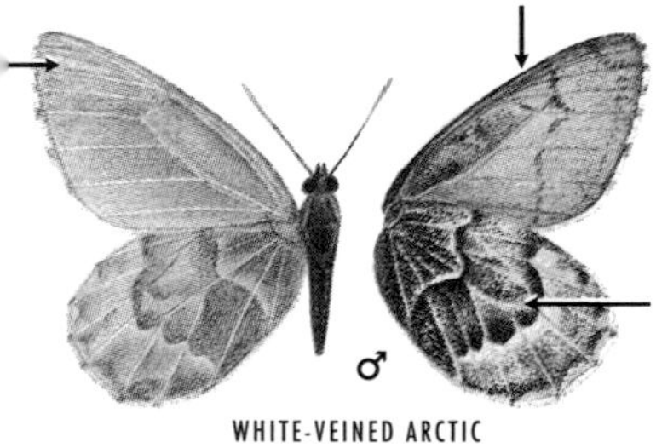

WHITE-VEINED ARCTIC

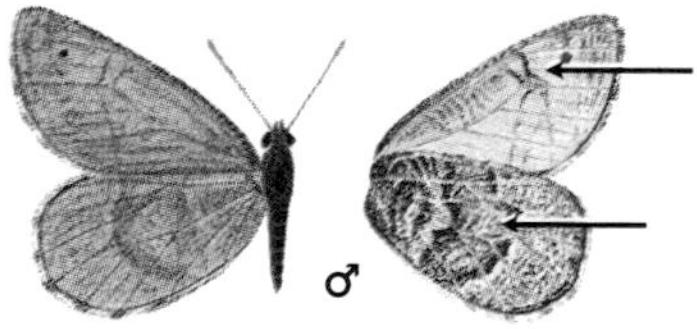

ALBERTA ARCTIC

MELISSA ARCTIC

POLIXENES ARCTIC

PLATE 30   × ⁴/₅

OPEN-WINGED SKIPPERS

MANGROVE SKIPPER *Phocides pigmalion,* male   **P. 318**
  Big Pine Key, Fla. Iridescent blue streaks.

GUAVA SKIPPER *Phocides palemon,* male   **P. 318**
  Cameron Co., Texas. White fringes and red discal bar.

MERCURIAL SKIPPER *Proteides mercurius,* male   **P. 318**
  Mexico. White frosting on outer margins.

SILVER-SPOTTED SKIPPER *Epargyreus clarus,* male   **P. 319**
  Decatur, Ill. Pointed forewing; lobe on hindwing. Gold forewing
  spots. Silver band on underside of hindwing. Widespread.

HAMMOCK SKIPPER *Polygonus leo,* male   **P. 320**
  Big Pine Key, Fla. Blackish with 3 white square patches.

GOLD-SPOTTED AGUNA *Aguna asander,* male   **P. 322**
  Cerro Campana, Panama. Gold spots paler than Silver-spotted Skip-
  per. Rare stray.

ZESTOS SKIPPER *Epargyreus zestos,* male   **P. 319**
  Dade Co., Fla. Hindwing red-brown with only trace of silver.

WHITE-STRIPED LONGTAIL *Chioides catillus,* male   **P. 321**
  Kerr Co., Texas. Forewing apex blunt. Long white stripe below.

ZILPA LONGTAIL *Chioides zilpa,* male   **P. 322**
  Tamaulipas, Mexico. White trapezoidal patch on hindwing.

LONG-TAILED SKIPPER *Urbanus proteus,* female   **P. 324**
  Brunswick Co., N.C. Body and basal wing area iridescent blue-green.
  Commonest of the longtails.

EIGHT-SPOTTED LONGTAIL *Polythrix octomaculata,* male   **P. 323**
  Mexico. Hindwing tail short. One submarginal brown spot on fore-
  wing.

TAILED AGUNA *Aguna metophis,* male   **P. 322**
  Veracruz, Mexico. Wing bases blue-green. Narrow white band below.

BROWN LONGTAIL *Urbanus procne,* male   **P. 327**
  Cameron Co., Texas. Brown. Narrow band across forewing or almost
  no marks.

DORANTES SKIPPER *Urbanus dorantes,* male   **P. 326**
  Hidalgo Co., Texas. Fringes checkered. Body and wings brown with
  transparent spots.

TELEUS LONGTAIL *Urbanus teleus,* male   **P. 326**
  Mexico D.F., Mexico. Brown with thin band across forewing. Fore-
  wing apex has 4 tiny spots. Lacks costal fold.

MOTTLED LONGTAIL *Typhedanus undulatus,* female   **P. 323**
  Mexico. Hindwing striated with broken black bands.

TWO-BARRED FLASHER *Astraptes fulgerator,* male   **P. 328**
  Hidalgo Co., Texas. Transverse white band across forewing. Wing
  bases and body iridescent blue.

WHITE-TAILED LONGTAIL *Urbanus doryssus,* male   **P. 328**
  Motzorongo, Mexico. Hindwing with white outer margin and short
  tails.

PLATE 30

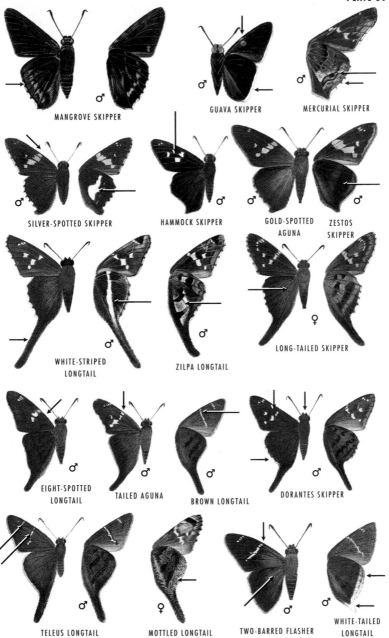

MANGROVE SKIPPER

GUAVA SKIPPER

MERCURIAL SKIPPER

SILVER-SPOTTED SKIPPER

HAMMOCK SKIPPER

GOLD-SPOTTED AGUNA

ZESTOS SKIPPER

WHITE-STRIPED LONGTAIL

ZILPA LONGTAIL

LONG-TAILED SKIPPER

EIGHT-SPOTTED LONGTAIL

TAILED AGUNA

BROWN LONGTAIL

DORANTES SKIPPER

TELEUS LONGTAIL

MOTTLED LONGTAIL

TWO-BARRED FLASHER

WHITE-TAILED LONGTAIL

PLATE 31   × ³⁄₄

OPEN-WINGED SKIPPERS

GOLD-BANDED SKIPPER *Autochton cellus,* female, Thorofare Gap, Va. **P. 330**
   Golden band across forewing. Small white patch near apex.

HOARY EDGE *Achalarus lyciades,* female, Willard, Mo.   **P. 330**
   Upperside with gold patch. Underside of hindwing with outer half
   hoary white.

COYOTE CLOUDYWING *Achalarus toxeus,* male   **P. 331**
   Hidalgo Co., Texas. Forewing pointed; brown with darker spots.
   Hindwing fringe white.

NORTHERN CLOUDYWING *Thorybes pylades,* female   **P. 332**
   Sussex Co., N. J. Forewing with triangular, non-aligned hyaline spots.

SOUTHERN CLOUDYWING *Thorybes bathyllus,* male   **P. 332**
   Quantico, Va. Broad hyaline spot band on forewing. Pale fringe.

FALCATE SKIPPER *Spathilepia clonius,* female, Panama   **P. 335**
   Squared-off apex. White band across forewing.

CONFUSED CLOUDYWING *Thorybes confusis,* male   **P. 333**
   Carteret Co., N.C. Male forewing without costal fold. Hyaline spots
   elongate. Hindwing underside strongly marked.

MIMOSA SKIPPER *Cogia calchas,* male   **P. 335**
   Hidalgo Co., Texas. Forewing pointed. Underside of hindwing with
   gray anal fold and pale vermiculations.

OUTIS SKIPPER *Cogia outis,* male, Dallas Co., Texas   **P. 335**
   Forewing with tiny white spots. Hindwing outer fringe checkered.

STALLINGS' FLAT *Calaenorrhinus stallingsi,* female   **P. 334**
   Tamaulipas, Mexico. Forewing with irregular white band. Hindwing
   fringe brown. Flies at dusk; rests during daylight.

SOUTHERN SCALLOPWING *Staphlyus mazans,* male   **P. 338**
   Hidalgo Co., Texas. Hindwing scalloped. Dark band on wings.

HAYHURST'S SCALLOPWING *Staphylus hayhurstii,* male   **P. 338**
   Benedict, Md. Hindwing scalloped. Dark band. Fringe checkered.

HAYHURST'S SCALLOPWING *Staphylus hayhurstii,* female   **P. 338**
   Kerr Co., Texas. Female browner with more contrast.

GLAZED PELLICIA *Pellicia arina,* female, Panama   **P. 337**
   Forewing pointed. Wings mottled with purple or violet sheen.

POTRILLO SKIPPER *Cabares potrillo,* male, Hidalgo Co., Texas **P. 334**
   Forewing with U-shaped hyaline spot. Hindwing with shallow lobes.

GOLDEN-HEADED SCALLOPWING *Staphylus ceos,* male   **P. 338**
   Pima Co., Ariz. Head and palpi covered with golden-orange scales.

MOTTLED BOLLA *Bolla clytius,* male, Panama   **P. 337**
   Forewing apex with tiny white spots. Darker mottling on wings.

HOARY SKIPPER *Carrhenes canescens,* female   **P. 339**
   El Salvador. Wings semi-transparent with complex pattern.

TEXAS POWDERED-SKIPPER *Systasea pulverulenta,* male   **P. 340**
   New Braunfels, Texas. Forewing with hyaline transverse band. Hindwing with 2-lobed projection.

SICKLE-WINGED SKIPPER *Achlyodes tamenund,* male   **P. 340**
   Hidalgo Co., Texas. Forewing with hooked apex. Dark brown with
   paler spots and purple sheen.

PLATE 31

GOLD-BANDED SKIPPER ♀

HOARY EDGE ♀

COYOTE CLOUDYWING ♂

NORTHERN CLOUDYWING ♀

SOUTHERN CLOUDYWING ♂

FALCATE SKIPPER ♀

CONFUSED CLOUDYWING ♂

MIMOSA SKIPPER ♂

OUTIS SKIPPER ♂

STALLINGS' FLAT ♀

SOUTHERN SCALLOPWING ♂

HAYHURST'S SCALLOPWING ♂

GLAZED PELLICIA ♀

POTRILLO SKIPPER ♂

GOLDEN-HEADED SCALLOPWING ♂

MOTTLED BOLLA ♂

HOARY SKIPPER ♀

TEXAS POWDERED-SKIPPER ♂

SICKLE-WINGED SKIPPER ♂

PLATE 32   × ¾

OPEN-WINGED SKIPPERS

GLASSY-WINGED SKIPPER *Xenophanes tryxus,* male   **P. 339**
    Cameron Co., Texas. Gray-black with transparent patches.

FALSE DUSKYWING *Gesta invisus,* male   **P. 342**
    Santiago, Dominican Republic. Forewing banded brown-black with
    submarginal blue-gray band.

HERMIT SKIPPER *Grais stigmaticus,* male   **P. 340**
    Veracruz, Mexico. Dark brown with darker spots.

FLORIDA DUSKYWING *Ephyriades brunnea,* male   **P. 342**
    Big Pine Key, Fla. Black with silky sheen. Forewing with circle of
    white spots.

WHITE-PATCHED SKIPPER *Chiomara georgina,* male   **P. 341**
    Cameron Co., Texas. Brown-black with irregular white patches.

MERIDIAN DUSKYWING *Erynnis meridianus,* male   **P. 345**
    Washington Co., Utah. Black with apical white spots. Little pattern
    contrast.

SLEEPY DUSKYWING *Erynnis brizo,* male   **P. 343**
    Sussex Co., Del. Forewing with complete, distinct bands. Near oaks.

JUVENAL'S DUSKYWING *Erynnis juvenalis,* male   **P. 344**
    Sussex Co., Del. Forewing with scattered white hairs. Hindwing un-
    derside with 2 round light spots near apex.

HORACE'S DUSKYWING *Erynnis horatius,* male   **P. 345**
    Craven Co., N.C. Forewing without white hairs and little pattern
    contrast. Underside of hindwing usually lacks 2 spots.

MOTTLED DUSKYWING *Erynnis martialis,* male   **P. 347**
    Plymouth Co., Iowa. Both wings with strong mottling above.

ZARUCCO DUSKYWING *Erynnis zarucco,* male   **P. 347**
    Carteret Co., N.C. Forewing pointed with faint reddish patch at end
    of cell. Hindwing fringe brown (except Florida Keys).

BROWN-BANDED SKIPPER *Timochares ruptifaciata,* male   **P. 341**
    Veracruz, Mexico. Hindwing orange-brown with 3 dark bands.

WILD INDIGO DUSKYWING *Erynnis baptisiae,* male   **P. 349**
    Adelphi, Md. Male with reddish brown spot at end of discal cell.
    Outer half of wings lighter.

PERSIUS DUSKYWING *Erynnis persius,* male   **P. 349**
    Lawrence Co., S.D. Male forewing with numerous raised white hairs
    and gray patch at end of cell.

COLUMBINE DUSKYWING *Erynnis lucilius,* male   **P. 348**
    Mansfield, Conn. Small. Brown patch at end of cell on forewing in-
    distinct. Underside of both wings with marginal and submarginal
    rows of distinct pale spots.

DREAMY DUSKYWING *Erynnis icelus,* male   **P. 343**
    West Kingston, R.I. Labial palpi long. Lacks transparent spots. Fore-
    wing grizzled gray with darker median and postmedian bands.

FUNEREAL DUSKYWING *Erynnis funeralis,* male   **P. 348**
    Harris Co., Texas. Forewing pointed with red-brown patch at end of
    cell. Hindwing triangular with white fringe.

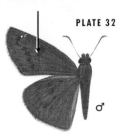

PLATE 32

GLASSY-WINGED SKIPPER

FALSE DUSKYWING

HERMIT SKIPPER

FLORIDA DUSKYWING

WHITE-PATCHED-
SKIPPER

MERIDIAN
DUSKYWING

SLEEPY
DUSKYWING

JUVENAL'S DUSKYWING

HORACE'S DUSKYWING

MOTTLED DUSKYWING

ZARUCCO DUSKYWING

BROWN-BANDED
SKIPPER

WILD INDIGO
DUSKYWING

PERSIUS DUSKYWING

COLUMBINE DUSKYWING

DREAMY DUSKYWING

FUNEREAL DUSKYWING

PLATE 33   × 1

VARIOUS SKIPPERS

GRIZZLED SKIPPER *Pyrgus centaureae*, male   **P. 350**
    Fort Churchill, Man. Small. Fringes checkered.

GRIZZLED SKIPPER *Pyrgus centaureae wyandot*, female   **P. 350**
    Fox Hunter's Paradise, Va. Small. Fringes checkered.

COMMON STREAKY-SKIPPER *Celotes nessus*, male   **P. 353**
    Bexar Co., Texas. Outer portion of wings with dark brown streaks.

COMMON CHECKERED-SKIPPER *Pyrgus communis*, male   **P. 350**
    Gillespie Co., Texas. Checkered black and white above. Paler below.

TROPICAL CHECKERED-SKIPPER *Pyrgus oileus*, male   **P. 351**
    Palm Beach Co., Fla. Male has overlying mat of long blue-gray hairs.
    Hindwing underside shows little contrast between bands and pale
    ground.

DESERT CHECKERED-SKIPPER *Pyrgus philetas*, male   **P. 352**
    Kerr Co., Texas. Small. Marginal and submarginal spots minute. Un-
    derside of hindwing pale gray-white.

COMMON SOOTYWING *Pholisora catullus*, male   **P. 354**
    Richmond Co., N.C. Black with tiny white spots in outer portion of
    forewing. Waste areas.

COMMON SOOTYWING *Pholisora catullus*, female   **P. 354**
    Cape May Co., N.J. Female has more white spots including sub-
    marginal row on hindwing.

ERICHSON'S WHITE-SKIPPER *Heliopetes domicella*, male   **P. 352**
    Hidalgo Co., Texas. Broad white median band on both wings.

SALTBUSH SOOTYWING *Hesperopsis alpheus*, male   **P. 355**
    Cameron Co., Texas. Upperside with mottled gray pattern. Fringes
    checkered.

ARCTIC SKIPPER *Carterocephalus palaemon*, male   **P. 356**
    Augusta, Me. Hindwing red-orange with black-outlined cream spots.

REDUNDANT SKIPPER *Corticea corticea*, male   **P. 358**
    Rio Palenque, Ecuador. Forewing with pale band.

PALE-RAYED SKIPPER *Vidius perigenes*, male   **P. 358**
    Los Fresnos, Texas. Brown on upperside.

VIOLET PATCH SKIPPER *Monca tyrtaeus*, male   **P. 358**
    Hidalgo Co., Texas. Dark brown above. Upperside of forewing with
    white spot on costa. Hindwing with 2 gray bands.

TURK'S CAP WHITE-SKIPPER *Heliopetes macaira*, male   **P. 353**
    Hidalgo Co., Texas. Underside of hindwing diffusely patterned with
    olive-brown band on outer margin.

MALICIOUS SKIPPER *Synapte pecta*, male   **P. 357**
    Volcan Santa Maria, Guatemala. Upperside of forewing with diffuse
    dusky yellow or orange band. Underside of hindwing light brown with
    minute dark striations.

LAVIANA WHITE-SKIPPER *Heliopetes laviana*, male   **P. 352**
    Hidalgo Co., Texas. Outer third of hindwing olive-brown linearly cut
    off from paler median area.

PLATE 33

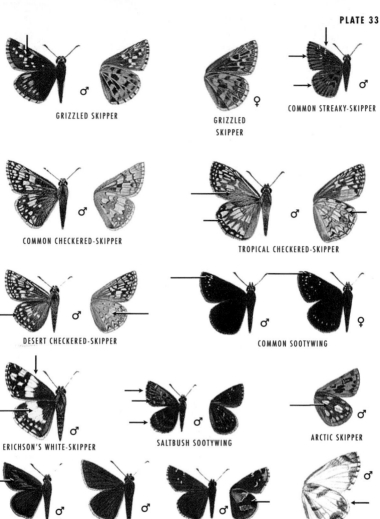

GRIZZLED SKIPPER

GRIZZLED SKIPPER ♀

COMMON STREAKY-SKIPPER ♂

COMMON CHECKERED-SKIPPER ♂

TROPICAL CHECKERED-SKIPPER ♂

DESERT CHECKERED-SKIPPER ♂

COMMON SOOTYWING ♂ ♀

ERICHSON'S WHITE-SKIPPER ♂

SALTBUSH SOOTYWING ♂

ARCTIC SKIPPER ♂

REDUNDANT SKIPPER ♂

PALE-RAYED SKIPPER ♂

VIOLET PATCH SKIPPER ♂

TURK'S CAP WHITE-SKIPPER ♂

MALICIOUS SKIPPER ♂

LAVIANA WHITE-SKIPPER ♂

PLATE 34   × 1¼

BRANDED SKIPPERS

SWARTHY SKIPPER *Nastra lherminier,* male   **P. 359**
Fairfax Co., Va. Upperside dark brown, sometimes trace of 2 light spots. Underside of hindwing yellow-brown with veins lighter.

NEAMATHLA SKIPPER *Nastra neamathla,* male   **P. 359**
Levy Co., Fla. Underside of forewing yellow-brown on more than half; hindwing yellow-brown without light scaling on veins.

JULIA'S SKIPPER *Nastra julia,* male, Bexar Co., Texas   **P. 359**
Underside of forewing yellow brown on less than half; 2-5 pale spots on outer half. Hindwing yellow-brown without paler veins.

DOUBLE-SPOTTED SKIPPER *Decinea percosius,* male   **P. 362**
Cameron Co., Texas. Forewing with angled transparent spot in discal cell. Hindwing with small central transparent spot.

THREE-SPOTTED SKIPPER *Cymaenes tripunctus,* male   **P. 360**
Palm Beach Co., Fla. Underside of forewing shows 3 small transparent spots near apex. Hindwing yellow-brown with faint, pale spots.

FAWN-SPOTTED SKIPPER *Cymaenes odilia,* male   **P. 360**
Yucatan, Mexico. Underside of hindwing with 2 pale bands.

CLOUDED SKIPPER *Lerema accius,* male, Dallas Co., Texas   **P. 360**
Underside of hindwing variegated with violet-blue sheen.

SOUTHERN SKIPPERLING *Copaeodes minimus,* male   **P. 364**
Madras, Ga. Tiny. Underside of hindwing with white ray.

ORANGE SKIPPERLING *Copaeodes aurantiacus,* male   **P. 364**
Bexar Co., Texas. Orange. Lacks white ray.

GARITA SKIPPERLING *Oarisma garita,* male   **P. 364**
Miniota, Man. Underside of hindwing light brown with lighter veins.

POWESHIEK SKIPPERLING *Oarisma poweshiek,* male   **P. 363**
Dickinson Co., Iowa. Hindwing pale brown, veins white.

UNCAS SKIPPER *Hesperia uncas,* male, Jefferson Co., Colo.   **P. 367**
Hindwing with macular band extended along veins.

LEAST SKIPPER *Ancyloxypha numitor,* male   **P. 362**
Hampshire Co., W. Va. Upper hindwing yellow-orange with black margin. Underside of forewing black with orange apex and costa.

OTTOE SKIPPER *Hesperia ottoe,* male   **P. 368**
Monona Co., Iowa. Male with black stigma with black or gray felt. Hindwing underside yellow-orange, unmarked.

COMMON BRANDED SKIPPER *Hesperia comma,* male   **P. 367**
Oquiasor, Me. Forewing stigma with black felt (see text). Underside of hindwing with normal macular band.

APACHE SKIPPER *Hesperia woodgatei,* female, Kerr Co., Texas   **P. 368**
Underside of hindwing brown to dark olive-green; small spots.

LEONARD'S SKIPPER *Hesperia leonardus,* male   **P. 369**
Martha's Vineyard, Mass. Red-orange with broad black borders above. Underside of hindwing brick red with distinct spots.

PAWNEE SKIPPER *Hesperia leonardus pawnee,* male   **P. 369**
Pilger, Neb. Underside of hindwing yellow-orange with faint macular band.

COBWEB SKIPPER *Hesperia metea,* male   **P. 370**
Sussex Co., N. J. Underside of hindwing with cobweb effect.

PLATE 34

SWARTHY SKIPPER

NEAMATHLA SKIPPER

JULIA'S SKIPPER

DOUBLE-SPOTTED SKIPPER

THREE-SPOTTED SKIPPER

FAWN-SPOTTED SKIPPER

CLOUDED SKIPPER

SOUTHERN SKIPPERLING

ORANGE SKIPPERLING

GARITA SKIPPERLING

POWESHIEK SKIPPERLING

UNCAS SKIPPER

LEAST SKIPPER

OTTOE SKIPPER

COMMON BRANDED SKIPPER

APACHE SKIPPER

LEONARD'S SKIPPER

PAWNEE SKIPPER

COBWEB SKIPPER

PLATE 35   × 1¼

BRANDED SKIPPERS

INDIAN SKIPPER *Hesperia sassacus,* male   **P. 373**
Pendleton Co., W. Va. Upperside with black border clear-cut. Underside of hindwing with yellow macular band.

EUROPEAN SKIPPER *Thymelicus lineola,* male   **P. 365**
Presque Isle, Mich. Brassy orange. Outer portion of wings with veins black-lined.

PAHASKA SKIPPER *Hesperia pahaska,* male   **P. 369**
Weston Co., Wyo. Distinct white pattern.

LONG DASH *Polites mystic,* male, Nepigon, Ont.   **P. 377**
Black stigma on upperside of forewing long, slightly curved. Underside of hindwing with macular band of equal-sized yellow spots.

GREEN SKIPPER *Hesperia viridis,* male   **P. 371**
Woodward Co., Okla. Hindwing with well-developed spot pattern. Macular band concave with respect to outer margin.

DOTTED SKIPPER *Hesperia attalus,* male   **P. 371**
Ocean Co., N.J. Forewing pointed. Hindwing with tiny pale spots.

FIERY SKIPPER *Hylephila phyleus,* male   **P. 365**
Fairfax Co., Va. Antennae short. Upperside with dentate black margins. Underside of hindwing with scattered small black spots.

FIERY SKIPPER *Hylephila phyleus,* female   **P. 365**
Cecil Co., Md. Hindwing pale brown with paler checks.

MESKE'S SKIPPER *Hesperia meskei,* male   **P. 372**
Big Pine Key, Fla. Hindwing bright yellow-orange with faint macular band.

WHIRLABOUT *Polites vibex,* male   **P. 377**
Baldwin Co., Ala. Upperside of hindwing with smooth black margin. Underside of hindwing with large black spots.

WHIRLABOUT *Polites vibex,* female   **P. 377**
Summerville, S.C. Hindwing gray with pale central patch.

DAKOTA SKIPPER *Hesperia dacotae,* male   **P. 372**
Dickinson Co., Iowa. Hindwing yellow-orange with faint macular band.

TAWNY-EDGED SKIPPER *Polites themistocles,* male   **P. 375**
Marathon Co., Wis. Upperside of forewing with orange along costa invading end of cell. Male stigma sinuous. Underside of hindwing brassy without spots.

TAWNY-EDGED SKIPPER *Polites themistocles,* female   **P. 375**
Marathon Co., Wis. Hindwing brassy gray without spots.

CROSSLINE SKIPPER *Polites origenes,* female   **P. 376**
Westchester Co., N.Y. Hindwing with faint spot band.

PECK'S SKIPPER *Polites peckius,* male   **P. 375**
Pendleton Co., W. Va. Underside of hindwing with yellow central patch.

CROSSLINE SKIPPER *Polites origenes,* male   **P. 376**
Westchester Co., N.Y. Upperside of forewing with long, relatively straight stigma. Underside of hindwing with faint spot band.

PLATE 35

INDIAN SKIPPER ♂

EUROPEAN SKIPPER ♂

PAHASKA SKIPPER ♂

LONG DASH ♂

GREEN SKIPPER ♂

DOTTED SKIPPER ♂

FIERY SKIPPER ♂

FIERY SKIPPER ♀

MESKE'S SKIPPER ♂

WHIRLABOUT ♂

WHIRLABOUT ♀

DAKOTA SKIPPER ♂

TAWNY-EDGED SKIPPER ♂

TAWNY-EDGED SKIPPER ♀

CROSSLINE SKIPPER ♀

PECK'S SKIPPER ♂

CROSSLINE SKIPPER ♂

PLATE 36   × 1¼

BRANDED SKIPPERS

NORTHERN BROKEN-DASH *Wallengrenia egeremet,* male   **P. 378**
Middlesex Co., Conn. Upperside of forewing with cream or yellow spot at end of discal cell. Underside of hindwing dark brown or purple-brown with paler spot band.

NORTHERN BROKEN-DASH *Wallengrenia egeremet,* female   **P. 378**
Middlesex Co., Conn. Forewing with a few elongate cream or yellow spots.

BARACOA SKIPPER *Polites baracoa,* male, Escambia Co., Fla.   **P. 375**
Small. Upperside of forewing with very short stigma.

SOUTHERN BROKEN-DASH *Wallengrenia otho,* male   **P. 377**
Chatham Co., Ga. Upperside of forewing with red-orange or orange areas along costa and at end of discal cell. Underside of hindwing orange or red-orange with faint spot band.

SOUTHERN BROKEN-DASH *Wallengrenia otho,* female   **P. 377**
Tarrant Co., Texas. Forewing with a few pale orange spots.

AROGOS SKIPPER *Atrytone arogos,* male   **P. 380**
Plymouth Co., Iowa. Both wings with black borders. Prairies.

LITTLE GLASSYWING *Pompeius verna,* male   **P. 379**
Westchester Co., N.Y. Upperside of forewing with black stigma and several transparent spots. Underside of hindwing purple-brown with distinct pale spot band.

LITTLE GLASSYWING *Pompeius verna,* female   **P. 379**
Washington Co., R.I. Forewing with a distinct square transparent spot at end of cell.

DELAWARE SKIPPER *Anatrytone logan,* male   **P. 381**
Wakulla Co., Fla. Outer margins black, wing veins black just inside borders. Forewing with thin black bar at end of cell.

BYSSUS SKIPPER *Problema byssus,* male   **P. 382**
Johnson Co., Kan. Both wings with black borders. Upperside of forewing with thin black bar at end of cell. Underside of hindwing dull yellow with band of paler spots.

RARE SKIPPER *Problema bulenta,* male, Wilmington, N.C.   **P. 382**
Both wings with black borders. Underside of hindwing clear yellow.

HOBOMOK SKIPPER *Poanes hobomok,* male   **P. 385**
Bronx Co., N.Y. Irregular black borders; lacks stigma.

HOBOMOK SKIPPER *Poanes hobomok,* female, Bronx Co., N.Y.   **P. 385**
Normal form. Similar to male but orange ground less extensive.

HOBOMOK SKIPPER *Poanes hobomok,* female, Augusta, Me.   **P. 385**
Form "pocohontas." Purple-black with few clouded white spots.

TAXILES SKIPPER *Poanes taxiles,* male, Larimer Co., Colo.   **P. 386**
Hindwing with brown in discal area. Anal fold orange or brown.

ZABULON SKIPPER *Poanes zabulon,* male, Cape May Co., N. J. **P. 385**
Forewing pointed. Upperside bright orange with black borders. Underside of hindwing with base and outer margin dark brown.

ZABULON SKIPPER *Poanes zabulon,* female   **P. 385**
Cape May Co., N.J. Hindwing two-toned brown and purple-gray.

AARON'S SKIPPER *Poanes aaroni,* male   **P. 386**
Atlantic Co., N.J. Hindwing orange-tan with a pale central streak.

PLATE 36

NORTHERN BROKEN-DASH

BARACOA SKIPPER

SOUTHERN BROKEN-DASH

AROGOS SKIPPER

LITTLE GLASSYWING

DELAWARE SKIPPER

BYSSUS SKIPPER

RARE SKIPPER

HOBOMOK SKIPPER

TAXILES SKIPPER

ZABULON SKIPPER

AARON'S SKIPPER

PLATE 37   × ³⁄₄

BRANDED SKIPPERS

SACHEM *Atalopedes campestris,* male   **P. 380**
Palm Beach Co., Fla. Upperside of forewing with large square black stigma. Found in weedy areas and gardens.

MULBERRY WING *Poanes massasoit,* male   **P. 384**
Kent Co., R.I. Black with irregular yellow central patch.

SACHEM *Atalopedes campestris,* female   **P. 380**
Big Pine Key, Fla. Square white transparent spot at end of cell on forewing.

YEHL SKIPPER *Poanes yehl,* male, Charleston Co., S.C.   **P. 387**
Upperside of forewing with straight linear stigma. Underside of hindwing orange-brown with a few distinct spots. Wooded swamps.

BLACK DASH *Euphyes conspicuus,* female   **P. 390**
Chester Co., N.J. Hindwing red-brown with curved spot band.

BROAD-WINGED SKIPPER *Poanes viator,* male   **P. 387**
Essex Co., Va. Large. Dark brown with paler yellow-orange and orange patches.

DION SKIPPER *Euphyes dion,* male   **P. 389**
Omaha, Neb. Male forewing with restricted orange and black stigma. Hindwing with broad orange streak or patch. Underside of hindwing red-brown or orange-brown with 2 yellow-orange rays.

BAY SKIPPER *Euphyes bayensis,* male   **P. 389**
Hancock Co., Miss. Hindwing yellow-orange.

DION SKIPPER *Euphyes dion,* female   **P. 389**
Omaha, Neb. Dark. Forewing with pale yellow spots.

MEXICAN MELLANA *Quasimellana eulogius,* male   **P. 387**
Mexico. Hindwing with dark brown streak running from cell to border. Rare stray to s. Texas.

BLACK DASH *Euphyes conspicuus,* male   **P. 390**
Litchfield Co., Conn. Hindwing red-brown with central curved yellow patch.

YEHL SKIPPER *Poanes yehl,* female   **P. 387**
Craven Co., N.C. Hindwing with few distinct cream spots.

BLACK DASH *Euphyes conspicuus,* female   **P. 390**
Litchfield Co., Conn. Upperside black with curved yellow patch on hindwing.

DUKE'S SKIPPER *Euphyes dukesi,* male   **P. 390**
North Landing River, Va. Sooty black above. Hindwing pale brown with yellow streak.

PALATKA SKIPPER *Euphyes pilatka,* male   **P. 389**
Craven Co., N.C. Extensive orange with black borders. Underside of hindwing dull brown. Coastal marshes.

PALMETTO SKIPPER *Euphyes arpa,* male   **P. 388**
Big Pine Key, Fla. Forewing with restricted tawny yellow. Underside of hindwing bright yellow-orange.

BERRY'S SKIPPER *Euphyes berryi,* male   **P. 391**
Volusia Co., Fla. Upperside with limited tawny area. Underside of hindwing pale brown with veins whitened.

PLATE 37

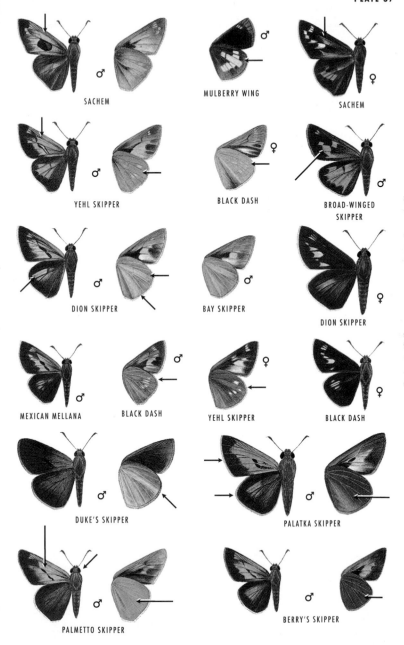

SACHEM ♂

MULBERRY WING ♂

SACHEM ♀

YEHL SKIPPER ♂

BLACK DASH ♀

BROAD-WINGED SKIPPER ♂

DION SKIPPER ♂

BAY SKIPPER ♂

DION SKIPPER ♀

MEXICAN MELLANA ♂

BLACK DASH ♂

YEHL SKIPPER ♀

BLACK DASH ♀

DUKE'S SKIPPER ♂

PALATKA SKIPPER ♂

PALMETTO SKIPPER ♂

BERRY'S SKIPPER ♂

PLATE 38   × 1

BRANDED SKIPPERS

TWO-SPOTTED SKIPPER *Euphyes bimacula*, male   **P. 391**
     Burlington Co., N.J. Upperside of forewing with limited tawny patch.
     Underside of hindwing with veins paler. Anal fold white.

TWO-SPOTTED SKIPPER *Euphyes bimacula*, female   **P. 391**
     Burlington Co., N.J. Forewing with two pale spots.

DUN SKIPPER *Euphyes vestris*, female   **P. 391**
     Westchester Co., N.Y. Forewing cell with 2 tiny diffuse spots.

DUN SKIPPER *Euphyes vestris*, male   **P. 391**
     Westchester Co., N.Y. Head and foreward part of thorax with golden-
     orange scaling. Wings brown-black with darker black stigma.

MONK SKIPPER *Asbolis capucinus*, male, Key Largo, Fla.   **P. 392**
     Forewing with gray stigma. Hindwing dull brick red and black.

DUSTED SKIPPER *Atrytonopsis hianna*, male   **P. 392**
     Washington Co., R.I. Underside of hindwing gray, lighter outwardly.
     At least a single white spot at base.

LINDA'S ROADSIDE-SKIPPER *Amblyscirtes linda*, male   **P. 394**
     Faulkner Co., Ark. Forewing brown — lacks reddish. Hindwing dark
     with a few light spots.

OSLAR'S ROADSIDE-SKIPPER *Amblyscirtes oslari*, male   **P. 394**
     Kerr Co., Texas. Hindwing underside light gray with paler spot band.

BRONZE ROADSIDE-SKIPPER *Amblyscirtes aenus*, female   **P. 393**
     Randall Co., Texas. Underside of forewing with red-brown basally.
     Hindwing with pale spot band.

BRONZE ROADSIDE-SKIPPER *Amblyscirtes aenus*, male   **P. 393**
     Form "erna," Randall Co., Texas. Hindwing has pale spots reduced.

CAROLINA ROADSIDE-SKIPPER *Amblyscirtes carolina*, male   **P. 395**
     Suffolk Co., Va. Forewing with small yellow spots. Underside of hind-
     wing dull yellow with dark spots. Wooded swamps with cane.

REVERSED ROADSIDE-SKIPPER *Amblyscirtes reversa*, female   **P. 396**
     Wendall, N.C. Hindwing rust-brown with yellow spots.

LACE-WINGED ROADSIDE-SKIPPER *Amblyscirtes aesculapius*   **P. 395**
     Female, Suffolk Co., Va. Fringes strongly checkered. Hindwing with
     pale yellow or white cobweb pattern.

NYSA ROADSIDE-SKIPPER *Amblyscirtes nysa*, male   **P. 396**
     Jim Wells Co., Texas. Fringes checkered. Hindwing variegated.

DOTTED ROADSIDE-SKIPPER *Amblyscirtes eos*, male, Kerr Co., Texas   **P. 397**
     Hindwing gray-brown with round white spots.

PEPPER AND SALT SKIPPER *Amblyscirtes hegon*, male   **P. 394**
     Bristol Co., Mass. Hindwing light gray-green with paler spot band.

COMMON ROADSIDE-SKIPPER *Amblyscirtes vialis*, male, Sussex Co.,   **P. 397**
     Va. Forewing apex and outer half of hindwing dusted violet-gray.

DUSKY ROADSIDE-SKIPPER *Amblyscirtes alternata*, male   **P. 398**
     Suffolk Co., Va. Fringes checkered. Forewing with pale spots.

CELIA'S ROADSIDE-SKIPPER *Amblyscirtes celia*, male   **P. 398**
     Hidalgo Co., Texas. Hindwing gray with white spot pattern.

BELL'S ROADSIDE-SKIPPER *Amblyscirtes belli*, male   **P. 398**
     Fulton Co., Ga. Fringes strongly checkered. Hindwing gray-black
     with pale gray spots.

PLATE 38

TWO-SPOTTED SKIPPER

DUN SKIPPER

DUN SKIPPER

MONK SKIPPER

DUSTED SKIPPER   LINDA'S   OSLAR'S   BRONZE   BRONZE

ROADSIDE-SKIPPERS

CAROLINA   REVERSED   LACE-WINGED   NYSA

ROADSIDE-SKIPPERS

DOTTED   PEPPER AND SALT   COMMON   DUSKY   CELIA'S   BELL'S

ROADSIDE-SKIPPERS

PLATE 39 × 1

BRANDED SKIPPERS AND YUCCA SKIPPERS

OCOLA SKIPPER *Panoquina ocola,* male, Escambia Co., Fla. **P. 401**
Forewings extend beyond hindwings. Hindwing without spots.

EUFALA SKIPPER *Lerodea eufala,* male, Wakulla Co., Fla. **P. 399**
Hindwing gray-brown, rarely with faint spots.

OLIVE-CLOUDED SKIPPER *Lerodea arabus,* male **P. 399**
San Luis Potosi, Mexico. Hindwing has central dark patch. Rare
stray. to s. Texas.

HECEBOLUS SKIPPER *Panoquina hecebola,* male, El Salvador **P. 402**
Underside of hindwing with veins lightened. Rarely with spot band or
purple sheen.

TWIN-SPOT SKIPPER *Oligoria maculata,* male, Big Pine Key, Fla. **P. 399**
Wings rounded. Hindwing pale red-brown with 3 distinct white spots
— one separate and two adjacent.

VIOLET-BANDED SKIPPER *Nyctelius nyctelius,* Cameron Co., Fla. **P. 403**
Male. Large pointed forewing with pattern of transparent spots.

CHESTNUT-MARKED SKIPPER *Thespieus macareus,* male **P. 403**
Veracruz, Mexico. Forewing with large white spots. Hindwing with
large white patch.

OBSCURE SKIPPER *Panoquina panoquinoides,* male **P. 401**
Cameron Co., Texas. Small. Hindwing plain brown with 3 pale spots.
Salt or brackish marshes.

PURPLE-WASHED SKIPPER *Panoquina sylvicola,* male **P. 402**
Hidalgo Co., Texas. Forewing with elongate spot in cell. Hindwing
with straight line of white or blue spots.

SALT MARSH SKIPPER *Panoquina panoquin,* male **P. 400**
Brunswick Co., N.C. Hindwing with light veins and white dash at
end of cell. Salt marshes.

YUCCA GIANT-SKIPPER *Megathymus yuccae coloradensis,* male **P. 404**
Hidalgo Co., Texas. Large. Forewing pointed with yellow band. Hindwing with yellow band on outer margin. Underside of hindwing gray
with white marks on costa.

BRAZILIAN SKIPPER *Calpodes ethlius,* male **P. 400**
Arlington, Va. Forewing with large translucent spots. Underside of
hindwing red-brown with distinct cream spots.

FUSINA SKIPPER *Panoquina fusina,* male **P. 403**
Florencia, Colombia. Hindwing with broad white band.

MANFREDA GIANT-SKIPPER *Stallingsia maculosa,* male **P. 406**
Bexar Co., Texas. Forewing with series of small, oval cream spots. Declining.

YUCCA GIANT-SKIPPER *Megathymus yuccae,* male, St. Johns Co., Fla. **P. 404**
Forewing pointed. Yellow submarginal band on forewing. Yellow band
on hindwing. Underside of hindwing gray with white spot on costa.

STRECKER'S GIANT-SKIPPER *Megathymus streckeri,* male **P. 405**
Cherry Co., Neb. Large. Yellow bands on both wings. Long erect
scales on hindwing. Underside of hindwing gray with white spots.

COFAQUI GIANT-SKIPPER *Megathymus cofaqui,* male **P. 405**
Hillsborough Co., Fla. Small. Yellow band on forewing broad.

PLATE 39

OCOLA SKIPPER

EUFALA SKIPPER

OLIVE-CLOUDED SKIPPER

HECEBOLUS SKIPPER

TWIN-SPOT SKIPPER

VIOLET-BANDED SKIPPER

CHESTNUT-MARKED SKIPPER

OBSCURE SKIPPER

PURPLE-WASHED SKIPPER

SALT MARSH SKIPPER

YUCCA GIANT-SKIPPER

BRAZILIAN SKIPPER

FUSINA SKIPPER

MANFREDA GIANT-SKIPPER

YUCCA GIANT-SKIPPER

STRECKER'S GIANT-SKIPPER

COFAQUI GIANT-SKIPPER

SPECIES
ACCOUNTS

7

TRUE BUTTERFLIES:
SUPERFAMILY PAPILIONOIDEA

The true butterflies have antennae with rounded clubs and are usually more slender-bodied and large-winged than skippers, the only other butterfly superfamily. The swallowtails (Papilionidae), whites and sulphurs (Pieridae), gossamer wings (Lycaenidae), metalmarks (Riodinidae), and brushfoots (Nymphalidae) are the true butterflies. Their wings are often covered with brightly colored scales. Androconia, scales that disseminate pheromones used in courtship, may be located in patches on almost any part of the wings, as scale tufts sheathed in the abdomen, or, rarely, on the abdomen itself. These butterflies may have two or three pairs of walking legs; in several families the front legs are modified in structure, reduced in size, and not used for walking.

Eggs may be turban-shaped, globular, or columnar, and are usually but not always deposited singly. Caterpillars undergo four to six instars, each of which may have a different color pattern. Caterpillars may be brightly colored, although many are predominantly green or brown, and many are ornamented with groups of bristles or spines. Caterpillars usually feed from the outside, but a few bore into fruits and seeds. Caterpillars lack narrowed neck-like areas. Pupae usually lack cocoons and those of most families hang from or are slung to objects such as stones, twigs, or bark with a silk girdle and hooks (cremaster) set into a silk mat.

SWALLOWTAILS: FAMILY PAPILIONIDAE

The swallowtails are worldwide in distribution and comprise about 560 species. They are richest in the tropics. Many are brilliantly colored and are favorites of collectors and photographers. Many species, especially those in the tropics, mimic other butterflies that are distasteful, while others are distasteful themselves and are emetic to birds and other vertebrate predators. The adults are medium to large and may or may not have tails (most of ours do). Adults have three pairs of walking legs. A unique trait is that forewing vein 3A ends on the inner margin. Adults of all species visit flowers for nectar. Males of most species patrol in search of mates, while males of one group, represented by the Black, Ozark, Short-tailed, Baird's, Old World, and Anise Swallowtails in our area, perch on hilltops or ridges instead of patrolling.

Eggs are globular. Caterpillars have repellent structures, the hornlike osmateria, that can be extruded from behind the head. They vary from yellow to red and are found only in the swallowtail family. In later stages, the caterpillars are smooth or have only relatively blunt fleshy structures and lack spines. The pupae are usually protectively colored (green or brown are the usual colors). They are attached at the posterior end by a silk button and slung by a silk girdle. All our species overwinter in the pupal stage. Some swallowtails may spend more than one year in the pupal stage, and it is thought that the endangered Schaus' Swallowtail may be one such species.

CATTLE HEART *Parides eurimedes*   **NOT SHOWN**
3–3½ in. (76–90 mm). Sexes dimorphic. Black. *Scalloped hindwings* having *pink fringe* between lobes. Upperside: Male forewing with *triangular green patch;* female forewing with white patch. Hindwing with large *red-pink patch* in center. **SIMILAR SPECIES:** Ruby-spotted Swallowtail (see Pl. 5) has pink postmedian patch on hindwing not centered; fringe is white, not pink. **EARLY STAGES:** Caterpillar velvety purple-brown with irregular black patches. **FOOD:** Pipe vines. **FLIGHT:** March–Nov. **RANGE:** Resident in American tropics from s. Mexico south through Cen. America to n. South America. Has strayed to Texas. **HABITAT:** In Mexico, openings and wide trails in a variety of mature tropical forests, 0–2700 ft. (0–800 m).

PIPEVINE SWALLOWTAILS: GENUS *Battus* SCOPOLI

This is a primarily tropical genus. The butterflies are primarily black with red or orange marks. The adults flutter their wings while nectaring and fly with rapid, shallow wingbeats. All of the species are distasteful, and they are mimicked by other distasteful or relatively palatable butterflies. The caterpillars feed on pipe vines (Family Aristolochiaceae) and have paired fleshy tubercles.

PIPEVINE SWALLOWTAIL *Battus philenor*   **PL. 5**
2¾–5⅛ in. (72–132 mm). The larvae and adults of this common butterfly are distasteful and emetic to birds, their would-be

Pipevine Swallowtail. Male imbibing moisture at wet spot, Davis Mts., Tex. Freshly emerged males of patrolling butterflies often take in moisture at sandy or muddy spots near streams or trails.

predators. The adult is the "model" for several mimics — Spicebush Swallowtail, Black and Ozark Swallowtails, Eastern Tiger Swallowtail (black female), Red-spotted Purple, and female Diana. Upperside: Black with *iridescent blue-green* hindwing (especially in male). Underside: Hindwing has submarginal row of seven round *orange spots* in an iridescent blue field. Flight rapid, wings flutter shallowly. Adults flutter wings rapidly when visiting flowers. **SIMILAR SPECIES:** (1) Spicebush Swallowtail has marginal row of oval green spots on both wings; round orange spot on outer hindwing angle above; two rows of smaller orange spots below. (2) Black Swallowtail and (3) Ozark Swallowtail females have red-orange eyespot at hindwing anal angle, 2 rows of yellow dots on abdomen, and upper hindwing has blue limited only to submarginal area. (4) Eastern Tiger Swallowtail dark female is usually larger with red-orange spot at anal angle, and shadows of tiger stripes can usually be seen on forewing, especially below. (5) Red-spotted Purple is usually smaller, lacks tails, and has basal red-orange markings on both wings below. **EARLY STAGES:** Larva brown or black with rows of fleshy tubercles, the 2 rows on back orange to red. **FOOD:** Various pipe vines (*Aristolochia* spp.). **FLIGHT:** Feb.–Nov. in Deep South and s. Texas (possibly 3–4 flights), April–Sept. in north (2 flights). **RANGE:** S. Canada (Ont.), s. Mich., and New England (rare) west to desert Southwest and south through much of our area to s. Mexico. **HABITAT:** Glades in woods in east, open fields and thorn scrub in west. Sea level to 5000 ft. (1500 m).

POLYDAMAS SWALLOWTAIL *Battus polydamas* **PL. 5**
3⅜–4½ in. (92–116 mm). *Lacks tails.* Hindwing has scalloped margin. Upperside: both wings with *submarginal yellow band.* Underside: hindwing has marginal row of red S-marks. **EARLY STAGES:** Larva similar to that of Pipevine Swallowtail, but has yellow lateral band on thorax. **FOOD:** Various pipe vines (*Aristolochia* spp.). **FLIGHT:** April–Nov. (2–3 flights). **RANGE:** Peninsular Fla. and s. Texas south through tropical Americas (including Antilles) to Argentina. Strays north as far as Mo. and Ky. **HABITAT:** Abandoned fields, open pine woods, suburbs, tropical forest edge. Sea level to 2000 ft. (600 m).

KITE-SWALLOWTAILS: GENUS *Eurytides* HÜBNER

There are more than 140 species in the kite-swallowtail group, which is found in most tropical regions. Adults of most kite swallowtails have extremely long tails. They fly close to the ground with shallow wingbeats. Freshly emerged males gather in groups at moist sand along rivers and streams. Caterpillars eat the leaves of plants in the annona family and are stout and without tubercles.

ZEBRA SWALLOWTAIL *Eurytides marcellus* **PL. 5**
2½–4 in. (64–104 mm). Upperside: Wings very *pale green-white* with black stripes and very *long tails.* Spring individuals are smaller and lighter in appearance. **SIMILAR SPECIES:** (1) Dark Kite-Swallowtail has more extensive black, found only once in s. Texas where the Zebra Swallowtail does not occur. (2) Cuban Kite-Swallowtail is smaller, greener, and with shorter, outcurved tails.

POLYDAMAS SWALLOWTAIL

ZEBRA SWALLOWTAIL

EARLY STAGES: Larva pea green with alternating yellow and black bands. **FOOD:** Paw-paw (*Asimina triloba*) and related plants in South. **FLIGHT:** In north, April–Aug. (2 flights); Feb.–Dec. in Deep South (possibly 3–4 flights). Less common later in year. **RANGE:** E. U.S. (exclusive of New England and northern part of Great Lakes states—rare in northern part of range) and s. Ont. west to e. Kans., Okla., and cen. Texas. **HABITAT:** Moist woods along rivers, wooded swamps, and pine flatwoods. Sea level to 1500 ft. (450 m).

DARK KITE-SWALLOWTAIL *Eurytides philolaus*   **NOT SHOWN**
3½–3¾ in. (90–95 mm). Long tails. Upperside: Forewing with *broad black longitudinal bars.* Also a rare all-black form. **SIMILAR SPECIES:** (1) Zebra Swallowtail has narrower black bars on forewing, and generally narrower black marginal areas. **EARLY STAGES:** Caterpillar with warm brown back and a white lateral band; it also has a central white blotch. **FOOD:** Leaves of various shrubs and small trees in the annona family (*Annona* and *Sapranthus*). **FLIGHT:** March–Nov. (2 flights). Most common after onset of rainy season. **RANGE:** S. Texas (once on South Padre I.) south to Costa Rica. **HABITAT:** Lowland tropical forests, usually deciduous or semideciduous. Sea level to 1000 ft. (300 m).

CUBAN KITE-SWALLOWTAIL *Eurytides celadon* **NOT SHOWN**
2⁹⁄₁₆–3⁵⁄₁₆ in. (66–85 mm). Small version of Zebra Swallowtail, greener, with all *black, outcurved tails.* Upperside: Forewing with antemedian black spot; hindwing has two parallel black stripes. **SIMILAR SPECIES:** (1) Zebra Swallowtail is larger, has tails white-tipped. **EARLY STAGES:** Not known. **FLIGHT:** July–Oct. (2 flights). **RANGE:** Resident on Cuba. Possible sightings of strays on Fla. Keys. Older specimens of dubious authenticity. **HABITAT:** Tropical forests.

FLUTED SWALLOWTAILS: GENUS *Papilio* LINNAEUS

This is the largest group of swallowtails, with more than 200 species found worldwide. The color patterns are quite variable, but our species usually feature black and yellow as predominant colors. The tails of many species are constricted at the base and may be spoon-shaped. Except for the Black Swallowtail and its relatives, the males patrol likely habitats in search of females. Freshly emerged males gather at moist sand or mud along streams or rivers. A wide variety of plants is eaten by caterpillars of different species; most are woody trees or shrubs. Each caterpillar instar is differently marked, with the younger stages often patterned after bird droppings. Other authors have divided this large group into several smaller genera, but these are best considered as species groups.

Black Swallowtail. Male basking on vegetation in Cameron Co., Tex. Butterflies often bask with open wings in early morning to raise their body temperatures to enable flight.

BLACK SWALLOWTAIL *Papilio polyxenes* **PLS. 2, 4, 5**

3⅛–4½ in. (79–113 mm). Upperside: Both sexes primarily black; male with *yellow submarginal band* of variable width; female with postmedian row of small yellow spots; hindwing with *black pupil centered* in red-orange eyespot at anal angle; hindwing of female has *iridescent blue submarginal band*. Abdomen with longitudinal rows of yellow dots. **SIMILAR SPECIES:** (1) Ozark Swallowtail usually has ventral postmedian band with more orange, black pupil of eyespot often touches wing margin, male has most apical yellow spot in upperside forewing, submarginal band short and single. The front is usually yellow. (2) Short-tailed Swallowtail has short tails and variable orange in dorsal submarginal band of male. (3) Baird's Swallowtail has yellow shoulders (tegulae) on thorax and black pupil of eyespot touching hindwing margin at anal angle. **EARLY STAGES:** Caterpillar green with black bands around the middle of each segment and 5 longitudinal rows of orange dots coinciding with the front edge of each black band. **FOOD:** Leaves of various low herbaceous plants in parsley family including cultivated Carrot and Wild Carrot, or Queen Anne's Lace (*Daucus carota*), Parsley, Dill, Celery, and many wild species. **FLIGHT:** April–Oct. (2–3 flights). **RANGE:** From Gaspé of Que. and N.S. west to s. Sask., Colo., and se. Calif. through most of the e. U.S., thence south through the mountains to n. South America. **HABITAT:** Open areas —fields, gardens, waste areas, marshes. Sea level to 7000 ft. (2150 m). **REMARKS:** In southern Man. there are populations with intermediates between Black Swallowtail and Old World Swallowtail. These have been treated by other authors either as a separate species (*P. kahli*) or as a subspecies of the Black Swallowtail.

BLACK SWALLOWTAIL

OZARK SWALLOWTAIL

OZARK SWALLOWTAIL *Papilio joanae*   **PL. 5**

3¼–4½ in. (82–113 mm). Very similar to Black Swallowtail, except *front yellow*. Upperside: Yellow postmedian band of male forewing with the most *apical spot short and single*; hindwing has *black pupil* in eyespot at anal angle *touching edge of wing*; female hindwing has costal spot of postmedian band small and obscured. Underside: Hindwing postmedian band with more extensive orange. **SIMILAR SPECIES:** Black Swallowtail, with which Ozark Swallowtail occurs, has a black face, a black pupil in eyespot at anal angle of hindwing centered, and less orange on postmedian band on underside of hindwing. **EARLY STAGES:** Similar to Black Swallowtail, but larva is bright green or light blue with segmental bands broken and the dots yellow-orange, yellow, or white. **FOOD:** Several plants in parsley family, including Yellow Pimpernel (*Taenidia integerrima*), Meadow Parsnip (*Thaspium barbinode*), and Golden Alexander (*Zizia aurea*). **FLIGHT:** April–Sept. (2 flights). **RANGE:** N. Ark., w. Ky., and Mo. **HABITAT:** Cedar glades and woodlands.

SHORT-TAILED SWALLOWTAIL *Papilio brevicauda*   **PL. 5**

2¾–3 in. (72–76 mm). Similar to Black Swallowtail except *very short tails* and upperside with variable amounts of *orange* in postmedian bands. **SIMILAR SPECIES:** (1) Black Swallowtail has longer tails and lacks orange in postmedian yellow bands. **EARLY STAGES:** Caterpillar similar to that of Black Swallowtail, but spots are yellow. **FOOD:** Cow Parsnip and Scotch Lovage. **FLIGHT:** June–July (1 flight). **RANGE:** Maritime Provinces of Canada. **HABITAT:** Open headlands and low hills with heath vegetation. **REMARKS:** Short-tailed Swallowtail and Black Swallowtail overlap in some areas with little evidence of hybridization.

BAIRD'S SWALLOWTAIL *Papilio bairdii*   **NOT SHOWN**
3 5/16–3 3/4 in. (85–95 mm). The *yellow tegulae* on the thorax and the
off-centered pupil in hindwing eyespot *touching wing margin*
should separate the Baird's from the similar Black Swallowtail
where the two might be encountered on the Great Plains. **SIMILAR
SPECIES:** Black Swallowtail lacks yellow tegulae and has centered
pupils in hindwing eyespot. **EARLY STAGES:** Caterpillar similar to that
of Black Swallowtail but shows more variability in yellow or
orange spotting. **FOOD:** Snakeroot (*Artemisia dracunculus*). **FLIGHT:**
May–Sept. (2 flights). **RANGE:** Rare stray in our area. Resident in w.
North America from s. Canada through Rocky Mts. and interior
ranges south to s. Calif. and s. N.M. **HABITAT:** Mountainous
foothills in w. U.S. Some populations along sand bars of rivers
leading east from Rocky Mts. into Great Plains. Rare stray east of
100th meridian. **REMARKS:** This is a close relative of the Old World
Swallowtail, whose North American populations have the same
larval host genus.

OLD WORLD SWALLOWTAIL *Papilio machaon*   **PL. 6**
2 5/8–3 in. (65–77 mm). Northern. Upperside: Hindwing with *red-
orange eyespot edged with black at lower margin*. **SIMILAR SPECIES:** (1)
Baird's Swallowtail (yellow form) has upperside hindwing eyespot
with black off-center pupil. Ranges not overlapping. **EARLY STAGES:**
Caterpillar similar to that of Black Swallowtail. **FOOD:** Arctic Sagebrush and possibly umbellifers. **FLIGHT:** Late May–July (1 flight).
RANGE: Holarctic. In North America from Alaska south and east
across subarctic Canada through n. Ont., isolated records in e.
Que. and n. Man. **HABITAT:** Barren rocky areas.

ANISE SWALLOWTAIL *Papilio zelicaon*   **NOT SHOWN**
3 5/16–3 1/2 in. (85–90 mm). Upperside: Hindwing eyespot with *cen-

OLD WORLD SWALLOWTAIL

ANISE SWALLOWTAIL

tered black pupil, otherwise similar to yellow form of Western Black Swallowtail. **SIMILAR SPECIES:** (1) Old World Swallowtail does not overlap in range in our area. Hindwing eyespot lacks centered black pupil. (2) Baird's Swallowtail (yellow form) has upperside hindwing eyespot with black pupil off-center. **EARLY STAGES:** Caterpillar very similar to that of Black Swallowtail: green with intersegmental black bands with yellow or orange spots. **FOOD:** Parsley family, many species including Mountain Parsley. **FLIGHT:** April–July (1 flight). **RANGE:** W. North America from w. cen. Alta. south to N.M., west to Pacific Coast, south to s. Calif. Rarely found in cen. Neb. and e. N.D. **HABITAT:** Foothills, gardens, river forests in plains.

GIANT SWALLOWTAIL *Papilio cresphontes*   **PLS. 2, 4, 6**
4–6¼ in. (102–154 mm). Large. Upperside: Forewing with *diagonal yellow spot band*. Hindwing with broad yellow band at base. Tails spoon-shaped, filled with yellow. Underside: Mostly yellow. **SIMILAR SPECIES:** (1) Thoas Swallowtail almost impossible to separate unless collected. Upper forewing has yellow postmedian band with quadrate spots in neat row. (2) Ornythion Swallowtail with upperside forewing yellow spot row close to outer margin; tails all black, not spoon-shaped. (3) Schaus' Swallowtail has narrower upperside forewing yellow band, underside hindwing with large chestnut postmedian patch. **EARLY STAGES:** Caterpillar ("orange dog") is brown with white mottled middle and anal saddles, closely resembling a fresh bird dropping. **FOOD:** Citrus family, mainly prickly-ash, but occasionally Hop Tree in north; in south, citrus, Hercules Club, and Torchwood. **FLIGHT:** All year in Deep South and s. Texas, May-Aug. in north (2 flights). **RANGE:** Americas from cen. and e. Canada (s. Man., s. Ont., rarely Que., N.B., N.S.) south through e. North America, desert Southwest south through Mexi-

Giant Swallowtail. Male basking in lower Rio Grande Valley, Tex. Giant Swallowtails are often found in southern gardens where they have a predilection for flowers of Bougainvillea, lantana, and other plants.

co, Cen. America, and most of South America. This species is rare and local in much of the Northeast. **HABITAT:** A variety of situations —rocky and sandy exposed hillsides near streams or gullies in north; pine flatwoods, towns, and citrus groves in the South.

THOAS SWALLOWTAIL *Papilio thoas*   **PL. 6**

4⅛–5 in. (105–128 mm). Upperside: Forewing with *diagonal yellow band* with *spots* more or less *square*, in a neat row. **SIMILAR SPECIES:** Giant Swallowtail has forewing upperside with center 2 spots in yellow postmedian row rounded or triangular. **EARLY STAGES:** Caterpillar like a large bird dropping—mottled olive green, dull white, brown, and yellow with a whitish thoracic saddle. **FOOD:** Citrus, Hop Tree, *Zanthoxylum*, and pipers. **FLIGHT:** All year in tropics, April–July in s. Texas. **RANGE:** Tropical America from s. Texas south to Brazil (very rare vagrant to Kans. and Okla.). **HABITAT:** Tropical

GIANT SWALLOWTAIL

THOAS SWALLOWTAIL

Schaus' Swallowtail. Male basking in Biscayne National Park, Fla. This butterfly is endangered by development of its hardwood hammock habitat and mosquito fogging. Efforts to restore the species are underway. Photo by George Krizek.

forests and edges in lowlands and mid elevations. **REMARKS:** Rare vagrant. Cannot be confidently separated from the more common Giant Swallowtail without capture.

SCHAUS' SWALLOWTAIL

SCHAUS' SWALLOWTAIL

Papilio aristodemus **PL. 6**
Endangered species. 3⅝–4⅝ in. (92–118 mm). Upperside: Forewing with narrow postmedian yellow band; hindwing with tails black, edged narrowly with yellow. Underside: Hindwing has broad chestnut median band. **SIMILAR SPECIES:** (1) Giant Swallowtail is larger, forewing has broader yellow band above; tails spoon-shaped, filled with yellow; (2) Bahaman Swallowtail forewing has yellow bar at end of cell; tails are yellow-centered. **EARLY STAGES:** Caterpillar has a pure white hood at the tail end and a lateral series of about six white and yellow patches; the thorax is somewhat swollen. **FOOD:** Primarily Torchwood, rarely Wild Lime. **FLIGHT:** Late April to mid-June, rarely July–Sept. (1 primary flight). **RANGE:** Greater Antilles north to Fla. Keys, formerly mainland near Miami. **HABITAT:** Tropical hardwood hammocks and associated scrub.

BAHAMAN SWALLOWTAIL *Papilio andraemon* **PL. 6**
3¾–4¹⁄₁₆ in. (96–106 mm). Upperside: Forewing with *yellow bar at end of cell,* submarginal yellow spots faint or lacking; hindwing with *long tails, yellow-centered.* **SIMILAR SPECIES:** (1) Giant Swallow-

tail is larger, lacks forewing cell bar above. Has yellow bands positioned quite differently. (2) Schaus' Swallowtail has forewing above with submarginal yellow spots. Tails without yellow centers. **EARLY STAGES:** Caterpillar dark olive or black with white saddle marks on the front and tail ends. There are two rows of blue spots along the back, and the prolegs and underneath are lilac. **FOOD:** Citrus, rue, Wild Lime. **FLIGHT:** April–Oct. (3 flights). **RANGE:** Bahamas, Cuba, and Jamaica. Rare stray or temporary colonist in Fla. Keys and mainland near Miami. **HABITAT:** In Fla., hammocks and scrub at sea level.

ORNYTHION SWALLOWTAIL   PL. 6
Papilio ornythion

3¼–4½ in. (82–114 mm). Female dimorphic, one form much like male, the other largely black (not illustrated). *Tails broad — all black.* Upperside: Forewing spots are *yellow-white* and *marginal spot row* is closer to outer margin. *Black female* hindwing upperside has marginal *row of large gray-green spots* and normal tails. **SIMILAR SPECIES:** (1) Giant and (2) Thoas swallowtails have hindwing tails broader, filled with yellow; ground color yellow, not yellow-white. (3) Broad-banded Swallowtail male has yellow spot at end of upperside forewing cell, hindwing underside with red spots in medial band. Female largely black with tails extremely short, submarginal band with blue. **EARLY STAGES:** Caterpillar very similar to that of King Swallowtail but smaller and with more yellow. **FOOD:** Citrus. **FLIGHT:** April–Sept. in Texas (probably 2 flights). **RANGE:** Guatemala and and Mexico. Strays north to cen. and s. Texas, s. N.M. (rarely s. Ariz. and Kans.). **HABITAT:** Gardens and citrus groves.

BROAD-BANDED SWALLOWTAIL *Papilio astyalus*   PL. 6

4⅝–4¹³⁄₁₆ in. (117–121 mm). Male upperside: Forewing with *diagonal band broad; small yellow spot* at end of cell. Hindwing with *tails narrow, all black.* Female primarily *black* with *very short tails*; upperside hindwing has *blue and gray-green submarginal band.* **SIMILAR SPECIES:** (1) Ornythion Swallowtail (male and yellow female), (2) Giant Swallowtail, and (3) Thoas Swallowtail all have narrower diagonal yellow band on upper forewing and more restricted yellow at base of hindwing. **EARLY STAGES:** Caterpillar similar to that of Thoas Swallowtail. **FOOD:** Citrus. **FLIGHT:** April–Oct. (probably 2 flights). **RANGE:** Mexico and Cen. America south to Argentina. Strays to s. Texas, rarely s. Ariz. and n. Texas. **HABITAT:** Seasonally dry tropical forests.

ANDROGEUS SWALLOWTAIL *Papilio androgeus* **PL. 6**
5¼–5½ in. (134–142 mm). A rare find in s. Fla. Sexes dimorphic.
Male with *elongated forewing*. Upperside: Extremely *broad yellow
bands* on both wings. No marginal rows of yellow spots as in close
relatives. Hindwing with *tails very narrow*. Female black. Upperside: Hindwing with much *blue iridescence; 3 narrow pointed tails*
on each hindwing. **SIMILAR SPECIES:** (1) Giant Swallowtail male has
marginal yellow spots and narrower diagonal yellow band. **EARLY
STAGES:** Caterpillar dark gray to black, with many white streaks and
blotches. True legs and prolegs dark brown, and thorax somewhat
swollen. **FOOD:** Orange and *Zanthoxylum*. **FLIGHT:** April–Oct. **RANGE:**
Resident in tropical America from Mexico and Greater Antilles
south to Argentina. Colonized s. Fla. in 1976. **HABITAT:** Overgrown
citrus groves in s. Fla.

EASTERN TIGER SWALLOWTAIL **PLS. 2, 5, 7**
Papilio glaucus
3⅝–6½ in. (92–165 mm). Male yellow, *tiger-striped*. Female
dimorphic—one form yellow like male and the other black,
although shadows of dark stripes can usually be seen. Upperside:
Both female forms have extensive blue iridescent scales on hindwing. Underside: Forewing marginal spot row *continuous*—not of
separate spots. Hindwing has *orange marginal spot*. **SIMILAR SPECIES:**
(1) Canadian Tiger Swallowtail is smaller, has black edging along
anal margin, and has continuous spot row on forewing underside
—black female form extremely rare. (2) Western Tiger Swallowtail has narrower forewings, upperside hindwing with uppermost
submarginal spot orange instead of yellow, underside hindwing
submarginal area without orange suffusion. No black female
form. (3) Two-tailed Swallowtail has narrower black stripes, has 2

*Eastern Tiger Swal-
lowtail. Male nectar-
ing at Joe-Pye Weed
at Callaway Gardens,
Ga. Many adult but-
terflies drink flower
nectar as their only
food. This provides
energy that allows
their flight and other
activities. Photo by
Evi Buckner.*

EASTERN TIGER SWALLOWTAIL

CANADIAN TIGER SWALLOWTAIL

tails on each hindwing. (4) Spicebush Swallowtail can only be confused with black female form, from which it differs in lower, more rapid flight, underside hindwing with postmedian orange spot row, upperside hindwing with round orange spot on costa, and spoon-shaped tails. **EARLY STAGES:** Caterpillar is dark green with 2 large eyespots on the swollen thoracic area. **FOOD:** Various trees and shrubs, especially Yellow Poplar, Wild Cherry, and Sweet Bay. **FLIGHT:** Feb.–Nov. in Deep South (3 flights), May–Sept. in north (2 flights). **RANGE:** E. North America from s. Ont. south to Gulf Coast, west to e. Colo. and cen. Texas. Rare in Sierra Madre of e. Mexico. **HABITAT:** Deciduous broadleaf forests, edges, and river valleys. **REMARKS:** The black form is believed to be an edible mimic of the distasteful and emetic Pipevine Swallowtail.

CANADIAN TIGER SWALLOWTAIL   PL. 7
Papilio canadensis

2⅝–3⅛ in. (65–80 mm). Northern. *Small.* Upperside: *Black stripes* relatively *broad*; hindwing with anal margin *black more than half distance to anal vein.* Underside: Forewing with marginal yellow spot band continuous. Hindwing has extensive *orange overscaling.* **EARLY STAGES:** Identical to those of Eastern Tiger Swallowtail. **FOOD:** Birch, aspen, and Black Cherry. **FLIGHT:** May to mid-July (1 flight). **RANGE:** Subarctic North America from cen. Alaska south and east across Canada and n. Great Lakes states to n. New England and the Maritimes. **HABITAT:** Northern deciduous and mixed evergreen-deciduous forests and associated edges. **REMARKS:** Black female form extremely rare. Eastern Tiger Swallowtail may have small spring individuals, but these are marked differently from the Canadian. Experts are divided on whether this is a truly separate species, but I classify it as such on the basis of biological evidence of flight periods and host plants.

WESTERN TIGER SWALLOWTAIL   **NOT SHOWN**
Papilio rutulus

2¾–3¹⁵⁄₁₆ in. (70–100 mm). Upperside: Hindwing with uppermost *marginal spot yellow or absent*. Underside: Forewing with marginal row composed of *separate* yellow spots. Hindwing has *marginal spots narrow* and postmedian area without orange suffusion. No black female form. **SIMILAR SPECIES:** (1) Eastern Tiger Swallowtail and (2) Canadian Tiger Swallowtail have upperside with marginal yellow spot clearly separate in a black field; uppermost marginal spot on hindwing orange, not yellow; and more orange postmedian suffusion on underside hindwing. **EARLY STAGES:** Caterpillar similar to that of Eastern Tiger Swallowtail but is usually brighter green. **FOOD:** Cottonwood, willows, aspen, Wild Cherry, and ash. **FLIGHT:** June–July (1 flight). **RANGE:** W. North America from e. B.C. south to n. Baja Calif. and s. N.M., e. to w. S.D. and se. Colo. Rare strays to cen. Neb. **HABITAT:** Woodlands near streams and rivers, wooded suburbs.

TWO-TAILED SWALLOWTAIL   **PL. 7**
Papilio multicaudatus

4⅜–5 in. (110–128 mm). Large. *Two tails* on each hindwing. Male with *narrow black stripes* on forewing. Adults have a high, floating flight. **SIMILAR SPECIES:** (1) Eastern Tiger Swallowtail has only a single tail on each hindwing. Forewing black stripes broader, orange suffusion on hindwing below. **EARLY STAGES:** Caterpillar is brown with a pair of green, black-edged oval eyespots on the swollen thorax. **FOOD:** Ash, Hop Tree, and Chokecherry. **FLIGHT:** Late May to mid-Aug. in North (1 flight), most of year in South. **RANGE:** W. North America from s. B.C. and s. Alta. east to cen. Neb. and cen. Texas and south to s. Mexico. **HABITAT:** Foothill canyons and slopes, cities, and suburbs.

SPICEBUSH
SWALLOWTAIL

PALAMEDES
SWALLOWTAIL

THREE-TAILED SWALLOWTAIL *Papilio pilumnus* **NOT SHOWN**
3⅛–3¾ in. (80–95 mm). *Three tails* on each hindwing, the longest
lined with yellow. Forewing with only 2 *black stripes*, marginal yellow spots coalesced into a solid band. **SIMILAR SPECIES:** (1) Two-tailed
Swallowtail has only 2 tails on each hindwing, black forewing
stripes much narrower. **EARLY STAGES:** Caterpillar like others in "tiger
group," but body green and head brown. **FOOD:** Laurel. **FLIGHT:**
Jan.–Oct. **RANGE:** El Salvador north to Mexico. Rare stray north to
s. Texas and se. Ariz. **HABITAT:** Not reported.

SPICEBUSH SWALLOWTAIL   *Papilio troilus*   **PLS. 2, 5**
3⅝–4⅞ in. (92–124 mm). *Black.* Upperside: Hindwing has *blue
iridescence* (female) or *blue-green pigment* (male). Underside:
Hindwing has marginal spots *pale green* and tails *spoon-shaped*,
with both marginal and postmedian orange spot rows. Usually
flies low. Flutters wings slowly when visiting flowers. **SIMILAR
SPECIES:** (1) Black and (2) Ozark Swallowtail males have postmedian row of yellow spots on upperside. Marginal spots yellow above;
tails linear, not spoon-shaped. Eyespot with black pupil. (3) Eastern Tiger Swallowtail (black female) tails are not spoon-shaped;
shadows of black stripes usually visible; hindwing below is without postmedian orange spot row. (4) Pipevine Swallowtail hindwing below has a single submarginal row of large, oval, red-
orange spots, entire hindwing above has highly reflective
blue-green iridescence. **EARLY STAGES:** Caterpillar is dark green
above and whitish laterally; it has 2 large, black, orange-edged
eyespots on the swollen thoracic dorsum, and 4 longitudinal lines
of black-edged blue spots on the abdominal dorsum. **FOOD:** Sassafras and Spicebush. Other reports need confirmation. **FLIGHT:**
April–Oct. (2 flights, sometimes a partial 3rd). **RANGE:** E. North
America from s. Ont. and s. New England south to Fla. and Gulf

Coast; resident west to Okla. and cen. Texas (rare stray to N. D. and cen. Colo.). **HABITAT:** Second-growth woods, deciduous woodlands, edges, wooded swamps, and pine barrens.

PALAMEDES SWALLOWTAIL *Papilio palamedes* **PL. 7**
4⁷⁄₁₆–5⅛ in. (112–132 mm). Sexes alike. Upperside: Both wings with *yellow postmedian band*; tails *filled with yellow*. Underside: Hindwing with *thin yellow stripe* at base and postmedian row of *orange crescents*. Flies slowly. **SIMILAR SPECIES:** (1) Black Swallowtail male has spotted abdomen and eyespot with black pupil. **EARLY STAGES:** Caterpillar is pale green with 2 black, orange-margined eyespots on the swollen thoracic dorsum. **FOOD:** Red Bay, possibly Sassafras. **FLIGHT:** March–Dec. (2 flights, partial 3rd in south). **RANGE:** Atlantic and Gulf of Mexico coastal plains from s. N.J. (rarely) south to cen. Mexico. Strays inland. **HABITAT:** Broadleaf evergreen swamp forests and wet woods near rivers.

VICTORINE SWALLOWTAIL *Papilio victorinus* **NOT SHOWN**
3¾–4⅜ in. (95–110 mm). *Tailless.* Mainly black. Forewing produced. Upperside: Hindwing with spot rows yellow. Underside: Hindwing of male with both marginal and postmedian rows of *red spots*. Female dimorphic. One form similar to male, the second with hindwing above with a *broad green band* instead of 2 yellow spot rows. **EARLY STAGES:** Caterpillar green, gray along sides variously marked with black, white, and pale blue; orange subdorsal eyespots at rear of humped thorax. **FOOD:** Avocado. **FLIGHT:** Jan.–Nov. **RANGE:** Cen. America from El Salvador north to Mexico. Has strayed to s. Texas on at least one occasion. **HABITAT:** In Mexico, moist to wet tropical forest at moderate elevations — 1000 to 3000 ft. (300–900 m).

PINK-SPOTTED SWALLOWTAIL **NOT SHOWN**
Papilio pharnaces
3⁵⁄₁₆–3¾ in. (85–95 mm). Sexes similar. Black. Normally tailed, but some examples lack tails. Upperside: Hindwing with postmedian and submarginal *rows of small pink spots*. **SIMILAR SPECIES:** Ruby-spotted Swallowtail lacks tails and has only a single pink patch on hindwing. **EARLY STAGES:** Unknown. **FOOD:** Citrus and other citrus family plants. **FLIGHT:** April in s. Texas; Feb.–Oct. in Mexico. **RANGE:** Cen. and s. Mexico. One reported stray in lower Rio Grande Valley, Texas. **HABITAT:** Wood edges at low or midelevations.

RUBY-SPOTTED SWALLOWTAIL *Papilio anchisiades* **PL. 5**
2¾–4 in. (70–102 mm). Sexes similar. Unmistakable. A *large, black, tailless* butterfly. Upperside: Forewing of female with dif-

fuse *white cell patch*. Hindwing has postmedian *pink patch*. **SIMILAR SPECIES:** (1) Polydamas Swallowtail has yellow submarginal band. (2) Pink-spotted Swallowtail is usually tailed and has two rows of pink spots on hindwing. **EARLY STAGES:** Caterpillar is green-brown with many cream or white streaks, lines, and flecks; there are also 5 longitudinal rows of short tubercles—each row with 1 tubercle on each abdominal segment. **FOOD:** Citrus, *Zanthoxylum*, and *Casimiroa*. **FLIGHT:** May–Oct. **RANGE:** Resident from s. Texas south through Mexico and Cen. America to Argentina. Rare strays north to Kans., se. Ariz., and w. Texas. **HABITAT:** Lowland tropical forests and nearby second growth, flower gardens.

8

TRUE BUTTERFLIES:
SUPERFAMILY PAPILIONOIDEA
WHITES AND SULPHURS:
FAMILY PIERIDAE

The whites and sulphurs are worldwide in distribution and comprise about 1100 species. They are richest in the tropics. Most have medium to small white, yellow, or orange wings with small amounts of black or red. Many have hidden ultraviolet patterns that are used in courtship. Fully developed wing appendages such as tails are absent, although a few species have falcate forewing apexes or short projections from the hindwings. Adults of both sexes have 3 pairs of walking legs. Most of our species with more than one generation have distinct seasonal variations. The more temperate species have smaller, darker individuals in the spring and fall, while the tropically affiliated species have distinct dry (winter) and wet (summer) season forms. Adults of all species visit flowers for nectar.

Males of our species patrol likely environments in search of receptive mates. Eggs are laid singly on leaves, buds, or stems of appropriate food plants. Most species are narrow in their choice of caterpillar hosts, usually selecting plants within a single genus, but rarely more than two closely related families. The vast majority of North American whites and sulphurs feed on either legumes or crucifers (plants in the mustard family). Eggs are columnar. The caterpillars are relatively smooth and are covered with short, fine setae, often clumped onto low tubercles. Like swallowtails, the pupae are attached to a silk mat and are slung in a girdle. Most temperate species overwinter in the pupal or larval stage. Tropical species overwinter as adults in warm, southern areas and then recolonize northward during spring or early summer.

MIMIC WHITES: SUBFAMILY DISMORPHIINAE

This primarily neotropical group comprises about 100 species. With the exception of the Old World wood whites (*Leptidea*), the adults of most are brightly colored and usually display strong sexual dimorphism in wing color, pattern, and shape. The tropical species, especially the females but often both sexes, are mimics of distasteful heliconiine and ithomiine butterflies. Adults often feed at bird droppings and seldom visit flowers. The males of most species patrol forest gaps and edges in search of receptive females.

COSTA-SPOTTED MIMIC WHITE   NOT SHOWN
Enantia albania

⅞–1⅛ in. (22–28 mm). Dimorphic. Both sexes with *forewing distinctly smaller than hindwing*. Male yellow. Upperside: Hindwing of male with large scaleless patch; forewing of female yellow with black on apex and outer margin. **EARLY STAGES:** Not reported. **FLIGHT:** Sept. in s. Texas; longer period in Mexico. **RANGE:** Tropical Mexico. Rare stray to lower Rio Grande Valley, Texas. **HABITAT:** Tropical lowland to mid-elevation forests, coffee plantations.

WHITES, MARBLES, ORANGETIPS:
SUBFAMILY PIERINAE

This worldwide group comprises some 1200 species. In North America 21 whites, orangetips, and marbles are included. The adults of most species are predominantly white above with some black pattern elements. Below, their hindwings often have a pattern of yellow and black scales (appearing green). The two sexes of most are only slightly dimorphic, although male orangetips have bright orange wing-tips. The adults are avid flower visitors, often selecting flowers of their host plants when available. The males of our species patrol open, sunny habitats in search of receptive females, although males of some tropical whites, e.g. *Leodonta*, perch along ravines. Most of our eastern whites select mustards (Family Brassicaceae) as their caterpillar host plants, although the related capers (Family Capparidaceae) are used by some, such as the Tropical White. Pine White caterpillars eat pine needles. Eggs are laid singly on host plant leaves or flowering parts. The young caterpillars feed externally and develop directly. Winter is passed by the chrysalis stage. Orangetips and marbles may pass several unfavorable years in the chrysalis stage before hatching.

PINE WHITE   *Neophasia menapia*   PL. 7

1¹⁵⁄₁₆–2⁹⁄₁₆ in. (50–66 mm). White. Upperside: Forewing with *costa lined black from base to cell*. Apical area extensively black. Underside: Hindwing of male has *veins lined narrowly with black*, that of female more heavily marked, margin lined with red, submarginal black stripe. High, floating flight near conifers. **SIMILAR SPECIES:** (1) Checkered White lacks black costa and has more checkered appearance. Has low, rapid erratic flight. **EARLY STAGES:** Caterpillar is dark green with a broad white lateral band and a narrow white dorsal stripe. **FOOD:** Usually Yellow or Lodgepole Pine, occasionally Douglas-fir or Balsam Fir. **FLIGHT:** Mid-July through Aug. (1 flight). **RANGE:** W. U.S. and s. Canada from s. B.C. and sw. Alta. south to cen. Ariz. and N.M. Rare stray to n. Minn. **HABITAT:** Pine forests in most of range; mixed Douglas-fir forests in north coastal Calif.

TROPICAL WHITE *Appias drusilla*   **PL. 7**

2⅛–2¹⁵⁄₁₆ in. (54–74 mm). Sexes *dimorphic*. Male has elongate forewing, white above and below. Upperside: Forewing has *costa and outer margin edged very narrowly with black*. Underside: Hindwing has satiny sheen. Female may be almost completely white (dry-season form) or with black outer margin and yellow-orange upper hindwing, especially at base (wet-season form). Flight is rapid and erratic, often in shade. **SIMILAR SPECIES:** (1) Great Southern White male upperside forewing has black outer margin extended along veins. White female form has black cell spot. **EARLY STAGES:** Caterpillar with head yellow-green with blue-green tubercles; body dark green above and pale gray-green laterally, the two tones divided by a thin white lateral line. **FOOD:** Capers. **FLIGHT:** All year in areas of residence; Oct.–April (dry-season form), May-Sept. (wet-season form). **RANGE:** Resident in tropical America from Brazil north, including the Antilles, as well as s. peninsular Fla. and the Keys. Frequent immigrant to coastal Texas, more rarely north to Colo. and Neb. **HABITAT:** Lowland tropical evergreen or semideciduous forests.

TROPICAL WHITE

Checkered White. Male long-day (summer form) nectaring at Alfalfa, Fort Collins, Colo. This species has both long-day and short-day (spring–fall) forms. The latter may be confounded with Western Whites.

CHECKERED WHITES: GENUS *Pontia* FABRICIUS

The checkered whites are found primarily in arid habitats throughout the Northern Hemisphere. There are four species in North America. Our two eastern species have been confused, but may be easily separated with practice. Their caterpillars are striped with yellow and purple-green; they feed on the seed pods of plants in the mustard family.

CHECKERED WHITE *Pontia protodice*   PL. 7

1 ¾–2 ⁷⁄₁₆ in. (44–62 mm). Upperside: Forewing of male with *black checkered pattern* on outer half, hindwing white; female heavily checkered above. Underside: Hindwing of male faintly checkered; female has yellow-tan pattern on hindwing and forewing apex. Short-day (spring, fall) form with underside hindwing veins outlined with gray-green. Flight low and erratic. Males patrol on flats. SIMILAR SPECIES: (1) Western White with upperside forewing submarginal band fully connected, underside hindwing veins always outlined with gray-green, at least faintly. (2) Cabbage White with underside forewing apex and hindwing uniformly yellow-green or gray-green. EARLY STAGES: Caterpillar alternately striped yellow and purple-green; body with many small black tubercles. FOOD: Various plants in mustard family—peppergrasses, Winter Cress, tumble mustards, etc. FLIGHT: March–Nov. (3 flights, partial 4th in South). RANGE: Resident in s. U.S. and n. Mexico, regularly colonizes and establishes temporary populations in most of U.S. and extreme s. Canada. Absent from most of New England. HABITAT: Open, relatively dry areas, often weedy; pastures, sandy lots, railroad beds.

WESTERN WHITE *Pontia occidentalis*   **PL. 7**
1¾–2⅛ in. (44–54 mm). Primarily western. Upperside: Forewing
has *marginal chevrons lighter and contrasting* with submarginal
band. Underside: Forewing apex and hindwing with *veins outlined
with gray-green*. Spring and fall short-day forms are more heavily
marked. Males patrol ridges and hilltops. **SIMILAR SPECIES:** Checkered White is the species found throughout most of our territory.
It lacks the contrast between the black marginal chevrons and
submarginal band. **EARLY STAGES:** Caterpillar is dull green with alternating dark and light stripes. **FOOD:** Mustard family, native rock
cresses, peppergrasses, and tumble mustards are most likely in
eastern part of range. **FLIGHT:** May–Aug. (2 flights), only 1 flight
(June–July) in far north. **RANGE:** In boreal North America from
Alaska, Yukon and w. N.W. Terr. south to cen. Calif., n. Ariz., and
n. N.M., east to cen. Ont. (James Bay), Wis. (rare), Mich. (rare),
n. Minn., and S.D. **HABITAT:** Subarctic and montane slopes and
peaks, open plains, railyards.

MUSTARD WHITES: GENUS *Pieris* SCHRANK

These butterflies of the Northern Hemisphere include our most
widespread butterfly, the Cabbage White. Most species are predominantly white with small black marks. Some species have
green or gray veining below. Caterpillars are green with or without small yellow marks; they eat the leaves of plants in the mustard family.

MUSTARD WHITE *Pieris napi*   **PL. 4, 8**
1⅜–2¼ in. (34–57 mm). Summer form *immaculate white above
and below*. Spring form, the only one in subarctic, has upper fore-

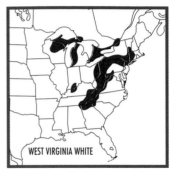

wing tipped with black. Underside: Forewing apex and hindwing with *veins sharply outlined with gray-green or yellow-green*. Flight weak. **SIMILAR SPECIES:** (1) West Virginia White has forewing apex rounded, underside hindwing with veins blurrily outlined with brown or gray-brown. (2) Cabbage White has upperside forewing with one or two black submarginal spots; underside hindwing lacks dark scaling on veins. **EARLY STAGES:** Caterpillar is green with a lateral yellow stripe along each side. **FOOD:** Various mustard family plants, including toothwort, Water Cress, rock cresses, mustards, and Winter Cress. **FLIGHT:** Late April to mid-Sept. in Mich., New England (2 flights), June–July to north (1 flight). **RANGE:** Holarctic. In North America from Alaska, Yukon, and w. N.W. Terr. south to cen. Calif. and s. N.M., east to N.S. and n. New England. Isolated population along Lab. coast and n. Nfld. **HABITAT:** Deciduous woods, bogs, open fields, open subarctic slopes and tundra.

WEST VIRGINIA WHITE *Pieris virginiensis* **PL. 8**

1 ¹³/₁₆–2 ⅛ in. (46–54 mm). *Wings translucent.* Flight weak. Forewing rounded. Underside: Hindwing *veins indistinctly lined with brown or brown-gray*. **SIMILAR SPECIES:** (1) Mustard White has veins more sharply outlined (spring form) or butterfly completely white (summer form). (2) Cabbage White has black spots on forewing upperside and uniformly colored hindwing underside. **EARLY STAGES:** Caterpillar is yellow-green with a green stripe along each side. **FOOD:** Toothworts. **FLIGHT:** Late March to mid-June, depending on latitude (1 flight). **RANGE:** Extreme s. Canada (s. Ont. and Montreal) and the e. U.S. in n. Great Lakes states and from s. New England southwest along Appalachians to n. Ga. and ne. Ala. **HABITAT:** Moist, rich, deciduous woodland or mature mixed woods. **REMARKS:** This butterfly and the Mustard White were formerly believed to

be the same species. Detailed studies of their biology and structure have shown they are distinct.

CABBAGE WHITE *Pieris rapae*   **PLS. 2, 4, 7**
1¾–2¼ in. (45–58 mm). White. Upperside: *Forewing tip black*, and there are one (male) or two (female) submarginal black spots. Underside: Forewing apex and hindwing uniformly *yellow-green or gray-green*. Spring forms weakly marked. Flight floating and fluttery. **SIMILAR SPECIES:** (1) Checkered White has checkered forewing; hindwing underside is either plain white (summer male) or patterned. Flight more direct. (2) Mustard White either immaculate white or underside hindwing veins evenly outlined with gray-green. (3) West Virginia White has rounded forewing; hindwing underside with faintly outlined brown or gray-brown veins. **EARLY STAGES:** Caterpillar is green with a thin broken yellow line on each side and a thin yellow dorsal line. **FOOD:** Many mustard family plants—including cabbage and other cole crops, mustard, Winter Cress, peppergrass, also rarely caper family and Nasturtium. **FLIGHT:** April or May to early Sept. (3 flights) to all year in South (7–8 flights). **RANGE:** Holarctic. Introduced to North America (about 1860) in Que., Canada. Has since spread to cen. Canada (s. Lab., cen. Que., s. N.W. Terr.), throughout the conterminous U.S. except Fla. Keys, extreme s. La., s. Texas, and some offshore islands, south to nw. Mexico. **HABITAT:** Many kinds of open, weedy habitats—cities and suburbs, gardens, power lines, marshes, road edges, etc. **REMARKS:** One of our commonest and most widespread butterflies. Its caterpillars occasionally cause economic damage to cole crops such as Cabbage, Broccoli, and Collards—especially in home gardens.

CABBAGE WHITE

Great Southern White. Male nectaring at Blue Boneset, lower Rio Grande Valley, Tex. This butterfly is common in southern and tropical coastal locations where it occasionally undertakes mass migrations.

GREAT SOUTHERN WHITE *Ascia monuste* **PL. 8**

2⁷⁄₁₆–3⅜ in. (62–86 mm). Male white with upperside forewing *zigzag black outer margin*. Female dimorphic. One form (dry season) similar to male with upperside forewing black more extensive on outer margin, also with *small black spot in cell*. Wet-season female almost completely *clouded* above and below with black scaling. **SIMILAR SPECIES:** (1) Cabbage White is smaller and has tip of forewing black. (2) Tropical White male has elongated all-white forewing without zigzag black outer margin. See (3) Giant White. **EARLY STAGES:** Caterpillar's body has 5 longitudinal orange bands or lines separated by areas of mottled gray. The head is tan-yellow with an orange front. **FOOD:** Beach Cabbage and Saltwort along the coast, but others such as peppergrasses, cultivated Cabbage, Collards, and Kale are used at inland sites. Plants in caper family are also used. **FLIGHT:** All year in peninsular Fla., Gulf Coast, and s. Texas. **RANGE:** Migratory along Southeast coastlines. Resident

GREAT SOUTHERN WHITE

GIANT WHITE

along s. Atlantic and Gulf coasts south through much of tropical America. Strays north to Md. in East and to Kans. and ne. Colo. on Great Plains. **HABITAT:** Primarily coastal salt marshes, dunes, also open sites such as fields and gardens. Migrants appear in a variety of open habitats.

GIANT WHITE *Ganyra josephina* **PL. 8**

3⁵⁄₁₆–3¹¹⁄₁₆ in. (85–93 mm). *Very large.* Forewing apex bulges outward slightly. Upperside: Forewing of male with prominent *round black cell spot*; in addition to black cell spot, wet-season female has blurred black postmedian spots. Marginal portions of veins outlined with black. Dry-season female marked less prominently. **SIMILAR SPECIES:** (1) Great Southern White is smaller, has zigzag black outer margin, and lacks prominent black forewing cell spot. (2) Tropical White lacks black forewing cell spot. **EARLY STAGES:** Caterpillar dark green with a yellow lateral line; back covered with tiny black tubercles. **FOOD:** Capers. **FLIGHT:** All year in lowland tropics, Sept.–Dec. in s. Texas. **RANGE:** Greater Antilles, Cen. America, and Mexico. Strays regularly to s. Texas, very rarely to N.M. and Kans. **HABITAT:** Forest edges, usually in seasonally dry tropical lowlands.

MARBLES: GENUS *Euchloe* HÜBNER

Marble butterflies are found only in the Northern Hemisphere. The five North American species are usually found in arid or boreal habitats. The green marbling on the underside of their hindwings is composed of a mix of black and yellow scales. Adults are early spring fliers and are never found visiting moist spots as are many other whites. The caterpillars are striped with bands of yellow, white, and gray; they feed on flowers and young pods of plants in the mustard family, most often rock cresses.

LARGE MARBLE

OLYMPIA MARBLE

LARGE MARBLE *Euchloe ausonides* PL. 8

1¼–2 in. (38–51 mm). Upperside: Forewing with black-patterned apex. Underside: Hindwing with *complex green marbling.* Flight low, direct. Males patrol hillsides or valley bottoms. **SIMILAR SPECIES:** (1) Olympia Marble is smaller, with marbling less complex and with rose-pink highlights (these fade after death) along underside hindwing costa. Forewing upperside with less black. (2) Falcate Orangetip has falcate forewing having small black cell spot in both sexes. Marbling highly fractured. **EARLY STAGES:** Caterpillar is gray with subdorsal yellow stripes and sublateral white stripes subtended by yellow. **FOOD:** Mustard family plants, rock cresses in east, others in west. **FLIGHT:** May–June (1 flight). **RANGE:** Boreal w. North America south to cen. Calif. and n. N.M., east to sw. Man. Isolated populations in Man. along Hudson Bay coast and east from n. Minn. and se. Man. to cen. Ont. (n. shore Lake Huron). **HABITAT:** A variety of open sunny areas, usually along valleys or hillsides.

OLYMPIA MARBLE *Euchloe olympia* PLS. 3, 8

1⅜–1¹⁵⁄₁₆ in. (34–50 mm). Underside: Hindwing has *simplified marbling* and ephemeral *rose-pink* highlight along costa. Males patrol ridges and hilltops. **SIMILAR SPECIES:** (1) Large Marble is larger with more complex marbling. (2) Falcate Orangetip has falcate forewing and underside hindwing with green pattern highly fractured. **EARLY STAGES:** Caterpillar is virtually identical to that of the Large Marble. **FOOD:** Various rock cresses. **FLIGHT:** Early April–late June (1 flight), early in Texas, progressively later northward. **RANGE:** S. Canada and U.S. from s. Alta., s. Ont., and sw. Que. south to cen. Texas. Isolated population in Appalachians from s.-cen. Pa. southwest to ne. Tenn. **HABITAT:** Very local, various open areas, including shale barrens, lakeshore dunes, and prairie hills.

Olympia Marble. Male nectaring at mustard in Rocky Mt. foothills, Colo. These butterflies are very sensitive to light conditions and fly only in sunlight. The males patrol along ridgetops or bluffs.

FALCATE ORANGETIP *Anthocharis midea* **PL. 8**

1 ⁷⁄₁₆–1 ¹³⁄₁₆ in. (36–46 mm). *Forewing apex falcate.* Upperside: Forewing of both sexes with *small round black cell spot*; male forewing *apex orange-tipped.* Underside: Hindwing has dark green marbling highly fractured. **SIMILAR SPECIES:** Olympia Marble has rounded forewing apex and simpler marbling; lacks orange forewing tip. **EARLY STAGES:** Caterpillar is blue-green with a white stripe along each side and a dorsal greenish orange line. **FOOD:** Various plants in mustard family, including rock cresses, Shepherd's Purse, Winter Cress, and others. **FLIGHT:** Early March to June (1 flight); earlier in south, later in north. Reportedly 2 generations in s. Appalachians. **RANGE:** E. U.S. from s. New England west to e. Kans., south to Ga., s. Miss., and s. Texas. Strays or local populations to s. Wis., e. Neb., and Fla. panhandle. **HABITAT:** Wet, open woods along rivers and streams, open swamps; sometimes dry woods and ridgetops.

Falcate Orangetip. Male nectaring at Winter Cress in Fairfax Co., Va. These delicate butterflies are one of the first signs of spring. The males patrol through open woods, swamps, and along streams.

Clouded Sulphur. Male nectaring at yellow composite, Campbell Co., Wyo. Clouded Sulphurs seem capable of overwintering at more northern locations than Orange Sulphurs, their closest relatives.

SULPHURS: SUBFAMILY COLIADINAE

The sulphurs may be responsible for the name "butter fly." Most genera are tropical. There are about 300 species worldwide. Most yellow species also have a white or pale female form. The males are often larger than the females—an unusual trait in butterflies. There are usually distinctly separate winter (or dry season) and summer (or wet season) forms. Freshly emerged males often cluster at moist spots to imbibe. Adults perch with their wings closed above their backs and never open them except in flight. The caterpillars are usually green with lateral stripes or marks. Legumes are their usual food plants, but other plant families are used by some genera.

SULPHURS: GENUS *Colias* FABRICIUS

This is a predominantly temperate group, with most species found in mountainous or alpine habitats. Among our most familiar butterflies are the Clouded and Orange sulphurs, which have greatly benefited from the alfalfa and clover fields planted as fodder for livestock. You will have to travel to the Arctic to see most of our species. Caterpillars of different species specialize on legumes, heaths, or willows.

CLOUDED SULPHUR *Colias philodice* PL. 9

1 5/16–2 3/4 in. (50–70 mm). A common, widespread butterfly. Upperside: Male *clear yellow* with solid black outer margins. Underside: Forewing with at least some *small dark submarginal spots*; hindwing with silver *cell spot* pink-rimmed, *almost always*

double. Female dimorphic—yellow form with black outer margins uneven with enclosed yellow spots. White form ("alba") identical but green-white instead of yellow. Spring and fall forms small, less prominently marked. Low, direct flight. **SIMILAR SPECIES:** (1) Orange Sulphur has at least some orange above; white female form cannot be reliably separated. (2) Pink-edged Sulphur has upperside forewing black cell spot smaller, and underside hindwing cleaner with silver cell spot single—less prominently pink-rimmed. **EARLY STAGES:** Caterpillar is dark green, blue-green, or yellow-green with a lateral white stripe subtended by black. The lateral white stripe may contain red spots. **FOOD:** Various legumes, especially White Clover in the East, also trefoils, other clovers, White Sweet Clover, and Alfalfa. **FLIGHT:** May–Oct. (3 flights in north), March–Nov. in south (4–5 broods), occasionally emerges during warm spells in midwinter. **RANGE:** North America from Alaska, Yukon, and w. N.W. Terr. south through w., cen., and se. Canada; Maritime Provinces; all of conterminous U.S. except much of Fla., s. Texas, and on e. slopes of Calif. mountains. Also occurs in nw. Mexico and has an isolated population in Guatemalan highlands. **HABITAT:** Many open habitats, open fields, lawns, road edges, rights of way, clover fields. **REMARKS:** Hybridizes with Orange Sulphur under crowded situations.

ORANGE SULPHUR *Colias eurytheme*   PLS. 2, 9
1⅞–2¹¹⁄₁₆ in. (48–68 mm). Highly variable. Upperside: At least *some orange* on male and normal female, otherwise as described for Clouded Sulphur. **SIMILAR SPECIES:** (1) Clouded Sulphur lacks any orange above. White female cannot be reliably separated. (2) Hecla Sulphur does not overlap in range or habitat. Underside hindwing is deep green usually with elongate pink cell spot. (3) Sleepy Orange has black margins more irregular, lacks underside

hindwing cell spot. **EARLY STAGES:** Caterpillar is dark green with a lateral white line subtended by black. **FOOD:** Various legumes, especially Alfalfa, White Sweet Clover, White Clover, and vetches. Others used less frequently. **FLIGHT:** June–Oct. (2–3 flights in north), March–Nov. (4–5 broods) further south. Adults sometimes emerge during warm spells in midwinter. **RANGE:** S. Canada south through conterminous U.S. to cen. Mexico. Rare in peninsular Fla. Strays north to n. Man., n. Ont., and cen. Que. **HABITAT:** A variety of open habitats, alfalfa fields, lawns, fields, road edges. **REMARKS:** One of the East's commonest butterflies. An occasional pest of alfalfa fields.

WESTERN SULPHUR *Colias occidentalis* PL. 9

1¾–2⅝ in. (45–65 mm). In Man. and Black Hills of the Dakotas, upperside is *orange with wing bases yellow*; underside has hindwing *cell spot* usually *single*. In the West, this sulphur is often pale lemon yellow. White females are uncommon. **SIMILAR SPECIES:** (1) Orange Sulphur has wing bases orange (except white female), underside hindwing cell spot double. **EARLY STAGES:** Caterpillar is yellow-green covered with tiny black points and has a white lateral line containing orange dashes; head yellow-green. **FOOD:** Various legumes, milk vetches, golden banner, *Oxytropis*. **FLIGHT:** Mid-June to mid-July (1 brood) in Man., 2 broods in Sask. **RANGE:** W. North America from cen. Yukon and w. N.W. Terr. east to sw. Man. and south to cen. Ariz. and cen. N.M. **HABITAT:** Wide variety of open situations including forest openings, prairies, and power-line cuts.

HECLA SULPHUR *Colias hecla* PL. 9

1⁷⁄₁₆–1¹³⁄₁₆ in. (36–46 mm). Upperside: *Deep orange*. Underside: Hindwing *dusky green* usually with *elongate pink cell spot*. **SIMILAR**

WESTERN SULPHUR

HECLA SULPHUR

LABRADOR SULPHUR

SPECIES: (1) Orange Sulphur and (2) Western Sulphur (in our area) have hindwing underside yellow, not green, and their ranges do not overlap the Hecla Sulphur's in East. **EARLY STAGES:** Caterpillar green with light lateral line and tiny black points. **FOOD:** Alpine Milk Vetch. **FLIGHT:** Late June to mid-Aug. (1 brood). **RANGE:** Holarctic. Greenland coast, Canadian Arctic Archipelago, Alaska, Yukon, and N.W. Terr. south to n. Que. Isolated occurrence on Nfld. Rocky Mt. populations in Alta. and B.C. are now considered a separate species, the Canadian Sulphur (*Colias canadensis*). **HABITAT:** Arctic tundra. **REMARKS:** Hybrids with Labrador Sulphur have been considered a separate species ("Booth's Sulphur," *C. hecla* × *nastes*).

LABRADOR SULPHUR *Colias nastes*   **PL. 9**

1⅛–1⅝ in. (28–41 mm). Small, variable. Upperside: Both sexes *dirty white or dingy green-yellow.* Black borders with *enclosed white or green-yellow spots.* Underside: Both wings with submarginal black spot rows. **SIMILAR SPECIES:** (1) Hybrids between this species and the Hecla Sulphur ("Booth's Sulphur") have upperside yellow or pale orange with very narrow black borders. **EARLY STAGES:** Not reported. **FOOD:** Legumes, including Alpine Milk Vetch, *Oxytropis*. **FLIGHT:** Late June–early Aug. (1 brood). **RANGE:** Arctic America including n. Alaska, Yukon, N.W. Terr., and Canadian Arctic Archipelago south in Rocky Mts. to n.-cen. Wash., nw. Mont., n. Que., and coastal Lab. **HABITAT:** Arctic tundra.

GIANT SULPHUR *Colias gigantea*   **PL. 9**

2⁷⁄₁₆–2⁹⁄₁₆ in. (61–66 mm). Large. Upperside: Male yellow with *narrow black borders*. Underside: Forewing *lacks* submarginal black spots. Females dimorphic—yellow form common in Riding Mts., Man., while white form is commoner to the north at Churchill, Man. *Black border often absent.* **SIMILAR SPECIES:** (1) Clouded Sulphur has submarginal black spot row on forewing underside. Female has broad black border on both wings. (2) Pink-edged Sulphur is smaller, with upperside forewing black cell spot small. Female with broad black upperside forewing apical area. (3) Palaeno Sulphur with upper black border wide, upperside forewing cell spot missing, underside hindwing green with silver spot not pink-rimmed. (4) Pelidne Sulphur has small black upperside forewing cell spot, underside hindwing heavily marked with black. **EARLY STAGES:** Not reported. **FOOD:** Willows (*Salix reticulata* at Churchill). **FLIGHT:** Late June–July (1 brood). **RANGE:** Arctic and subarctic America from Alaska east to w. N.W. Terr., south along Rockies to n. Wyo., east to Man. Isolated population in n. Ont. along Hudson Bay. **HABITAT:** Willow bogs in taiga. **REMARKS:** Some consider this butterfly a subspecies of Scudder's Willow Sulphur.

PELIDNE SULPHUR *Colias pelidne*   **PL. 9**

1¼–1½ in. (32–38 mm). Upperside: Forewing has *broad black border* and *small black cell spot*. Small hindwing cell spot heavily

GIANT SULPHUR

PELIDNE SULPHUR

PINK-EDGED SULPHUR

rimmed with dark pink. Underside: Hindwing with *heavy black scaling*. White females commoner than yellow forms. SIMILAR SPECIES: (1) Palaeno Sulphur upperside often has wider black borders, is usually missing upperside forewing cell spot, and has underside hindwing white cell spot not rimmed with pink. (2) Pink-edged Sulphur has underside hindwing plain yellow without heavy black markings. (3) Giant Sulphur has narrower black borders, plain yellow underside hindwing. EARLY STAGES: Not reported. FOOD: Blueberry and *Gaultheria*. FLIGHT: Late June–July (1 brood). RANGE: Several disjunct populations: (1) Northern Rocky Mts. from w.-cen. Alta. south to nw. Wyo.; (2) coastal areas of extreme s. Hudson and James bays; (3) w. Nfld., Lab., and ne. Que. Isolated records in w. Arctic (Yukon). HABITAT: Subarctic forest openings and arctic tundra.

PINK-EDGED SULPHUR *Colias interior* PL. 9

1 ⅞–2 ⁹⁄₁₆ in. (48–66 mm). Both sexes with *prominent pink fringes*. Upperside: Forewing with small black cell spot. Female apical area black; hindwing without black. Underside: Hindwing *clear yellow with single, pink-rimmed silver cell spot*. White females very rare. SIMILAR SPECIES: (1) Clouded Sulphur underside hindwing has submarginal black spot row. (2) Giant Sulphur is larger, males very similar, females with black borders often absent. EARLY STAGES: Caterpillar is yellow-green with a merged white and red longitudinal line along each side. FOOD: Various blueberries and bilberry. FLIGHT: Mid-June to late Aug. (1 flight). RANGE: North America from B.C. and e. Ore. east across subarctic Canada through the Great Lakes area to the Maritime Provinces and n. New England. Isolated population in cen. Appalachians of ne. Pa., w. Md., e. W. Va., and nw. Va. HABITAT: Boggy or scrubby areas dominated by blueberries and other heaths. Often in recovering burns or logged sites.

PALAENO SULPHUR

PALAENO SULPHUR *Colias palaeno* PL. 9

1 ⁷⁄₁₆–1 ¾ in. (36–44 mm). Upperside: Male with *wide black border*; forewing black cell spot usually *missing*. Underside: Hindwing *dusky green* with white spot *not* rimmed with pink. White females predominate, have upperside forewing apical area black. **SIMILAR SPECIES:** (1) Pelidne Sulphur usually has small black upperside forewing cell spot and has underside hindwing silver cell spot rimmed with pink. Male upperside forewing and hindwing black borders usually narrower. (2) "Booth's Sulphur" (hybrid between Hecla Sulphur and Labrador Sulphur) usually shows some orange and has narrower black border. **EARLY STAGES:** Not reported. **FOOD:** Arctic Bilberry. **FLIGHT:** Late June–early Aug. (1 brood). **RANGE:** Holarctic. Arctic America from Alaska east to e. N.W. Terr. and n. Ont.; s. Baffin I. and isolated records on Victoria and Southampton islands. **HABITAT:** Subarctic bogs, taiga openings, and arctic tundra.

SOUTHERN DOGFACE *Colias cesonia* PL. 10

2¼–2¹⁵⁄₁₆ in. (58–74 mm). Forewing apex slightly falcate, not rounded. Upperside: Forewing of both sexes usually shows central *yellow dog's head* surrounded by black. Female with black areas diffuse. Two seasonal forms. Underside: Summer form has hindwing yellow, that of winter form has dark and pink mottling. **SIMILAR SPECIES:** (1) Orange Sulphur has at least some orange on upperside forewing; has black borders but never in shape of dog's head; (2) Mexican Yellow has dog's head pattern on upperside forewing but ground color is cream, not yellow. **EARLY STAGES:** Caterpillars variable, usually green and covered with black hairy bumps —body unmarked or with yellow and black longitudinal lines or crossbands. **FOOD:** Many legumes, including lead plant, indigo bush, prairie clovers, false indigo, and others. **FLIGHT:** All months in Deep South and s. Texas, 2 flights during May–Aug. and overwin-

Southern Dogface. Female resting on vegetation. Larimer Co., Colo. Basically a southern and tropical butterfly, these attractive insects colonize large areas of the Great Plains each summer.

tering adults (Aug.–April). Colonists to north either do not reproduce or bring off only 1 adult generation before winter. **RANGE:** Resident from South America north through Cen. America and s. U.S. (s. Texas and peninsular Fla.). Irregular colonist and temporary resident northward, occasionally reaching s. Man., s. Ont., and N.J. **HABITAT:** Various open places; brushy hills, prairie hills, and weedy pastures. **REMARKS:** These butterflies are unlike the other sulphurs in wing shape and pattern; some consider that the Southern Dogface belongs in another genus, *Zerene*.

ANGLED SULPHURS: GENUS *Anteos* HÜBNER

This is a small genus of the New World tropics. Both our species are strong fliers, usually found flying high over the canopy or along rivers. Adults may occasionally be seen visiting moist sand along rivers or streams.

WHITE-ANGLED SULPHUR *Anteos clorinde* PL. 10

2¾–3½ in. (70–89 mm). Large. Forewing *apex falcate*; hindwing with short marginal projection. Ground *pale green*, turning white with age, with *yellow-orange bar* across forewing cell. Flies high and swiftly. **SIMILAR SPECIES:** (1) Yellow-angled Sulphur has pale yellow ground and lacks yellow-orange bar. (2) Giant White lacks hindwing projections. **EARLY STAGES:** Caterpillar is yellow-green, with an interrupted yellow lateral line above the spiracles and a wide whitish green line below the spiracles. **FOOD:** *Cassia spectabilis*. **FLIGHT:** Aug.–Dec. in s. Texas, all year in tropics. **RANGE:** Resident in mainland tropical America from Argentina north to Mexico, regular vagrant to s. Texas. Also in Great Plains to Neb. and ne. Colo. **HABITAT:** Open, sunny areas in a variety of tropical plant formations. Migrants almost anywhere.

YELLOW-ANGLED SULPHUR *Anteos maerula* PL. 10

3¹¹⁄₁₆–4⅝ in. (93–117 mm). Large. Forewing *apex falcate*; hindwing with short marginal projection. Male *bright yellow* above, female slightly paler. Upperside: Forewing cell with black spot. Flies high and swiftly. **SIMILAR SPECIES:** (1) White-angled Sulphur ground color is pale green or white, upperside forewing has yellow-orange bar across cell. (2) Cloudless Sulphur is smaller and has regular wing shape. **EARLY STAGES:** Caterpillar is olive-green, with a broad yellow buff lateral stripe, and 2 irregular rows of subdorsal blotches. **FOOD:** *Cassia*. **FLIGHT:** April, Aug.–Dec. in s. Texas; all year in tropics. **RANGE:** Resident in tropical America from Peru north to Mexico, irregular rare vagrant to Fla., Miss., s. Texas, se. Ariz., sw. N.M., and e. Neb. **HABITAT:** Open sunny places in a variety of tropical plant formations. Migrants almost anywhere.

GIANT SULPHURS: GENUS *Phoebis* HÜBNER

These are the most conspicuous tropical sulphurs. They are common and are found in open areas and along forest edges. The adult males cluster on moist sand along rivers and streams. These

CLOUDLESS SULPHUR

Cloudless Sulphur. Male nectaring at lantana. Lower Rio Grande Valley, Tex. In contrast to other families, male whites and sulphurs are often significantly larger than their female counterparts. Cloudless Sulphurs have differing seasonal forms.

butterflies may partake in extensive migrations often noted along coastlines. The adults may appear far to the north of their usual habitats. Caterpillars feed on leaves of *Cassias* and mimosa family plants.

CLOUDLESS SULPHUR *Phoebis sennae*   PL. 10

2½–3¹⁄₁₆ in. (63–78 mm). This is by far the commonest giant sulphur. Upperside: Male is *clear lemon yellow*; female dimorphic, yellow or white (rarer in East). Forewing of female with *hollow black cell spot*, outer margins of both wings edged irregularly with black. Underside: Both sexes have hindwing with *2-centered pink-rimmed silver spots*. **SIMILAR SPECIES:** (1) Statira Sulphur male has upperside forewing with outer portions paler yellow. Female has only upperside forewing edged in black, and black cell spot is smaller, not hollow. (2) Large Orange Sulphur male has upperside bright orange. Female has upperside forewing with interrupted diagonal row of black smudges. (3) Orange-barred Sulphur is larger, male has upperside forewing with red-orange costal bar, and hindwing red-orange outer margin. Female upperside forewing with broken line of diagonal smudges. Yellow female form has outer half of upperside hindwing red-pink. **EARLY STAGES:** Caterpillar is yellow or green with tiny black tubercles and a yellow longitudinal stripe with small blue dots along each side. **FOOD:** *Cassias*. **FLIGHT:** All year in Deep South, late summer immigrant to north. **RANGE:** Permanent resident in tropical America from Argentina north through Cen. America and the Caribbean to s. Texas and the Deep South. Regular vagrant and occasional colonist to the Southwest and much of the eastern U.S. **HABITAT:** A wide variety of open, weedy tropical and subtropical situations.

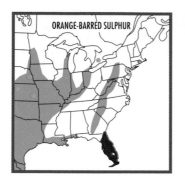

ORANGE-BARRED SULPHUR *Phoebis philea*   **PL. 10**

2¹¹⁄₁₆–3⅞ in. (68–98 mm). Upperside: Male forewing with *red-orange bar* and hindwing with *red-orange outer margin*. Female much larger than male, dimorphic: one form yellow-orange, the other off-white. Both female forms have forewing with solid black cell spot and a broken, offset, submarginal line of black smudges. Yellow form with outer half of hindwing red-orange. Flies high and swiftly. **SIMILAR SPECIES:** (1) Large Orange Sulphur is smaller, male bright orange above; female upperside forewing with continuous diagonal row of black smudges. (2) Cloudless Sulphur is smaller, male bright yellow above, female upperside forewing without row of black smudges. **EARLY STAGES:** Caterpillar is yellow-green with black tubercles and lateral black and yellow bands, the latter with included white-ringed reddish-black spots. **FOOD:** *Cassias*. **FLIGHT:** All year in Fla. (2–3 flights). Vagrants mainly in mid- to late summer. **RANGE:** Resident in much of lowland tropical America south to Brazil, and in peninsular Fla. and the Keys (since around 1928). Irregular vagrant to s. Texas, extremely rare vagrant northward to Colo., Minn., Wis., and Conn. **HABITAT:** Forest edges, city gardens.

LARGE ORANGE SULPHUR *Phoebis agarithe*   **PL. 10**

2¾–3⅜ in. (70–86 mm). Upperside: Male *bright orange*. Female dimorphic, yellow-orange or pink-white. Underside: Forewing of both sexes with *straight submarginal line*, not offset as in all other *Phoebis*. **SIMILAR SPECIES:** (1) Apricot Sulphur underside has submarginal line on forewing broken and offset. (2) Cloudless Sulphur male is pure yellow above; female upperside forewing lacks submarginal smudges. (3) Orange-barred Sulphur is larger; male has upperside with red-orange bar on forewing and red-orange outer margin on hindwing. Female has upperside submarginal spot line on forewing interrupted and offset. **EARLY STAGES:** Caterpil-

Large Orange Sulphur. White phase female nectaring at fleabane in lower Rio Grande Valley, Tex. This species is the commonest "large sulphur" in south Texas, where white form females are prevalent over the yellow form.

lar is green with a lateral yellow line edged with black below. **FOOD:** Woody plants in pea or legume family—*Pithecellobium* and *Inga* are known host genera. **FLIGHT:** All year in s. Fla. and s. Texas, strays north in mid- to late summer. Has recognizable seasonal forms. **RANGE:** Resident in much of lowland tropical America from Peru north to peninsular Fla. and s. Texas. Rare vagrant north to Colo., S.D., Wis., and N.J. **HABITAT:** Many open, lowland tropical situations including forest edges, pastures, and city gardens.

APRICOT SULPHUR *Phoebis argante*   **NOT SHOWN**
2⅛–2⅝ in. (53–65 mm). Upperside: Male *bright orange*. Female dimorphic. Underside: Both sexes with forewing *submarginal line broken and offset*. **SIMILAR SPECIES:** Large Orange Sulphur has underside forewing submarginal line straight, not offset. **EARLY STAGES:** Caterpillar is green or yellow-green with many small creamy granulations and a white or yellow stripe along each side; back with short reddish hairs. **FOOD:** Woody plants in pea or legume family, including *Pentaclethra* and *Inga*. **FLIGHT:** All year in tropics. Strays to Texas from June–Oct. **RANGE:** Paraguay north to Mexico. Extremely rare vagrant (twice) to s. Texas and w. Kans. **HABITAT:** Tropical forest clearings, roadsides, gardens, pastures.

TAILED SULPHUR   **NOT SHOWN**
Phoebis neocypris
1½–1⅝ in. (38–40 mm). Large. Both sexes with *triangular tail-like extension* on each hindwing. Female dimorphic. **SIMILAR SPECIES:** (1) Cloudless Sulphur is smaller, lacks hindwing extensions. (2) Yellow-angled Sulphur has falcate forewing apex, hindwing with shorter projections. **EARLY STAGES:** Unknown. **FLIGHT:** All year in trop-

ics, seen during Sept. in Texas. **RANGE:** Resident at moderate elevations in Cen. America and Mexico. Strayed once to s. Texas. **HABITAT:** In tropics, seen especially at mid-elevation forests.

STATIRA SULPHUR *Phoebis statira* PL. 10

2⁷⁄₁₆–3⅛ in. (62–80 mm). Upperside: Male *two-toned* with ridged scale line down middle of both wings. Outer portion beyond scale ridge is pale yellow-cream, inner portion lemon yellow. Female with even black borders on apex and outer margin of forewing. Cell spot solid black. **SIMILAR SPECIES:** (1) Cloudless Sulphur is solid yellow, lacks scale ridge. Female with apex and outer margin unevenly edged with black, forewing cell spot hollow, filled with yellow or white. **EARLY STAGES:** Caterpillar pale orange with a green tinge; blue-black band along each side. **FOOD:** Legumes—*Dalbergia* and *Cassia* in Fla. **FLIGHT:** June–early Feb. (summer flight and overwintering adults). **RANGE:** Resident in lowland tropical America north to peninsular Fla. Vagrant in s. Ga., s. Texas, N.M., and Kans. **HABITAT:** Second growth or scrub habitats in tropical lowlands. Vacates seasonally dry habitats, and large migrations have been seen in the tropics.

ORBED SULPHUR *Phoebis orbis* NOT SHOWN

2¼–3 in. (63–76 mm). Dimorphic. Upperside: Male forewing with *basal area orange, outer half pale lemon yellow*. Female with only one form, deep ocher above with *large brown patch* on underside hindwing. **SIMILAR SPECIES:** Cloudless Sulphur is solid yellow above, yellow female form is paler and without underside hindwing brown patch. **EARLY STAGES:** Caterpillar green with yellow tubercles, each segment tending orange behind, white lateral line on each side bordered above with dark olive. **FOOD:** Royal Poinciana. **FLIGHT:** Usually April–Aug. on Hispaniola, but also other

STATIRA SULPHUR

LYSIDE SULPHUR

Lyside Sulphur. Resting adult. Lower Rio Grande Valley, Tex. The greenish underside of these tropical butterflies blends well when they rest on vegetation, often in sun-dappled situations. They undergo periodic vast migrations.

months. **RANGE:** Resident on Cuba and Hispaniola, rarely strays to Fla. Keys. **HABITAT:** Usually tropical moist forest above 500 m on Hispaniola, but also in other situations.

LYSIDE SULPHUR *Kricogonia lyside* PL. 8

1 ¹¹⁄₁₆–2⅜ in. (42–60 mm). Extremely variable. Forewing apex abruptly *squared off*. Upperside: Base of forewing *yellow*; male often with black bar on hindwing costa. Underside: Hindwing with satiny sheen and raised veins. Female dimorphic, with both yellow and white forms. **SIMILAR SPECIES:** (1) Cabbage White upperside forewing has one (male) or two (female) black spots. (2) Great Southern White upperside forewing has black outer margin in both sexes. (3) Cloudless Sulphur has normal wing shape, male upperside is uniformly yellow, while female upperside forewing has black outer margin and black cell spot. **EARLY STAGES:** Caterpillar dull green with dorsal and lateral gray or silver lines, the dorsal line bordered on both sides by chocolate brown and the sides with variegated brown and golden yellow. **FOOD:** Lignum Vitae in much of range, *Porliera* in Texas. **FLIGHT:** All year in s. Texas, April–Aug. elsewhere to north and east (including Fla.). **RANGE:** Resident in lowland tropical America from Antilles and Venezuela north to s. peninsular Fla. (rare) and s. Texas (abundant). Migrates and found regularly north to Colo., Neb., and Ky. **HABITAT:** Lowland scrub and seasonally dry forest edges.

SMALL YELLOWS: GENUS *Eurema* HÜBNER

These include the most common tropical butterflies. They are found in semitropical and tropical habitats throughout the world. Many have such strikingly different seasonal forms that they have

BARRED YELLOW

MEXICAN YELLOW

been described as different species. They may undertake extensive local migrations at the beginning of the dry season in the tropics. Caterpillars of most species eat legumes, but some species feed on other plants. They all overwinter as adults.

BARRED YELLOW *Eurema daira*   PL. 11
1 ¼–1 ⅝ in. (32–40 mm). Sexually dimorphic and with 2 seasonal forms. Summer (wet-season) form smaller. Upperside: Male forewing with *black bar* along inner margin and extensive black on apical area. Female forewing with gray-black on apex as in male and black patch on hindwing outer margin. Summer (wet-season) form with black more extensive. Occasional individuals in s. Fla. with white hindwing, showing Caribbean influence. Underside: Hindwing satiny white (summer form), or brick red or tan with 2 black spots in cell (winter form). SIMILAR SPECIES: (1) Dainty Sulphur is smaller, has elongated forewing; upperside black bar along hindwing costal margin; underside hindwing more patterned. (2) Little Yellow upperside has small black forewing cell spot, lacks black bar on forewing inner margin. EARLY STAGES: Caterpillar light green above and translucent green below with a pale stripe on each side. FOOD: Joint vetch, also pencil flower and other legumes. FLIGHT: All year in Deep South, late summer and fall as vagrant. RANGE: Widespread resident and migrant from Argentina north through Caribbean, Cen. America, and Mexico. Resident in Deep South. Vagrant north to s. Texas, s. Ariz., S.D., and Washington, D.C. HABITAT: Pastures, dunes, forest edges in subtropical and tropical zones.

BOISDUVAL'S YELLOW *Eurema boisduvalianum*   PL. 11
1 ⅝–2 in. (40–52 mm). Sexes dimorphic. Upperside: *Lemon yellow* with *black borders* and *slight projection* on each hindwing. Male

with weakly expressed *dog's head* pattern on forewing; hindwing with black border projecting into yellow ground. Female forewing with black apical area, narrow black margin on hindwing. **SIMILAR SPECIES:** (1) Mexican Yellow has ground pale cream, dog's snout more pronounced, and hindwing projections more accentuated. (2) Dina Yellow is deeper yellow, upperside forewing lacks dog's-head pattern. No tail-like projections on hindwing. **EARLY STAGES:** Not known. **FLIGHT:** All year in tropics, April–Nov. in s. Texas. **RANGE:** Resident from Costa Rica north to Mexico and the Antilles. Regular vagrant north to se. Ariz., sw. N.M., and s. Texas, rarely to s. Fla. **HABITAT:** Thorn scrub, pastures, and roadsides.

MEXICAN YELLOW *Eurema mexicanum*   PL. 11

1¾–2⁷⁄₁₆ in. (44–62 mm). Sexes dimorphic. Upperside: Ground *pale cream*; forewing of both sexes with *dog's head* pattern, which is more accentuated in male. Triangular *tail-like projections* from hindwing outer margin. **SIMILAR SPECIES:** (1) Boisduval's Yellow has ground yellow with less pronounced tail-like projections. **EARLY STAGES:** Caterpillar is variable pale green to dark green. **FOOD:** Acacia and *Diphysa*; reports of *Cassia* may be in error. **FLIGHT:** All year in tropics, midsummer to fall as vagrant. **RANGE:** Resident in n. South America north to s. Texas. A common vagrant in the Southwest and Great Plains, rarely north to s. Man. and s. Ont., east to Miss. and Ill. **HABITAT:** Dry open hillsides, thorn scrub, prairies.

SALOME YELLOW *Eurema salome*   NOT SHOWN

1⁵⁄₁₆–2³⁄₁₆ in. (49–55 mm). Sexes dimorphic. Ground yellow. Hindwing with pronounced *tail-like projections*. Upperside: Male forewing with barely recognizable shallow *"monkey's head"* indentation into black border; hindwing with *black border* of more or less *even width*, with indentation. Female without hindwing black border. **SIMILAR SPECIES:** (1) Boisduval's Yellow has hindwing projections less pronounced. Male upperside has forewing black border with more recognizable dog's head; hindwing black border with indentation into yellow area. Female with narrow black border on hindwing. (2) Dina Yellow lacks hindwing projections; underside has red-orange spots on forewing and hindwing apexes. **EARLY STAGES:** Not known. **FOOD:** *Diphysa*. **FLIGHT:** All year in tropics; Aug.–Sept. in s. Texas. **RANGE:** Resident in tropical America, extremely rare vagrant to lower Rio Grande Valley, Texas. **HABITAT:** Forest edges and openings; road edges. Middle elevations in tropics.

TAILED ORANGE *Eurema proterpia*   PL. 11

1¹¹⁄₁₆–2³⁄₁₆ in. (42–55 mm). Sexually dimorphic and with 2 seasonal forms. Summer (wet-season) form without tails. Winter (dry-sea-

son) form with distinct triangular projection on hindwing. Upperside: *Orange* with black edges. Forewing apex *squared off*. Male with forewing costa black; females with arced black forewing costa, apex, and outer margin. Underside: Hindwing *unpatterned*. **SIMILAR SPECIES:** Sleepy Orange has rounded forewing apex; upperside forewing has small black cell spot, underside hindwing with faintly mottled pattern. **EARLY STAGES:** Caterpillar is grass green. **FOOD:** *Desmodium* and Mesquite. **FLIGHT:** All year in tropics; Aug.–Nov. in Texas. **RANGE:** Resident in the Greater Antilles, South America from Peru north through lowland Cen. America and Mexico, especially dry-season zones; strays regularly north to se. Ariz., sw. N.M. and s. Texas, very rarely to Kans. and Neb. **HABITAT:** Seasonally dry scrub, forest edges, pastures. **REMARKS:** As recently as 1951, the seasonal forms were still considered separate species.

Little Yellow. Female nectaring at white aster in Fairfax Co. Va. These butterflies temporarily colonize more northern locations each summer, especially in the East, where their caterpillars feed on Partridge Pea.

MIMOSA YELLOW

LITTLE YELLOW *Eurema lisa*   PL. 11

1¼–1¹¹⁄₁₆ in. (32–42 mm). Sexually dimorphic. Upperside: Forewing of both sexes with *small black cell spot*. Male yellow with broad black forewing apex. Hindwing with *black border*. Female also dimorphic—yellow form much more common than white form. **SIMILAR SPECIES:** (1) Mimosa Yellow lacks forewing cell spot; forewing black apical area is less extensive on male. Female and winter male upperside usually with black border on hindwing. (2) Dina Yellow is larger, with narrower black borders on forewing upperside, usually none on hindwing. (3) Dainty Sulphur is smaller, with more complex pattern above and below. Both sexes with black bar along upperside forewing inner margin. **EARLY STAGES:** Caterpillar is grass green with one or two lateral white lines. **FOOD:** *Cassias*, especially Partridge Pea and Wild Sensitive Plant. **FLIGHT:** All year in Deep South and s. Texas (4–5 broods), late spring to early fall further north (1–3 broods). **RANGE:** Resident in lowland tropical America and s. U.S. from Texas eastward, strays and temporarily colonizes much of eastern North America including areas far to north, se. N.D. and Minn. east across s. Ont. and s. Que. to N.S. **HABITAT:** Dry sandy fields, roadsides, old fields, rights of way.

MIMOSA YELLOW *Eurema nise*   PL. 11

¹³⁄₁₆–¹⁷⁄₁₆ in. (30–36 mm). Sexually dimorphic. Ground yellow in both sexes—no white female form. Upperside: Forewing lacks black cell spot and has narrow black outer margins. Hindwing black margin lacking in female, infrequent in male. **SIMILAR SPECIES:** (1) Little Yellow upperside has forewing black cell spot and broader black margins on both wings. **EARLY STAGES:** Caterpillar is green with short white setae and a white lateral line. **FOOD:** Sensitive plant. **FLIGHT:** All year in tropics; May–Aug. in s. Fla.; Sept.–Nov. in

Sleepy Orange. Male nectaring at lantana in Callaway Gardens, Ga. With their rapid flight, these butterflies are anything but sleepy, although the winter- or dry-season form spends more time resting in shady locations. Photo by Evi Buckner.

s. Texas. **RANGE:** Resident in lowland tropical America south to Argentina, irregular stray northward to se. Ariz., cen. Texas, and s. Fla., rarely s. Calif., s. Colo., and Kans. **HABITAT:** Brushy edges of woods, rarely pastures.

SHY YELLOW *Eurema messalina*   NOT SHOWN
1–1¼ in. (26–38 mm). Ground color *white*. Upperside: Male with black outer margins on both wings. Female with black apical area. **SIMILAR SPECIES:** (1) Cabbage White has 1 or 2 black spots on forewing. **EARLY STAGES:** Not reported. **FOOD:** *Desmodium*. **FLIGHT:** Most common May–Aug., also Feb. **RANGE:** Resident in West Indies, very rare vagrant to s. Fla. (Oct.). **HABITAT:** Brushy areas.

DINA YELLOW *Eurema dina*   PL. 11
1⁵⁄₁₆–2³⁄₁₆ in. (33–55 mm). Sexually dimorphic. Upperside: Male orange-yellow with very *narrow black* on forewing costa and outer margin, hint of black outer hindwing margin on summer form. Female with black forewing apex. Underside: Hindwing has *three black spots* on underside hindwing. **EARLY STAGES:** Caterpillar is light green with a dark green lateral line. **FOOD:** Woody members of simarouba family, Mexican Alvaradoa in Fla., *Picramnia* in Costa Rica. **FLIGHT:** All year in s. Fla. (3–4 broods, including long winter generation). **RANGE:** Resident in Cen. America, Mexico, and Caribbean north to peninsular Fla. (since 1962). Regular vagrant to s. Texas and se. Ariz. **HABITAT:** Edges of brushy fields and open forest.

SLEEPY ORANGE *Eurema nicippe*   PL. 11
1⅜–2³⁄₁₆ in. (35–56 mm). Sexually dimorphic and seasonally diphenic. Upperside: Both wings *orange* with irregular *black bor-*

Dainty Sulphur. Short-day form male nectaring at white aster in Larimer Co., Colo. Each summer, these small butterflies move up from the South and Southwest, temporarily colonizing a vast territory before the onset of winter.

ders on costal and outer margins. Orange-yellow form rare. Male with black border sharply defined, female with black border edge diffuse. Forewing with small black cell spot. Underside: Hindwing of summer form orange-yellow, that of winter form brick red, brown, or tan. **SIMILAR SPECIES:** (1) Orange Sulphur male has more regular black borders on outer margin. Female has pale yellow spots enclosed within black border. Both sexes have at least a small amount of yellow above. Hindwing underside with silver cell spots. **EARLY STAGES:** Caterpillar green with lateral white and yellow stripe subtended by black. **FOOD:** Various *Cassias*. **FLIGHT:** All year in Deep South and s. Texas (4–5 broods, including 1 of overwintering adults). Mid- to late summer further north. **RANGE:** Resident in the West Indies, Mexico, and s. U.S. Regular vagrant and temporary colonist north to central states, rarely strays to Colo., S.D., Conn., and n. Ont. (James Bay). May also migrate south to

Costa Rica. **HABITAT:** Low areas in lower austral and subtropical zones, including open woods, pines, open fields, and roadsides.

DAINTY SULPHUR *Nathalis iole* PL. 10

1–1¼ in. (25–32 mm). *Small*. Forewings elongated. Sexually dimorphic and seasonally diphenic. Upperside: Black and yellow. Female with more extensive black. Hindwing with some orange infusion. White form rare. Underside: Forewing showing *orange* or *yellow basal patch* with *black spots* on outer edge. Hindwing of summer form pale yellow, that of winter form dusky green. **SIMILAR SPECIES:** (1) Barred Yellow is larger and lacks black cell spot on forewing upperside. (2) Little Yellow is larger and lacks black bar along inner margin of upperside forewing. **EARLY STAGES:** Caterpillar is dark green with purple dorsal stripe and a fused black and yellow line along each side. **FOOD:** Low plants in aster family, especially Fetid Marigold and Shepherd's-Needle. **FLIGHT:** All year in peninsular Fla. and s. Texas (number of broods indefinite). No more than 6 months in colonized areas to north. **RANGE:** Resident from Guatemala and the West Indies north to peninsular Fla. and the Southwest. Regular vagrant and colonist north to se. Wash., se. Idaho, cen. Man., Minn., and s. Ont. **HABITAT:** Dry open areas, including weedy fields, sandy coastal flats, and hillsides. **REMARKS:** The Dainty Sulphur is unique among our sulphurs in several structural features, so much so that some feel it belongs in a separate subfamily.

9

TRUE BUTTERFLIES:
SUPERFAMILY PAPILIONOIDEA
HARVESTERS, COPPERS, HAIRSTREAKS,
AND BLUES: FAMILY LYCAENIDAE

Butterflies of this family are worldwide in distribution, with about 4,700 species, but the proportions of species differ in different regions. Coppers are especially dominant in north temperate regions, blues are richest in the Old World tropics and north temperate zone, and hairstreaks are particularly abundant and diverse in the New World tropics. The adults are usually small to tiny and are often brilliantly colored. Iridescent blues, bright reds, and oranges are frequent colors on the upper surfaces. Front legs of most males lack a pretarsus and their tarsomeres are fused into one segment, but their legs are still used for walking. Females have three pairs of normal walking legs. Adults of most of our species visit flowers for nectar, but adults of harvesters feed on woolly aphid honeydew, and adults of some hairstreaks never visit flowers but probably feed on aphid honeydew or bird droppings.

Eggs are usually laid singly on host leaves or flower buds (but see the Harvester, *Feniseca tarquinius*), although the cycad hairstreaks (Genus *Eumaeus*) lay theirs in groups, and the caterpillars feed communally. Most of our species are relatively specific in their caterpillar host choice, usually limited to plants of the same family, but many species of tropical affinities are catholic in their choice of hosts. In fact, the Gray Hairstreak (*Strymon melinus*) has one of the broadest host ranges of any butterfly. The eggs of most species are sea-urchin–shaped. Most caterpillars are slug-shaped with retracted heads; their bodies are covered with short fine setae. The caterpillars of many species depend upon ants for protection. These caterpillars have abdominal glands that produce sugary secretions collected by the ants. In fact, the early stages of some species are actually maintained inside ant nests. Caterpillars of the Harvester, our only carnivorous species, feed on woolly aphids.

The pupae are stout and may be attached to the surface by a

Harvester. Male perching on leaf along small stream in Fairfax Co., Va. The caterpillars are carnivorous—an unusual trait for a butterfly—and eat woolly aphids found on alders and other trees.

fine girdle. Pupae of some species have a mechanism for producing sounds that are probably related to protection from predators by ants. Overwintering is accomplished in either the egg or pupal stage.

HARVESTERS: SUBFAMILY MILETINAE

This group is composed of about 50 species, most of which are found in Africa and Asia. Only a single species, the Harvester, occurs in North America. These butterflies are carnivorous and have close associations with ants and with Homoptera. The adults are found near colonies of their hosts and obtain nutrition from the "honeydew" secretions of their hosts. The butterflies perch with their wings closed, and males take prominent perches where they await the appearance of females. They occasionally

HARVESTER

American Copper. Male nectaring at flowers of Butterfly Milkweed in western Iowa. The late Alexander Klots felt that eastern U.S. populations were introduced in hay shipments during Colonial times. Evidence supports this idea.

visit moist sand or mud to imbibe moisture. Eggs are laid in the middle of Homoptera colonies, usually aphids but sometimes scale insects or treehoppers. The caterpillars are predaceous or parasitic on their hosts, at least in their early stages. The young caterpillars of some species are carried into ant nests, where they complete their development by feeding on ant brood. The chrysalis is tied to the surface from which it hangs with a silken girdle, and its underside usually resembles a monkey face.

HARVESTER *Feniseca tarquinius* PL. 12

1 ⅛–1 ¼ in. (28–34 mm). Adults unique. Upperside: *Orange-brown with black areas and spots.* Underside: Hindwing brown or orange-brown with *faint white scrawls.* **EARLY STAGES:** Caterpillar is greenish brown with faint longitudinal olive lines; long white hairs originate from the intersegmental areas. **FOOD:** Woolly aphids, especially on alders. **FLIGHT:** Mid-May to mid-Aug. in North (2 broods); Feb. or March to Sept. in South (3 broods). **RANGE:** S. N.S. and Me. west to se. Man. and e. N.D., south to cen. peninsular Fla., the Gulf Coast and s. Texas. **HABITAT:** Woodlands, usually deciduous, near slow-moving or swampy streams. **REMARKS:** Our only butterfly with carnivorous caterpillars. Adults are usually found near woolly aphid colonies; never visit flowers.

COPPERS: SUBFAMILY LYCAENINAE

Most coppers are found in sunny, open habitats throughout the temperate zone, with 50 species found in Eurasia and North America. One isolated species, *Lycaena pyhrrias*, lives on volcanos in Guatemala. A few species occur in New Guinea, New Zealand, and northern Africa. The upper surface of wings is iridescent pur-

AMERICAN COPPER

GRAY COPPER

ple or red-orange in most species. Our species may bask with open wings. Males perch and interact, seemingly aggressively with other males, while they await receptive females. No species are known migrants, but several are good colonists at least on a local basis. Most species are single-brooded, but the American Copper may have two or three broods in the East. They overwinter as eggs or as first instar caterpillars within the egg. The caterpillars feed on leaves of the host plants, which in our area are docks, knotweeds, bush cinquefoil, or cranberries.

AMERICAN COPPER *Lycaena phlaeas* **PL. 12**

1–1 ⅜ in. (25–35 mm). Small. Sexes similar. Upperside: Forewing *iridescent fiery orange-red*; hindwing *gray with red-orange border* on outer margin. Underside: Hindwing gray with small black spots and a red-orange zigzag submarginal line. **EARLY STAGES:** Caterpillar varies from green to rose red; some have a red dorsal stripe. **FOOD:** Sheep Sorrel in eastern temperate areas, rarely Curled Dock; *Oxyria digyna* in Arctic. **FLIGHT:** May–Sept. (2 broods) in ne. U.S. and se. Canada, in southern part of range from mid-April through Sept. (3 broods). In arctic Canada during July and early Aug. **RANGE:** Holarctic. In North America probably introduced to the e. U.S. and s. Canada from the Gaspé and N.S. east to w.-cen. Ont. and n. Minn., south to n. Ga. and n. Ark. Rare vagrants, possibly moved as early stages in hay shipments, have been found to s. Sask., w. S.D., and cen. Colo. Native populations in Arctic and western alpine habitats—tundra of N.W. Terr. and Arctic Archipelago, isolated alpine populations in cen. and n. Rockies, Sierra Nevada, Blue Mts., Yukon, and Alaska. **HABITAT:** Old fields, roadsides, pastures, and landfills in East; tundra in arctic habitats; rocky areas in alpine habitats. **REMARKS:** Although the eastern temperate butterfly is called the American Copper, circumstantial

Gray Copper. Male basking in field, Larimer Co., Colo. This is a close relative of the more western Edith's Copper and Great Copper. Its range is gradually spreading eastward and southward.

evidence now points to an Old World introduction by man, perhaps in the Colonial period. The butterfly is more similar to European populations than to those of w. North America and the Arctic. The copper's eastern populations are found almost entirely in habitats disturbed by man, and its primary food plant in the East is Sheep Sorrel, a plant introduced from Europe.

GRAY COPPER *Lycaena dione*   **PLS. 3, 12**
1½–1⅞ in. (37–47 mm). Large. Upperside: *Dark gray*. Forewing has 2 black cell spots; hindwing has pale *orange and black border* on outer margin. Underside: Pale gray-white with pattern of small black spots and repetition of hindwing border, but with orange-red. **SIMILAR SPECIES:** Bronze Copper is quite different on upperside. Underside hindwing similar, but forewing orange, not gray. **EARLY STAGES:** Caterpillar is green with a darker green or red dorsal stripe. **FOOD:** Several docks, including Broad Dock. **FLIGHT:** Mid-June through July, occasionally Aug. (1 brood). **RANGE:** Cen. and w. North America. In central plains and prairies from s. Man., Sask., and Alta. south to cen. Ill., cen. Mo., and n. Texas. Also in Calif. and adjacent parts of Baja Calif. Norte and s. Ore. **HABITAT:** Weedy fields, pastures, open grassy areas along ditches and streams.

BRONZE COPPER *Lycaena hyllus*   **PL. 12**
1½–1⅞ in. (37–47 mm). Large. Sexually dimorphic. Upperside: Male iridescent brown-purple; female with forewing yellow-orange with *black spots*. Underside: Both sexes have orange forewing with black spots; hindwing is *off-white with black spots and wide orange* outer margin. **EARLY STAGES:** Caterpillar is yellow-green with a blackish middorsal stripe. **FOOD:** Water Dock and Curled

BRONZE COPPER

Bronze Copper. Male resting on vegetation. Larimer Co., Colo. Although rare or disappearing in the Northeast, in the West they are spreading into disturbed and agricultural areas.

Dock. **FLIGHT:** Mid-June to late Sept. in north and west (2 broods); mid-May to as late as early Nov. in southernmost part of range (3 broods). **RANGE:** Cen. North America from cen. Man. and Mont. south and east in a band through Midwest to the Atlantic Coast from Me. south to Md. **HABITAT:** Open areas with low vegetation in or near marshes, bogs, wet meadows, and seeps.

RUDDY COPPER *Lycaena rubidus*   **PL. 12**
1 ⅜–1 ⅝ in. (35–41 mm). Primarily western. Sexually dimorphic. Upperside: Male *fiery red-orange;* female dull orange-brown. Underside: Both sexes *gray-white or pale tan-white;* hindwing with only *faint black spots.* Our other plains coppers are more strongly patterned below. **EARLY STAGES:** Not well recorded. **FOOD:** Several dock species. **FLIGHT:** Mid-June through Aug. (1 brood). **RANGE:** Plains and intermountain west from s. Alta. and sw. Sask. west to interior portions of Pacific Slope states, east to cen. N.D. and Neb. **HABITAT:** Dry sandy or gravelly areas, usually near streambeds or alluvial washes.

BOG COPPER *Lycaena epixanthe*   **PL. 12**
⅞–1 in. (23–25 mm). Small. Sexes dimorphic. Upperside: Male with purplish iridescence; female mouse gray-brown. Underside:

Pale tan or white. Hindwing has *tiny black spots* and *zigzag red-orange border* on outer margin. **SIMILAR SPECIES:** (1) Dorcas Copper and (2) Purplish Copper are larger, have upperside with more black spots and underside with the ground color orange-brown. **EARLY STAGES:** Caterpillar is blue-green covered with short white setae; a dark-green middorsal band, dark oblique dashes, and a light lateral line. **FOOD:** Cranberries. **FLIGHT:** Late June to late Aug. (1 brood); exact dates depending on locality. **RANGE:** Se. Canada and ne. U.S. from cen. Ont. and Nfld. south to W. Va. and N.J. **HABITAT:** Acid bogs with cranberries and other low heath family plants. **REMARKS:** Colonies relatively uncommon, but butterflies are often abundant when found. Geographically variable but quite uniform at any single locality.

DORCAS COPPER *Lycaena dorcas* PL. 12

1–1 ³⁄₁₆ in. (26–30 mm). Sexually dimorphic. Upperside: Male has blue-purple iridescence; female brown with *limited light areas.* Red-orange border on hindwing limited to a *few spots near anal angle.* Underside: Orange-brown. **SIMILAR SPECIES:** (1) Purplish Copper is larger; upperside of male lighter, that of female with extensive light areas. Orange border on hindwing extends over much of outer margin. (2) Bog Copper is smaller, has much paler underside. **EARLY STAGES:** Caterpillar is pale green with faint white oblique dashes, a dark green middorsal line, diamond-shaped shield on prothorax, head tan. **FOOD:** Shrubby Cinquefoil. **FLIGHT:** Mid-June to late Sept. (1 brood), flies earlier in southern part of range. **RANGE:** Boreal Alaska and Canada south and east to e. Ont. and n. Great Lakes states. Isolated populations from Lab. and Nfld. south to N.B. (*L. d. dospassosi*) and Me. (*L. d. claytoni*). Some believe that the western U.S. mountain populations are closest to the Purplish Copper. **HABITAT:** Brushy old fields, fringes of bogs, open areas near small streams.

RUDDY COPPER

BOG COPPER

DORCAS COPPER

PURPLISH COPPER

PURPLISH COPPER *Lycaena helloides*   **PL. 12**

1 ⅛–1⁷⁄₁₆ in. (28–36 mm). Sexually dimorphic. Upperside: Male has purplish iridescence on both wings; female has extensive orange areas on both wings. Marginal *orange band* on hindwing of both sexes *extensive*. **SIMILAR SPECIES:** Dorcas Copper has less extensive marginal orange band on hindwing, and female has smaller light areas. **EARLY STAGES:** Caterpillar is green with many oblique yellow lines; body covered with short white hairs. **FOOD:** Various docks and knotweeds, rarely cinquefoils. **FLIGHT:** Mid-May to late Oct. (2 broods) in Mich. **RANGE:** Great Lakes region from se. Ont. and w. N.Y. (rarely) through n. Midwest and n. plains to West Coast from s. B.C. south to Baja Calif. Norte. **HABITAT:** Damp stream courses, marshes, wet fields, roadsides. **REMARKS:** More variable in pattern within populations than Dorcas Copper. Summer brood individuals and those found on the plains can be much paler.

Purplish Copper. Male perching in territorial posture. Fort Collins, Colo. This western butterfly barely enters the East but is widespread in the West, where it may hybridize with Dorcas Coppers — creating much confusin.

Hairstreaks are richest in tropical habitats throughout the world, but they are especially numerous in the Americas, with about 1,000 species. We have a number of tropical species that barely reach the southern limits of our area. In tropical species, the upperside of the small to medium-sized adults is often iridescent blue. The iridescent colors are due to reflected light from the physical structure of the wing scales and are not pigmental. Few of our species are so colored; most of ours are brown above. Males perch with their wings closed over their back, and most perch to await the appearance of receptive females. Most species are local in their occurrence, and migration is rare, even though a few species, e.g. *Strymon melinus*, are good long-distance colonists. Eggs are usually laid singly, although those of *Eumaeus* are laid in clusters. Caterpillars feed on leaves or reproductive structures of a wide variety of plants, usually woody trees or shrubs. Those of *Calycopis* are exceptional in their consumption of recently dead leaves. The pupae of several species can produce sounds between abdominal segments. The butterflies overwinter in either the egg or pupal stage.

ATALA *Eumaeus atala*   **PL. 12**

1⅝–2 in. (41–51 mm). Unmistakable. A tailless butterfly with a *red-orange abdomen*. Upperside: Both wings are *iridescent blue-green* on a field of velvety black. Underside: Both wings dull black; hindwing has a red-orange basal spot and 3 rows of irregular iridescent blue-green spots. **EARLY STAGES:** Caterpillar is brilliant red with two rows of yellow spots along the back. Caterpillars feed in groups. **FOOD:** Coontie and several introduced cycads. **FLIGHT:** All year, most common in early summer. **RANGE:** Se. Fla. and Keys,

ATALA

Great Purple Hairstreak. Female at moisture. Fort Davis State Park, Tex. This is our only eastern butterfly whose caterpillars eat mistletoe, an unusual diet. Mistletoes are parasites that grow in the crowns of large trees.

Bahamas, and Cuba. **HABITAT:** Shaded, subtropical hardwood hammocks and adjacent open areas, botanical gardens with ornamental cycads. **REMARKS:** Considered endangered by the State of Florida, where populations are thought to have gone extinct from time to time. Possibly the butterflies recolonize from Bahamian populations, as in the late 1970s and 1980s when, after a long absence, the butterflies became locally abundant and a minor pest of ornamental cycads.

MEXICAN CYCADIAN *Eumaeus toxea* **NOT SHOWN**
1⅜–2 in. (34–51 mm). Tailless. Abdomen is black above, redorange below. Upperside: Iridescent blue on a field of black. Underside: Black; hindwing has basal red-orange spot and rows of iridescent blue spots. **SIMILAR SPECIES:** Atala's abdomen is solid red, and the two do not occur together. **EARLY STAGES:** Caterpillar glossy red with yellow on dorsal ridges. **FOOD:** Cycads. **FLIGHT:** March in Texas, April–Dec. in Mexico. **RANGE:** S. Texas (rare) and n. Mexico south to Honduras.

STROPHIUS HAIRSTREAK *Allosmaitia strophius* **NOT SHOWN**
1⁵⁄₁₆–1¼ in. (24–32 mm). Upperside: Forewing of male with *blue limited to inner margin*; scent scales scattered over basal half. Hindwing blue with *scent patch* on base of radial vein. Female gray. Underside: *Pale brown* with pattern similar to Golden-bordered Hairstreak. **EARLY STAGES:** Not reported. **FOOD:** Flowers of Malpighia family plants. **FLIGHT:** Late Oct. to early Nov. in Texas, all year in Cen. America. **RANGE:** Mexico from Sinaloa south, Cen. America, and South America to s. Brazil. Rare vagrant in s. Texas. **HABITAT:** Subtropical dry and wet woods and scrub as high as 1200 m. **REMARKS:** Formerly known as *A. pion.*

GREAT PURPLE HAIRSTREAK

GREAT PURPLE HAIRSTREAK *Atlides halesus*   **PL. 12**
1¼–2 in. (31–51 mm). Large. Abdomen is black above, *red-orange*
below. Upperside: Extensive *iridescent blue* (not purple!). Underside: *Black* with iridescent *gold* marks near tails. **SIMILAR SPECIES:**
White M Hairstreak is only other iridescent blue hairstreak in
Southeast and most of Texas, but it has a very different underside
pattern. **EARLY STAGES:** Caterpillar is green and covered with short
green or yellow-orange hairs. **FOOD:** Mistletoe (*Phoradendron*).
FLIGHT: Late March to late Nov. (3 flights) in Southeast, rarely seen
in midwinter. **RANGE:** Central U.S. from N.J. (rarely) and Md. west
through s. Mo. and Texas to cen. Calif., thence south to Cen.
America (Guatemala). **HABITAT:** Wooded areas with trees infested
with mistletoe: wooded swamps, oak woods, mesquite, etc.

MARIUS HAIRSTREAK *Rekoa marius*   **NOT SHOWN**
⅞–1¼ in. (22–32 mm). Rare stray to s. Texas. Sexually dimorphic.
Upperside: Male iridescent dark blue; female gray, hindwing with
orange marginal *eyespot* near tail. Underside: Exceedingly similar
to Gray Hairstreak. **EARLY STAGES:** Not reported. **FOOD:** Many plants in
several families, especially legumes and malpighias. **FLIGHT:** Mid-
Sept. to Dec. in s. Texas; probably flies all year in Mexico, but
specific records are June–Aug., Sep.–Dec. **RANGE:** Mexico from
Sonora south, Cen. America and South America to s. Brazil and
Paraguay. **HABITAT:** Disturbed areas in several tropical zones, from
sea level to 2000 m.

GOLD-BORDERED HAIRSTREAK   **NOT SHOWN**
Rekoa palegon
⅞–1⅛ in. (22–29 mm). Rare stray to s. Texas. Underside: Distinctive—gray with *orange-brown outer margins* and *irregular stripes*.
EARLY STAGES: Not reported. **FOOD:** Many plants in several families,
especially those of the Asteraceae family. **FLIGHT:** Early Nov. in s.

Texas, May–Dec. in Mexico. **RANGE:** Mexico from Tamaulipas south, Cen. America and South America to Argentina. **HABITAT:** Disturbed areas in a wide variety of tropical environments.

AMETHYST HAIRSTREAK *Chlorostrymon maesites*   **PL. 13**
⅞–1 in. (23–25 mm). Small. Sexually dimorphic. Upperside: Male deep iridescent purple-blue; female dull gray-blue. Underside: *Yellow-green* with *thin postmedian line*. **SIMILAR SPECIES:** Silver-banded Hairstreak is larger, with silver-white postmedian band below. **EARLY STAGES:** Not reported. **FOOD:** Raised in the laboratory from Woman's Tongue (*Albizia lebbeck*). **FLIGHT:** Dec. to late July (2 or 3 broods). **RANGE:** Se. peninsular Fla. and Keys, West Indies. **HABITAT:** Evergreen or semideciduous forest and hammocks.

TELEA HAIRSTREAK *Chlorostrymon telea*   **NOT SHOWN**
¹¹⁄₁₆–⅞ in. (17–21 mm). Rare vagrant in s. Texas. Underside: Postmedian line forms a W *near inner margin*; marginal brown patch. **SIMILAR SPECIES:** Very similar to Amethyst Hairstreak. **EARLY STAGES:** Not reported. **FOOD:** Flowers of Central American Soapberry (Peru) and Guazuma (Costa Rica). **FLIGHT:** June in s. Texas, Jan.–July, especially April–June, in Cen. America. **RANGE:** Mexico from Sinaloa south, Cen. America and South America to s. Brazil. **HABITAT:** Stream valleys in seasonal semideciduous dry forest. Usually found at flowers.

SILVER-BANDED HAIRSTREAK   **PL. 13**
Chlorostrymon simaethis
1–1³⁄₁₆ in. (26–30 mm). Sexually dimorphic. Upperside: Male suffused iridescent purple; female dull gray. Underside: Green with *silver-white postmedian band* on both wings. **EARLY STAGES:** Caterpillar light green to light brown covered with fine short black setae, with an irregular wavy black longitudinal and dorsal green-black

AMETHYST HAIRSTREAK

SILVER-BANDED
HAIRSTREAK

SOAPBERRY HAIRSTREAK

stripe; head same color as body with two black eyespots. Caterpillars feed inside pods of host. **FOOD:** Balloon vine (*Cardiospermum*). **FLIGHT:** Aug.–Dec. (2 broods). **RANGE:** U.S. from s. Fla. and Keys, s. Texas, and s. Ariz. south through the West Indies, Mexico, Cen. America, and South America to Argentina. **HABITAT:** Open areas or edges in or near seasonally dry tropical forest or scrub.

BLACK HAIRSTREAK *Ocaria ocrisia*   NOT SHOWN

⅞–¹⁵⁄₁₆ in. (22–24 mm). Rare stray to s. Texas. Distinctive, although there may be 2 species masquerading under this name. Upperside: Charcoal gray to charcoal black with *narrow blue margin* on hindwing. **EARLY STAGES:** Not reported. **FOOD:** Cen. American Lowland Live Oak (Costa Rica), flowers of *Paullinia* (Brazil). **FLIGHT:** Early Nov. in s. Texas; all year in Cen. America. **RANGE:** Mexico south from Tamaulipas, Cen. America, and South America to Brazil and Argentina. **HABITAT:** Disturbed habitats at low to moderate elevations.

SOAPBERRY HAIRSTREAK *Phaeostrymon alcestis*   PL. 14

¹⁵⁄₁₆–1¼ in. (33–35 mm). Sexes similar. Upperside: Plain brown; hindwing without orange anal spot. Underside: Forewing and hindwing cells have *narrow white bars* bounded by black. Postmedian band has a sharply jagged VW mark. **SIMILAR SPECIES:** Banded Hairstreak underside has lines thicker; lacks VW on hindwing postmedian band. **EARLY STAGES:** Not reported. **FOOD:** Western Soapberry. **FLIGHT:** late May through June (1 brood). **RANGE:** S. Midwest from sw. Mo., s. Kans., se. Colo., and cen. Ariz. south to n. Mexico. **HABITAT:** Mixed oak scrub, prairie valleys, hedgerows.

BROWN HAIRSTREAKS: GENUS *Satyrium* SCUDDER

The brown hairstreaks are found in North America, usually in

Coral Hairstreak. Male. Fairfax Co. Va. Although they lack tails, Coral Hairstreaks are close relatives of other eastern brown hairstreaks. Territorial males may be found in late afternoon, often on hilltops.

woods, along woodland edges, or by streams and rivers. All of our species are brown or gray-brown on the upperside, and their chief identifying features are on the underside. Adults readily visit flowers, often those of milkweeds or dogbane. Caterpillars usually feed on reproductive structures and young leaves of their host plants. Caterpillars of several species are tended by ants. Woody plants are selected, especially the beech, poplar, rose, and heath families. The winter is passed in the egg stage.

CORAL HAIRSTREAK *Satyrium titus*   **PL. 14**
1–1 ¼ in. (26–38 mm). Tailless. Underside: Hindwing brown with marginal row of *coral red spots* capped inwardly with a white-edged black line, as well as a postmedian row of 8 black spots and dashes circled with white. **EARLY STAGES:** Caterpillar has a black head and a dull green body tinted with rose or yellow toward the

CORAL HAIRSTREAK

front. During the day, full-grown caterpillars hide in litter at the base of small sprouts or saplings of the host. **FOOD:** Wild Cherry, Wild Plum, and Chokeberry. **FLIGHT:** Mid-May to late Aug. (1 brood), flies earlier in more southern latitudes. **RANGE:** Canada and U.S. from s. Que. and s. Ont. west to Alta. and B.C., south to cen. Ga., cen. Ark., cen. Texas, and cen. N.M. Isolated record in Fla. panhandle. **HABITAT:** Barrens, neglected pastures, sparsely wooded hills, copses near prairie streams.

ACADIAN HAIRSTREAK *Satyrium acadicum*   PL. 14

1 3/16–1 7/16 in. (30–36 mm). Tailed. Underside: Hindwing gray with a row of orange submarginal spots capped with black. Blue tail-spot *capped with orange*. Postmedian row of *round black spots*. **SIMILAR SPECIES:** Edwards' Hairstreak is usually found in different habitat. Hindwing underside much less gray, with blue tail-spot not capped with orange and postmedian spots dark brown, not black. **EARLY STAGES:** Caterpillar has a brown head and a green body with paired longitudinal yellow stripes along each side. **FOOD:** Willows. **FLIGHT:** June–Aug. (1 brood). **RANGE:** N.S. and Prince Edward I. south to N.J. and Md., west across the Great Lakes region, n. Midwest, and n. Plains to se. B.C. and e. Wash. **HABITAT:** On or near willows along stream courses and in marshes.

Acadian Hairstreak. Male perching. Dickinson Co., Iowa. Acadian Hairstreaks are found perching on willows, their caterpillar hosts, or nectaring at flowers of plants such as dogbane, milkweeds, or White Sweet Clover.

ACADIAN HAIRSTREAK

Edwards' Hairstreak. Male perching on vegetation. The adults are often seen nectaring at flowers, especially milkweeds, or resting on their host plants, often Scrub Oak. Photo by Jim Ebner.

EDWARDS' HAIRSTREAK *Satyrium edwardsii*   PL. 14

1 ³⁄₁₆–1 ⁷⁄₁₆ in. (30–36 mm). Tailed. Underside: Hindwing pale brown, blue tail-spot *not capped with orange*, postmedian row of separate *oval dark brown spots*. SIMILAR SPECIES: (1) Banded Hairstreak underside hindwing has postmedian row of short white-edged darkened dashes, not spots. (2) Acadian Hairstreak underside is pale gray with round postmedian spots, and blue tail-spot is capped with orange. EARLY STAGES: Caterpillar has a black head and a brown body with pale yellow-brown marks. During the day the nearly full-grown caterpillars hide in ant nests at the base of host trees. FOOD: Scrub Oak, occasionally Black Oak. FLIGHT: Late June to late July in North; mid-May to early July in South. RANGE: E. U.S. and extreme s. Canada. S. Me. west through s. Ont. to extreme se. Sask. and south to n. Ga., cen. Mo., and ne. Texas. HABITAT: On or near scrub oaks in sand barrens, shale barrens, limestone ridges, and similar open areas.

BANDED HAIRSTREAK *Satyrium calanus* **PL. 14**

1 ³⁄₁₆–1 ⁷⁄₁₆ in. (30–36 mm). Tailed. Underside: Hindwing brown with postmedian line of *dark, white-edged dashes*. Blue tail-spot not capped with orange. **SIMILAR SPECIES:** (1) Hickory Hairstreak underside usually has both wings with postmedian dashes wider and more offset; hindwing with blue lunule at anal angle extends further inward and thinner black cap on orange spot. (2) Edwards' Hairstreak has underside paler and postmedian row of dark oval spots, not dashes. (3) King's Hairstreak is larger; underside hindwing has orange cap on blue tail-spot. Outer margin indented above second tail. **EARLY STAGES:** Caterpillar is green with white oblique lines. **FOOD:** Oaks, walnuts, and hickories. **FLIGHT:** July–Aug. in North, April–May in Fla. (1 brood). **RANGE:** E. U.S., s. Canada, and s. Rocky Mts; s. N.S. and Me. west to se. Sask., south to cen. Fla., the Gulf states, and s.-cen. Texas. **HABITAT:** Forests with oaks or hickories and adjacent edges or fields. **REMARKS:** Widespread, common, and geographically variable. Abundance fluctuates wildly from year to year, but it may be consistently common in some areas. There may be more than one species in the Southeast, but further study is required.

HICKORY HAIRSTREAK *Satyrium caryaevorum* **PL. 14**

1 ³⁄₁₆–1 ⅜ in. (30–34 mm). Usually very rare, occasionally abun-

Banded Hairstreak. Male nectaring at dogbane. Fairfax Co., Va. This is our commonest hairstreak through much of the East, even in urban parks. Adults are most easily found nectaring at milkweeds near forest edges.

BANDED HAIRSTREAK

dant. Tailed. Underside: Both wings with postmedian dashes *broader and more offset*. Hindwing with *blue crescent-shaped marking*. Orange eyespot has *thin black cap*. SIMILAR SPECIES: Banded Hairstreak underside has postmedian dashes narrower and less offset; orange spot at anal angle of hindwing has thicker black cap, and blue tail-spot is thinner. EARLY STAGES: Caterpillar is yellow-green with 2 parallel dorsal white lines and oblique yellow-white lines. FOOD: Predominantly hickories, but oak, chestnut, and ash also reported. FLIGHT: Late June to early Aug. (1 brood). RANGE: Ne. quadrant of U.S. from s. New England and s. Que. west to se. Minn. and e. Kans. Extends south in Appalachians to e. Tenn. HABITAT: Deciduous forests, second-growth woods. REMARKS: Often found with Banded Hairstreak.

KING'S HAIRSTREAK *Satyrium kingi*   PL. 14
1 3/16–1 7/16 in. (30–36 mm). Tailed. Underside: Both wings brown with postmedian dashes; hindwing with *blue tail-spot capped with orange* and outer margin *indented* above second tail. SIMILAR SPECIES: (1) Banded Hairstreak underside hindwing lacks orange cap on blue tail-spot and lacks indentation of outer margin. (2) Striped Hairstreak is smaller, and underside has widely separated lines, not dashes. EARLY STAGES: Caterpillar is light green with oblique yellow-green lines. FOOD: Common Sweetleaf. FLIGHT: Mid-May to early June (1 brood). RANGE: Atlantic coastal plain from Md. south and Gulf states west to s. Ark. and e. Texas. HABITAT: Hardwood hammocks, wooded swamp edges. REMARKS: Rare and local.

STRIPED HAIRSTREAK *Satyrium liparops*   PL. 14
1 1/8–1 7/16 in. (28–36 mm). Tailed. Underside: Both wings have median and postmedian rows of *widely separated white lines* (stripes); hindwing underside with blue tail-spot *capped with*

Striped Hairstreak. Female nectaring at New Jersey Tea, Fairfax Co., Va. Although widespread, this hairstreak is usually less common than the Banded. They nectar at many of the same flowers but also an additional wider variety.

orange, and outer margin *indented above second short tail.* **SIMILAR SPECIES:** King's Hairstreak is larger; undersides of both wings have series of dashes, not widely separated lines. **EARLY STAGES:** Caterpillar like that of King's Hairstreak but darker green. **FOOD:** Woody plants in rose and heath families, also reports for oak, willow, and hornbeam. **FLIGHT:** July to early Aug. in North, May in South (1 brood). **RANGE:** N.S. and Me. west across s. Canada to cen. Man., south to cen. Fla., e. Texas, and s. Colo. **HABITAT:** Deciduous forest openings and edges, prairie copses, acid barrens, swamp woods, etc. **REMARKS:** Widespread but seldom abundant.

SOUTHERN HAIRSTREAK *Satyrium favonius* **PL. 13**
1 5/16–1 1/2 in. (24–38 mm). Highly variable over geographic range, especially in amount of orange above and below. Tailed. Underside: Hindwing is gray-brown with *narrow orange cap* on blue tail-

SOUTHERN HAIRSTREAK

spot, and postmedian line with *white-edged black* W near inner margin. Along south Atlantic coast and peninsular Fla., the butterfly has longer tails and more extensive orange and blue markings on the hindwing underside. **SIMILAR SPECIES:** (1) Gray Hairstreak has hindwing underside grayer, blue tail-spot indistinct, lacks W in postmedian line. (2) White M Hairstreak upperside is iridescent blue, and underside of hindwing has prominent white spot on costal margin and white M mark near tail. **EARLY STAGES:** Caterpillar is pale green with a narrow dark green median stripe, lateral oblique green stripes, and a yellow stripe along each side. **FOOD:** Various oaks. **FLIGHT:** Mid-March to early July (1 brood). **RANGE:** S. New England and Atlantic Coast west to cen. Ill., se. Colo., and cen. Ariz., south to peninsular Florida, the Gulf Coast, and s. Texas. **HABITAT:** A variety of woods or edges with evergreen or deciduous oaks, oak hammocks in Deep South. **REMARKS:** These southern populations were previously considered to be a species separate from more northern and western butterflies, which were called *Satyrium favonius ontario*, the Northern Hairstreak.

TROPICAL GREEN HAIRSTREAKS: GENUS *Cyanophrys*

This is a group of similar tropical butterflies that are green on the underside and steely blue or brown on the upperside. They are usually tailed, but some species lack tails.

CLENCH'S GREENSTREAK *Cyanophrys miserabilis*   PL. 13
⅞–1 1⁄16 in. (23–27 mm). Locally common in lower Rio Grande Valley. *Face brown.* Upperside: Steel blue. Underside: Yellow-green, with several *red-brown submarginal spots* on hindwing outer margin. Hindwings *tailed*. **SIMILAR SPECIES:** (1) Goodson's Greenstreak has green face and is tailless; hindwing underside has only one red-brown spot at anal angle. (2) Tropical Greenstreak nearly identical to Clench's Greenstreak but face is green and hindwing underside has only a single red-brown spot at anal angle. **EARLY STAGES:** Not reported. **FOOD:** *Parkinsonia aculeata*. **FLIGHT:** April–Dec. (2–3 broods), from Feb. in Cen. America. **RANGE:** S. Texas and n. Mexico south through Cen. America to Costa Rica. **HABITAT:** Seasonally dry subtropical woodland and thorn scrub.

GOODSON'S GREENSTREAK *Cyanophrys goodsoni*   PL. 13
⅞–1 1⁄16 in. (22–27 mm). *Face green.* Underside: Hindwing with only a *single red-brown spot* at anal angle. Hindwing tailless. **SIMILAR SPECIES:** Clench's Greenstreak is tailed; hindwing underside has more than one red-brown submarginal spot. **EARLY STAGES:** Not reported. **FOOD:** *Rivinia humilis*. **FLIGHT:** May to Dec. in s. Texas,

from Feb. in Cen. America. **RANGE:** S. Texas and e. Mexico south to Guanacaste Province, Costa Rica. **HABITAT:** Seasonally dry tropical forest edges and thorn scrub.

TROPICAL GREENSTREAK   PL. 13
Cyanophrys herodotus

⅞–1 1/16 in. (22–27 mm). Rare vagrant to s. Texas. *Face green.* Underside: Green. Hindwing has only a *single red-brown spot* at anal angle. *Tailed.* Reliably identified only by experts. **SIMILAR SPECIES:** (1) Clench's Greenstreak has brown face and several red-brown spots at anal angle of hindwing. (2) Goodson's Greenstreak lacks tails. **EARLY STAGES:** Not reported. **FLIGHT:** Late May to late Oct. in s. Texas, all year in Mexico and Cen. America. **RANGE:** Mexico from Sinaloa and Tamaulipas south through Cen. America and South America to Brazil. **HABITAT:** Seasonally wet and dry tropical forest and associated edges.

Cedar Hairstreaks and Elfins: Genus *Callophrys* Scudder

This is a group of North American butterflies whose species feed on either conifers in the cypress group or on mistletoes. Our species are green with white marks on the underside. They are very similar, but each is restricted to different host plants. Adults usually perch directly on the host but occasionally visit flowers or moist mud or sand.

JUNIPER HAIRSTREAK *Callophrys gryneus*   PL. 13

1 1/16–1 1/4 in. (27–32 mm). Tailed. Underside: Forewing postmedian *white spot row aligned.* Hindwing *apple green* (eastern) to *yellow-green* (western) with 2 *white antemedian spots*, and outer margin with white trim (eastern) or with irregular postmedian white line

edged inwardly with red-brown (western). **SIMILAR SPECIES:** Hessel's Hairstreak found only on Atlantic White-cedar. Underside is more blue-green, with white lines more broken into spots and surrounded by more extensive brown. **EARLY STAGES:** Caterpillar green with subdorsal oblique white or yellow bars along each side. **FOOD:** Redcedar, junipers. **FLIGHT:** May–Aug. in North, Mar.–July in West, Feb.–Sept. in South (2 broods). **RANGE:** New England and s. Ont. west to s. B.C., s. Calif., and nw. Mexico, south to n. peninsular Fla. and cen. La. **HABITAT:** Old fields, bluffs, juniper forests, and breaks. **REMARKS:** Formerly considered a species separate from the Juniper Hairstreak (*Callophrys siva*). The occurrence of hybrid populations in w. Texas and s. N.M. indicates that *gryneus* and *siva* should be treated as a single widespread, variable species. Sweadner's Hairstreak (*Callophrys gryneus sweadneri*), found in peninsular Florida, may be distinct enough to be considered a separate species. Usually found by tapping redcedars or junipers with a net handle or pole.

HESSEL'S HAIRSTREAK *Callophrys hesseli*   **PL. 13**

1–1 ⅛ in. (26–28 mm). Tailed. Underside: *Blue-green* with *patches of red-brown* surrounding white spot lines. Forewing has *costal white spot* in postmedian spot row *set outwardly*. **SIMILAR SPECIES:** Juniper Hairstreak is much commoner. Its underside is apple green to yellow-green, without patches of red-brown near white spot lines; forewing has costal white spot in postmedian row set inward. **EARLY STAGES:** Caterpillar is dark blue-green with oblique white bars along the sides. **FOOD:** Atlantic White-cedar. **FLIGHT:** Late May (1 brood) in New England, mid-April to late July (2 broods) to South. **RANGE:** Very local. Atlantic coastal plain from s. Me. south and west to cen. Ga.; peninsular Fla. on Gulf Coast. **HABITAT:** Atlantic White-cedar swamps and associated barrens. Local and often difficult to observe closely.

XAMI HAIRSTREAK *Callophrys xami*

¾–1¼ in. (19–32 mm). Tailed. Underside: Hindwing is *yellow-green*, with postmedian white line *formed into a W* toward tails. **SIMILAR SPECIES:** Silver-banded Hairstreak hindwing underside has broad silver-white postmedian line and hoary patch on outer margin. **EARLY STAGES:** Caterpillar is yellow-green with rose markings. **FOOD:** Succulents, including *Echeveria*. **FLIGHT:** April–Dec. **RANGE:** Cen. Texas and se. Ariz. south to Guatemala. **HABITAT:** Rocky slopes and canyons, levees.

BROWN ELFIN *Callophrys augustinus*

¹⁵⁄₁₆–1⅛ in. (24–28 mm). Tailless. Sexes similar. Underside: *Chestnut brown* with irregular dark postmedian line. Hindwing *darker at base*. **SIMILAR SPECIES:** Henry's Elfin hindwing has tail-like extension. Hindwing underside has some white in postmedian line and hoary, white-scaled submarginal patch. **EARLY STAGES:** Caterpillar is bright green with a yellow-green dorsal stripe and oblique lateral stripes and dashes. **FOOD:** Primarily plants in the heath family. **FLIGHT:** May–July in north; mid-March to mid-April in south (1 brood). **RANGE:** Much of boreal North America. Lab. and Nfld. west through prairie provinces, north to w. N.W. Terr. and s. Yukon, south in Appalachians to n. Ga. and n. Ala. Absent from Midwest and plains. South through western mountain archipelago to Chihuahua and Baja Calif. Norte. **HABITAT:** Acid soil habitats with heath family plants—barrens, bogs, mixed conifer woods, sandy coasts.

HOARY ELFIN *Callophrys polios*

⅞–1⅛ in. (22–28 mm). Small. Tailless. Sexes similar. Underside: Forewing has *irregular white postmedian line* and white "frosted"

Brown Elfin. Male perching. Lebanon State Forest, N.J. The elfins, harbingers of spring, usually perch on or near to their caterpillar hosts. Brown Elfins use various heaths and often nectar at their flowers.

Hoary Elfin. Male perching on ground, Rocky Mt. National Park, Colo. Adults spend most of their time perching on or near Bearberry, also called Kinnikinnick, a matlike shrub. They use their dark colors to absorb the sun's rays early in spring.

outer margin. Hindwing has *outer half frosted light gray*. **SIMILAR SPECIES:** (1) Frosted Elfin and (2) Henry's Elfin are larger, have tail-like extensions on their hindwings. **EARLY STAGES:** Caterpillar is green. **FOOD:** Bearberry, probably also Trailing Arbutus. **FLIGHT:** April–May, occasionally early June (1 brood). **RANGE:** Much of boreal North America. N.S. and Me. south to N.J., south in Appalachians to Va., west across Great Lakes region and s. prairie provinces, thence north to Yukon and Alaska. South in Rockies to n. N.M. and along Pacific Coast to n. Calif. **HABITAT:** Sunny glades in barrens, dunes, forest edges, rocky ridges. Colonies are very local.

FROSTED ELFIN *Callophrys irus*   PL. 14
1–1¼ in. (26–32 mm). Tailed. Sexes similar. Underside: Forewing has *irregular postmedian line*. Hindwing postmedian line faint,

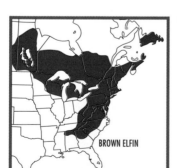

BROWN ELFIN

HOARY ELFIN

and with *black* submarginal *spot above tail*. **SIMILAR SPECIES:** (1) Henry's Elfin underside has forewing submarginal line straight; hindwing has stronger postmedian line and lacks submarginal black spot. (2) Hoary Elfin has marginal gray-white area. **EARLY STAGES:** Caterpillar is pale blue-green with 3 whitish dorsal lines, whitish oblique dashes, and whitish lateral line. **FOOD:** Wild indigo and lupine, occasionally Blue False Lupine and rattlebox. **FLIGHT:** In North mid-May to early June (1 brood); mid-March to April in South. **RANGE:** S. Me. west across N.Y., s. Ont., and s. Mich. to cen. Wis. and ne. Ill., south along Atlantic Coast and Appalachians to n. Ala. and Ga. Isolated population (*C. i. hadros*) in e. Texas, nw. La., and sw. Ark. **HABITAT:** Edges and fields near woods and scrub.

HENRY'S ELFIN *Callophrys henrici*   PL. 14

1 – 1 ³⁄₁₆ in. (26–30 mm). Tailed. Sexes similar. Upperside: Male is the only elfin to *lack forewing stigma*. Underside: Forewing has *postmedian line relatively straight*; hindwing with some *white* in postmedian line, especially at costal and inner margins. **SIMILAR SPECIES:** (1) Frosted Elfin male has stigma on forewing; forewing below has irregular postmedian line, and hindwing postmedian line is faint and never has white. There is a black spot above tail at anal angle. (2) Hoary Elfin lacks tails and has white "frosted" area on hindwing below. **EARLY STAGES:** Caterpillars are light green or redbrown with lighter lateral bars and stripes. **FOOD:** Redbud, huckleberries, hollies, viburnum, Mexican Buckeye (*Ungnadia speciosa*), persimmon. Usually only one host in any area, but several used in central Texas. **FLIGHT:** Mid-Feb. to late May (1 brood). **RANGE:** E. North America from N.S. and Me. west through s. Que. and cen. Ont. to se. Man. south to cen. peninsular Fla., the Gulf Coast and Texas. **HABITAT:** Edges and openings in barrens, wooded swamps, etc.

FROSTED ELFIN

HENRY'S ELFIN

BOG ELFIN   *Callophrys lanoraieensis*   **PL. 14**

⅞–1⁵⁄₁₆ in. (22–24 mm). Small. Tailless. Underside: Hindwing has *pattern reduced* and outer margin *frosted gray*. **SIMILAR SPECIES:** (1) Eastern Pine Elfin and (2) Western Pine Elfin are larger with more complex banding. The Eastern is not likely to be found in same habitat, while the Western Pine Elfin is extremely rare in Me. **EARLY STAGES:** Caterpillar green with a wide white lateral stripe. **FOOD:** Black Spruce. **FLIGHT:** Mid-May to early June (1 brood). **RANGE:** N.B. south through coastal Me. to e. N.H. Isolated populations in e. Ont., s. Que., and N.S. **HABITAT:** Black Spruce–tamarack bogs.

EASTERN PINE ELFIN   *Callophrys niphon*   **PL. 14**

1⅛–1¼ in. (28–32 mm). Tailless. Sexes similar. Underside: Hindwing has submarginal *gray band* just outside of *black inverted crescents*. **SIMILAR SPECIES:** (1) Bog Elfin is smaller, has reduced pattern, and frosted outer margin on underside of hindwing. (2) Western Pine Elfin hindwing underside lacks gray submarginal band and has strong zigzag submarginal dark band. **EARLY STAGES:** Caterpillar is pale green with 2 cream stripes along each side. **FOOD:** Pines such as Scrub, White, and Jack pines. **FLIGHT:** Early March (Ga., Texas) or late April through June (1 brood). **RANGE:** S. Canada from N.S. and N.B. west to n. Alta. Eastern U.S. south to n. Fla., the Gulf Coast, and e. Texas. **HABITAT:** Fields, edges, or openings with small to medium pines.

WESTERN PINE ELFIN   *Callophrys eryphon*   **PL. 14**

1⅛–1⁵⁄₁₆ in. (29–33 mm). Tailless. Sexes similar. Underside: Both wings have strongly *jagged submarginal dark bands*. **SIMILAR SPECIES:** Eastern Pine Elfin has gray band just outside inverted crescents on underside of hindwing, and submarginal dark bands are less jagged. **EARLY STAGES:** Caterpillar is very similar to that of the East-

Eastern Pine Elfin. Female nectaring at fleabane, Fairfax Co., Va. The eggs are laid on the tips of young pine foliage and the striped caterpillars blend well while eating the needles. The males perch and seek females all day.

ern Pine Elfin. **FOOD:** Young leaves of hard pines such as Yellow Pine, also Black Spruce. **FLIGHT:** Mid-May to early June (1 brood). **RANGE:** W. North America from cen. B.C. and cen. Alta. east to cen. Ont., n. Mich., and Me. Isolated population in N.W. Terr. **HABITAT:** Black Spruce bogs, pine woods. **REMARKS:** Although eastern populations that feed on Black Spruce are considered a geographical form of the Western Pine Elfin, this arrangement is uncertain. They may be a geographical form of the Bog Elfin or a distinct species.

WHITE M HAIRSTREAK *Parrhasius m-album* PL. 15

1 ¼–1 ⅝ in. (32–41 mm). Tailed. Upperside: *Iridescent blue.* Underside: Gray-brown; hindwing with white, black-edged postmedian line forming a *white* M (or W) near anal angle; small *white spot on costa* near base. **SIMILAR SPECIES:** (1) Great Purple Hairstreak is black below, abdomen red-orange. Tails double and long. (2) Southern Hairstreak upperside is brown, not blue, and has an extensive submarginal orange patch on hindwing underside. **EARLY STAGES:** Caterpillar is green with a dark dorsal stripe and dark green oblique lateral stripes. **FOOD:** Oaks. **FLIGHT:** Feb.–Oct. in south (3 broods, 4 in Fla.). **RANGE:** Se. U.S. from Conn., Pa., se. Iowa, and Mo. south to peninsular Fla., Gulf Coast, and e. Texas. Rare

WHITE M HAIRSTREAK

AZIA HAIRSTREAK

vagrant north to s. Ont., Mich., and Wis. Related butterflies occur in the mountains of Cen. America and South America. **HABITAT:** Various woods with broad-leafed trees.

AQUAMARINE HAIRSTREAK *Oenomaus ortygnus* **NOT SHOWN**
1⅛–1½ in. (29–37 mm). Rare vagrant to s. Texas. Large. Tailed. Underside: Gray with pinkish sheen. Hindwing with 3 *or 4 black spots*. *No* postmedian or submarginal lines. **EARLY STAGES:** Not reported. **FOOD:** Buds, flowers, and fruits of *Annona*. **FLIGHT:** Mid-Dec. in s. Texas, Jan.-Nov. in Mexico. **RANGE:** Mexico from Tamaulipas south through Cen. America to Brazil. **HABITAT:** Wet and dry tropical forests from sea level to 1,000 m.

ECHION HAIRSTREAK *Tmolus echion* **PL. 13**
¹⁵⁄₁₆–1 in. (24–26 mm). Rare vagrant to s. Texas. Tailed. Underside: Pale gray; irregular *orange* postbasal and postmedian *spot rows*. **SIMILAR SPECIES:** Silver-banded Hairstreak is smaller; forewing underside has median dash. **EARLY STAGES:** Not reported. **FOOD:** A wide variety of tropical plants. **FLIGHT:** May in s. Texas, all year in Mexico. **RANGE:** Mexico south from Sinaloa and Tamaulipas, Cen. America and South America to Brazil. Strays to lower Rio Grande Valley, Texas. **HABITAT:** Open scrubby areas, wood edges. **REMARKS:** This butterfly was introduced to Hawaii to control lantana.

AZIA HAIRSTREAK *Ministrymon azia* **PL. 13**
⅞–¹⁵⁄₁₆ in. (22–24 mm). Tailed. Tiny. Underside: Gray. Hindwing with *narrow orange white-edged postmedian line*. **EARLY STAGES:** Not reported. **FOOD:** Plants in pea family, *Mimosa malacophylla* in lower Rio Grande Valley. **FLIGHT:** March–Sept.; flies all year in most of the tropics; broods not determined. **RANGE:** S. Texas, s. Fla. and

CLYTIE HAIRSTREAK

Keys, south through the West Indies, Mexico, and Cen. America to s. Brazil. **HABITAT:** Subtropical thorn scrub.

CLYTIE HAIRSTREAK *Ministrymon clytie*   PL. 14

¾–⅞ in. (19–22 mm). Small. Tailed. Underside: Pale gray. Forewing has *orange median dash*. Hindwing has both postbasal and postmedian *orange lines*. **SIMILAR SPECIES:** Echion Hairstreak is larger, and underside of hindwing has series of spots, not dashes. **EARLY STAGES:** Not reported. **FOOD:** Legumes, especially *Prosopis reptans* in s. Texas. **FLIGHT:** Feb.–Dec. in s. Texas. **RANGE:** S. Texas south through Mexico to nw. Costa Rica, possibly Venezuela. **HABITAT:** Openings in various tropical forests.

TEPHRAEUS HAIRSTREAK *Siderus tephraeus*   NOT SHOWN

⅞–1⅛ in. (22–28 mm). Rare stray to s. Texas. Upperside: Male *iridescent blue*; forewing with apical 1/3 black; large *oval sex patch* in cell, divided black and brown. Female dull blue; forewing apex blackish. Underside: Pale gray; submarginal and postmedian areas with *white streaks* barely contrasting with ground. **EARLY STAGES:** Not reported. **FLIGHT:** Nov. in s. Texas; although it may fly throughout the year, specific records are May–Dec. in Mexico. **RANGE:** Mexico south to Brazil. **HABITAT:** Tropical lowland forests, especially along rivers. Has strayed to lower Rio Grande Valley, Texas.

EARLY HAIRSTREAK *Erora laetus*   PL. 15

⅞–1⅟₁₆ in. (22–24 mm). Tailless. Upperside: Black and blue. Female has most blue. Underside: *Jade green or gray-green*; hindwing has irregular *orange postmedian line* and submarginal row of *small orange spots*. **EARLY STAGES:** Caterpillar varies from pale green to rusty brown, has reddish, brown, and dark green patches. **FOOD:** Beaked Hazel and beech. **FLIGHT:** April–early Sept. (2 broods, 3 in South). **RANGE:** The Maritime Provinces west across s. Que. and s. Ont. to n. Mich. and n. Wis., south along the Appalachians to Tenn. and N.C. Extremely rare in most locations. **HABITAT:** Deciduous or mixed woods—often found along dirt roads or open ridgetops.

RED-BANDED HAIRSTREAK *Calycopis cecrops*   PL. 13

1⁵⁄₁₆–1³⁄₁₆ in. (24–30 mm). Tailed. Underside: Both wings are gray-brown with *postmedian line edged inwardly with red-orange*. **SIMILAR SPECIES:** Dusky-blue Groundstreak has thinner red-orange edging and has larger red cap on black eyespot between tails. **EARLY STAGES:** Caterpillar is identical to that of Dusky-blue Groundstreak and develops very slowly. **FOOD:** Fallen leaves of sumacs, Wax Myrtle, and oaks. **FLIGHT:** April to early Oct. (2 broods), all year in peninsular Fla. **RANGE:** Se. U.S. from Long I. west to Mo. and se. Kans. south through entire area to s. Texas. Strays north to Mich. and e. Nebr. **HABITAT:** Overgrown fields, coastal hammocks, edges.

DUSKY-BLUE GROUNDSTREAK *Calycopis isobeon*   PL. 13

⅞–1¼ in (22–33 mm). Tailed. Underside: Both wings gray-brown with postmedian line *edged narrowly* on inner edge with *red-orange*. Eyespot at anal angle of hindwing with orange equal to black. **SIMILAR SPECIES:** Red-banded Hairstreak has broader red-orange edging on postmedian line below, and eyespot at anal angle has more black than orange. **EARLY STAGES:** Caterpillar is dark brown; has 2 black dorsal lines and long dark brown hairs. **FOOD:** Dead leaves, fruits, and detritus on ground, especially under trees in Anacardium family. **FLIGHT:** Jan.–April, June–July, Sept. in Texas, Mexico. **RANGE:** Cen. and s. Texas south through Mexico and Cen. America to n. South America (Venezuela). Strays east to Miss.

EARLY HAIRSTREAK

RED-BANDED HAIRSTREAK

Red-banded Hairstreak. Adult perching on foliage. Fairfax Co., Va. Eggs are usually laid on dead leaves, which the blackish caterpillars eat. This is a most unusual diet for butterflies.

and north to Kans. **HABITAT:** Lowland forest edges, valley bottoms. **REMARKS:** Some individuals in s. Texas appear to be intergrades between this species and the Red-banded Hairstreak, suggesting that they are the same species.

RUDDY HAIRSTREAK *Electrostrymon sangala* PL. 13
⅞–1 in. (22–26 mm). Tailed. Upperside: *Orange and black.* Underside: Pale brown; hindwing has *postmedian line very thin.* **SIMILAR SPECIES:** (1) Muted Hairstreak male lacks sharply cut dorsal pattern. Females indistinguishable without capture and dissection. (2) Dusky-blue Groundstreak underside has broader postmedian band, grayer ground color. **EARLY STAGES:** Not reported. **FOOD:** Flowers of *Erythrina tristan* (Costa Rica). **FLIGHT:** Dec.–April, June–July, Sept. in Cen. America (3 broods?). **RANGE:** S. Texas and Mexico south through Cen. America to South America (Venezuela). **HABITAT:** Tropical semideciduous river forest, edges.

DUSKY-BLUE GROUNDSTREAK

FULVOUS HAIRSTREAK *Electrostrymon angelia* PL. 13
¾–1⅛ in. (18–28 mm). Small. Tailed. Upperside: Red-orange, bordered by black. Underside: Hindwing gray-brown with *white-edged black postmedian line*, and *large eyespot* near anal angle. **EAR-LY STAGES:** Caterpillar red-brown with bluish tinge. **FOOD:** Brazilian Pepper. **FLIGHT:** Jan. to mid-Nov. **RANGE:** S. Fla. and Keys, West Indies. **HABITAT:** Tropical hardwood hammock edges.

MUTED HAIRSTREAK *Electrostrymon canus* **NOT SHOWN**
¹⁵⁄₁₆–1³⁄₁₆ in. (24–30 mm). Previously confounded with Ruddy Hairstreak. Tailed. Like Ruddy Hairstreak but male with upper surface *pale orange-brown*; female inseparable from that of Ruddy Hairstreak. **SIMILAR SPECIES:** See (1) Ruddy Hairstreak. (2) Dusky-blue Groundstreak has underside grayer with narrower post-median bands. **EARLY STAGES:** Not reported. **FOOD:** Flowers of *Psiguria racemosa* and mangos (*Mangifera indica*), both in Venezuela. **FLIGHT:** April–Aug., Dec.–Jan. in Cen. America (3 broods?). **RANGE:** S. Tex. south through Mexico, Cen. America, and South America to Peru. **HABITAT:** Edges and openings in semideciduous tropical river forests.

Scrub-Hairstreaks: Genus *Strymon* Hübner

This is a primarily tropical group with a number of species along the U.S.-Mexico boundary. Most species are gray on the upperside, with distinctively patterned hindwings on the underside. The Gray Hairstreak is our most widespread hairstreak and one of the most catholic in its choice of host plants. Legumes, mallows, and crotons are frequent host plant choices by scrub-hairstreaks.

GRAY HAIRSTREAK *Strymon melinus* PLS. 3, 15

1 ⅛–1 ⅜ in. (28–34 mm). Our most widespread hairstreak. Tailed. Upperside: Navy gray. Underside: Paler gray (except for dark spring/fall form). Hindwing postmedian line often *edged inwardly with orange*, usually *relatively straight*. SIMILAR SPECIES: (1) Southern Hairstreak has upperside of both wings with orange patches. Underside browner, usually with more submarginal orange. (2) Balloon Vine Hairstreak underside hindwing has postmedian line orange and white, without black; whitish submarginal dashes. EARLY STAGES: Caterpillar extremely variable, ranging from green to yellow to red-brown with oblique marks of various colors. FOOD: Flowers and fruits of an almost infinite variety of plants, most often from pea and mallow families. FLIGHT: Late May through Sept. in North (2 broods), mid-Feb. through Nov. in South. RANGE: U.S. and s. Canada south through Mexico and Cen. America to South America. Must recolonize northern portions of range each spring and summer. HABITAT: A wide variety of open, sunny situations with suitable host plants.

RED-CRESCENT SCRUB-HAIRSTREAK PL. 15
Strymon rufofusca

1–1 ⅛ in. (26–28 mm). Underside: Hindwing gray, postmedian line *red-orange*, broken into *short dashes*. SIMILAR SPECIES: Red-lined Scrub-Hairstreak is larger, with hindwing underside postmedian line more continuous. EARLY STAGES: Not reported. FOOD: *Malvastrum*. FLIGHT: July, late Oct. through late Dec. in s. Texas; all year in neotropics. RANGE: S. Texas south through Mexico, Cen. America, and South America to Argentina; also found on Grenada. HABITAT: Open weedy fields and pastures.

Gray Hairstreak. Adult perching. Solano Co., Calif. This is our widest ranging hairstreak, whose caterpillars feed on a wide range of plants. Spring and fall adults are smaller and much darker than this summer individual.

RED-LINED SCRUB-HAIRSTREAK *Strymon bebrycia* **PL. 15**

1–1 3/16 (25–30 mm). Underside: Hindwing gray with white submarginal spots and postmedian line *red-orange, lined outwardly with white*. **SIMILAR SPECIES:** Gray Hairstreak hindwing underside postmedian line usually has some black and relatively little orange. **EARLY STAGES:** Not reported. **FOOD:** Balloon vine (*Cardiospermum*). **FLIGHT:** Feb., June, Sept. to Dec. in s. Texas (3 broods?). **RANGE:** Mexico from Sonora and Nuevo Leon south through Cen. America to nw. Costa Rica. Rare vagrant to s. Ariz. and s. Texas. **HABITAT:** Subtropical thorn scrub.

MARTIAL SCRUB-HAIRSTREAK *Strymon martialis* **PL. 15**

1 1/8–1 3/8 in. (28–34 mm). Upperside: Both sexes black with some blue. Underside: Hindwing gray with strong *black and white postmedian line*; submarginal *orange eyespot large and blurred*, smudged. Submarginal black line extending parallel to outer margin, often mixed with orange scales. **SIMILAR SPECIES:** Bartram's Scrub-Hairstreak upperside dark gray. Hindwing underside more clean-cut, submarginal line straight, 2 basal white spots, and large orange anal eyespot. **EARLY STAGES:** Caterpillar is dull green with short white hairs on the back. **FOOD:** Florida Trema and Bay Cedar. **FLIGHT:** Feb.–Dec.; generations not determined. **RANGE:** S. Fla. and Keys, West Indies. **HABITAT:** Fields and sunny areas near coast.

YOJOA SCRUB-HAIRSTREAK *Strymon yojoa* **PL. 15**

7/8–1 1/4 in. (22–31 mm). Rare vagrant to s. Texas. Upperside: Gray. Underside: Gray with faint *irregular postmedian line* bounding submarginal *gray-white band*. **SIMILAR SPECIES:** Lacey's Scrub-Hairstreak is small; hindwing underside has complex pattern but lacks submarginal gray-white band. **EARLY STAGES:** Not reported. **FOOD:** A

MARTIAL SCRUB-HAIRSTREAK

BARTRAM'S SCRUB-HAIRSTREAK

wide variety of tropical plants. **FLIGHT:** Late Oct. to mid-Dec. in s. Texas, all year in neotropics. **RANGE:** Mexico south from Tamaulipas through Cen. America to s. Brazil. **HABITAT:** Lightly disturbed areas, scrub.

WHITE SCRUB-HAIRSTREAK *Strymon albata* **PL. 15**
1 ⅛–1 ⁵⁄₁₆ in. (28–33 mm). Upperside: Both wings with extensive white patches. Underside: Hindwing *pale gray* with faint postmedian line; anal *eyespot without orange*. **SIMILAR SPECIES:** Yojoa Scrub-Hairstreak upperside is darker gray and has contrasting gray-white submarginal band. Underside is similar. **EARLY STAGES:** Not reported. **FOOD:** *Abutilon*. **FLIGHT:** June–Dec. (2 broods?). **RANGE:** S. Tex. (rarely) and Mexico south through Cen. America to Colombia and Venezuela. **HABITAT:** Shrubby fields and second growth in seasonally dry tropical lowlands.

BARTRAM'S SCRUB-HAIRSTREAK *Strymon acis* **PL. 15**
¹⁵⁄₁₆–1 ⅛ in. (24–28 mm). Distinctive. Underside: Hindwing has straight *bold white postmedian line lined with black*, large orange submarginal eyespot, and 2 *white basal spots*. **SIMILAR SPECIES:** Martial Scrub-Hairstreak hindwing underside lacks the 2 basal white spots, postmedian band is less distinctive. **EARLY STAGES:** Caterpillar variable — green-white, yellow-green, or yellow-tan covered with short tan setae; body with pale bumps, light lateral lines, and a dark middorsal band edged with white. **FOOD:** Narrow-leafed Croton. **FLIGHT:** Feb.–Nov. (3–4 generations). **RANGE:** S. Fla. and the Keys, West Indies. **HABITAT:** Openings in pine forests.

LACEY'S SCRUB-HAIRSTREAK *Strymon alea* **PL. 15**
¾–1 ⅛ in. (21–28 mm). Small. Underside: Hindwing is gray with *complex pattern* — postbasal *blotches*, irregular brown postmedian *line*, submarginal band of *small, brown triangular spots*. **SIMILAR SPECIES:** Mallow Scrub-Hairstreak hindwing underside has small, round, black basal spot and postmedian line of separate black spots. **EARLY STAGES:** Not reported. **FOOD:** *Bernardia*. **FLIGHT:** April–Dec. (4 broods?). **RANGE:** Cen. and s. Texas south through Mexico to nw. Costa Rica. **HABITAT:** Subtropical thorn scrub.

MALLOW SCRUB-HAIRSTREAK *Strymon istapa* **PL. 14**
⅞–1 ³⁄₁₆ in. (22–30 mm). Small. Underside: Hindwing is gray with *single round, black basal spot* on costa; postmedian line of small *black spots*. Tails short. **SIMILAR SPECIES:** Disguised Scrub-Hairstreak has pointed forewing; hindwing underside has 2 basal spots. **EARLY STAGES:** Caterpillar is green with a darker dorsal line and a dirty white patch near the head. **FOOD:** Mallows. **FLIGHT:** All year, broods not determined. **RANGE:** Peninsular Fla., s. Texas, s. Ariz., and s.

Calif. south through Mexico and Cen. America to South America. **HABITAT:** Open waste areas, roadsides, and weedy pastures.

DISGUISED SCRUB-HAIRSTREAK *Strymon limenia*   **PL. 14**
$^{15}/_{16}$–1 $^{3}/_{16}$ in. (24–30 mm). Has not been found on Fla. Keys since 1976. Forewing pointed. Underside: Hindwing is brown with 2 *basal black spots* and postmedian line also of *black spots*. **SIMILAR SPECIES:** Mallow Scrub-Hairstreak has underside of hindwing gray with a single black basal spot. **EARLY STAGES:** Not reported. **FLIGHT:** April, May, Dec. (2 broods?). **RANGE:** Fla. Keys, West Indies. **HABITAT:** Weedy openings and fields.

TAILLESS SCRUB-HAIRSTREAK *Strymon cestri*   **PL. 15**
$^{7}/_{8}$–1 $^{1}/_{8}$ in. (22–29 mm). Tailless. Forewing apex *squared off*. Underside: Hindwing is *marbled gray and white*, with black submarginal spot on outer margin. **SIMILAR SPECIES:** Lantana Scrub-Hairstreak has forewing more pointed; hindwing underside lacks submarginal black spot. **EARLY STAGES:** Not reported. **FLIGHT:** March, Oct. in s. Texas. **RANGE:** S. Texas south through Mexico to Guanacaste Province, Costa Rica. **HABITAT:** Seasonal mid-elevation tropical forests and edges.

LANTANA SCRUB-HAIRSTREAK *Strymon bazochii*   **PL. 15**
$^{15}/_{16}$–1 in. (24–26 mm). Tailless. Underside: Hindwing with prominent postbasal *costal spot*; dark *apical and basal patches*. **SIMILAR SPECIES:** Tailless Scrub-Hairstreak has squared-off forewing apex; underside of hindwing has a submarginal black spot. **EARLY STAGES:** Caterpillar is dull green. **FOOD:** Flowering parts of lantana, lippias, and several mints. **FLIGHT:** May–Dec. (2–3 broods). **RANGE:** S. Texas

MALLOW SCRUB-HAIRSTREAK

WESTERN PYGMY-BLUE

and Mexico, Cen. America, and South America to Paraguay; Greater Antilles. Introduced into Hawaii to control lantana. **HABITAT:** Openings in subtropical thorn scrub.

BLUES: SUBFAMILY POLYOMMATINAE

Blues are tiny to small butterflies found throughout the world, but they are most diverse in Southeast Asia, tropical Africa, and north temperate regions. Although 32 species are found in North America, there are only two widespread species (Eastern Tailed-Blue and Spring Azure) in most of the East. Adult males are predominantly blue above, while females and males of a few species are predominantly brown. The blue of the males is due to reflected light rather than pigmentation. Below, the wings are usually gray-white with black spots or streaks. Adults are usually found near their host plants, and they do not fly long distances. Our tropical and subtropical species (*Brephidium*, *Hemiargus*, and *Leptotes*) are exceptional, since their species may undertake long migrations and are often long-distance colonists. Adult males are frequent visitors to moist sand or mud, and the adults avidly visit flowers for nectar. Eggs are laid singly on host plant leaves or flowers. The caterpillars usually feed on external plant parts, but those of some species bore into succulent host plants. Caterpillars have glands that secrete sugary secretions to attract ants. The caterpillars of some species are raised in ant nests. Host plants occur in many plant families, but legumes are frequent choices. The winter is usually passed by the pupal stage, but for tropical species development may be continuous with adults overwintering.

WESTERN PYGMY-BLUE *Brephidium exile*   **PL. 15**
⅝–¾ in. (15–19 mm). *Tiny.* Upperside: Both wings with basal blue. Underside: Hindwing is *white at base, fringe mostly white.* **SIMILAR SPECIES:** Eastern Pygmy-Blue has hindwing underside dark brown, fringe dark. **EARLY STAGES:** Caterpillar is yellow-green with many small brown tubercles. **FOOD:** Saltbushes and pigweed. **FLIGHT:** All year in s. Texas, July–Sept. northward. **RANGE:** W. U.S. east to Mo. and Ark., south to n. Mexico. **HABITAT:** Waste areas and deserts.

EASTERN PYGMY-BLUE *Brephidium isophthalma*   **PL. 15**
¾–⅞ in. (19–23 mm). *Tiny.* Underside: *Hindwing and fringes all dark brown.* **SIMILAR SPECIES:** Western Pygmy-Blue has wing fringe mostly white, and base of hindwing beneath is white. **EARLY STAGES:** Caterpillars vary from green to yellow-green with many brown tubercles. **FOOD:** Glassworts. **FLIGHT:** All year in Fla., May–Aug. in

Ga., broods not determined. **RANGE:** South Atlantic coastal plain, peninsular Fla. and Keys, Gulf Coast, West Indies. Stray inland. **HABITAT:** Upper limits of tidal marshes.

CASSIUS BLUE *Leptotes cassius*   PL. 16

¾–¹⁵⁄₁₆ in. (20–33 mm). Upperside: Males pale blue; females with much white. Underside: Both wings have *pale lines broken*; forewing with *blank areas* along inner margin. **SIMILAR SPECIES:** Marine Blue is larger; uppersides of both wings have violet-blue overcast. Undersides of both wings have pale brown lines more continuous. **EARLY STAGES:** Caterpillar is green with a russet overtone. **FOOD:** Ornamental leadwort, Hairy Milk Pea, Lima Bean, rattlebox. **FLIGHT:** All year in s. Fla. and s. Texas, broods not determined. **RANGE:** Fla., including Keys, and Texas south through West Indies, Mexico, and Cen. America to South America. Strays north to S.C., Mo., Kans., and N.M. **HABITAT:** Residential areas, weedy fields, thorn scrub, edges.

MARINE BLUE *Leptotes marina*   PL. 16

1–1⅛ in. (26–28 mm). Upperside: Both wings of male have violet overcast; females lack white. Underside: Forewing with most *pale brown lines continuous* from costa to inner margin. **SIMILAR SPECIES:** Cassius Blue underside has paler lines broken, with blank areas on margin of forewing. Above, the male is blue, and female has extensive white areas. **EARLY STAGES:** Caterpillar is green or brownish with dark brown oblique stripes and spots. **FOOD:** Leadwort and legumes including milk vetch, clover, and Alfalfa. **FLIGHT:** All year in s. Texas, April–Sept. northward. **RANGE:** Southwest south through Mexico to Guatemala. Vagrant and temporary colonist north and east reaching Wis., Ind., Ky., and La. **HABITAT:** Mesquite thorn scrub, town gardens, and waste areas.

MARINE BLUE

MIAMI BLUE

CYNA BLUE *Zizula cyna*   PL. 15

⅝–⅞ in. (16–21 mm). Tiny. Wings rounded. Upperside: Pale violet-blue with broad black borders. Underside: Hindwing pale gray
with *minute black dots*. **EARLY STAGES:** Not reported. **FOOD:** Flower
buds of Acanthaceae. **FLIGHT:** March to early Nov., broods not
determined. **RANGE:** S. Texas south through Mexico, Cen. America,
and South America to Argentina. Strays north to Kans. and n.
Texas. **HABITAT:** Open scrub in desert and subtropics. **REMARKS:**
Apparently not an accidental introduction from Africa, as was
previously believed.

MIAMI BLUE *Hemiargus thomasi*   PL. 15

⅞–1⅛ in. (22–28 mm). Upperside: Female hindwing has *orange
spot* at anal angle. Underside: Both wings have *white submarginal
band*; hindwing anal angle has 2 *eyespots* on outer margin. **SIMILAR
SPECIES:** Ceraunus Blue female upperside hindwing lacks orange
spot. Underside lacks white submarginal band; individuals from
Fla. population have only a single anal eyespot on hindwing
underside. **EARLY STAGES:** Not reported. **FOOD:** Balloon vine, possibly
also *Chiococca*; reared from *Cesalpinia bahamensis* in the
Bahamas. **FLIGHT:** All year in Fla., long winter generation of diapause adults. **RANGE:** Species has become more restricted because
of loss of habitat. S. peninsular Fla. (formerly) and Keys, West
Indies. **HABITAT:** Tropical hardwood hammock openings and edges.

CERAUNUS BLUE *Hemiargus ceraunus*   PL. 15

¾–1⅛ in. (20–28 mm). Underside: Both wings have postmedian
row of dark dashes. Fla. individuals have only one submarginal
eyespot on hindwing (*H. c. antibubastus*); Southwest individuals
have 2 (*H. c. zachaeina*). **SIMILAR SPECIES:** (1) Miami Blue has white
submarginal band and 2 black eyespots at anal angle of hindwing

underside. (2) Reakirt's Blue has forewing underside with post-median chain of prominent round, black spots. **EARLY STAGES:** Caterpillars vary from green to yellow to red, with short silver white hairs. **FOOD:** Flower buds of woody legumes—pea, mimosa, and cesalpinia. **FLIGHT:** All year in s. Fla. and Texas, late summer elsewhere. **RANGE:** Fla. and Keys, s. Texas, and Southwest south through West Indies, Mexico, and Cen. America to South America. Vagrants north to Nev., Kans., Mo., and N.C. **HABITAT:** Thorn scrub, beach dunes, second growth, pastures, etc.

REAKIRT'S BLUE *Hemiargus isola* PL. 15

¾–1⅛ in. (20–28 mm). Forewing *apex sharply cut off*. Underside: Forewing with postmedian row of 5 *prominent round, black spots*. **SIMILAR SPECIES:** Ceraunus Blue has forewing apex rounded, as in most blues, and forewing below has a submarginal row of black dashes instead of rounded black spots. **EARLY STAGES:** Not reported. **FOOD:** Many plants in pea family. **FLIGHT:** March–Nov. (3 broods), all year in s. Texas. **RANGE:** Texas and the Southwest south through Mexico and Cen. America to Costa Rica. Vagrant and warm-season colonist north and east to se. Sask., Wis., Ohio, and Miss. **HABITAT:** Open weedy areas, pastures, fields.

EASTERN TAILED-BLUE *Everes comyntas* PL. 16

¹³⁄₁₆–1⅛ in. (20–29 mm). One of the 2 common, widespread eastern blues. *Tailed.* Upperside: Male iridescent blue, female brown but with much blue at wing base in spring individuals. Underside: Hindwing pale gray with *distinct black spots*, black *bar at end of cell*, 2 *large orange spots* on outer margin, one at tail. **SIMILAR SPECIES:** Western Tailed-Blue often larger; hindwing underside often has black spots lacking or indistinct; lacks bar at end of cell; only single reduced marginal orange spot by tail. **EARLY STAGES:** Caterpillar is

CERAUNUS BLUE

REAKIRT'S BLUE

Eastern Tailed-Blue. Male perching on vegetation, Fairfax Co., Va. One of the East's commonest butterflies. Adults nectar at many small flowered plants. Caterpillars eat flowers of a wide variety of legumes.

dark green with a dark dorsal stripe and faint oblique lateral stripes. **FOOD:** Flowers and young seeds of a wide variety of herbaceous legumes. **FLIGHT:** April or May to Oct. or Nov. in North (3 broods), Feb.–Nov. in South. **RANGE:** E. U.S. and se. Canada extending west to s. Man., w. N.D., cen. Colo., and cen. Texas. Isolated populations in cen. Calif., possibly introduced. Also ranges from w. Texas, w. N.M., and se. Ariz. south through Mexico and Cen. America to Costa Rica. **HABITAT:** Open, sunny, weedy environments.

WESTERN TAILED-BLUE *Everes amyntula* PL. 16
⅞–1⅛ in. (22–28 mm). Tailed. Variable. Underside: Hindwing black *spots lacking or indistinct*, and only a *single reduced orange spot* near tail. **SIMILAR SPECIES:** Eastern Tailed-Blue is usually (but not always) smaller; there are two large orange spots on outer margin, including one near tail; black spots beneath are lacking or indistinct. **EARLY STAGES:** Caterpillars vary from green to yellow-green to straw; they may have pink or maroon marks. **FOOD:** Flowers and young seeds of various legumes, usually those with inflated pods. **FLIGHT:** May–June (1 brood). **RANGE:** W. North America, Alaska south to Baja Calif. Norte, in all western mountains,

extends east across prairie provinces to n. Mich. and Ont. Isolated population on Gaspé Peninsula, Que. **HABITAT:** Open areas with low shrubs, found in native situations much more often than Eastern Tailed-Blue.

Azures: Genus *Celastrina* Tutt

The azures are found throughout the Northern Hemisphere and are all very similar. In North America this may be our most poorly understood group. Before 1972, when it was shown that *Celastrina nigra* was a separate species, we thought there was only one azure. Now we know there are at least three, and very probably there are at least several other sibling host-plant specialists. Our commonest species, *Celastrina argiolus*, is quite variable geographically and seasonally. The caterpillars are tended by ants. The winter is spent in the chrysalis.

SPRING AZURE *Celastrina argiolus* PL. 16

1⅛–1⁵⁄₁₆ in. (29–33 mm). Variable. Sexually dimorphic and seasonally variable. Upperside: *Males blue*; females with at least *some black* on outer portion of forewing. Late spring and summer individuals with *white patches* on hindwing. Underside: Hindwing gray-white with *faint small black spots*, darker gray with larger black spots, or with black-gray margins and blotches in center. **SIMILAR SPECIES:** (1) Appalachian Azure is larger; hindwing underside has pattern reduced but with 2 or 3 submarginal black spots near anal angle. (2) Dusky Azure males have upperside black-gray; hindwing underside of both sexes has full row of distinct submarginal black spots. **EARLY STAGES:** Caterpillars vary from yellow-green to pink with a dark dorsal stripe and oblique lateral stripes.

APPALACHIAN AZURE

FOOD: Flowering parts of dogwoods, Wild Cherry, New Jersey Tea, viburnums, other woody plants, and occasionally some herbaceous plants such as *Collinsia* and *Verbesina virginica*. **FLIGHT:** May–Aug. in Canada (1 or 2 broods) — progressively longer flight southward, late Jan.–Oct. along Gulf Coast. **RANGE:** Most of Canada and the U.S. south of the tundra except peninsular Fla., southern plains, and Texas coast; extends south in mountains to Colombia. **HABITAT:** Deciduous woods and nearby openings or edges. **REMARKS:** Often the first spring butterfly. One of 2 common, widespread eastern blues. Species relationships remain unclear. There may be as many as three species covered by our current concepts.

APPALACHIAN AZURE *Celastrina neglecta-major* **PL. 16**
1 ⁵⁄₁₆–1 ½ in. (33–37 in.). Large. Upperside: Male completely blue. Female *lacks* extensive *white scaling* on hindwing. Underside: Hindwing largely *chalk white*, submarginal row *reduced to 1 or 3 clear-cut black spots*. **SIMILAR SPECIES:** Spring Azure is smaller, hindwing underside grayer, with heavier spotting. Late spring form has white on hindwing upperside. **EARLY STAGES:** Not reported. **FOOD:** Flowering parts of Bugbane (*Cimicifuga racemosa*). **FLIGHT:** Mid-May to early June in Appalachians (1 brood). **RANGE:** Cen. and s. Appalachians from s. Pa. south to ne. Tenn. and n. Ga. Also s. Ohio, cen. Ky., e. Tenn., and sw. Mo. **HABITAT:** Rich, deciduous woods.

DUSKY AZURE *Celastrina ebenina* **PL. 16**
⅞–1 ¼ in. (22–32 mm). Upperside: *Male black-gray*; female dark, *restricted* light areas of *gray-blue*. Underside: Hindwing of both sexes with *black spots* in submarginal row *pronounced*. **SIMILAR**

SPECIES: Spring Azure males are blue above, and females are never as dark as those of the Dusky Azure. **EARLY STAGES:** Caterpillar is whitish blue-green with 1 dorsal and 2 lateral yellow-white stripes. **FOOD:** Young leaves of Goat's Beard. **FLIGHT:** April to early May (1 brood), rarely later in summer. **RANGE:** Southern Appalachians and Ohio River Valley, also cen. Ill. and nw. Ark. **HABITAT:** Shady, rich, deciduous woods.

SILVERY BLUE *Glaucopsyche lygdamus* PL. 16

⅞–1¼ in. (22–32 mm). Upperside: Both wings have pronounced *black margin with white fringe*. Male with bright iridescent silver-blue; female dark with blue basally. Underside: Both wings are gray-brown with submarginal *rows of round, black, white-edged spots*. **EARLY STAGES:** Caterpillars vary from green to purplish with a dark dorsal stripe and white oblique lateral lines. Caterpillars are tended by ants. **FOOD:** Usually vetches, occasionally other legumes. **FLIGHT:** March–June (1 brood); flies later at northern latitudes. **RANGE:** Most of boreal North America south of tundra. Alaska south to Baja Calif. Norte and cen. N.M., east across Canada and Great Lakes region to Que., Nfld., and N.S. Also apparently isolated populations in (1) central and southern Appalachians, (2) Mo. and w. Ark., and (3) w. Kans. and n. Okla. **HABITAT:** Open areas near woods, prairie hills, bogs.

ORANGE-MARGINED BLUES: GENUS *Lycaeides* HÜBNER

This is another Northern Hemisphere group, with most species found in Eurasia. The caterpillars of our species feed on legumes.

DUSKY AZURE

SILVERY BLUE

NORTHERN BLUE *Lycaeides idas*   PL. 16

1 3/16–1 7/16 in. (30–36 mm). Geographically variable. Sexually dimorphic. Upperside: Male blue, female brown with submarginal orange spots. Underside: Hindwing has black terminal line broken into *small spots at vein endings*, submarginal orange *spots reduced*. Reliably identified only by locality and by dissection of male genital structures. SIMILAR SPECIES: Melissa Blue has continuous black subterminal line on underside of both wings. In our area, the two species are never found in the same locality. EARLY STAGES: Not reported for eastern populations. FOOD: Several plants in heath family, including crowberry, laurel, and Labrador Tea. FLIGHT: July to early Aug. (1 brood). RANGE: Holarctic. W. North America from Alaska south to cen. Calif., s. Idaho, and sw. Colo., east across s. Canada to the n. Great Lakes region and ne. Ont. An isolated group of populations in se. Lab., Nfld., s. Que., and N.S. HABITAT: Mixed evergreen forest openings, headlands with low heaths.

MELISSA BLUE *Lycaeides melissa*   PL. 16

1–1 3/8 in. (26–34 mm). Sexes dimorphic. The subspecies Karner Blue (*L. m. samuelis*) is extirpated or endangered in several states. Underside: Both wings have a *continuous black subterminal line*. Red-orange submarginal row either continuous (*L. m. melissa*) or broken into separate spots (*L. m. samuelis*). SIMILAR SPECIES: Northern Blue has the subterminal line broken into small black spots at the vein endings on both wings below. The two species are never found together in our area. EARLY STAGES: Caterpillar is green with short pale lines. The caterpillars are tended by ants. FOOD: Lupine

for Karner Blue, various pea family plants for more western populations. **FLIGHT:** late May–Aug. (2 broods) for Karner Blue, April–Oct. for more western areas (3 broods). **RANGE:** Intermountain West, prairies, and plains east to sw. Minn. and nw. Iowa (*L. m. melissa*), isolated pine barrens populations from Wis. east to cen. N.Y. and s. N.H. (*L. m. samuelis*). **HABITAT:** Pine-oak barrens in East (*L. m. samuelis*), prairies, open weedy areas in West (*L. m. melissa*).

DIADEM BLUES: GENUS *Plebejus* KLUK

Named for the iridescent spots on the outer margin of the hindwing underside, these blues are richest in the West and are also found in Eurasia. The adults are usually found in direct association with their caterpillar host plants. Winter is passed in the chrysalis.

GREENISH BLUE *Plebejus saepiolus*   **PL. 16**

1–1¼ in. (26–32 mm). Sexes dimorphic. Upperside: Males green-blue; females brown with blue at base. Underside: Gray-white with postbasal and submarginal rows of *irregular black spots*. **EARLY STAGES:** Caterpillars green or red. **FOOD:** Flowering parts of various clovers, especially Alsike Clover. **FLIGHT:** Mid-May–July (1 brood). **RANGE:** Boreal w. North America south in mountains to s. Calif. and sw. N.M., east across s. Canada and the n. Great Lakes region to N.B., s. N.S., and n. Me. Expanded range into se. Canada and n. New England after 1912. **HABITAT:** Stream edges, bogs, roadsides, open fields.

GREENISH BLUE

ACMON BLUE

ACMON BLUE *Plebejus acmon*   **PL. 19**
¹⁵⁄₁₆–1⅛ in. (24–29 mm). Sexually dimorphic. Upperside: Males
blue; female brown. The only eastern blue with both sexes having
red-orange submarginal band on hindwing above and below. **SIMI-**
LAR SPECIES: (1) Northern and (2) Melissa blues have males without
orange on upperside; females have submarginal orange on *both*
wings. **EARLY STAGES:** Caterpillar is pale green with coalesced pink
and white stripes along each side. **FOOD:** Flowers and developing
seeds of buckwheats, lupines, and milk vetches. **FLIGHT:** July–Sept.
(1 brood). **RANGE:** W. North America from sw. Canada through all
of the western U.S. (except highest mountain areas) to nw. Mexico east to cen. Great Plains, strays to se. Minn. Once was established in s. N.J. **HABITAT:** Prairie hills, weedy areas, roadsides.

CRANBERRY BLUE *Vacciniina optilete*   **PL. 17**
⅞–1 in. (22–25 mm). Sexually dimorphic. Upperside: Violet-blue;
female marked with dark scales. Underside: Both wings with
strong, *black postmedian spot rows*; hindwing with 1 *black-edged*
orange submarginal *spot* near anal angle. **SIMILAR SPECIES:** Silvery
Blue is iridescent silver-blue on upperside and has round black
white-edged postmedian spots on underside. **EARLY STAGES:** Not
reported. **FOOD:** Cranberries and low blueberries. **FLIGHT:** July (1
brood). **RANGE:** Holarctic. In North America from Alaska east to
cen. N.W. Terr. and nw. Man. **HABITAT:** Spruce bogs in taiga, wet
coniferous woods.

ARCTIC BLUE *Agriades glandon*   **PL. 17**
⅞–1 in. (22–26 mm). Geographically variable. Sexually dimorphic. Forewings pointed. Upperside: Male gray-blue; female or-

CRANBERRY BLUE

ARCTIC BLUE

ange-brown. Underside: Hindwing has postmedian *black spots obsolete or surrounded by white patches* in darker background. **EARLY STAGES:** Not reported. **FLIGHT:** Late June to mid-Aug. **RANGE:** Holarctic. Most of boreal North America, including tundra and Arctic Archipelago. South to cen. Calif., se. Ariz., and cen. N.M., east to Lab. and Nfld. **HABITAT:** Gravelly hills, domes, low ridges.

True Butterflies:
Superfamily Papilionoidea
Metalmarks: Family Riodinidae

With a few exceptions, metalmarks are denizens of tropical latitudes, especially those of the Americas. About 1,300 species are known. Our species are small to medium butterflies. The butterflies vary widely in their patterns, postures, and behavior. The front legs of males are reduced in size and are not used for walking. The adults usually perch with their wings spread open or cocked slightly. The adults of many tropical species habitually perch upside down on the lower surface of large leaves. Males locate their mates by perching in likely sites rather than by patrolling. Adults of our species feed on flower nectar. Eggs are widely variable but are generally sea-urchin–shaped. Caterpillars of our species are slug-shaped and have dense tufts of long fine setae. Pupae are usually stout and without silk. Overwintering is in either the larval or pupal stage.

Scintillant Metalmarks: Genus *Calephelis*
Grote and Robinson

This group is limited to the Americas, with most species found in the tropics. Most of the species are bewilderingly similar, and the taxonomy is in disarray. The adults perch near their host plants with their wings open. The caterpillars have long hairs, and feed on plants in the Family Asteraceae. Winter is passed by the caterpillar.

LITTLE METALMARK *Calephelis virginiensis*   PL. 17
¼–1 in. (12–25 mm). The only metalmark in its range. *Small.*
Upperside: Rusty orange; *fringes dark*, not checkered. **EARLY STAGES:**
Caterpillar is pale green with rows of long white hairs. **FOOD:** Yellow
Thistle. **FLIGHT:** Mid-March to mid-Oct. (3–5 broods). **RANGE:** Se.
Atlantic coastal plain and piedmont from Md. (rarely) south to

Fla., including the Keys, thence west to se. Texas. **HABITAT:** Grassy areas in open, sandy pine woods.

NORTHERN METALMARK *Calephelis borealis* **PL. 17**

1 ⅛–1 ¼ in. (28–32 mm). Large. Male forewing relatively *rounded*. Upperside: Both wings with *dark median band.* **SIMILAR SPECIES:** Swamp Metalmark is smaller and brighter; male with pointed forewing. **EARLY STAGES:** Caterpillar is green with black dots and rows of long white hairs. **FOOD:** Roundleaf Ragwort, possibly other ragworts and fleabane. **FLIGHT:** Mid-June to late July (1 brood). **RANGE:** W. Conn. south to nw. N.J. and w.-cen. Pa., cen. Appalachians and Ohio Valley, isolated colonies in sw. Mo. and e. Okla. **HABITAT:** Small stream valleys amid shale, serpentine, or limestone barrens. **REMARKS:** Highly localized. May co-occur only with Swamp Metalmark.

FATAL METALMARK *Calephelis nemesis* **PL. 17**

¾–1 in. (18–26 mm). Occurs with Rounded and Rawson's metalmarks. Male has *pointed forewing.* Upperside: Both sexes usually have *dark brown median band*, wings paler beyond band to give it more contrast. Fringes *checkered.* **SIMILAR SPECIES:** (1) Rounded Metalmark has indistinctly checkered fringes; male has rounded forewing. (2) Rawson's Metalmark is relatively large, has absent or weak expression of dark median band on upperside. Male has pointed forewing. **EARLY STAGES:** Caterpillar is dark gray with silvery tubercles and long buff and gray-white hairs. **FOOD:** Seep Willow, possibly *Clematis.* **FLIGHT:** All year in s. Texas. **RANGE:** Southwest east to cen. Texas and south to s. Mexico. **HABITAT:** Weedy or brushy areas along streams, washes, ditches, or roadsides.

LITTLE METALMARK

NORTHERN METALMARK

ROUNDED METALMARK *Calephelis nilus*   PL. 17

¹¹⁄₁₆–¹⁵⁄₁₆ in. (17–24 mm). Male has *rounded* forewing apex. Upperside: May have dark median band and *indistinctly checkered fringes*. **SIMILAR SPECIES:** (1) Fatal Metalmark has distinctly checkered wing fringes, and both species usually have dark median bands on upperside of both wings. (2) Rawson's Metalmark is relatively large, brighter, and usually lacks dark median band on upperside. **EARLY STAGES:** Not reported. **FOOD:** Boneset (*Eupatorium odoratum*). **FLIGHT:** All year in s. Texas. **RANGE:** Cen. Texas south to cen. Mexico. **HABITAT:** Thorn scrub, fence rows, roadsides. **REMARKS:** Formerly called Lost Metalmark (*C. perditalis*), but *perditalis* is now considered a subspecies of *C. nilus*.

SWAMP METALMARK *Calephelis mutica*   PL. 17

¹⁵⁄₁₆–¹³⁄₁₆ in. (24–30 mm). Small. Wing fringes lightly checkered. Upperside: Bright, little darkening of central portion of wings. Male has *pointed* forewing. **SIMILAR SPECIES:** Northern Metalmark is larger and duller, and male has rounded forewing. **EARLY STAGES:** Caterpillar is green with black dots and rows of long white hairs. **FOOD:** Swamp and Roadside thistles. **FLIGHT:** Late June to mid-Aug. (1 brood) in Great Lakes region, late May to early Sept. (2 broods) further south. **RANGE:** Populations in s. Mich., s. Wis., Ohio, Mo., and n. Ark. Isolated records in e. Iowa and cen. Ky. **HABITAT:** Wet meadows, marshes, bogs. **REMARKS:** Found in localized colonies. Sometimes found at same localities (but different habitats) as Northern Metalmark.

RAWSON'S METALMARK *Calephelis rawsoni*   PL. 17

¹³⁄₁₆–1 in. (19–26 mm). Large. Upperside: *Median band weak or absent*, fringes *checkered*. Male forewing pointed. **SIMILAR SPECIES:**

FATAL METALMARK

ROUNDED METALMARK

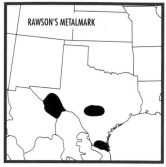

RAWSON'S METALMARK

SWAMP METALMARK

(1) Fatal Metalmark has pointed forewing (in male), dark median band above, and checkered wing fringes. (2) Rounded Metalmark has rounded forewing apex (both sexes), may or may not have darkened median band, and weakly checkered wing fringes. **EARLY STAGES:** Not reported. **FOOD:** Several bonesets (*Eupatorium havanense* and *E. greggii*). **FLIGHT:** June–Nov. (2 broods?). **RANGE:** S. and w. Texas south to cen. Mexico. **HABITAT:** Moist areas on shaded limestone outcrops, subtropical woods.

RED-BORDERED METALMARK *Caria ino*   PL. 17

¾–¹⁵⁄₁₆ in. (20–24 mm). Sexually dimorphic. Both sexes have base of *forewing costal margin arched*. Upperside: Male dark brown with postmedian *line of metallic spots* extending backward from costal margin. Underside: Male checkered red below; female orange. **SIMILAR SPECIES:** Scintillant metalmarks (Genus *Calephelis*) have straight costal margin, not as strongly patterned. **EARLY STAGES:** Not reported. **FOOD:** *Celtis pallida*. **FLIGHT:** March–Nov. in s. Texas. **RANGE:** S. Texas south through Mexico to Costa Rica. **HABITAT:** Subtropical thorn forest.

BLUE METALMARK *Lasaia sula*   PL. 17

⅞–¹³⁄₁₆ in. (22–30 mm). Sexually dimorphic. Upperside: Male *blue-green* above; female *checkered gray* with submarginal black spots. **EARLY STAGES:** Not reported. **FLIGHT:** April–Dec. in s. Texas. **RANGE:** Extreme s. Texas (lower Rio Grande Valley) south to Honduras. **HABITAT:** Open subtropical woods, edges.

RED-BORDERED PIXIE *Melanis pixe*   PL. 17

1½–1¹³⁄₁₆ in. (37–46 mm). Unique. Usually perches under leaves with wings open. Upperside: Black. Forewing apex *yellow-orange with red spot at base*. Hindwing with *band of red spots* along outer

RED-BORDERED
METALMARK

margin. **EARLY STAGES:** Not reported. **FOOD:** Guamuchil (*Pithecellobium dulce*). **FLIGHT:** Jan. to early Nov. in s. Texas. **RANGE:** Extreme s. Texas (lower Rio Grande Valley) south to Costa Rica. **HABITAT:** Lowland tropical riparian forest, city parks.

CURVE-WINGED METALMARK *Emesis emesia*　　**PL. 17**
1–1¼ in. (26–32 mm). Forewing *costa curved*, concave in middle, with *translucent white dash*. **EARLY STAGES:** Not reported. **FOOD:** *Cesalpinia mexicana.* **FLIGHT:** Oct.–Nov. in s. Texas, July–Jan. in Mexico. **RANGE:** Extreme s. Texas (lower Rio Grande Valley) south to Guatemala. **HABITAT:** Subtropical woods, seasonally dry thorn forest.

FALCATE METALMARK *Emesis tenedia*　　**NOT SHOWN**
1⅛–1⅜ in. (29–35 mm). Rare resident in s. Texas. Dimorphic. Forewing apex of both sexes *extended slightly outward*. Upperside: Male black-brown. Female brown with large pale cream to gray patch beyond end of cell. Underside: Male orange with dark checks; female yellow-brown. **EARLY STAGES:** Not reported. **FLIGHT:** Aug. and Oct. in s. Texas; July–Jan. in Mexico and Cen. America. **RANGE:** S. Texas and Mexico south to Panama.

NARROW-WINGED METALMARK　　**PL. 17**
Apodemia multiplaga
1⅛–1 5/16 in. (28–33 mm). Rare. Forewing *pointed*. Outer margin concave just below apex. Upperside: *Black-brown with white spots and checks*. **EARLY STAGES:** Not reported. **FLIGHT:** June, mid-Oct. to Nov. in s. Texas; also March and Aug. in Mexico and Cen. America. **RANGE:** Rare vagrant in extreme s. Texas (lower Rio Grande Valley) south through Mexico and Cen. America to nw. Costa Rica. **HABITAT:** Open tropical woods.

¾–1 in. (19–25 mm). Small. Upperside: *Gray* with *smeared* white submarginal band. Underside: White with *small black marks* and *orange marginal band*. **EARLY STAGES:** Not reported. **FLIGHT:** Early June, Oct. in s. Texas. **RANGE:** Extreme s. Texas (lower Rio Grande Valley) south to nw. Costa Rica. **HABITAT:** Subtropical woods and scrub.

11

True Butterflies:
Superfamily Papilionoidea
Brushfoots: Family Nymphalidae

Butterflies of this highly variable family are found worldwide, but they are especially rich in the tropics; there are more species in this family than in any other. Some prefer to split this family into several smaller ones, but this book follows the conservative approach of recognizing the major groups as subfamilies. The adults vary from small to large. The male's front pair of legs is reduced and not used for walking—hence the family name. Wing shape is highly variable; some species have irregular margins (Genus *Polygonia*), and others have long tail-like projections (Genus *Marpesia*). Browns, oranges, yellows, and blacks are frequent colors, while iridescent structural colors such as blues and purples are rare. Both perching and patrolling mate-location strategies occur. Adults of some groups feed primarily on flower nectar, while those of others do not visit flowers at all, but instead feed on sap flows, rotting fruit, dung, or animal carcasses. Adults of the heliconians (Genus *Heliconius*) are unusual in their habit of collecting pollen and then absorbing proteins through the proboscis. Adults of some groups are the longest lived butterflies, surviving 6–11 months. Eggs are laid in clusters, in columns, or singly, sometimes not directly on the host plant. The caterpillars of some are communal, feeding in groups during their early instars. Caterpillars of many species have rows of bristly tubercles, while others have only scattered short setae. Pupae of most species hang from a silk mat. Overwintering may be as larvae or adults.

Snouts: Subfamily Libytheinae

This small family has one to a few medium-sized species in each of the world's temperate and tropical regions. The family contains only about 10 species. In North America there is only one species.

The male front legs are reduced and are not used for walking. Periodically, adults migrate in massive numbers.

SNOUTS: GENUS *Libytheana* MICHENER

The snouts are found worldwide, with one or a few species on each continent. Adults often perch head down on twigs or small branches, where they mimic dead leaves. Males patrol host plants in search of females. Eggs are laid in small groups on host leaves. Winter is passed by adults. Adults visit flowers for nectar. Our species may undergo vast emigrations, especially in Texas and Arizona. Here I consider that our snouts represent a single species.

AMERICAN SNOUT *Libytheana carinenta*   PL. 18

1 ⅝−2 in. (41 −51 mm). Sexes are similar. Forewings *squared off*, extended at apex; *beaklike* labial palps. Upperside: Forewing with white spots on apical third and orange patches along inner margin and base. Underside: Hindwing either mottled or uniformly violet-gray. The species sometimes engages in huge migrations. Previously, our species was referred to as *L. bachmanii*, but it has been shown that our butterfly is the same as that in the American tropics. **EARLY STAGES:** Caterpillar is dark green with lateral and middorsal yellow stripes. Front swollen, with 2 black tubercles; last segment tapered abruptly. **FOOD:** Hackberries and sugarberry. **FLIGHT:** 2 broods annually; adults overwinter in South and in tropics. First flight mid-May through June, 2nd brood emerges early Aug. **RANGE:** Resident from s. U.S., and in Mexico south through the lowland tropics to Argentina. Also in the West Indies. Periodic migrant and colonist north through most of e. U.S. and s. Ont. In West

American Snout. Adult nectaring at goldenrod, Fairfax Co., Va. The long snout helps complete the "dead leaf" appearance of the butterfly when at rest on twigs or small branches. They often participate in mass migrations.

north to Colo., s. Nev., and cen. Calif. **HABITAT:** Thorn scrub, river woods, wooded swamps, brushy fields, edges. **REMARKS:** When resting on twigs, adults resemble dead leaves. The snout (palpi) looks like a leaf petiole.

HELICONIANS: SUBFAMILY HELICONIINAE

This group is richest in the American tropics, but several genera are prominent in the Northern Hemisphere. The adults of some are long-lived, and several are distasteful. Many other species mimic the distasteful butterflies of this group. Males patrol in search of recently emerged females or chrysalids that are about to produce an adult. Life span is long, as long as six months in some instances. The adults of *Heliconius* are unique in that they intentionally collect pollen in their proboscis. The proteins in the pollen are absorbed through the wall of the proboscis. The eggs are laid singly on passion-vines.

GULF FRITILLARY *Agraulis vanillae*   **PL. 19**
2⅝–3¾ in. (66–96 mm). Flies steadily with shallow wingbeats. Forewings pointed. Upperside: Bright orange with black marks, and 3 white, black-rimmed spots. Underside: Hindwing and apex with *elongated, iridescent silver spots.* **EARLY STAGES:** Caterpillar glossy black with red-orange lateral and dorsal stripes; 4 longitudinal rows of long complex spines. **FOOD:** Maypops and other passion-vine species. **FLIGHT:** All year in s. Fla. and s. Texas; number of broods not determined. Found northward Jan. to early Nov. **RANGE:** Resident in southern U.S., Mexico, Cen. America, West Indies, and South America. Regular vagrant north to cen. U.S., rare further north. Only 1 record for Canada (sw. Man.). **HABITAT:** Subtropical second growth, woodland edges, brushy fields, city gardens.

Gulf Fritillary. Male nectaring at lantana, Callaway Gardens, Ga. The species spreads northward in the summer, laying eggs on Maypops and ornamental passionvines. This insect is often propagated in butterfly houses.

MEXICAN SILVERSPOT *Dione moneta* PL. 19

3–3¼ in. (76–82 mm). Upperside *dull orange, darker* at wing base; veins *lined with black.* **SIMILAR SPECIES:** Gulf Fritillary is bright orange. **EARLY STAGES:** Caterpillar is dark brown with orange and gray spots; body with 4 rows of spines. **FOOD:** Passion-vines. **FLIGHT:** All year in tropics; April–Dec. in Texas. **RANGE:** Periodic stray to cen. and w. Texas, s. N.M., occasionally reproduces in s. Texas; resident throughout mainland tropical America. **HABITAT:** Openings and edges of mid-elevation evergreen forests in tropics; known from several habitats in Texas.

BANDED ORANGE HELICONIAN *Dryadula phaetusa* PL. 19

3⁷⁄₁₆–3½ in. (88–90 mm). Male upperside *bright orange* with *black stripes.* Female duller; black stripes smeared. **EARLY STAGES:** Caterpillar is dull purple with 4 rows of long spines; top of head with 2 spiny horns. **FOOD:** Passion-vines. **FLIGHT:** All year in tropics; July, Dec. in Tex. **RANGE:** Tropical America from cen. Mexico south to Brazil. Rare vagrant north to Texas and Kans. **HABITAT:** Open brushy areas in seasonal tropical lowlands.

JULIA *Dryas iulia* PL. 19

3¼–3⅝ in. (82–92 mm). Forewings pointed. Male *bright orange* above and below. Upperside: *Narrow black border* on outer margin of hindwing. Female duller, with more extensive black markings above. **EARLY STAGES:** Caterpillar is dark brown with fine, transverse black lines and spots. Head white with black marks and 2 black tubercles. **FOOD:** Passion-vines (*Passiflora lutea* in Texas). **FLIGHT:** All year in s. Fla. and s. Texas; strays north in summer.

RANGE: Resident in s. Texas and peninsular Fla., West Indies, Mexico, and Cen. America south to Brazil. Strays north to e. Neb. Does not stray in East. **HABITAT:** Openings and edges of subtropical hammocks; often found in nearby fields.

ISABELLA'S HELICONIAN *Eueides isabella*   **PL. 20**

3¹⁄₁₆–3½ in. (78–90 mm). Forewing elongated but with apex rounded. Wings similar above and below. Apical half of forewing *black with yellow patches.* Black stripe through orange area along inner margin. Hindwing orange with 2 *black stripes* across median area and black, white-dotted outer margin. **SIMILAR SPECIES:** The unrelated Tiger Mimic-Queen, one of a large group of similar distasteful mimics, has a nearly identical pattern, but the 2 hindwing stripes are connected outwardly. **EARLY STAGES:** Caterpillar with upper body black with narrow white transverse bands on back and yellow lateral stripes; orange patch on segments 8 and 9. Head black, spotted white with 2 black tubercles. **FOOD:** Passion-vines. **FLIGHT:** All year in tropics; April–July in Texas. **RANGE:** Mexico and West Indies south to Brazil. Periodic immigrant to cen. Texas. **HABITAT:** Subtropical scrub, woodland edges, and brushy fields.

LONGWINGS: GENUS *Heliconius* KLUK

Our commonest species, the Zebra, roosts in small to large clusters. The adults return to the same roost night after night.

ZEBRA *Heliconius charithonius*   **PL. 19**

2¾–3¹⁵⁄₁₆ in. (72–100 mm). Unique. Wings *long and narrow*; *black* with narrow, pale yellow stripes. **EARLY STAGES:** Caterpillar is creamy white with many fine transverse bands and 6 rows of branched black spines. Head pale yellow. **FOOD:** Passion-vines.

Zebra. Male nectaring at blue eupatorium flowers. Lower Rio Grande Valley, Tex. Every evening the adults fly to locations where they form clusters for protection overnight. The long-lived adults can collect pollen grains from flowers.

FLIGHT: All year in s. Fla. and s. Tex., found in warmer months northward. **RANGE:** Resident from peninsular Fla. and s. Texas through West Indies, Mexico, and Cen. America to South America. Periodic vagrant north to S.C., Neb., and N.M. **HABITAT:** Tropical hammocks, river forests, edges.

ERATO HELICONIAN *Heliconius erato* PL. 19

2¹¹⁄₁₆–3⅛ in. (68–80 mm). Black with pink patch on forewing and *yellow* lateral *stripe* on hindwing. **EARLY STAGES:** Caterpillar white with black spots and spines, head buff with 2 black tubercles. **FOOD:** Passion-vines. **FLIGHT:** All year in tropics; June, Aug.–Sept. in s. Texas. **RANGE:** Tropical America from Mexico south to Brazil. Rare vagrant to s. Texas. **HABITAT:** Tropical and subtropical woods and edges.

ZEBRA

VARIEGATED FRITILLARY

Variegated Fritillary.
Female nectaring at
Alfalfa. Fort Collins,
Colo. A common
colonist far north of
its normal southern
breeding range, eggs
are laid on a variety of
plants, especially vio-
lets and garden pan-
sies.

VARIEGATED FRITILLARY *Euptoieta claudia* **PLS. 3, 20**
1¼–3⅛ in. (44–80 mm). Flies low with shallow wingbeats. Often flutters wings when at flowers. Orange with black markings. Forewing pointed, hindwing apex and outer margin with *angles.* Upperside: Black marginal spots between veins. Underside: Hindwing mottled *without silver spots.* **EARLY STAGES:** Caterpillar red-orange with dorsal and lateral stripes of alternating black and white patches, 6 rows of black spines. **FOOD:** Violets, Maypops, and a wide variety of plants in other families. **FLIGHT:** Feb. or March to Nov. or Dec. (4 broods) in South, April–Oct. (3 broods) northward. **RANGE:** Resident from s. U.S. south through higher elevations in tropical America to Argentina. Also highlands of Cuba and Jamaica. Regular colonist north through most of U.S. (except Pacific Northwest) to southern Canada. **HABITAT:** Wide variety of open, sunny areas—waste fields, prairies, pastures, etc.

MEXICAN FRITILLARY *Euptoieta hegesia* **PL. 20**
2⁹⁄₁₆–2¹⁵⁄₁₆ in. (66–74 mm). Hindwing margins *without strong angles.* Upperside: Wings lack contrast between basal and outer portions. Basal half *plain orange, unpatterned.* Underside: Hindwing orange-brown with pattern evident. **EARLY STAGES:** Caterpillar with head and body shining red, dorsal and lateral black-edged silver lines, 6 rows of black spines, head with 2 black, clubbed horns. **FOOD:** *Turnera*, passion-vines, and morning glories. **FLIGHT:** All year in tropics and s. Texas, Sept.–Oct. in cen. Texas. **RANGE:** Resident in lowlands of Mexico, Cen. America, and West Indies. Vagrant to cen. Texas, cen. Ariz., and s. Calif. **HABITAT:** Fields, openings, edges in tropical lowlands and foothills.

This New World group comprises 14 species. In some western areas, several species occurring together may be difficult to identify, but our eastern species usually pose no problems. The silver spots on the underside of the hindwings owe their metallic appearance to reflected light rather than to pigment. The adults are often found at flowers, especially those of milkweeds, mints, and thistles. All species are single-brooded. Females of some species display delayed maturation of their eggs so that they may be laid at the end of the summer. Males patrol suitable habitats in search of females. The females drop their eggs in the vicinity of dried-up violets, foretelling the presence of fresh foliage the following spring. The eggs hatch in the fall, and the young first-instar caterpillars overwinter without feeding. In the spring when the violets leaf out, the caterpillars complete their development, feeding primarily at night.

DIANA *Speyeria diana*   PL. 20

3⁷⁄₁₆–4⁷⁄₁₆ in. (88–112 mm). Unique. Large. Upperside: Male with wing *black* at base, *orange* outwardly; female *black with blue* on outer portion of hindwing. Underside: Lacks spot pattern typical of other *Speyeria*. **EARLY STAGES:** Caterpillar velvety black with rows of black fleshy orange-based spines, double row of white dots along back. **FOOD:** Violets. **FLIGHT:** Mid-June to early Sept., extreme dates broader in s. Appalachians (1 brood). **RANGE:** Cen. Appalachians west to Ozarks, formerly Atlantic coastal plain of Va. and N.C., and Ohio River Valley. **HABITAT:** Openings and fields in wet, rich forested valleys and mountainsides. Males wander to a wider

Diana. Male nectaring at Swamp Milkweed, Bath Co., Va. The spectacular iridescent blue females appear at flower patches in the afternoon, presumably after laying their eggs in the morning.

range of habitats. **REMARKS:** Female is a mimic of the distasteful Pipevine Swallowtail.

GREAT SPANGLED FRITILLARY *Speyeria cybele* **PL. 20**

3–3¹⁵⁄₁₆ in. (76–100 mm). Large. Upperside: Tawny. Male with *black scaling* on forewing *veins*. Underside: *Broad pale submarginal band* on hindwing. **SIMILAR SPECIES:** See (1) Aphrodite Fritillary. (2) Atlantis Fritillary is smaller, darker; upperside forewing has black band on outer margin, and underside hindwing has elongated postmedian silver spots. **EARLY STAGES:** Caterpillar is velvety above and chocolate brown below, black spines are red-yellow at base. A dorsal double row of gray dots. **FOOD:** Violets. **FLIGHT:** Mid-June to mid-Aug., occasionally early Oct. (1 brood). **RANGE:** Cen. Canada and n. U. S. south to n. Ga., cen. Ark., n. N.M., and cen. Calif. **HABITAT:** Open fields and valleys, power-line rights of

Great Spangled Fritillary. Male nectaring at Butterfly Milkweed, Fairfax Co., Va. Males patrol to find females. Females, who survive for several months, scatter their eggs near withered violets in the fall.

Aphrodite Fritillary. Male nectaring at Echium, Pendleton Co., W. Va. A common butterfly of tallgrass prairie. Butterflies of such habitats can disappear after overenthusiastic use of fire for plant conservation.

way, brushy pastures. **REMARKS:** The commonest fritillary in most of our area.

APHRODITE FRITILLARY *Speyeria aphrodite* PL. 20

2⁹⁄₁₆–3⁵⁄₁₆ in. (66–84 mm). Geographically variable. Upperside: Male forewing with *small black spot below cell* and *without black scaling* on veins. Underside: Hindwing with pale *submarginal band narrow or lacking*. **SIMILAR SPECIES:** (1) Great Spangled Fritillary is larger, has broader submarginal band on underside hindwing. (2) Atlantis Fritillary is smaller, has black margins above, and narrower pale submarginal band on underside hindwing. **EARLY STAGES:** Caterpillar brown-black with a dorsal black line, spines ocher or brown. **FOOD:** Violets. **FLIGHT:** Mid-June to mid-Sept. (1 brood). **RANGE:** Canada south of the taiga from N.S. and Prince Edward I. west across s. Que., Ont., and the prairie provinces to

APHRODITE FRITILLARY

REGAL FRITILLARY

Regal Fritillary. Male basking on vegetation. Orange Co., Va. Regal Fritillaries have disappeared from almost all their haunts east of the Mississippi River but are common in prairies to the west. Photo by George Krizek.

se. B.C., thence south in the Rockies to e.-cen. Ariz. and n. N. M., south in Appalachians to n. Ga. **HABITAT:** Moist prairies, mountain pastures, barrens.

REGAL FRITILLARY *Speyeria idalia* PL. 20

3⅛–4⅛ in. (79–106 mm). Unique. Large. Upperside: Forewing *red-orange* with *ornate black marks*. Hindwing black with post-median row of *white spots* and submarginal row of orange (male) or white (female) spots. **EARLY STAGES:** Caterpillar velvety black with ocher-yellow or dull orange mottlings. Dorsal spines black-tipped silver-white. **FOOD:** Bird's-foot Violet. **FLIGHT:** Mid-June to mid-Aug., occasionally mid-Oct. (1 brood). **RANGE:** Formerly from N.B. south to nw. N.C., west to se. Mont. and ne. Colo. Rapidly declining, now rare or absent from areas east of the Appalachians. Still common only in tall-grass prairie reserves. **HABITAT:** Wet fields, marshes, tall-grass prairie. **REMARKS:** Disappearing or declining in abundance over most of its range.

EDWARDS' FRITILLARY *Speyeria edwardsii* PL. 20

2¾–3⅜ in. (70–86 mm). Large. Forewing pointed. Upperside: Bold *black border* on outer margins of both wings. Underside: *Green* or *gray-green* with metallic silver marks and narrow buff submarginal band. **SIMILAR SPECIES:** Callippe Fritillary is usually smaller, lacks black border above, and underside hindwing ground is blue-green, not gray-green. **EARLY STAGES:** Caterpillar dark yellow above, gray along sides with a black dorsal line. **FOOD:** Violets. **FLIGHT:** Late June to early Sept. (1 brood). **RANGE:** Short-grass prairie and w. portions of Rockies from s. Alta. east to the cen. Dakotas and w. Neb., south to ne. N.M. **HABITAT:** Foothills, short-grass prairie valleys. **REMARKS:** A typical short-grass prairie species.

CORONIS FRITILLARY *Speyeria coronis*   PL. 21

2½–3⅜ in. (64–86 mm). Underside: Hindwing with silver spots in marginal row *rounded* inward and with discal silver spots *elongated*. SIMILAR SPECIES: Aphrodite Fritillary has hindwing below with marginal silver spots pointed inwardly and discal silver spots more rounded. EARLY STAGES: Caterpillar mottled brown and black; lateral spine row orange, others black. FOOD: Violets. FLIGHT: Mid-June to Sept. (1 brood). RANGE: Pacific Coast from s. Wash. south to nw. Baja Calif. Norte east through Great Basin and cen. Rockies to high plains of cen. S.D., w. Neb., and cen. Colo. HABITAT: Wooded hills, prairie valleys.

CALLIPPE FRITILLARY *Speyeria callippe*   PL. 20

2–2¹⁵⁄₁₆ in. (52–74 mm). Males patrol hilltops awaiting females; other *Speyeria* males patrol meadows and hillsides. Underside: Hindwing ground color *bright blue-green*. SIMILAR SPECIES: Mormon Fritillary is more delicately marked, smaller, has large round antennal knobs, and has the underside of hindwing darker at base. EARLY STAGES: Caterpillar mottled brown and black with a black dorsal line. FOOD: Violets. FLIGHT: Mid-June to mid-Aug. (1 brood). RANGE: Pacific Coast (se. B.C. south to nw. Baja Calif. Norte) west through Great Basin and Rockies to s. Man., w. S.D., and cen. Colo. HABITAT: Brushy hillsides, prairie ridges.

ATLANTIS FRITILLARY *Speyeria atlantis*   PL. 20

2⅜–2¾ in. (60–70 mm). Smallest and most northern of our three most familiar fritillaries. Upperside: Forewing has *black outer margin* and male has black scaling on veins. Underside: Hindwing has *dark disk* with *narrow pale submarginal band*. SIMILAR SPECIES: Aphrodite Fritillary has pale outer margins, males do not have darkened veins, and the hindwing disk below is not darkened. EARLY STAGES: Caterpillar yellow-green on top with a black dorsal line,

green-gray below, spines gray. **FOOD:** Violets. **FLIGHT:** Late June to early Sept. (1 brood). **RANGE:** Maritime Provinces and ne. U.S. (south to W. Va.) west across Great Lakes region and s. Canada. Widespread in w. North American mountain archipelago from Yukon south to Ariz. and N.M. **HABITAT:** Upland pastures, openings in coniferous woods, and bogs.

MORMON FRITILLARY *Speyeria mormonia* **PL. 21**
2–2⅜ in. (52–60 mm). Small. *Antennal clubs relatively large,* rounded. Forewing apex *rounded.* Upperside: Forewing without black scaling on veins. Underside: Hindwing *disk sometimes greenish,* but not as bright or as solid as on Callippe Fritillary. **EARLY STAGES:** Caterpillar variable yellow to orange with black blotches and lines. **FOOD:** Violets. **FLIGHT:** Mid-June to Sept. (1 brood). **RANGE:** Western mountain archipelago from s. Alaska south to cen. Calif. and e.-cen. Ariz., extends east to sw. Man. and the Dakotas. **HABITAT:** Mountain meadows, moist prairie valleys.

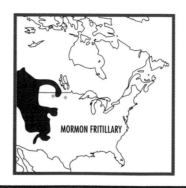

Our lesser fritillaries belong to an assemblage found in cooler portions of the Northern Hemisphere, especially in the arctic and higher mountains. Most of our species are Holarctic, being found in both the New and Old worlds. The males patrol continuously in search of receptive females and stop only briefly to imbibe nectar, often at yellow composite flowers. Caterpillars use a variety of host plants. Several arctic and alpine species require two years to complete their development.

MOUNTAIN FRITILLARY *Boloria napaea* **PL. 18**

1½–1⅞ in. (37–47 mm). Forewing is pointed, *outer margin* of hindwing *arched*. Upperside: Male delicately marked orange; female with heavy black pattern. Underside: Hindwing with *faint pattern*. Found in our area only in arctic Canada. **EARLY STAGES:** Not reported. **FOOD:** Smartweeds (*Polygonum bistortoides* and *P. viviparum*). **FLIGHT:** Late June–July (1 brood). **RANGE:** Holarctic. Alaska and w. Yukon, Victoria I., tundra of N.W. Terr. east to Dist. of Keewatin. Isolated alpine populations in Canadian Rockies and Wyo.'s Wind R. Mts. **HABITAT:** Moist tundra.

BOG FRITILLARY *Boloria eunomia* **PL. 18**

1⅝–1¾ in. (39–45 mm). Underside: Hindwing with *nonmetallic* white pattern; submarginal row of *white, black-outlined spots*. **SIMILAR SPECIES:** See (1) Silver-bordered Fritillary. **EARLY STAGES:** Caterpillar red-brown with reddish spines. **FOOD:** Scrubby willows, smartweed, and violets. **FLIGHT:** Mid-June to Aug., 1 month at any locality (1 brood). **RANGE:** Throughout most of Canada and Alaska and in the bordering U.S., in n. Me., n. Great Lakes region, and alpine Rocky Mts. south to Colo. **HABITAT:** Wetlands including acid bogs, and dwarf willow seeps.

BOG FRITILLARY

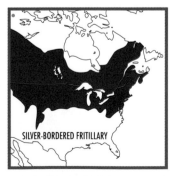

SILVER-BORDERED FRITILLARY

Meadow Fritillary. Adult resting. Western Iowa. The butterfly is found in disturbed pastures and roadsides in the East and is spreading southward. In the West it is limited to native mountain meadows.

SILVER-BORDERED FRITILLARY *Boloria selene*   **PL. 18**
1⅝–2⅛ in. (41–53 mm). Underside: Our only lesser fritillary with *metallic silver spots* on hindwing; submarginal spots are black. **SIMILAR SPECIES:** Bog Fritillary has underside of hindwing with nonmetallic white pattern, and submarginal spots are white, not black. **EARLY STAGES:** Caterpillar mottled dark gray with pale yellow spines, except front thoracic pair black. **FOOD:** Violets. **FLIGHT:** Late June–July (1 brood) in North, May or June–Sept. (2–3 broods) in e. U.S. **RANGE:** Holarctic. N. third of conterminous U.S. and Canada south of the taiga, extending northwest to cen. Alaska. **HABITAT:** Wet meadows, marshes, or bogs.

MEADOW FRITILLARY *Boloria bellona*   **PL. 18**
1⅝–2 in. (39–51 mm). Unique *squared-off forewing apex.* Underside: Hindwing mottled purple-brown without off-white basal patch. **SIMILAR SPECIES:** Frigga Fritillary has rounded forewing apex,

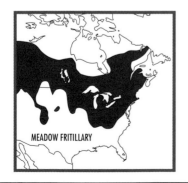

MEADOW FRITILLARY

FRIGGA FRITILLARY

DINGY FRITILLARY

POLARIS FRITILLARY

and there is an off-white basal patch on costal margin of hind-wing below. **EARLY STAGES:** Caterpillar shiny green with yellow-brown spines. **FOOD:** Violets. **FLIGHT:** Late April to mid-Oct. (2 or 3 broods). **RANGE:** S. Canada exclusive of the Maritimes west to e. B.C., south in U. S. to n.-cen. Ore., cen. Colo., ne. Tenn., and nw. N.C. Expanding southward in Southeast. **HABITAT:** Moist meadows, pastures, hayfields. **REMARKS:** Range expanding south and eastward. Unusual among lesser fritillaries in its ability to adapt to disturbed habitats.

FRIGGA FRITILLARY *Boloria frigga* PL. 18

1 ⅝–1 ⅚ in. (41 – 49 mm). Forewing *apex pointed*, not squared off. Underside: Hindwing with *basal off-white patch* along costal margin. Adults feed on nectar of Labrador Tea. **SIMILAR SPECIES:** Meadow Fritillary has squared-off forewing apex and lacks off-white patch on hindwing costal margin below. **EARLY STAGES:** Caterpillar body and spines black with pale purplish lateral line. **FOOD:** Cranberry and Bog Rosemary, possibly also dwarf birch and scrub willows. **FLIGHT:** Late May (Wis.) to early Aug. (Lab.) (1 brood). **RANGE:** Holarctic. Most of Canada, Arctic Archipelago, and Alaska, south in bordering U.S. to n. Great Lakes region, and, as isolated populations, to Wyo. and s.-cen. Colo. **HABITAT:** Sphagnum bogs, sedge bogs.

DINGY FRITILLARY *Boloria improba* PL. 18

1 ⅛–1 ⅜ in. (28 – 35 mm). Small. Dingy. Pattern *muted*, unsilvered. Underside: *Outer half* of hindwing often *grayish*. **EARLY STAGES:** Caterpillar mottled dark brown with red-brown spines; head black. **FOOD:** Dwarf willows. **FLIGHT:** Late June to early Aug. (1 brood). Probably biennial but flies every year. **RANGE:** Holarctic. Arctic tundra of N.W. Terr. east to Dist. of Keewatin and s. Victo-

ria I.; Yukon and Alaska; isolated populations in c. Canadian Rockies, sw. Wyo., and sw. Colo. **HABITAT:** Wet tundra with dwarf willows.

POLARIS FRITILLARY *Boloria polaris*   **PL. 18**
1⅓–1½ in. (33–38 mm). Distinctive. Underside: Hindwing with *frosted white appearance*. White marginal slashes between veins, and postmedian *black spots surrounded with white*. **EARLY STAGES:** Not reported. **FOOD:** Mountain Avens, probably also blueberry (*Vaccinium uliginosum*). **FLIGHT:** Biennial, late June–July, mid-Aug. in Lab. Odd-numbered years at a few locales, even-numbered years at most places. **RANGE:** Holarctic. Tundra of Alaska, n. Canada (incl. Arctic Archipelago), and ne. Greenland. **HABITAT:** Tundra ridges or flat areas below summits.

FREIJA FRITILLARY *Boloria freija*   **PL. 18**
1½–1⅝ in. (37–39 mm). Underside: Hindwing with diagnostic median *zigzag black line*, arrowhead-shaped white spots in center of wing and at edges. Arctic populations dark above (*B. f. tarquinius*). **EARLY STAGES:** Caterpillar dark brown with black spines. **FOOD:** Various heath family plants, possibly also crowberry and rose family plants. **FLIGHT:** Late May to mid-July, to mid-Aug. in Lab. (1 brood). **RANGE:** Holarctic. Most of Canada and Alaska; south in U. S. to n. Great Lakes region, and in Rockies to n. N.M. **HABITAT:** Open Leatherleaf bogs, margins of open black spruce bogs, Jack Pine and Lodgepole Pine forests.

TITANIA FRITILLARY *Boloria titania*   **PL. 18**
1⅝–1⅞ in. (41–47 mm). Underside: Hindwing with *thin marginal white spots capped inwardly with brown*, and median band usually with pale marks obliterated. Black markings heavy above.

ARCTIC FRITILLARY

DOTTED CHECKERSPOT

EARLY STAGES: Caterpillar gray with black stripes and orange spines; head black. **FOOD:** Possibly scrub willows, smartweed, and violets —North American hosts are undocumented. **FLIGHT:** Mid-July– Aug. (1 brood). **RANGE:** Holarctic. Most of Canada south of the tundra, Alaska, and south in the U.S. to N.H. (White Mts.), n. Minn., in Rockies to n. N.M., and in n. Cascades. **HABITAT:** Damp subalpine streamsides, acid bogs, taiga. **REMARKS:** Species relationship with Arctic Fritillary is unclear.

ARCTIC FRITILLARY *Boloria chariclea* PL. 18

1¼–1⅜ in. (31–34 mm). Small. Underside: Hindwing with marginal row of *thin white streaks*, median row with at least discal and costal spots distinctly pale white. Upperside: Black markings *delicate*. **SIMILAR SPECIES:** Titania Fritillary has heavier black spotting. **EARLY STAGES:** Caterpillar not described. **FOOD:** Dwarf willows and Mountain Avens. **FLIGHT:** Late June to early Aug. in odd-numbered years. **RANGE:** Holarctic. Tundra of n. Canada (including Arctic Archipelago), Alaska, and Greenland. **HABITAT:** Tundra and subarctic bogs.

Brushfoots: Subfamily Nymphalinae

This subfamily is the most prevalent in the family and is found throughout the world. It is a diverse group and contains several tribes, each with somewhat different structural and biological features. Adults of our species are predominantly orange, brown, and black, and wing shape is variable. Mating systems are variable; patrolling is predominant in the checkerspots and crescentspots, while perching or perching and patrolling is the rule for the remainder. Some of the strongest migrants are found among the lady butterflies, tortoiseshells, and anglewings, but most of the other species are local in their occurrence. Host plants span a wide variety of families, but most species limit their choice to plants of a single family. The Painted Lady, in contrast, has one of the widest host palettes in the subfamily. Eggs may be laid singly but are often clustered in groups, sometimes near the host or on an adjacent plant. Caterpillars feed singly or communally, often at night or in folded leaf shelters. Winter is passed by young caterpillars or by hibernating adults.

DOTTED CHECKERSPOT *Poladryas minuta*   PL. 18

1 ¹¹⁄₁₆–1 ⅞ in. (42–48 mm). Texas populations highly localized. Upperside: Bright red-orange. Underside: Hindwing with *double row of marginal white spots*, and median white band containing *double row of black dots*. EARLY STAGES: Caterpillar white with longitudinal black bands; head orange-brown. FOOD: Beardtongues. FLIGHT: Jan.–Sept. (several broods) in cen. Texas, June to early Sept. northward (1 brood). RANGE: Southwest from se. Wyo. and extreme nw. Neb. south to s.-cen. Texas, Chihuahua, and n. Sonora west to e.-cen. Calif. HABITAT: Limestone ridges in mesquite woodland, foothill ridges. REMARKS: Males establish perches on low vegetation in ridgetop clearings.

THEONA CHECKERSPOT *Thessalia theona*   PL. 19

1 ⁵⁄₁₆–1 ¾ in. (33–43 mm). Upperside: Checkered pattern with yellow-orange antemedian band and orange postmedian band. Underside: Hindwing cream with veins *outlined in black*, overlain by a *red-orange* postbasal blotch and *postmedian band*. SIMILAR SPECIES: Definite Patch is smaller and has black lines between postbasal orange blotch and postmedian band. EARLY STAGES: Caterpillar

Theona Checkerspot. Male nectaring on small composite. Laguna Atascosa National Wildlife Refuge, Tex. Males perch and patrol on hilltops or along ridges to seek females. Caterpillars live in small clusters.

velvety brown-black with small cream dots and a yellow lateral band; head orange. **FOOD:** Ceniza Blanca (*Leucophyllum texanum*). **FLIGHT:** All year in tropics. April–Oct. in Southwest (several broods). **RANGE:** Cen. Ariz. east to e.-cen. Texas and thence south through Mexico and Cen. America to Colombia. **HABITAT:** Subtropical scrub, desert foothills, limestone ridges.

FULVIA CHECKERSPOT *Thessalia fulvia* **PL. 19**
1 5⁄16–1 15⁄16 in. (33–49 mm). Variable within and between populations. Underside: Hindwing with combination of *black-lined veins* on *cream background* and black submarginal *band* enclosing series of *cream dots*. **EARLY STAGES:** Caterpillar ocher-yellow with longitudinal black lines and bands; head red-brown. **FOOD:** Paintbrush. **FLIGHT:** April–Oct. (3 broods). **RANGE:** Southwest from cen. Neb., cen. Kans., and cen. Texas (*T. f. fulvia*) west to s. Ore. and Calif. (*T. f. leanira*) and south to nw. Mexico. **HABITAT:** Prairie hills, rocky ridgetops.

PATCHES: GENUS *Chlosyne* BUTLER

This large, wholly New World genus comprises both the patches (more southern) and small checkerspots (more northern). Most species occur in the tropics, where many species mimic distasteful butterflies. Eggs are laid in clusters under host plant leaves, and young caterpillars feed in groups. Usual hosts belong to the Asteraceae and acanthus families.

BORDERED PATCH *Chlosyne lacinia* **PL. 21**
1 3⁄4–2 3⁄8 in. (44–60 mm). Highly variable geographically. Upperside: Black with *broad transverse orange band* on hindwing. **EARLY STAGES:** Caterpillar polymorphic—black to orange with black

spines; head black. **FOOD:** Sunflower, ragweed, crownbeard, and other composites. **FLIGHT:** All year in s. Texas (many broods), only during warm months to north. **RANGE:** Resident from s. Ariz. east to s. Texas south through Mexico, Cen. America, and South America to Argentina. Vagrant and temporary colonist north to Neb., s. Nev., and s. Calif. **HABITAT:** Desert washes, low ridges, openings in moist thorn scrub.

DEFINITE PATCH *Chlosyne definita*   **PL. 21**
¹⁵/₁₆−1⁵/₁₆ in. (24−33 mm). Small. Upperside: Checkered pattern of red-orange, yellow-orange, and dark brown checks and bands. Underside: Hindwing submarginal *orange band* with one *included white spot.* **EARLY STAGES:** Not reported. **FOOD:** *Stenandrium barbatum.* **FLIGHT:** April−Oct. (several broods). **RANGE:** Resident from s. N.M. and s. Texas south to s. Mexico. **HABITAT:** Openings in subtropical thorn scrub.

BANDED PATCH *Chlosyne endeis*   **PL. 21**
1⅛−1½ in. (29−38 mm). Underside: Forewing has outer half *black* with *cream white spots.* Hindwing is cream white with postbasal and submarginal red-orange bands separated by two black irregular lines. **SIMILAR SPECIES:** Definite Patch is smaller, underside of forewing is predominantly orange. **EARLY STAGES:** Not reported. **FLIGHT:** March−Nov. (several broods). **RANGE:** S. Texas to s. Mexico, rare stray to cen. Texas. **HABITAT:** Subtropical thorn forest.

CRIMSON PATCH *Chlosyne janais*   **PL. 21**
1⅞−2⅝ in. (47−65 mm). Upperside: Forewing black with *small white spots.* Hindwing black with *large orange-red patch* on basal half. **EARLY STAGES:** Caterpillar gray-green with complex black markings and black spines; head red-orange. **FOOD:** Scrubby acanthus

Gorgone Check-erspot. Male perching on thistle, Sioux Co., Iowa. Females lay eggs in clusters on sunflower leaves, and the young caterpillars feed shoulder to shoulder in large groups.

family. **FLIGHT:** All year in tropics, July–Nov. in s. Texas (several broods). **RANGE:** Resident from s. Texas south through Mexico and Cen. America to Colombia. Strays north to se. N.M. and n. Texas. **HABITAT:** Weedy fields and edges in lowland tropical forests.

ROSITA PATCH *Chlosyne rosita*   PL. 21

1 7/16–1 11/16 in. (36–42 mm). Rare. Upperside: Hindwing *patch yellow* at base, *red-orange* near edge. Underside: Hindwing pattern *simpler* than that of the Crimson Patch. **SIMILAR SPECIES:** Crimson Patch is larger, patch on hindwing is entirely red-orange—lacks yellow at base. **EARLY STAGES:** Not reported. **FOOD:** Several low acanthus family plants. **FLIGHT:** Most of year in s. Texas (4 broods?). **RANGE:** Mexico south to El Salvador, periodic colonist in s. Texas (lower Rio Grande Valley). Rare stray to n. Texas and se. Ariz. **HABITAT:** Openings in subtropical forest.

CRIMSON PATCH

GORGONE CHECKERSPOT

RED-SPOTTED PATCH *Chlosyne marina* **PL. 21**

1 ⁵⁄₁₆–1 ⅜ in. (33–35 mm). Black. Upperside: Forewing with white spots; hindwing with *yellow at base* in addition to a *red sub-marginal band.* **EARLY STAGES:** Not reported. **FLIGHT:** Most of year in Mexico, late Oct. in s. Texas. **RANGE:** Resident in Mexico, rare stray in s. Texas and s. Ariz. **HABITAT:** Openings in subtropical thorn scrub.

GORGONE CHECKERSPOT *Chlosyne gorgone* **PL. 19**

1 ⁵⁄₁₆–1 ¼ in. (33–43 mm). Underside: Hindwing with *zigzag pattern* of alternating brown and white *bars and scallops.* **SIMILAR SPECIES:** (1) Pearl Crescent and (2) Silvery Checkerspot are similar above, but both have much plainer patterns below. **EARLY STAGES:** Caterpillar yellow with longitudinal black stripes; black head and spines. **FOOD:** Sunflowers, crosswort, and other composites. **FLIGHT:** July–Aug. in north (1 brood), May to mid-Sept. in most of range (2 broods), early April to late Sept. in South (3 broods). **RANGE:** Resident in most of cen. U.S. south to cen. N.M., cen. Tex., La., and cen. Ga. and s. Canada from cen. Alta. east to sw. Man. and s. Ont. **HABITAT:** Prairies, open ridges, glades in deciduous woods, waste areas. **REMARKS:** This species and the following *Chlosynes* were formerly included in *Charidryas.*

SILVERY CHECKERSPOT *Chlosyne nycteis* **PL. 19**

1 ⅝–2 in. (40–52 mm). Common. Hindwing with at least some *white-centered submarginal spots* above and below. Underside: Hindwing pale, with marginal crescent. **SIMILAR SPECIES:** (1) Pearl Crescent and (2) Northern Crescent are smaller, have small black spots in the submarginal row on the upperside of hindwing, and have relatively plain, uncheckered hindwing patterns below. **EARLY STAGES:** Caterpillar brown-black to black dotted with white, some

SILVERY CHECKERSPOT

HARRIS' CHECKERSPOT

Silvery Checkerspot. Male basking, Rockingham Co., Va. This species' life history is similar to Gorgone Checkerspot, but the butterflies live in moister habitats along streams and moist meadows.

yellow tubercles. **FOOD:** Wingstem, sunflowers, asters, Black-eyed Susan, and crownbeard. **FLIGHT:** June–July (1 brood) in North, May–Sept. (2 broods) further south, possibly 3–4 flights in Deep South and Texas. **RANGE:** E. North America from N.B. and s. Que. west to se. Sask. south to the Fla. panhandle (rarely), s.-cen. Texas, s. N.M., and cen. Ariz. **HABITAT:** Openings near stream courses; second-growth scrub.

HARRIS' CHECKERSPOT *Chlosyne harrisii*   **PL. 19**

1 ⁷⁄₁₆–2 in. (36–52 mm). The only butterfly in the East that is primarily orange and black. Underside: Hindwing has a white, orange, and black *checkered pattern*. **EARLY STAGES:** Caterpillar deep red-orange with dorsal black stripe; cross stripes on each segment. **FOOD:** Flat-topped White Aster. **FLIGHT:** June–July (1 brood). **RANGE:** S. Canada from N.S. and Prince Edward I. west to se. Sask., south to W. Va., s. Ohio, and ne. Ill. **HABITAT:** Moist pastures, marshes, bog edges, damp meadows.

SAGEBRUSH CHECKERSPOT *Chlosyne acastus*   **PL. 18**

1 ⅝–2 in. (40–52 mm). Western. Underside: Hindwing white spots in checkered pattern have a *pearly sheen*. **SIMILAR SPECIES:** Pattern like that of Harris' Checkerspot, but the two do not occur together. **EARLY STAGES:** Caterpillar black with gray stripes and black spines. **FOOD:** Aster (*Machaeranthera*) and rabbitbrush. **FLIGHT:** June–Aug. (2 broods). **RANGE:** S. Alta. and s. Sask. south through the cen. Dakotas to cen. N.M. and se. Calif. **HABITAT:** Streambeds, dry washes in sagebrush-juniper woodland.

ELF *Microtia elva*   PL. 21

   1–1⅛ in. (26–36 mm). Rounded forewings. Upperside: Both
   wings *black* with one or two large *yellow-orange patches*. Flutters
   weakly near ground. EARLY STAGES: Not reported. FLIGHT: All year in
   tropics, late July in s. Texas. RANGE: Resident from Mexico south
   through Cen. America to Venezuela (?). Rare stray to e. Mo., s.
   Ariz., and s. Texas. HABITAT: Open, weedy fields in seasonal lowland
   tropics.

TINY CHECKERSPOT *Dymasia dymas*   PL. 18

   ⅞–1¼ in. (23–32 mm). Small. Underside: Hindwing with *terminal black line* and *marginal white spots*. EARLY STAGES: Caterpillar
   gray with black and white mottling, dorsal black line and white
   bands. FOOD: Tube-tongue. FLIGHT: Feb.–Nov. in s. Texas (3 or 4
   broods). RANGE: Resident from s. Texas west to s. Calif. south to
   cen. Mexico. HABITAT: Desert and subtropical scrub, especially
   adjacent to washes and valleys.

ELADA CHECKERSPOT *Texola elada* PL. 18

⅞−1⅛ in. (22−29 mm). Small. Upperside: Orange and black checkered pattern. Underside: Hindwing checkered black and white with *red-orange marginal band*. **SIMILAR SPECIES:** Tiny Checkerspot is larger, has hindwing underside with terminal black line. **EARLY STAGES:** Not reported. **FOOD:** Yellow-flowered Asteraceae in Mexico. **FLIGHT:** April−Oct. (several broods). **RANGE:** Resident from cen. Texas west to cen. Ariz. and south to s. Mexico. **HABITAT:** Subtropical scrub and thorn forest.

CRESCENTS: GENUS *Phyciodes* HÜBNER

Like *Chlosyne*, this genus is found only in the Americas, where most species are tropical. Our more temperate species are primarily orange and black, and some species are confusingly similar. Males of some species patrol, and those of others perch. Like the patches, females lay their eggs in clusters, and the young caterpillars feed in groups.

TEXAN CRESCENT *Phyciodes texana* PL. 21

1 5/16−1⅞ in. (33−47 mm). Forewing outer margin concave below apex. Upperside: Black with white spots, and at least some *red-brown near base*. Seminole Crescent, *P. t. seminole*, has larger spots and a broader cream band on hindwing. **EARLY STAGES:** Not reported. **FOOD:** Low acanthus family plants. **FLIGHT:** All year in tropics and s. Texas. **RANGE:** Resident from S.C., Ga., and n. Fla. west across the s. U.S. to s. Calif., thence south through Mexico to Guatemala; strays north to cen. Ill., S.D., and cen. Nev. **HABITAT:** Stream courses, dry gulches, city parks.

Texan Crescent. Female resting, Cochise Co., Ariz. Males perch and patrol along stream-courses, washes, or small clearings. Adults visit yellow composite flowers, and females lay their eggs in clusters.

CUBAN CRESCENT *Phyciodes frisia*

PL. 21

1¼–1¾ in. (31–44 mm). Geographically variable. Fla. individuals (*P. f. frisia*) orange and black above; hindwing with *zigzag black submarginal line*; Texas individuals (Tulcis Crescent, *P. f. tulcis*) are black and white above. Forewing *outer margin only slightly indented*. **EARLY STAGES:** Caterpillar is yellow and gray, mottled with black (most) or yellow. **FOOD:** Shrimpflower (*Beloperone guttata*). **FLIGHT:** All year in tropics, most of year in s. Fla., May–Nov. in s. Texas. **RANGE:** Resident in s. peninsular Fla. and West Indies; strays to n. Fla. (*P. f. frisia*). Also resident from s. Texas (*P. f. tulcis*) south through mainland tropical America to Argentina, strays to w. Texas and s. Ariz. **HABITAT:** Open fields and second growth.

BLACK CRESCENT *Phyciodes ptolyca*

PL. 21

1¼–1⅜ in. (31–35 mm). Upperside: Black and yellow. Underside: Distinctly patterned; forewing with *narrow white or yellow marginal patch*. **SIMILAR SPECIES:** A black subspecies of Cuban Crescent (*P. f. tulcis*) is less distinctly patterned below and has wider white marginal patch on underside of forewing. **EARLY STAGES:** Not reported. **FLIGHT:** All year in tropics, mid-Dec. in s. Texas. **RANGE:** Resident from Mexico to Venezuela. Rare stray to s. Texas. **HABITAT:** Open fields and pastures in tropical lowlands.

VESTA CRESCENT *Phyciodes vesta*

PL. 21

1¼–1½ in. (31–37 mm). Upperside: Orange finely marked with black lines. Underside: Forewing with postmedian and submarginal *series of orange circles on dark background*. **EARLY STAGES:** Not reported. **FOOD:** Hairy Tubetongue. **FLIGHT:** All year in lowland Mexico, most of year in Texas, summer only to north. **RANGE:** Resident from cen. Texas west to se. Ariz., south to Guatemala. Strays

TEXAN CRESCENT

CUBAN CRESCENT

PEARL CRESCENT

VESTA CRESCENT

and temporary colonist north to Ark., Colo., and Neb. **HABITAT:** Mesquite and thorn woodland, roadside verges, streambeds.

PHAON CRESCENT *Phyciodes phaon* **PL. 21**

1¼–1½ in. (31–37 mm). Upperside: Forewing with *pale cream median band*. Black markings *more extensive* than on similar southern crescents. Underside: Spring and fall individuals have gray hindwing ("marcia" form). **EARLY STAGES:** Caterpillar variable — olive green to olive-brown with both white and darker bands. **FOOD:** Fog Fruit and Mat Grass. **FLIGHT:** All year in tropics, s. Texas, and s. Fla., more restricted at northern stations. **RANGE:** Resident from coastal S.C. west to w. Texas, and s. Calif. south to Cuba and through Mexico to Guatemala. Strays and occasionally colonizes as far north as e. Colo., Neb., and Mo. **HABITAT:** Open areas with closely cropped vegetation, pastures, dunes, road verges.

Vesta Crescent. Adult perching, lower Rio Grande Valley, Tex. Eggs are laid in clusters on the leaves of Fog Fruit and Matgrass. Adults nectar at flowers of several plants, including those of their caterpillar hosts.

PEARL CRESCENT *Phyciodes tharos*   PL. 22

1¼–1⅝ in. (31–41 mm). One of our commonest, most wide-spread temperate butterflies. Geographically and seasonally variable. Small. Males have black antennal knobs in most of range. Upperside: Males with postmedian and submarginal orange areas *broken by fine black marks.* Underside: Hindwing with crescent in *dark marginal patch.* Spring and fall brood individuals have gray, mottled hindwing underside ("marcia" form). **EARLY STAGES:** Caterpillar is dark chocolate brown; spines brown. Head with white patches. **FOOD:** Asters. **FLIGHT:** All year in Deep South and Mexico (6 broods?), April or May to Oct. or Nov. to north (2–4 broods). **RANGE:** Extreme s. Canada from s. Ont. west to se. Alta., south through e. 2/3 of the U.S. to s. Mexico. **HABITAT:** Open, weedy areas, pastures, vacant lots, roadsides.

NORTHERN CRESCENT *Phyciodes cocyta*   PL. 22

1½–1⅞ in. (37–47 mm). Very similar to Pearl Crescent but known to be a separate species since the two overlap in range without hybridizing. Adults are larger. Male *antennal knobs orange.* Upperside: Males have relatively large open orange post-median and submarginal areas above. Underside: Hindwing usu-

Phaon Crescent. Male nectaring at Shepherd's-Needle, Gainesville, Fla. Adults have same caterpillar hosts as Vesta Crescent and nectar at a similar array of flowers.

PHAON CRESCENT

*Northern Crescent.
Male resting. Pendle-
ton Co., W. Va. Long
confused with the
more widespread
Pearl Crescent, much
remains to be learned
about this species and
its relationships to
other crescents. It
may be a complex of
similar species.*

ally with *pale tan marginal crescent patch* and pale orange worm-like markings. Females darker but often inseparable from those of Pearl and Tawny Crescents. "Marcia" form exceedingly rare. **EARLY STAGES:** Caterpillar is similar to that of Pearl Crescent, but body is pinkish and spines are pinkish gray. **FOOD:** Asters. **FLIGHT:** June–July, rarely Aug. (1 brood), possibly 2 broods in s. Canada. **RANGE:** In the East from Nfld. south to nw. N.J., in the mountains to N.C. and W. Va., and in Great Lakes states west across Canada to the MacKenzie Delta and south through the w. mountain archipelago to se. Ariz. and s. N.M. **HABITAT:** Openings in woods near streams, shale barrens, marsh edges.

TAWNY CRESCENT *Phyciodes batesii* PL. 22

1 5/16–1 3/4 in. (33–43 mm). Antennal knobs black and white. Upperside: Males darker than the Pearl Crescent and the North-

NORTHERN CRESCENT

TAWNY CRESCENT

Painted Crescent. Female resting in vegetation, Washington Co., Colo. Butterfly of the plains and arid Southwest. Bindweed is one of the caterpillar hosts and is an unlikely choice for a crescent as related butterflies use other plant families.

ern Crescent with forewing postmedian band pale orange, contrasting with orange submarginal band. Underside: Forewing *black patch* on *inner margin larger* than subapical patch on costa. Hindwing of male with *yellow-tan ground*, that of female with submarginal row of *black points*. The species has disappeared from most of its former haunts in the East. **EARLY STAGES:** Caterpillar brown with pinkish tinge and pale, broad dorsal stripe. **FOOD:** Wavy-leafed Aster. **FLIGHT:** June–July (1 brood), May in Ga. mountains. **RANGE:** Cen. Alta. east to cen. Ont. and sw. Que., south to n. Ga., Mich., and Wis. Isolated populations in the Black Hills and Neb. Pine Ridge. Many older records are based on misidentifications. **HABITAT:** Moist meadows and pastures, dry rocky ridges.

FIELD CRESCENT *Phyciodes pratensis*   **NOT SHOWN**
1⅜–1¾ in. (35–45 mm). Western. Upperside: Dark, very similar to Tawny Crescent. Underside: Forewing with *yellow discal bar* and *smaller black patches*. Hindwing more heavily patterned. **EARLY STAGES:** Caterpillar brown-black with faint dorsal stripes; head black. **FOOD:** Asters. **FLIGHT:** May–Sept. on plains (2 broods). **RANGE:** Boreal w. North America from Alaska south to s. Calif., s. Ariz. and s. N.M., east to sw. Man. and cen. Kans.(?). **HABITAT:** Open areas and flats.

PAINTED CRESCENT *Phyciodes pictus*   **PL. 21**
1¼–1½ in. (31–37 mm). Small. Upperside: Dark. Underside: Forewing apex and hindwing *clear yellow-cream*. **EARLY STAGES:** Caterpillar yellow-brown with faint dorsal lines; head brown and cream. **FOOD:** Hairy Tubetongue and bindweed. **FLIGHT:** April to early Oct. (2–3 broods). **RANGE:** W. Neb. and cen. Kans. south to w.

PAINTED CRESCENT

BALTIMORE CHECKERSPOT

Texas and n. Mexico, west to w. Ariz. **HABITAT:** Marsh and stream edges in short-grass prairie.

CHECKERSPOTS: GENUS *Euphydryas* SCUDDER

BALTIMORE CHECKERSPOT *Euphydryas phaeton*   **PL. 22**
1¾–2¾ in. (44–70 mm). Upperside: Black with several rows of *cream white spots* on outer half of both wings. Outer margin of both wings with *red-orange crescents*. **EARLY STAGES:** Caterpillar orange-red striped with black; spines black. **FOOD:** Turtlehead, beardtongue, False Foxglove, and, rarely, English Plantain. **FLIGHT:** Late June to mid-Aug. in North, mid-May to late June in South (1 brood). **RANGE:** Very local. N.S. and N.B. west across s. Que. and the Great Lakes region to se. Man., south through e. U.S. to n. Ga., n. Miss., and ne. Okla. Isolated records in Neb. and ne.

Baltimore Checkerspot. Male perching, Pendleton Co., W. Va. This is the official state butterfly of Maryland and was featured on a U.S. postage stamp. Eggs are laid in masses on Turtlehead and related plants.

Texas. **HABITAT:** Usually marshes, bogs, sandy oak barrens, dry open or wooded hillsides. **REMARKS:** Geographically variable. Some question whether there might be two cryptic species instead of one widespread butterfly.

VARIABLE CHECKERSPOT   NOT SHOWN
Euphydryas chalcedona

1 ⁵⁄₁₆−2 in. (33 −52 mm). Upperside: *Checkered black, red-orange, and cream.* Underside: Hindwing with postmedian and marginal red-orange bands *separated by median and submarginal cream bands.* **EARLY STAGES:** Caterpillar black with variable amounts of white; rows of variably colored bristly tubercles. **FOOD:** Besseya, Indian paintbrush, penstemon, and snowberry. **FLIGHT:** May−June. **RANGE:** Resident in much of w. North America; stray to sw. Man. and possibly nw. Minn. **HABITAT:** Sagebrush flats and hills, high prairie with mixed conifers. **REMARKS:** The Variable and Chalcedona checkerspots are now considered to be one species.

ANGLEWINGS: GENUS *Polygonia* HÜBNER

The anglewings are so-named because of the highly irregular outline of their wings. A few species are seasonally diphenic above with a black hindwing summer form and an orange hindwing winter form. Most anglewings have one of two underside hindwing patterns, either plain or finely lined. Several species also occur in Eurasia, and one unusual endemic, *Polygonia haroldi*, is found in central Mexico. Most species are found in wooded habitats. The adult males are unusual in that they set up their territories in late afternoon. Adults rarely visit flowers but feed on rotting fruit, sap flows, or animal dung. Adults are readily attracted to bait traps. Our species overwinter as adults in hollow logs or in outbuildings. Some have just one brood annually, and others have two. Our two commonest species, the Question Mark (*Polygonia interrogationis*) and the Eastern Comma (*P. comma*) migrate south in the fall and return in the spring. Females lay their eggs singly or in short stacks, often on plants adjacent to their true hosts, and the young caterpillars must find their way to food after hatching.

QUESTION MARK *Polygonia interrogationis*   PLS. 4, 22

2 ¼−3 in. (58 −76 mm). Widespread. Large. Upperside: Hindwing of summer form largely black with short tail-like projections, while that of the winter form is orange and black with longer violet-tipped projections. Upperside: Forewing with *"extra" black dash* not present in the similar Eastern Comma. Underside: *Pearly silver question mark* on hindwing is diagnostic. Sexes are

Eastern Comma. Male, winter form, perching, Fairfax Co., Va. The butterfly has a black-hindwing summer form and an orange-hindwing winter form. The adults feed at fermenting fruits and dung instead of flowers.

similar, but there are two seasonal forms. **EARLY STAGES:** Caterpillar variable, body and spines black to yellow; back with 8 metallic silver spots. **FOOD:** Nettle, false nettle, Japanese hops, elms, and hackberry. **FLIGHT:** Two broods—late fall to early spring (winter form), late spring to summer (summer form). Winter form adults overwinter. **RANGE:** N.S. and s. N.B. across s. Canada to e. Alta., thence south throughout e. 60% of U.S. (absent from s. peninsular Fla. and Keys) to cen. Mexico. Immigrant and seasonal colonist to northern and western portions of range. **HABITAT:** River woods, wooded swamps, city parks, and other wooded situations. Migrants may be found in virtually any location.

EASTERN COMMA *Polygonia comma*   **PL. 22**

2–2⅞ in. (52–62 mm). Small with stubby tail-like projections on hindwing. Upperside: Forewing has a single dark postmedian spot

QUESTION MARK

EASTERN COMMA

near bottom edge. Dark border on hindwing encloses pale spots and is broader than forewing border. Hindwing is either primarily black (summer form) or orange with black spots (winter form). Underside: Hindwing has a central silver or white *comma mark* that is *swollen at both ends*. SIMILAR SPECIES: (1) Question Mark is larger, has long violet-tipped tail-like projections from hindwing, and has a question mark in center of hindwing below. (2) Satyr Comma has more extensive orange, has 2 dark postmedian spots near bottom edge of forewing above, and has hindwing below golden brown with a relatively straight median line. EARLY STAGES: Caterpillar variable, black to green-brown and white, spines black to white, rising from yellow tubercles. FOOD: Nettle, false nettle, elms, and hops. FLIGHT: Two broods. Sept.–May (winter form), late May–August (summer form). RANGE: S. N.B. west across s. Canada to s. Man., thence south throughout e. half of U.S. to Gulf Coast and cen. Texas. HABITAT: Woods near rivers, swamps, marshes, moist woods, etc.

SATYR COMMA *Polygonia satyrus* PL. 22

1 15/16–2 7/16 in. (50–62 mm). Upperside: Forewing usually has *two black postmedian spots* near bottom edge. Hindwing with marginal dark border only as broad as forewing outer margin; has *black spot in center*. Underside: Golden brown with *median line relatively straight*. SIMILAR SPECIES: Eastern Comma's upperside usually has only one dark postmedian spot along bottom edge of forewing; median line on hindwing underside not as straight. EARLY STAGES: Caterpillar with green-white dorsal band and lateral lines; spines black (laterals) or green-white (dorsal and subdorsal). Lives in folded leaf shelter. FOOD: Nettles. FLIGHT: Adults emerging in late July, overwintering to June in East (1 long flight). RANGE: S. N.S. and n. New England west across n. Great Lakes region and

SATYR COMMA

GREEN COMMA

s. Canada to w. North America from s. Yukon and sw. N.W. Terr., south through w. boreal Canada and w. U.S. to Baja Calif., s. Ariz., and sw. N.M. **HABITAT:** Openings in riparian woods, marshes, nearby fields and edges, wooded ravines in prairies.

GREEN COMMA *Polygonia faunus* PL. 22

1 ¹⁵⁄₁₆–2⁷⁄₁₆ in. (50–62 mm). Wing *outline* exceptionally *irregular.* Upperside: Forewing with inner 2 costal black spots fused or almost so. Underside: Both wings have outer half lighter and with submarginal *green spots.* **EARLY STAGES:** Caterpillars yellow-brown to brick red with the back white, broken double orange lateral bands, and transverse black and yellow bands or spots; most spines white; head black with white W on front. **FOOD:** Small Pussy Willow, Black Birch, alder, gooseberry, blueberry. **FLIGHT:** Adults emerge in mid- to late summer, overwinter, and reproduce the following spring. Adults live 9–10 months. **RANGE:** Boreal North America south of the tundra. In the East from the Maritimes and New England west across the n. Great Lakes region and Ont. to Man. and ne. Minn., a separate isolated population in s. Appalachians (*P. f. smythi*). **HABITAT:** Canadian zone woods.

HOARY COMMA *Polygonia gracilis* PL. 23

1 ¹⁵⁄₁₆–2³⁄₁₆ in. (49–56 mm). Upperside: Hindwing with *light sub-marginal spots in dark band.* Underside: Wing surfaces gray-brown, *outer half distinctly pale,* often hoary white or silver-gray. The *comma mark is abruptly curved* in a fish-hook shape. The western Zephyr Comma is now considered a subspecies. **EARLY STAGES:** Caterpillar black with upper part of rear half of abdomen white. **FOOD:** Currants. **FLIGHT:** Adults emerge in July, fly until Sept.,

Green Comma. Male at moist sand. Red Lodge, Mont. Adults emerge in summer, hibernate, and repro-duce the following spring. Thus, they have a long lifespan of 9–10 months. They have a variety of caterpillar hosts. Pho-to by George Krizek.

HOARY COMMA

GRAY COMMA

overwinter, and fly until May or June the following spring. **RANGE:** Boreal North America south of the tundra. In the East from N.S., N.B., and n. New England west across s. Canada and Mich. upper peninsula to s. Man. and n. Minn. In the West the species is found in most boreal wooded habitats south to cen. Calif. **HABITAT:** Open boreal woodland near stream courses.

GRAY COMMA *Polygonia progne* PL. 22

2⅛–2⁷⁄₁₆ in. (54–62 mm). Upperside: Hindwing with outer half black, enclosing 3–5 *yellow-orange dots*. Underside: *Fine gray-brown striations*. Hindwing has little or no contrast between basal and outer portions. Comma is shaped like a fish hook. **EARLY STAGES:** Caterpillar yellow-brown with dark olive-brown blotches and lines; head orange-brown; spines black or yellow. **FOOD:** Gooseber-

Gray Comma. Male perching, Pendleton Co., W. Va. The butterfly has two annual generations, each a different seasonal form. A close relationship of this butterfly to a dissimilar western butterfly has been suggested.

COMPTON
TORTOISESHELL

CALIFORNIA
TORTOISESHELL

ry, rarely azalea or elm. **FLIGHT:** Jan.–Aug. (summer form), Oct.–May (winter form) (2 broods). **RANGE:** From Maritimes west across s. Que., Ont., prairie provinces, sw. N.W. Terr. to the Pacific Northwest; south in the Appalachians to w. N.C., n. Ark., and sw. Kans. to the Southwest. **HABITAT:** Rich Canadian and transition zone woods, aspen parklands.

TORTOISESHELLS: GENUS *Nymphalis* KLUK

Tortoiseshells are found in temperate and subarctic regions of both Eurasia and North America. Adults have one generation annually, although sometimes a partial second generation is produced. Adults overwinter and sometimes estivate (pass the summer in a dormant state) as well. Courtship and egg-laying occurs in the spring after hibernation. The Milbert's Tortoiseshell readily visits flowers, but adults of the other species visit sap flows and animal dung and are readily attracted to artificial baits. All of our species are occasionally migratory or regularly change elevations. Eggs are laid in clusters, and the caterpillars feed communally.

COMPTON TORTOISESHELL   PL. 23
Nymphalis vau-album

2¾–3¹⁄₁₆ in. (72–78 mm). Upperside: *Single white spots* on forewing and hindwing costal margins. **SIMILAR SPECIES:** Vaguely reminiscent of anglewings (*Polygonia*) in that it has somewhat irregular wing outlines, although the inner margin of forewing is straight, not curved as in anglewings. **EARLY STAGES:** Caterpillar light green with black spines. **FOOD:** Aspen, birches, or willows. **FLIGHT:** Adults emerge in July, fly until Oct. or Nov., overwinter, and fly until the following June (1 brood). **RANGE:** N.S., N.B., New England, and N.Y. west across s. Canada and the Midwest, thence northwest to

Compton Tortoise-shell. Adult imbibing moisture from wet sand. Tioga Co., Pa. This butterfly is unusual in that it periodically migrates to locations south of its normal range. A relative of similar butterflies found in Eurasia. Photo by George O. Krizek.

w. Canada, including s. Yukon and se. Alaska, extending south in mountains to ne. Colo. (rare) and n. Utah. Vagrants to Dist. of Keewatin, Nfld., Neb., and Fla. **HABITAT:** Upland boreal forests, especially deciduous.

CALIFORNIA TORTOISESHELL   PL. 23
Nymphalis californica

2⅜–2¾ in. (60–70 mm). Upperside: Orange with large black spots. **SIMILAR SPECIES:** Milbert's Tortoiseshell is smaller and has black basal and orange outer portions of forewing above sharply divided. **EARLY STAGES:** Caterpillar velvety black with white dots; spines black except for a yellow dorsal row. **FOOD:** Wild lilacs (*Ceanothus*). **FLIGHT:** Adults emerge in late June, fly until fall, overwinter, and fly until the following April or May (1 brood). **RANGE:** Pacific Coast from s. B.C. south to extreme nw. Baja Calif. Norte (rarely); east to cen. Alta., cen. Colo., and e. N.M. in most boreal western ranges. Migrants rarely found east to Mich., Pa., N.Y., and Vt. **HABITAT:** Ridgetops (males), open brushy areas and open woods. **REMARKS:** Undergoes periodic massive population outbreaks and emigrations in the far West. Strays in our area may result from such irruptions.

MOURNING CLOAK *Nymphalis antiopa*   PL. 23

3⅛–4 in. (80–102 mm). One of our most familiar butterflies. Outer margins irregular, with a short tail-like projection on hindwing. Upperside: Purplish black with a broad, bright yellow marginal border on both wings (fading to white with age) and a row of iridescent blue spots just inside border. **EARLY STAGES:** Caterpillar black with minute white flecks; a dorsal row of dull red spots; red-

Mourning Cloak. Male. Fairfax Co., Va. Although it occasionally has a small second generation, most adults are of a single annual brood and can live at least 11 months, our longest lived butterfly. May migrate southward but also can overwinter in cold climates.

orange prolegs; and black spines. **FOOD:** Willows, birch, cottonwood, elm, hackberry. **FLIGHT:** Adults emerge in June or July, estivate until fall, overwinter, and then fly until the following May or June (1 brood, rarely 2). **RANGE:** Holarctic. Throughout North America south of the tundra (except peninsular Fla., s. La., and s. Texas); extends irregularly south to cen. Mexico. **HABITAT:** Stream courses, woodland glades, city parks, swamp forests. Migrants are seen in a wide variety of habitats. **REMARKS:** Mourning Cloak may be our longest lived butterfly—adults live 10−11 months. Most adults overwinter; apparently, some of the population migrates south each fall.

MILBERT'S TORTOISESHELL *Nymphalis milberti* **PLS. 4, 23**
1⅞−2⁷⁄₁₆ in. (48−62 mm). Outer margins are irregular with a short tail-like projection on hindwing. Upperside: *Basal ⅔ of both*

Milbert's Tortoise-shell. Male resting on vegetation, Fort Collins, Colo. Females lay masses of eggs on nettle leaves, and the young caterpillars feed in large groups. This is a close relative of the European Small Tortoise-shell.

wings black (except for 2 costal orange marks on forewing). *Outer third* of both wings *orange* grading to yellow-orange at inner edge. There is a narrow black marginal border on both wings that sometimes includes blue points on hindwing. **EARLY STAGES:** Caterpillar usually black with minute white flecks and a broken lateral green-yellow stripe. **FOOD:** Nettles. **FLIGHT:** May–Oct., rarely Nov. (2 broods). **RANGE:** Boreal North America south of the taiga. Occasionally migrating south of breeding range to s. Calif., s. N.M., s. Ind., and Pa.—rarely to Mo., Ga., S.C., and N.C. **HABITAT:** Moist pastures, marshes, wet areas near woods. **REMARKS:** Local and altitudinal movements are not well understood. Adults overwinter. Males establish perches on hilltops where available.

SMALL TORTOISESHELL *Nymphalis urticae*   **NOT SHOWN**
1 ⁵⁄₁₆–2⅜ in. (50–60 mm). Rare stray from Europe. Upperside: Forewing costal margin with *alternating black and yellow 4-sided patches*; hindwing with *irregular black patch*. **EARLY STAGES:** Caterpillar usually black with minute white flecks and a white lateral stripe. **FOOD:** Nettles. **FLIGHT:** Mar.–Oct. (1–3 broods). **RANGE:** Eurasia from w. Europe across Russia to Pacific Coast. Has strayed twice to N.Y. **HABITAT:** Weedy places and gardens. Migrant on high mountains.

LADY BUTTERFLIES: GENUS *Vanessa* FABRICIUS

Some of the lady butterflies, notably the Painted Lady and the Red Admiral, are among the most widespread butterflies in the world. In fact, the Painted Lady is also known as the Cosmopolitan. Adults of all our species regularly engage in migratory move-

RED ADMIRAL

AMERICAN LADY

ments, but it is the Painted Lady whose migrations, usually originating in the deserts of northern Mexico, are most dramatic because of their extent and immense numbers. Adult males take up perches in late afternoon—often on promontories or in the lee of large trees. Eggs are laid singly on host plant leaves, and the caterpillars live within webbed leaf shelters.

RED ADMIRAL *Vanessa atalanta*   PL. 23

2¼–3 in. (58–76 mm). Common and widespread. Upperside: *Black.* Forewing with white apical spots and *red-orange median band*; hindwing with *red-orange marginal band.* **EARLY STAGES:** Caterpillars variable black to yellow-green with black and yellow lateral stripes. **FOOD:** Nettles, false nettle, wood nettle, pellitory, possibly hops. **FLIGHT:** March or April to Sept. or Oct. in North (2 broods), Oct.–March in s. Texas as wintering population. **RANGE:** Holarctic. North America south of the taiga and south through Mexican highlands to Guatemala. Migrant and temporary colonist in n. part of range. **HABITAT:** Openings in or near stream courses, marshes, seeps, moist fields, city parks, ridge tops (males). May be found in a wide variety of habitats during migration. **REMARKS:** A regular migrant that probably cannot survive the coldest winters and must recolonize more northern areas.

AMERICAN LADY *Vanessa virginiensis*   PL. 23

2⅛–2⅝ in. (53–67 mm). Formerly called the Hunter's Butterfly or Virginia Lady. Upperside: Forewing with a *white dot in orange field* just below black apical patch. Underside: Hindwing with 2 *large submarginal eyespots.* Whether or not adults can survive cold winters is not clearly documented, and it may be necessary for migrants to colonize much of the East each year. **EARLY STAGES:** Caterpillar has a complex pattern—black with transverse white

American Lady. Adult nectaring on French Marigold, Fairfax Co., Va. Adults overwinter in the south and migrate to the north each spring. The harlequin-like caterpillars eat leaves of everlastings and related plants.

bands; a pair of subdorsal silver-white spots on rear half; 4 rows of black spines, each arising from a broad red base. **FOOD:** Everlastings, pussy toes, rarely other Asteraceae. **FLIGHT:** May–Nov. (3–4 broods), all year in Deep South and s. Texas. **RANGE:** Resident in s. U.S., Mexico, and highlands of Cen. America south to Colombia. Migrant and sometimes temporary colonist to s. Canada, West Indies, oceanic islands, and Europe. Strays periodically to Nfld. and once to Lab. **HABITAT:** Open areas with low vegetation; meadows, dunes, vacant lots.

PAINTED LADY *Vanessa cardui*   **PLS. 3, 23**

2³⁄₁₆–2⅞ in. (55–73 mm). Forewing pointed. Upperside: Orange with pinkish overtone when freshly emerged. Forewing has black apical area with included white spots. Hindwing has a submarginal row of 5 small black spots, occasionally with some blue

PAINTED LADY

Painted Lady. Adult nectaring at flowers of Mock Orange, Fort Collins, Colo. This widespread butterfly cannot survive freezing winters in any of its life stages, but it makes up for the deficiency by having periodic massive migrations.

scaling. Underside: Mottled gray, brown, and black with *4 small submarginal eyespots.* **SIMILAR SPECIES:** (1) American Lady has small white spot in orange field below black apical forewing patch, and always has some blue in upper hindwing submarginal spots. Hindwing below has 2 very large submarginal eyespots. (2) West Coast Lady (very rare in our area) has 4 equal blue-filled submarginal eyespots on upper hindwing. **EARLY STAGES:** Caterpillar variable; lilac to yellow-green with black mottlings and a black head. **FOOD:** More than 100 plants, esp. thistles, mallows, and legumes. **FLIGHT:** May–Oct. in East (1–3 broods), Oct.–April in s. Texas. **RANGE:** Occurs on all continents except Antarctica and Australia. Resident in Mexican plateau, migrant and temporary colonist throughout U. S. (commoner in West) and Canada north to s. Yukon, sw. N.W. Terr., n. Que., and Lab. **HABITAT:** Many open situations—fields, marshes, dunes, thorn scrub, gardens. **REMARKS:** Also called the Thistle Butterfly because of its preference for thistles and the Cosmopolitan for its virtually worldwide occurrence. Next to the Monarch, this is our most conspicuous migrant.

WEST COAST LADY *Vanessa annabella*   **PL. 23**

1 5/16–2 1/4 in. (50–58 mm). *Forewing apex squared off.* Upperside: Forewing *costal bar is orange—not white* as in our other ladies. Hindwing with *3 or 4 blue submarginal spots.* Underside: Hindwing with submarginal *eyespots obscured.* **EARLY STAGES:** Caterpillars variable, tan to black with large orange blotches. **FOOD:** Mallows, Hollyhock. **FLIGHT:** Strays east to the western part of our area during late Sept. to early Nov. **RANGE:** Resident in w. U.S., extreme w. Canada, and nw. Mexico, vagrants east to cen. Kans., e. N.D., and s. Ont. **HABITAT:** Weedy areas, roadsides, gardens.

WEST COAST LADY

COMMON BUCKEYE

MIMIC *Hypolimnas misippus*   **PL. 27**

2³⁄₁₆–3½ in. (56–90 mm). Sexes strongly dimorphic. Upperside: Male *purple-black* with a *large white spot* on each wing. Female has two forms—the commoner one is orange with black marginal borders. **EARLY STAGES:** Caterpillar may be either black or dark gray with light gray bands. **FOOD:** Several plants in acanthus, mallow, morning glory, and purslane families. **FLIGHT:** April–May, Sept.–Dec. **RANGE:** Resident in Africa and Asia. Probably was introduced to West Indies, rare vagrant to se. U.S. **HABITAT:** Open, weedy areas.

BUCKEYES: GENUS *Junonia* HÜBNER

Buckeyes are primarily a tropical group, and various species are found in the tropics worldwide. Many species have dramatically different dry- and wet-season forms. Males of our species patrol along streambeds, dirt roads, or relatively bare openings. The butterflies cannot survive freezing temperatures in any stage, but the adults are excellent colonists. Host plants are members of the snapdragon and acanthus families. Caterpillars live solitarily and eat host plant leaves.

COMMON BUCKEYE *Junonia coenia*   **PL. 23**

1⅝–2¹¹⁄₁₆ in. (39–68 mm). Upperside: Forewing with at least part of *white subapical bar inside the large eyespot.* Uppermost of two hindwing eyespots is *much larger* and has a magenta crescent. Underside: Hindwing tan-brown or rose-red (short-day form). **EARLY STAGES:** Caterpillar black with dorsal and lateral broken yellow lines; 4 rows of iridescent blue-black spines; head orange and black with 2 fleshy orange projections. **FOOD:** Snapdragon, Toadflax, False Foxglove, plantain, ruellia. **FLIGHT:** May–Oct. (2–3

Common Buckeye. Adult resting, Fairfax Co., Va. Male Common Buckeyes often perch and patrol along dirt roads, bare open areas, and sand dunes. They may occasionally participate in migrations — often along coastlines.

broods), all year in Deep South. **RANGE:** Resident in s. U.S. and north along the coasts to N.C. and cen. Calif.; south to Bermuda, Cuba, Isle of Pines, and s. Mexico; migrant and temporary colonist north to Ore., s. Man., s. Ont., and s. Me. **HABITAT:** Open, sunny situations —open fields, dunes, roadsides, thorn scrub.

MANGROVE BUCKEYE *Junonia evarete*   PL. 23

1⅜−2 in. (35−52 mm). Forewing apex slightly extended. Upperside: Forewing *band narrow, orange or orange-white*; large eyespot *ringed with orange*—never brown. Uppermost hindwing eyespot equal to or smaller than lowest forewing eyespot. Underside: Hindwing median line *slightly jagged*, ground color brown, seldom banded, usually lacks eyespots. **EARLY STAGES:** Caterpillar black with minute white flecks, a double row of broken orange spots along each side; spines black or yellow; head yellow above. **FOOD:**

TROPICAL BUCKEYE

WHITE PEACOCK

White Peacock. Adult perching on ground, lower Rio Grande Valley, Tex. Adult males perch and fly circular patrolling flights. This is a widespread tropical butterfly that resides and breeds only along the southern U.S. border.

Black Mangrove. **FLIGHT:** Several generations during warm part of year. **RANGE:** Extreme s. Fla., West Indies, and Atlantic coast of Mexico north to s. Texas. **HABITAT:** Black Mangrove swamps and tidal flats.

TROPICAL BUCKEYE *Junonia genoveva*   PL. 23

1¾–2³⁄₁₆ in. (44–55 mm). Upperside: Forewing *band wide, white diffused with orange or brown*; large eyespot *edged with brown internally*. Hindwing with uppermost eyespot equal to or smaller than lowest forewing eyespot. Underside: Hindwing median line *relatively straight*. A dark form, Dark Buckeye (*J. g. nigrosuffusa*), occurs along the s. Texas coast. **SIMILAR SPECIES:** Mangrove Buckeye has forewing apex more extended. Median line of hindwing underside slightly jagged. **EARLY STAGES:** Caterpillar black with faint dorsal and lateral rows of cream dots; spines black with blue bases; head black with 2 short fleshy projections. **FOOD:** Lippia, porterweed, ruellia, stemodia. **FLIGHT:** March–Oct. (3–4 broods), Oct.–March (adults overwinter). **RANGE:** Resident in s. Fla., s. Texas, s. Ariz., and s. N.M. south through the West Indies, Mexico, and Cen. America to Argentina. Rare vagrant to cen. Fla., se. Colo., and se. Calif. **HABITAT:** Open, tropical lowlands—weedy fields, beach dunes.

WHITE PEACOCK *Anartia jatrophae*   PL. 24

2³⁄₁₆–2¾ in. (55–69 mm). Mostly *white*. Upperside: Small round *black submarginal spot* on forewing and 2 *on slightly scalloped hindwing*. **EARLY STAGES:** Caterpillar dark brown to black, yellow-brown below; a transverse row of small silver spots on each segment; spines black with orange bases; head black with 2 long clublike projections. **FOOD:** *Bacopa*, lippia, ruellia, Water Hyssop. **FLIGHT:** All year in Deep South and s. Texas. **RANGE:** Resident from s. Fla. (including Keys) and s. Texas south through the West Indies, Mexico, and Cen. America to Argentina. Migrant and temporary colonist to coastal S.C. and cen. Texas. Rare vagrant to Neb., Mo., and N.C. **HABITAT:** Moist weedy fields, swamp edges, parks.

CARIBBEAN PEACOCK *Anartia chrysopelea*   **PL. 24**
2⅟₁₆–2¹⁵⁄₁₆ in. (62–74 mm). Brown with *white median band* or patches. Outer wing margins *scalloped*. **EARLY STAGES:** Not reported. **FOOD:** *Lippia*. **FLIGHT:** Jan.–Sept. in Cuba; late Feb. in Fla. **RANGE:** Resident on Cuba, Isle of Pines, and Swan I. Rare vagrant (once) to Fla. Keys. **HABITAT:** Disturbed scrubland.

BANDED PEACOCK *Anartia fatima*   **PL. 24**
2⅜–2⁹⁄₁₆ in. (60–66 mm). Usually lands on or near ground with wings open. Upperside: *Brown*. Forewing with white or cream-yellow median and submarginal bands. Hindwing slightly scalloped with *broken red median band*. **EARLY STAGES:** Caterpillar black with longitudinal rows of light dots; spines red-brown to black-brown; head purple-black. **FOOD:** Ruellia in s. Texas, other acanthus family plants further south. **FLIGHT:** All year in s. Texas. **RANGE:** Resident from Mexico through Cen. America to e. Panama. Vagrant and occasional colonist to s. and cen. Texas. **HABITAT:** Open weedy areas, fields, orchards, second growth.

MALACHITE *Siproeta stelenes*   **PL. 26**
3¼–3¹⁵⁄₁₆ in. (81–99 mm). This is our only *largely green* nymphalid. Forewing apex extended; hindwing has pointed tail-like projection. Upperside: Brown-black with translucent yellow-green or white-green marks. Underside: Gray with green windowlike

MALACHITE

marks. Has slow floating flight. **EARLY STAGES:** Caterpillar is velvety black with dark red divisions between segments; prolegs pink; 2 large spined horns on head. **FOOD:** Usually cafetin, but ruellia is also likely. **FLIGHT:** All year—2 or 3 flights during the summer; 1 brood of the dry-season form overwinters. **RANGE:** Resident from s. Fla. and s. Texas south through West Indies and mainland tropical America to Brazil. Rare vagrant to Kans. **HABITAT:** Clearings in river forest, overgrown orchards, weedy areas near houses. **REMARKS:** Florida populations have appeared in recent decades. Adults roost under leaves at night.

ADMIRALS: SUBFAMILY LIMENITIDINAE

These butterflies are found on most continents. The adults of most genera are characterized by their flap-and-glide flight. The butterflies share common traits of caterpillar and chysalid structure.

COMMON BANNER *Epiphile adrasta* PL. 25

2¼–2⅝ in. (58–65 mm). Sexes differ on upper wing surfaces, but lower surfaces are similar. Upperside: Forewing of both sexes with *squared-off* extended *apex* and *pale transverse median band*. **EARLY STAGES:** Caterpillar green with yellow lateral lines; spiracles yellow-orange; orange spines with black forks; 2 large recurved spiny horns on brown head. **FOOD:** Vines in Sapindaceae family. **FLIGHT:** All year in tropics; Oct. in s. Texas. **RANGE:** Mexico south to Panama; rare stray to s. Texas. **HABITAT:** Tropical rain and cloud forests.

ADMIRALS: GENUS *Limenitis* FABRICIUS

The admirals are a Northern Hemisphere group—the North American members of which are slightly differentiated. Some refer our species to a separate genus, *Basilarchia*, but I feel this is too fine a distinction. There are four North American species, one of which (*L. lorquini*) is restricted to the far West. Adults have a flap-and-glide flight and are associated with forests or adjacent open areas, often along stream courses. The males perch and occasionally patrol in search of females. The males readily visit moist spots by streams, and both sexes will imbibe fluids from animal dung, bird droppings, and rotting fruit. The butterflies only occasionally take nectar from flowers. Adults of the Viceroy and Red-spotted Purple mimic distasteful and emetic butterflies, the Monarch and the Pipevine Swallowtail, respectively. The adults select cottonwood, aspen, or willows for their caterpillar hosts. Eggs are laid singly at the tip of host leaves, and the cater-

White Admiral. Adult perching. Ontario, Canada. White Admirals hybridize freely with the Red-spotted Purple and are considered the same species. The former is common in the Northeast and across much of Canada. Photo by John R. Riggenbach.

pillars, which resemble bird droppings, eat leaves. The winter is passed by the young caterpillars, which live in small rolled leaf shelters.

WHITE ADMIRAL, RED-SPOTTED PURPLE   PL. 24
Limenitis arthemis

3–4 in. (75–101 mm). Our two very different forms were once considered separate species. WHITE ADMIRAL: Upperside of both wings black. Forewing with outwardly curved broad *white band* and a few white spots on apex. Hindwing has a postmedian *white band*, submarginal series of red spots, and a marginal row of blue dashes. Underside: White bands are repeated. Hindwing has reddish brown background. RED-SPOTTED PURPLE: Upperside is *blue to blue-green* with outer part of hindwing more iridescent. Underside: Forewing has two costal red-orange bars, and

WHITE ADMIRAL

RED-SPOTTED PURPLE

Red-spotted Purple. Male perching on ground, Fairfax Co., Va. This shows the marginal orange spots that help make this form a good mimic of the distasteful Pipevine Swallowtail. The iridescent upper wing surfaces (see Plates 5, 24) help complete the mimetic resemblance.

hindwing has 3 basal red-orange spots and a submarginal *row of red-orange spots*. The Banded Purple, form "proserpina," which is like the White Admiral with a submarginal blue band, is also shown on Pl. 24. The more northern White Admiral (*L. arthemis arthemis*) freely hybridizes with the more southern Red-spotted Purple (*L. arthemis astyanax*) in a belt across New England, s. Ontario, and the Great Lakes states (see map). Rarely, individuals looking like White Admirals show up far to the south amid Red-spotted Purple populations. **EARLY STAGES:** Caterpillar cryptic gray-brown and white; humped at thorax. **FOOD:** Leaves of trees and shrubs: Wild Cherry, poplar, aspens, black oaks, and others. **FLIGHT:** April or May to Oct. (2 broods). **RANGE:** Boreal and temperate North America from Alaska and subarctic Canada southeast of continental divide and high plains to peninsular Fla. and the Gulf states. Isolated populations (*L. a. arizonensis*) from Ariz., N.M., and w. Texas south into n. Mexico. **HABITAT:** Deciduous broad-leaf forest or mixed evergreen forest, associated edges, and clearings.

VICEROY *Limenitis archippus*   **PLS. 3, 24**
2⅝–3⅕ in. (67–85 mm). Upperside: Orange on burnt orange with postmedian *black line on hindwing* and a *single row of white spots* in the black marginal band. In Florida and the Southwest, where resident Monarchs are rare, Viceroys (*L. a. floridensis*) are brown instead of red-orange and are mimics of the Queen. **SIMILAR SPECIES:** (1) Monarch and (2) Queen both lack the hindwing postmedian black line and have two rows of white spots in the marginal bands. **EARLY STAGES:** Caterpillar olive green with a white dorsal blotch, white sides and a few black spots; antennae-like projections from second thoracic segment. **FOOD:** Leaves of various

willows. **FLIGHT:** May–Sept. (2–3 broods) in most of range; all year in Fla. **RANGE:** North America from sw. N.W. Terr. (rare) south through s. Canada and most of U.S. to cen. Mexico (Veracruz). **HABITAT:** Riparian and swampy areas, lake edges. **REMARKS:** A well-known mimic of the distasteful Monarch. The Viceroy itself may not be completely palatable.

WEIDEMEYER'S ADMIRAL *Limenitis weidemeyerii* PL. 24

2⁹⁄₁₆–3¾ in. (66–95 mm). Western. Upperside: Hindwing submarginal areas are *black*. Underside: Hindwing has *gray-white marginal spots*. Basal area is gray-white with dark lines. **SIMILAR SPECIES:** White Admiral has submarginal red spots on hindwing above, and background of hindwing below is red-brown. **EARLY STAGES:** Caterpillar humpbacked, yellow-green or gray with lighter mottling with bristly spines on second segment. **FOOD:** Willows, aspen, cottonwood, *Amelanchier*, and *Holodiscus*. **FLIGHT:** June to

Viceroy. Male perching, Fairfax Co., Va. This is a close model of the Monarch (see plates 24, 27). Despite its resemblance to the Monarch it periodically hybridizes with the Red-spotted Purple from which intermediate but sterile offspring result.

early Sept. (1 –2 broods). **RANGE:** W. North America from se. Alta. south to se. Ariz. and s. N.M., east to Neb. and w. to e.-cen. Calif. **HABITAT:** Streamsides, river forests, small towns, and subdivisions.

BAND-CELLED SISTER *Adelpha fessonia*   **PL. 24**
2³⁄₁₆–2¾ in. (55 –70 mm). The *white-banded* butterfly with *orange forewing apex* most likely to be found in the lower Rio Grande Valley. White median band reaches forewing costal margin. **SIMILAR SPECIES:** Silver Emperor male has a similar pattern, though it is unrelated. Wing shape is different, and median white band does not reach costa. **EARLY STAGES:** Not reported. **FOOD:** *Celtis lindheimeri.* **FLIGHT:** March–April, July–Dec.; flies from March through November in Mexico and Cen. America (all year in Costa Rica?). **RANGE:** Cen. Mexico south to Panama; periodic resident in lower Rio Grande Valley, Texas. **HABITAT:** Woodland edges and trails near streams.

SPOT-CELLED SISTER *Adelpha basiloides*   **NOT SHOWN**
2³⁄₁₆–2⅝ in. (55 –66 mm). Upperside: Black with median white band on both wings. Forewing has small orange apical patch, and white band does not reach costal margin. **SIMILAR SPECIES:** Band-celled Sister has larger orange apical patch, and white band reaches forewing costal margin. **EARLY STAGES:** Not reported. **FOOD:** Various shrubs in madder family (*Alibertia, Faramea,* and *Ixora*). **FLIGHT:** March–Nov. in Mexico; throughout the year in Cen. America. **RANGE:** S. Texas (once) south to Panama. A rare stray to lower Rio Grande Valley. **HABITAT:** Lowland tropical forests with a distinct dry season.

CALIFORNIA SISTER *Adelpha bredowii*   **PL. 24**
2⅝–3¹⁵⁄₁₆ in. (67 –99 mm). The California Sister has the flap-and-glide flight typical of admirals. It is likely to be the only black but-

terfly in its eastern range having a *white median band* and *orange forewing apex*. **EARLY STAGES:** Caterpillar is mottled green. **FOOD:** Leaves of oaks, especially evergreen species. **FLIGHT:** May–Sept. (2 broods). **RANGE:** Sw. U.S. from sw. Ore., n. Utah, and sw. Kans. south through Mexico to Honduras. Regular visitor to e.-cen. Texas. **HABITAT:** Oak groves and stream valleys.

MEXICAN BLUEWING *Myscelia ethusa* PL. 24

2¼–3 in. (64–76 mm). Forewing apex appears cut off. Upperside: Black with *transverse violet bands*. Outer half of forewing with irregular white spots. **EARLY STAGES:** Not reported. **FLIGHT:** All year in s. Texas. **RANGE:** Mexico south through Cen. America to Colombia. Periodic stray and temporary resident in lower Rio Grande Valley, Texas. **HABITAT:** Stream valleys with dry scrub or scattered forest.

DINGY PURPLEWING *Eunica monima* PL. 25

1⅞–2 in. (48–52 mm). Small size (for a brushfoot). Sexes similar. Purple wings perch with their wings tightly closed and rarely open them except in flight. Wing margins regular. *Dingy, smeared white spots* on forewing apex. Ground color black-brown with slight *purplish gloss*; underside without distinct pattern. **SIMILAR SPECIES:** Large Purplewing is larger, wing margins are more irregular, and white spots on outer half of forewing are distinct, not dingy. **EARLY STAGES:** Caterpillar olive green with black and yellow lateral stripes; head black and orange with 2 short stout horns on top of head. **FOOD:** Gumbo Limbo. **FLIGHT:** All year in tropics; June–Aug. in s. Texas. **RANGE:** Mexico and West Indies south through Cen. America to n. South America (Venezuela). Periodic immigrant to s. Fla. (occasional resident?), s. Texas, and s. Ariz. **HABITAT:** Hardwood hammocks in s. Fla.; river forests in seasonally dry tropics.

DINGY PURPLEWING

LARGE PURPLEWING

LARGE PURPLEWING *Eunica tatila*   PL. 25

1 %₆−2 %₆ in. (49−61 mm). Sexes similar. Medium size. Upperside: Bases of both wings with *violet iridescence*. Forewing margin irregular at apex; outer portion with 6−7 distinct white spots. Underside: Hindwing with 6 or 7 small white-pupiled *marginal eyespots*. **EARLY STAGES:** Not reported. **FLIGHT:** All year in s. Fla. **RANGE:** Resident from Fla., West Indies, Mexico, and mainland tropical America to Argentina. Strays north to Texas, rarely Kans. **HABITAT:** Hardwood hammocks on Fla. Keys, river forests elsewhere.

BLUE-EYED SAILOR *Dynamine dyonis*   PL. 25

1 ⅜−1 ⅞ in. (39−48 mm). Small. Sexes dimorphic. Upperside: Male bronze-green; female black with white bands and patches. Underside: Both sexes with similar pattern, including 2 *round, blue submarginal spots*. **EARLY STAGES:** Caterpillar pale green; black warts on thorax; rows of short spines on dorsum. **FOOD:** Noseburn (*Tragia neptifolia*) and *Dalechampia*. **FLIGHT:** May−Nov. in Texas; March−Nov. in Mexico. **RANGE:** Resident from cen. Mexico south through Cen. America to Colombia. Periodic colonist and occasional resident to n.-cen. Texas. **HABITAT:** Forest edges.

CRAMER'S EIGHTY-EIGHT *Diaethria clymena*   PL. 25

1 ½−1 ¹⁄₁₆ in. (38−41 mm). Upperside: Black with *iridescent blue marginal bands*. Underside: Forewing red; hindwing with *black-outlined "88" or "89."* **EARLY STAGES:** Not reported. **FOOD:** *Trema micrantha* (Brazil). **FLIGHT:** Feb.−July in Fla.; March−Nov. in South America. **RANGE:** Resident in South America, occasional stray in s. Fla. **HABITAT:** Wet tropical forests.

MEXICAN EIGHTY-EIGHT *Diaethria asteria*   PL. 25

1 ⅜−1 ¹¹⁄₁₆ in. (39−41 mm). Upperside: *Violet* with *white apical spot* on forewing. Underside: Hindwing with *black-outlined "88"* on gray-white background. **EARLY STAGES:** Not reported. **FLIGHT:** July in s. Texas, Sept. in Mexico. **RANGE:** Resident in s. Mexico and n. Cen. America. One reported stray to s. Texas. **HABITAT:** Wet tropical forests.

COMMON MESTRA *Mestra amymone*   PL. 25

1 ¹¹⁄₁₆−1 ¹⁵⁄₁₆ in. (41−49 mm). Sexes similar. Base of forewing costa vein swollen. Upperside: Gray-white. Hindwing with median *row of white spots* and *outer hindwing orange*. **EARLY STAGES:** Caterpillar brown with green diamonds on dorsum; 8 rows of spines; head capsule red with black on crown; 2 prominent head spines, each terminating in a knob. **FOOD:** Noseburn (*Tragia neptifolia*). **FLIGHT:** All year in s. Texas, especially June−Nov. **RANGE:** Resident from s.

COMMON MESTRA

Texas and Mexico south through Cen. America to Costa Rica. In the U.S., strays north through the plains to S.D. **HABITAT:** Weedy fields, roadsides, wood edges.

RED RIM *Biblis hyperia*   **PL. 25**

2⅝−3 in. (65−76 mm). Sexes similar. Upperside: Brown-black; forewing with pale outer area; hindwing with submarginal *pink-red band* and *scalloped* outer margin. **EARLY STAGES:** Caterpillar with fine brown, black, and gray lines; many finely branched spines terminating in rosettes; head gray with 2 prominent recurved horns. **FOOD:** Noseburn (*Tragia volubilis*). **FLIGHT:** Feb., July−Nov. in s. Texas; March−Nov. in Mexico and Cen. America. **RANGE:** Periodic resident in lower Rio Grande Valley, Texas, and south through West Indies, Mexico, and mainland tropical America to Paraguay. Periodic stray to cen. Texas. **HABITAT:** Open, subtropical woods.

CRACKERS: GENUS *Hamadryas* HÜBNER

The crackers are found in the American tropics. Only in the Florida Keys and Texas's lower Rio Grande Valley have up to six species been found as occasional vagrants or, rarely, as temporary colonists. Adults habitually perch with wings outspread and head down on tree trunks. Males seem to be territorial and fly at each other with a clicking noise, hence the name "cracker." This sound is thought to be made by spiny rods at the tip of the male's abdomen. Adults never visit flowers. Adults congregate at a focal tree just before dusk. As the sun sets, they leave the tree to roost under the leaves of adjacent trees or shrubs. The caterpillars of all species eat the leaves of various *Dalechampia*, a genus of tropical vines. There is no resistant overwintering stage, and adults may be found throughout the year.

VARIABLE CRACKER *Hamadryas feronia* PL. 26

2 ¹⁵⁄₁₆–3¼ in. (75–82 mm). Upperside: Forewing with dull red bar in discal cell; hindwing *eyespots* each have a *blue ring* surrounding a *white-centered black spot*. Underside: Hindwing white or tan-white with a series of *submarginal black rings*. SIMILAR SPECIES: (1) Gray Cracker has eyespots on hindwing upperside with orange scales outside of black crescent. Hindwing underside with submarginal eyespots, each with a brown ring surrounding a black crescent in a white center. (2) Brownish Cracker lacks red bar on forewing upperside. (3) Guatemalan Cracker has upperside hindwing submarginal eyespots with a blue ring, followed inwardly by a wide black ring, a blue ring, and finally, a mottled brown and white center. EARLY STAGES: Caterpillar dirty gray-green with a pale interrupted line along each side or black with brown dots and an interrupted reddish line along each side; some yellow spines. FOOD: *Dalechampia*. FLIGHT: All year in tropics, July–Dec. in s. Texas. RANGE: Resident from Mexico south through mainland tropical America to s. Brazil and Argentina. Periodic stray to lower Rio Grande Valley, Texas. HABITAT: Forest edges and cutover second growth.

GRAY CRACKER *Hamadryas februa* PL. 26

2¾–3⁵⁄₁₆ in. (72–85 mm). Upperside: Forewing discal cell bar with at least some red; hindwing eyespots have *orange scales outside of black crescent*. Underside: Forewing with a black submarginal patch on lower half. Hindwing white with submarginal eyespots, each a *brown ring* surrounding a *black crescent* in a *white center*. SIMILAR SPECIES: (1) Variable Cracker has duller red bar on upperside forewing, and submarginal eyespots on hindwing upperside have a blue ring surrounding a white-centered black spot. (2) Brownish Cracker lacks any red on forewing upperside. (3) Guatemalan Cracker has a distinct red bar on forewing above, and hindwing eyespots each have a blue ring followed inwardly by a wide black ring, a blue ring, and a mottled brown and white center. EARLY STAGES: Caterpillar black with light green spines and 6 yellow longitudinal lines; head capsule red-brown with 2 long recurved knobbed spines. FOOD: *Dalechampia* and *Tragia*. FLIGHT: All year in tropics; Aug.–Oct. in s. Texas. RANGE: Resident from s. Texas (periodic in lower Rio Grande Valley) south through Mexico and mainland tropical America to Argentina. HABITAT: Tropical seasonally dry forest and associated edges.

RED CRACKER *Hamadryas amphinome* PL. 26

3¹⁄₁₆–3⅜ in. (78–87 mm). Upperside: Forewing with broad white band, *ground blue*. Underside: *Hindwing brick red* with submarginal eyespots largely obscured. **EARLY STAGES:** Caterpillar with head, thoracic, and anal segments black with white spots; other segments with black-centered yellow rings; several rows of much-branched long spines. Head with long horns ending in round white knobs. **FOOD:** *Dalechampia*. **FLIGHT:** All year in tropics; Sept. in Texas. **RANGE:** Resident from cen. Mexico south through mainland tropical America to Argentina. Rare stray (once) to lower Rio Grande Valley, Texas. **HABITAT:** Second-growth scrub, forest edges.

BROWNISH CRACKER *Hamadryas iphthime*   **PL. 26**

2¾–3⅛ in. (72–79 mm). Upperside: Forewing *without red bar* in discal cell; hindwing submarginal spots each a *blue ring*, followed inwardly by a *narrow brown ring*, a *light blue ring*, then a *thin black center* containing a *white oval or crescent*. **SIMILAR SPECIES:** All other similar crackers likely to stray to s. Texas—(1) Variable, (2) Gray, and (3) Guatemalan—have a red bar or at least some red scaling in discal cell on forewing above. **EARLY STAGES:** Unreliably reported. **FOOD:** *Dalechampia*. **FLIGHT:** All year in tropics; Aug. in s. Texas. **RANGE:** Resident from cen. Mexico south through mainland tropical America to Brazil. One reported stray to cen. Texas. **HABITAT:** Trails and light gaps in wet forest.

GUATEMALAN CRACKER   **PL. 26**
Hamadryas guatemalena

3–3⅞ in. (76–97 mm). Upperside: Forewing with *red bar* in discal cell; hindwing submarginal eyespots with *blue ring*, followed inwardly by a wide *black ring*, a *blue ring*, then a *mottled brown-and-white center*. Underside: Forewing with white subapical spot nearest apex large; hindwing tan-white with series of submarginal black rings. **SIMILAR SPECIES:** (1) Variable Cracker has submarginal eyespots on hindwing upperside, each with a blue ring surrounding a white-centered black spot. (2) Gray Cracker has submarginal eyespots on hindwing upperside, each with orange scaling outside a black crescent. (3) Brownish Cracker lacks any hint of a red bar or red scaling in upperside forewing discal cell. **EARLY STAGES:** Caterpillar black with prominent yellow dorsal patches; head capsule black with 2 knobbed horns. **FOOD:** *Dalechampia*. **FLIGHT:** All year in tropics; Aug. in s. Texas. **RANGE:** Resident from Mexico south through Cen. America to Costa Rica. Rare stray to lower Rio Grande Valley, Texas. **HABITAT:** Cutover areas, forest edges, stream valleys.

PALE CRACKER *Hamadryas amphichloe*   **PL. 26**
2¹⁵⁄₁₆–3⅜ in. (74–86 mm). Thus far, the only cracker found in Fla. Upperside: Forewing with *red bar* in discal cell, males with

outer part whitish. Hindwing submarginal eyespots each with orange scaling outside a black crescent. **EARLY STAGES:** Not reported. **FLIGHT:** All year in West Indies. **RANGE:** Resident in West Indies and South America south to Ecuador. Rare stray or import on exotic plants to Fla. Keys. **HABITAT:** Forest edges near streams, trees in open fields.

ORION *Historis odius*   **NOT SHOWN**
4½–4¾ in. (114–120 mm). Large. Black and orange. Upperside: Forewing with apex extended, *white spot* on costal margin below apex. Hindwing *pointed* at anal angle. Underside: Orange-brown to purple-brown, *leaflike*. **EARLY STAGES:** Caterpillar light green with light brown transverse markings; dorsal spines black, lateral spines white. **FOOD:** Various cecropias. **FLIGHT:** June in Fla. (one report); all year in tropics. **RANGE:** West Indies and Mexico south through Cen. America to Argentina. Rare stray to Fla. (one report). **HABITAT:** Tropical forests.

BLOMFILD'S BEAUTY *Smyrna blomfildia*   **PL. 26**
3–3½ in. (76–90 mm). Adults sip fermented juices of rotting fruits. Upperside: Male rich orange, female brown. Forewing apex *black with three white spots*. Underside: Hindwing with many *wavy markings* and 2 *submarginal eyespots*. **EARLY STAGES:** Caterpillar black with white-branched spines; head capsule orange with 2 stout recurved horns. **FOOD:** *Urera*. **FLIGHT:** All year in tropics. **RANGE:** Resident from Mexico south through mainland tropical America to Peru. Periodic vagrant to s. Texas. **HABITAT:** Tropical forests.

DAGGERWINGS: GENUS *Marpesia* HÜBNER

Daggerwings are a moderately rich New World group. Only one species is resident in eastern North America, but three others have been found as strays from more tropical countries. Adults of all species have a long thin "dagger" projecting from the rear portion of each hindwing. The butterflies roost under large leaves, often in small groups. Adults may visit flowers or feed on rotting fruits. The caterpillars feed on leaves of trees in the fig family.

WAITER DAGGERWING *Marpesia zerynthia*   **PL. 25**
2¾–3⅛ in. (71–80 mm). Upperside: Brown-black. Underside: *Basal half* of both wings white — *outer half dark brown*. **EARLY STAGES:** Not reported. **FLIGHT:** July and Oct. in s. Texas; May–Nov. in Mexico. **RANGE:** Resident from cen. Mexico south through mainland tropical America to Brazil. Rare stray to s. Texas. **HABITAT:** Tropical forests.

MANY-BANDED DAGGERWING *Marpesia chiron* **PL. 25**
2⅞₆–2⅝ in. (62–67 mm). Periodically engages in mass emigrations or synchronous adult emergences in tropics. Upperside: Dark brown with 3 *paler stripes* and 3 *faint white dots* on forewing apex. Underside: Basal third pale gray with faint orange stripes. **EARLY STAGES:** Caterpillar yellow-orange above with reddish streaks and 2 black lines; sides yellow; dorsal spines black. Head yellow-green with 2 black spots at base of horns. **FOOD:** Fig and related tropical trees. **FLIGHT:** Feb., July–Oct. in s. Texas; May–Dec. in Mexico (all year in Cen. America?). **RANGE:** Resident from West Indies and Mexico south through mainland tropical America to Argentina. Frequent stray to s. Texas, rarely to Kans. and s. Fla. **HABITAT:** Tropical forests, especially river valleys.

RUDDY DAGGERWING *Marpesia petreus* **PL. 25**
2¹⁵⁄₁₆–3¾ in. (75–95 mm). Our only common daggerwing. Upperside: *Orange* with *thin black lines.* Forewing apex highly extended. Hindwing with *long thin tails.* Underside: Pattern somewhat cryptic, *leaflike.* **SIMILAR SPECIES:** Antillean Daggerwing has shorter tails, and median dark band is sharply angled. **EARLY STAGES:** Caterpillar purplish above, white below; abdominal segments yellow above; segments 5, 7, 9, 11 each with a weak upright threadlike appendage. **FOOD:** Figs. **FLIGHT:** Most of year in Fla., especially common May–July. **RANGE:** Resident from s. Fla., West Indies, Mexico, and mainland tropical America south to Brazil. Strays north to s. Texas, Kans., Neb., Colo., and Ariz. **HABITAT:** Hardwood hammocks or edges in s. Fla.; evergreen or semi-evergreen forests elsewhere.

ANTILLEAN DAGGERWING *Marpesia eleuchea* **PL. 25**
2⅝–3¼ in. (65–82 mm). Forewing *apex extended.* Hindwing with a long thin tail. Upperside: Orange with 3 black lines, the *central* of which is *sharply angled* inwardly. **SIMILAR SPECIES:** Ruddy Daggerwing has forewing apex more rounded, longer tail on hindwing, and median black line on forewing upperside is straight, not angled. **EARLY STAGES:** Not described. **FOOD:** Fig. **FLIGHT:** All months in West Indies. **RANGE:** West Indies, strays occasionally to Fla. Keys, presumably from Cuba. **HABITAT:** Tropical woodlands.

LEAF BUTTERFLIES: SUBFAMILY CHARAXINAE

This is a primarily tropical group of medium to large-sized, robust, fast-flying butterflies. Our species are limited to the leafwings (Genus *Anaea*).

RUDDY DAGGERWING

LEAFWINGS: GENUS *Anaea* HÜBNER

The leafwings are a wholly New World, primarily tropical, group. We have one common species, which occurs primarily in the southern states, but one other is resident in the Florida Keys, and three others have appeared as strays. The adults often have a sickle-shaped or squared-off forewing apex and a short pointed tail-like projection on each hindwing. All species have two seasonal forms — a summer or wet-season one and a winter or dry-season one. The dry-season adults pass the winter in reproductive arrest. The adults are rapid, direct fliers and are often found perching on tree limbs or trunks high in the canopy. Adults imbibe nutrients from animal dung, rotting fruit, or sap flows. They almost never visit flowers for nectar. Eggs are laid singly on host plant leaves, usually those of *Crotons* (goatweed, for example).

TROPICAL LEAFWING *Anaea aidea*   **PL. 25**

2⁷⁄₁₆–3¹⁄₁₆ in. (62−78 mm). Upperside: Dusky orange-red. Outer margin *slightly uneven*; marginal areas darkened with black scaling; hindwing with small *faint yellow marginal points*. Two seasonal forms; winter (dry-season) form with sickle-shaped forewing apex. **SIMILAR SPECIES:** Goatweed Leafwing is larger, not as red, and has a forewing with straight outer margin. **EARLY STAGES:** Not reported. **FLIGHT:** Sept.−April (dry-season form), April−Sept. (wet-season form). **RANGE:** Mexico south to Cen. America (nw. Costa Rica) with occasional strays to s. Texas, Kans., and Calif. **HABITAT:** Woods edges, trails, willows near river courses.

FLORIDA LEAFWING *Anaea floridalis*   **PL. 25**

3−3½ in. (76−90 mm). Pointed tail on hindwing. Outer margin straight. Upperside: Red with *dark* outer margins and bar in forewing discal cell. Has summer and winter forms. SIMILAR SPECIES: Goatweed Leafwing is similar, but the two do not occur together. EARLY STAGES: Caterpillar green-brown covered with many fine white tubercles; 2 yellow side stripes; black saddle mark and black anal plate; head with 7 orange and 2 black horns. FOOD: Woolly Croton. FLIGHT: Oct.–April (winter or dry-season form), May–Oct. (summer or wet-season form). RANGE: Fla. Keys and extreme s. peninsular Fla. HABITAT: Pine-palmetto scrub or its edges. REMARKS: This butterfly is closely related to the Troglodyte (*Anaea troglodyta*), an endemic Caribbean species.

GOATWEED LEAFWING *Anaea andria*   PL. 25

2⁷⁄₁₆–3¼ in. (62–84 mm). Our only widespread leafwing is both sexually and seasonally dimorphic. Upperside: *Red-orange*. Summer males with only faint black markings. Females with a broad irregular yellow submarginal band. Winter form has sickle-shaped forewing apex. SIMILAR SPECIES: Tropical Leafwing, an irregular vagrant in the Goatweed Leafwing's range, is smaller, redder, has heavier dark markings and slightly irregular outer margins. EARLY STAGES: Caterpillar gray-green, covered with small tubercles; orange tubercles on head. FOOD: Goatweed, Texas Croton, Prairie Tea. FLIGHT: Aug.–May (winter form), July–Aug. (summer form). RANGE: Resident in the s.-cen. and se. U.S., frequent vagrant outside its normal breeding range south to n. Mexico, west to cen. Ariz., north to Wyo., and east to Mich., S.C., and w. Va. HABITAT: Open deciduous woods and scrub, especially along streams, open fields, and many others.

ANGLED LEAFWING *Anaea glycerium*   PL. 25

2⁵⁄₁₆–3³⁄₁₆ in. (60–80 mm). Orange. Forewing apex pointed; outer margin *highly irregular*. Hindwing outer margin *concave* between

FLORIDA LEAFWING

GOATWEED LEAFWING

vein endings. **EARLY STAGES:** Caterpillar green with pale stripes, white band, and reddish patches; head capsule green with 2 black stubby horns. **FOOD:** *Croton jalapensis.* **FLIGHT:** June – Nov. (wet-season form), Oct.–June (dry-season form). July in s. Texas. **RANGE:** Mexico south through Cen. America to n. South America. Strays to s. Texas. **HABITAT:** Disturbed forest and edges.

PALE-SPOTTED LEAFWING *Anaea pithyusa* **PL. 25**

2¼–2¹⁵⁄₁₆ in. (56–74 mm). One of many tropical *blue and black* leaf wings, but the only one found regularly in the U.S. **EARLY STAGES:** Caterpillar green or brown with a black thoracic band; black anal plate; head capsule black with yellow-orange tubercles and 2 stubby black horns. **FOOD:** Cuala (*Croton lucidus*). **FLIGHT:** Nov. – March (dry-season form), May – Sept. (wet-season form). March, July, Sept., Nov. in s. Texas. **RANGE:** Mexico south through Cen. America to South America (Peru and Bolivia). Resident in lower Rio Grande Valley; one reported stray to Kenedy Co., Texas. **HABITAT:** Tropical forests.

CHESTNUT LEAFWING *Anaea echemus* **PL. 25**

2¼–2¾ in. (58–70 mm). Upperside: *Chestnut brown* suffused with black near edges. Hindwing with 2 or more *oval black white-tipped submarginal spots* near tail. **EARLY STAGES:** Not reported. **FOOD:** *Croton lucidus.* **FLIGHT:** Aug. – March (dry-season form), March – Nov. (wet-season form). May in s. Texas. **RANGE:** Cuba; windblown strays to nearby islands, rarely Texas. **HABITAT:** Wide range of tropical forests.

HACKBERRY BUTTERFLIES: SUBFAMILY APATURINAE

This is a group of closely related butterflies found worldwide. The adults are brightly colored and stout-bodied. As shown by their early stages, they are most closely related to the Charaxinae and Satyrinae. Our species are limited to the emperors (*Asterocampa*) and two species of *Doxocopa*.

EMPERORS: GENUS *Asterocampa* RÖBER

Our three emperors belong to a small New World group — one other species is found in Mexico. Our *Asterocampas* usually live in forests or along rivers. When they wander they may be found in cities or suburbs. Adults have a flap-and-glide flight, and often perch very high on branches of their host trees. Adults imbibe nutrients from animal dung, rotting fruits, and sap flows. They also take up minerals and salts on roads and moist spots. Flowers

Hackberry Emperor. Male perching. Woodbury Co., Okla. When perched on branches or tree trunks with their wings closed, the butterflies are difficult to spot. They visit flowers rarely.

are visited only on extremely rare occasions. Trees in the hackberry genus (*Celtis*) are the only hosts. Eggs are laid in groups, and the young caterpillars feed colonially. Winter is passed by small groups of caterpillars clustered inside dead rolled leaves.

HACKBERRY EMPEROR   *Asterocampa celtis*   PL. 26

1 ⅞–2 ¼ in. (48–64 mm). Our commonest, most widespread emperor. Highly variable geographically. Upperside: Forewing with postmedian row of white spots, only 1 *submarginal black spot* and 1 *solid black discal bar* with 2 *separate black spots*. SIMILAR SPECIES: (1) Empress Leilia has 2 submarginal black spots and 2 solid brown discal bars; (2) Tawny Emperor lacks submarginal black spots and has 2 solid black discal bars. EARLY STAGES: Caterpillar yellow-green; yellow spots along midline; 3 yellow lines along each side. FOOD: Sugarberry, hackberry. FLIGHT: May–Oct. (2 broods). RANGE: Resident in extreme s. Ont., most of e. U.S., cen. Plains states and sw. mountains as well as n. Mexico. Rare strays to s. Que. and w. N.D. HABITAT: Wooded streams, forest glades, towns.

EMPRESS LEILIA   *Asterocampa leilia*   PL. 26

2–3 in. (51–76 mm). Primarily southwestern. Upperside: Chestnut brown. Forewing has 2 *submarginal black spots* and 2 *solid*

Empress Leilia. Female perching. Cochise Co., Ariz. In the afternoon, males perch on shrubs or low tree branches, often their host hackberry, and await receptive females.

brown discal bars. **SIMILAR SPECIES:** Hackberry Emperor has forewing upperside with only 1 submarginal black spot and 1 black discal bar. **EARLY STAGES:** Caterpillar green with tiny yellow dots and a yellow stripe along each side. **FOOD:** *Celtis pallida.* **FLIGHT:** All year in s. Texas, least common Jan.–April. **RANGE:** Resident from s. Texas west to s. Ariz., ranging south to cen. Mexico. **HABITAT:** River forests and thorn scrub.

TAWNY EMPEROR *Asterocampa clyton*   PL. 26

1 $^{5}/_{16}$–2¾ in. (50–72 mm). Geographically variable. Upperside: Forewing *lacks white spots* and black submarginal spots, but has 2 *prominent black discal bars.* **SIMILAR SPECIES:** See Hackberry Emperor. **EARLY STAGES:** Caterpillar yellow-green with a narrow dark green or indigo blue dorsal stripe; head capsule white or black or a combination of the two. **FOOD:** Sugarberry, hackberry, *Celtis lindheimeri.* **FLIGHT:** June–Aug. (1 brood) in North, March–Nov. (2

EMPRESS LEILIA

TAWNY EMPEROR

*Tawny Emperor.
Male perching.
Gainesville, Fla.
Tawny Emperors have
several distinctive
geographic races that
were once considered
as separate species.
This is subspecies
flora.*

broods) in South. **RANGE:** E. U.S., extreme s. Ont., and ne. Mexico. Isolated populations in Fla. (*A. c. flora*), se. Ariz., and sw. N.M. **HABITAT:** Dense riverside woods, dry woods, cities, etc.

PAVON EMPEROR *Doxocopa pavon*   PL. 24
2³⁄₁₆ – 2¹¹⁄₁₆ in. (55 – 68 mm). Upperside: Male purple; forewing of both sexes with *small orange apical patch*. Female has squared-off forewing apex. Upperside: Orange patch near forewing apex and white median band tapering off and not reaching forewing costal margin. Underside: Both sexes *lack* silvery iridescence. **SIMILAR SPECIES:** Silver Emperor has silvery iridescence on hindwing below. Male has squared-off extended forewing apex and extensive orange median patch. **EARLY STAGES:** Caterpillar green with indistinct dorsal yellow-white blotches; yellow-white dorsal midline; head capsule green with white and black stripes on face; horns green. **FOOD:** Elm (vine). **FLIGHT:** May, Aug.–Dec. in s. Texas. **RANGE:** Lowland tropics from n. Mexico south to Bolivia. Occasional stray to lower Rio Grande Valley, Texas. **HABITAT:** Tropical forests.

SILVER EMPEROR *Doxocopa laure*   PL. 24
2³⁄₄ – 3¹⁄₄ in. (69 – 84 mm). Sexes similar, but male has upperside forewing median band invaded by orange. Underside: Hindwing of both sexes with *silvery iridescence*. **EARLY STAGES:** Caterpillar pale green with tiny yellow spots; head capsule green with a corona of short green spines. **FOOD:** Elm (vine). **FLIGHT:** All year in tropics; July –Dec. in s. Texas. **RANGE:** Lowland tropics from n. Mexico south to Brazil. Occasional in lower Rio Grande Valley, Texas. **HABITAT:** Wood edges and roadsides.

The satyrs are a worldwide group of medium-sized butterflies. They are most often brown with one or more marginal eyespots. One unifying structural feature is the swollen base of the costal vein, although a few other brushfoots share this feature. The males often have visible patches of specialized scales on the fore- or hindwings. Almost all species feed on grasses, including bamboos, rushes, and sedges, but some tropical species feed on club mosses. The adults have short proboscises and rarely visit flowers, but feed on rotting fruit, animal droppings, or sap flows instead. The adults usually perch with their wings closed but open them wide when basking early in the morning or during cloudy weather. Arctic species perch tilted over, facing the sun, with their wings closed. Males patrol in a characteristic slow, skipping flight. Except for arctic and prairie species, the butterflies are usually found in woodlands, often those associated with streams or swamps. Most species are localized and are not migratory. Eggs are laid singly on the hosts, and caterpillars feed within shelters of several leaves sewn together with silk. Development may require two years in arctic and alpine species. Winter is usually passed by partially grown caterpillars.

PEARLY-EYES: GENUS *Enodia* HÜBNER

There are three pearly-eyes, all of which are limited in their occurrence to eastern North America. All three pearly-eye species are very similar. These butterflies are found in densely forested swamps or along wooded streams. The males perch and patrol chiefly in the shade or in the open at dusk or on overcast days. They often rest on tree trunks. The adults never visit flowers, but feed at sap flows, bird droppings, and carrion. The caterpillars feed on stout grasses, including cane (*Arundinaria*) for our two southeastern species (*creola* and *portlandia*).

SOUTHERN PEARLY-EYE *Enodia portlandia*   PL. 27
2 3/16–2 3/4 in. (55–71 mm). Orange antennal clubs. Underside: Forewing with *curved* submarginal *row of 4* eyespots (Florida females may have 5), and postmedian dark line *straight* or *slightly zigzag.* SIMILAR SPECIES: (1) Northern Pearly-Eye has black antennal clubs; below, the forewing has a straight row of 4 submarginal eyespots, and the postmedian dark line is sinuous. (2) Creole Pearly-Eye has its forewing with a straight row of 5 submarginal eyespots below, and the postmedian dark line has an outward arched extension at the end of the discal cell. EARLY STAGES: Cater-

SOUTHERN PEARLY-EYE

NORTHERN PEARLY-EYE

pillar yellow-green, with 2 sets of red-tipped horns. **FOOD:** Giant Cane and Switch Cane. **FLIGHT:** March–Oct. (3 broods). **RANGE:** Se. U.S. west to e. Okla. and e. Texas. **HABITAT:** Shady, wooded areas near small streams leading into swamps.

NORTHERN PEARLY-EYE *Enodia anthedon*   **PL. 27**

2⅛–2⅝ in. (53–67 mm). The only pearly-eye northeast of s. Va. Antennal clubs are *black*. Underside: Forewing has *straight* submarginal *row of* 4 spots, postmedian dark line is *sinuous*. **SIMILAR SPECIES:** (1) Southern Pearly-Eye has orange antennal clubs; below, the forewing has a curved submarginal row of 4 eyespots, and the postmedian line is straight. (2) Creole Pearly-Eye has the underside of the forewing with a straight row of 5 submarginal eyespots, and the postmedian dark line has an outwardly arched extension near the discal cell. **EARLY STAGES:** Caterpillar yellow-green with green and yellow stripes; pairs of red-tipped horns at both

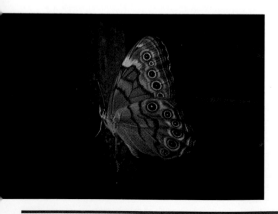

Creole Pearly-Eye. Perching. Great Dismal Swamp National Wildlife Refuge, Va. Adults are found only in forests near their caterpillar host Switch Cane. The adults are most active in late afternoon just before sunset.

CREOLE PEARLY-EYE

ends. **FOOD:** White Grass, Broadleaf Uniola, Bottlebrush. **FLIGHT:** June–Aug. (1 brood) in North, May–Sept. (2 broods) in South. **RANGE:** E. North America from cen. Sask. and e. Neb. east to N.S. and south to cen. Ala. and Miss. **HABITAT:** Damp deciduous woods, usually near streams or marshes; mixed transition zone woodlands.

CREOLE PEARLY-EYE *Enodia creola*   **PL. 27**

2⅚–2¾ in. (59–69 mm). Male has forewing apex extended. Upperside: Forewing of male with raised scale patches. Underside: Forewing with *straight* submarginal row of 5 *spots*; postmedian dark line with *outward arched extension* at end of discal cell. **SIMILAR SPECIES:** (1) Southern Pearly-Eye and (2) Northern Pearly-Eye have only 4 eyespots in submarginal row on forewing below. **EARLY STAGES:** Caterpillar similar to the Southern Pearly-Eye's. **FOOD:** Switch Cane. **FLIGHT:** June–Sept. (2 broods) in Va., April–Sept. (3 broods) in Miss. **RANGE:** Se. U.S. west to e. Okla. and e. Texas, peripheral records in se. Kans. and Del. Absent from Fla., s. Ga., and se. Ala. **HABITAT:** Usually dense moist woods near periphery of large swamps, but dense upland forests in s. Appalachians.

BROWNS: GENUS *Satyrodes* SCUDDER

There are only two browns, both limited to eastern North America. Species relationships require further study, and several additional species may need to be recognized. The adults are found in marshes and swamps, or along slow-moving streams and ditches. Males perch and occasionally patrol in their attempts to court females. The butterflies are most active in the early morning, and again in late afternoon and at dusk. Flower visitation is rare; the butterflies feed at bird droppings or sap flows. The caterpillars feed on various grasses and sedges.

Appalachian Brown. Male perching. Fairfax Co., Va. Adults are found in small grassy openings along small streams or in moist woods. They never visit flowers but feed at sap flows and probably on bird droppings and rotting fruit as well.

EYED BROWN *Satyrodes eurydice* PL. 27

1 ¹¹⁄₁₆–2⁷⁄₁₆ in. (43–61 mm). Underside: Forewing with *eyespots* in submarginal row approximately *equal*, usually touching or in *chainlike sequence*; hindwing with postmedian line distinctly *zigzag*. The Smoky Eyed Brown (*S. e. fumosa*) is larger, darker and has 5 eyespots in the underside hindwing submarginal row. There is a blend zone in nw. Neb. with the more typical northern form. **SIMILAR SPECIES:** Appalachian Brown has underside of forewing with uppermost and lowest eyespots in submarginal row larger than the middle two; postmedian line on underside of hindwing is sinuous, not sharply angled or zigzag. **EARLY STAGES:** Caterpillar yellow-green with red lateral stripes; red head horns. **FOOD:** Sedges. **FLIGHT:** June–Sept. (1 brood). **RANGE:** Temperate e. North America from se. Sask. and e. Neb. east across s. Canada and n. U.S. to Atlantic

EYED BROWN

APPALACHIAN BROWN

Coast from N.S. south to Del. Peripheral populations in n.-cen. Colo., e.-cen. Alta., and n. Que. **HABITAT:** Freshwater marshes, sedge meadows, slow-moving streams or ditches.

APPALACHIAN BROWN *Satyrodes appalachia*   PL. 27
1 ⅞–2¼ in. (47–57 mm). Underside: Forewing submarginal row usually with uppermost and lowest eyespots *larger than middle two*. Spots often *not touching*. Hindwing with postmedian line sinuous, not zigzag. **SIMILAR SPECIES:** Eyed Brown has eyespots in submarginal row on underside of forewing approximately equal, usually touching in chainlike sequence. On underside of hindwing, the dark postmedian line is zigzag, not gently sinuous. **EARLY STAGES:** Caterpillar similar to that of Eyed Brown, but red stripes on head do not extend below the horns. **FOOD:** Sedge, Giant Sedge. **FLIGHT:** July–Sept. (1 brood) in north, June–Oct. (2 broods) in south. **RANGE:** Se. Canada and e. U.S. from s. Que., s. Ont., and cen. Minn. south to cen. Gulf states and S.C. Isolated population in n. peninsular Fla. **HABITAT:** Wet wooded swamps, shrub swamp, forest edges.

GEMMED SATYR *Cyllopsis gemma*   PL. 28
1 ⅜–1 ¹¹⁄₁₆ in. (35–42 mm). *Lacks eyespots*. Underside: Hindwing with *silvery gray patch* on outer margin containing 4 small *black reflective spots*. **EARLY STAGES:** Caterpillar yellow-green with dark green stripes (summer) or brown with darker brown stripes (fall); long gray-brown horns at both ends. **FOOD:** Bermuda Grass. **FLIGHT:** April–Sept. (3 broods) in Va. All year in s. Tex. **RANGE:** Se. U.S. from se. Kans., cen. Okla., and cen. Texas east to the Atlantic Coast from Md. south to cen. peninsular Fla., along Gulf Coast to ne. Mexico. **HABITAT:** Wet, open woodland, often long-leafed pine woods.

GEMMED SATYR

CAROLINA SATYR

Carolina Satyr. Male perching. Lower Rio Grande Valley, Tex. Adults are usually found along the ground in various forests. In the South the adults survive the winter in reproductive arrest and then lay eggs in spring.

CAROLINA SATYR *Hermeuptychia sosybius*   **PL. 28**

1 ¼–1 ½ in. (32 –38 mm). Small. Upperside: *Unmarked.* Underside: Both wings with series of *many small yellow-rimmed eyespots.* **SIMILAR SPECIES:** (1) Little Wood Satyr and (2) Viola's Wood Satyr are both larger, have eyespots showing on upper surface, and have fewer larger eyespots below. **EARLY STAGES:** Caterpillar light green with darker green stripes covered with yellow tubercles. **FOOD:** Carpet Grass, Centipede Grass, probably other grasses. **FLIGHT:** April–Oct. in Va. (3 broods), all year in Deep South and s. Texas. **RANGE:** Se. U.S. north to s. N.J. (rare), south throughout mainland tropical America. **HABITAT:** Woodlands.

GEORGIA SATYR *Neonympha areolata*   **PL. 28**

1 ⁷⁄₁₆–1 ¹⁵⁄₁₆ in. (36 –50 mm). Small. Upperside: *Unmarked.* Underside: Hindwing with submarginal row of *elongated eyespots* and

GEORGIA SATYR

MITCHELL'S SATYR

red-orange lines. **EARLY STAGES:** Caterpillar yellow-green with yellow stripes and a green head capsule; red-brown tail-like projections. **FOOD:** Probably sedges. **FLIGHT:** June—July in N.J. (1 brood), April—Sept. (2 broods) in most of range. Most of year in Fla. **RANGE:** Se. U.S. from se. Okla. and se. Texas east to Atlantic Coast, isolated population in s. N.J. **HABITAT:** Openings in sandy pinewoods or pine barrens.

MITCHELL'S SATYR *Neonympha mitchellii*   PL. 28

Endangered species. 1⅜–1¼ in. (34–44 mm). Small. Fragile. Wings *translucent.* Underside: Both wings with submarginal rows of closely spaced *black, yellow-rimmed eyespots.* **SIMILAR SPECIES:** Carolina Satyr has more eyespots on the underside of both wings. The two might occur together only in a small area of North Carolina. **EARLY STAGES:** Caterpillar lime green with whitish stripes, covered with small whitish bumps. **FOOD:** Sedges and bulrush. **FLIGHT:** Late June—early July (1 brood). Total flight lasts only about 10 days. **RANGE:** Isolated populations in s. Mich., n. Ind., n. N.J. , and s.-cen. N.C., formerly in n. Ohio and Md. **HABITAT:** Sedge swamps. **REMARKS:** This is a declining, sensitive species in most of its range. Its small colonies may be eliminated by collecting.

Little Wood-Satyr. Adult perching. Fairfax Co., Va. Our commonest satyr. Adults may rarely feed at flowers but most often rely on sap flows and rotting fruit. Despite their abundance the species complex is not well understood.

LITTLE WOOD-SATYR

LITTLE WOOD-SATYR *Megisto cymela*   **PL. 27**

1 ⅝ − 1 ⅞ in. (39 − 47 mm). Our commonest satyr. Forewing with 2 prominent *yellow-rimmed black eyespots* above and below. Hindwing with 2 *major eyespots*, but smaller spots may be present below. The Little Wood-Satyr may consist of 2 reproductively isolated species that cannot be separated on external appearance. In much of the East, there are 2 apparent broods that fly in close succession, but the gap is so brief that the second flight could not possibly be the offspring of the first. There is evidence that each group has differently colored caterpillars that overwinter at different stages. **SIMILAR SPECIES:** (1) Viola's Wood-Satyr is larger and has the postmedian line below strongly bowed. (2) Red Satyr has only 1 eyespot and a strong reddish flush on each wing above and below. **EARLY STAGES:** Caterpillar pale brown tinged with green; median black stripe and lateral brown patches; head capsule and anal forks dirty white. **FOOD:** Grasses. **FLIGHT:** June−July (1 brood) in North, March−Sept. (2−3 broods) in Deep South. **RANGE:** E. North America from cen. plains eastward, absent from coastal La. and s. peninsular Fla. **HABITAT:** Woods, old fields, especially on basic soils.

VIOLA'S WOOD-SATYR *Megisto viola*   **PL. 27**

1 ¹¹⁄₁₆ − 1 ¹⁵⁄₁₆ in. (43 − 49 mm). Large. Upperside: Eyespots are relatively large. Underside: Both wings are strongly marked; the dark postmedian line is *strongly bowed*. **SIMILAR SPECIES:** Little Wood-Satyr is smaller, has relatively smaller eyespots, and has a relatively straight dark postmedian line on both wings below. **EARLY STAGES:** Caterpillar similar to Little Wood-Satyr but lighter brown. **FOOD:** Grasses. **FLIGHT:** April (1 brood) in Fla., later elsewhere. **RANGE:** Atlantic Coast from S.C. south to cen. Fla., remainder of range

COMMON RINGLET

not well-defined. **HABITAT:** Woods. **REMARKS:** This butterfly may occur with the Little Wood Satyr without hybridizing with it.

RED SATYR *Megisto rubricata*   **PL. 27**

1 ⅜–1 ⅞ in. (35–48 mm). Upperside: Dark brown. Each wing has only *1 eyespot* and an adjacent *reddish* area. Underside: Light brown. Forewing with *reddish flush* and only *1 eyespot near apex.* **SIMILAR SPECIES:** Little Wood Satyr lacks reddish flush and has 2 eyespots on each wing. **EARLY STAGES:** Caterpillar tan with darker and lighter stripes, the subdorsal dark stripe with white dots; head capsule light mottled tan. **FOOD:** Bermuda Grass, St. Augustine Grass. **FLIGHT:** April–Sept. (2 broods). **RANGE:** Southwest from s.-cen. Kans., e. Texas, cen. N.M., and cen. Ariz. south through Mexico to Guatemala. **HABITAT:** Open woodlands—mesquite, juniper, oak-pine.

COMMON RINGLET *Coenonympha tullia*   **PL. 28**

1 ⅓–1 ¼ in. (34–38 mm). Highly variable geographically. Different geographic forms blend over narrow areas. Some experts consider these forms to be separate species. The Inornate Ringlet (*C. t. inornata*) occurs in most of our area. Upperside: Wings range from *yellow-cream* to *orange-brown.* Underside: Forewing usually with a *round, black eyespot.* Hindwing gray-green with a *sinuous median white line.* **EARLY STAGES:** Caterpillar is dark green with pale green stripes and a white band below; head capsule green with small white bumps. **FOOD:** Grasses and rushes. **FLIGHT:** Mid-June to mid-Sept. (1–2 broods). **RANGE:** Holarctic. In North America from Alaska and w. N.W. Terr. south through w. mountains to Baja Calif. Norte, se. Ariz., and cen. N.M., ranges across s. Canada to Que. and New England south to Long I. and n. N.J.;

Common Wood-Nymph. Female perching. Fairfax Co., Va. Females live much longer than their male counterparts and lay eggs toward the end of their flight period — often in late summer or early fall. The role of the prominent eyespots is unknown.

range is still expanding, also isolated populations in N.B. (*C. t. nipisquit*) and Nfld. (and adjacent mainland). **HABITAT:** Open grassy areas in wide variety of settings.

COMMON WOOD-NYMPH *Cercyonis pegala*   PL. 28

1⅞–3 in. (48–76 mm). Geographically variable and sexually dimorphic. Forewing with 2 *large submarginal yellow-rimmed eyespots.* Underside: Hindwing with variable number of small postmedian eyespots. Coastal and southern population individuals are larger and have the outer portion of the forewing yellow or yellow-orange (*C. p. abbotti, C. p. pegala, C. p. texana*). Butterflies of inland populations are smaller and have yellow forewing patch reduced (*C. p. alope*) or absent (*C. p. nephele* and *C. p. olympus*). **EARLY STAGES:** Caterpillar green, becoming yellow-green at rear with paler stripes; head capsule green; anal forks reddish. **FOOD:** Purple-

COMMON WOOD-NYMPH

top and other grasses. **FLIGHT:** Late June–Oct., females flying later (1 brood). **RANGE:** S. Canada and U.S., except some southern areas including much of peninsular Fla., s. Midwest, e. and s. Texas. One record from n. Nueva Leon, Mexico. **HABITAT:** Prairies, old fields, pinewoods, bogs, open meadows.

ALPINES: GENUS *Erebia* DALMAN

The alpines are limited to subalpine, alpine, and arctic habitats throughout the Northern Hemisphere. Most species are found in mountainous Eurasia. In eastern North America six species occur, primarily in boreal portions of eastern Canada, but two bog species (*E. disa* and *E. discoidalis*) rarely reach the northern portions of the Great Lakes states. Males patrol low over grassy vegetation with a slow skipping flight. Adults occasionally visit flowers. The life histories of most of our species are unknown or little studied.

ROSS'S ALPINE *Erebia rossii*   **PL. 28**

1 ⅝–1 ¹³⁄₁₆ in. (39–46 mm). Upperside: Forewing with 1 to 3 subapical *black, white-centered eyespots* all surrounded by a *red-orange ring.* Underside: Hindwing with a *pale postmedian band.* **EARLY STAGES:** Not reported. **FOOD:** Sedges. **FLIGHT:** Mid-June to mid-July, rarely Aug. in far North (1 brood). **RANGE:** Holarctic. In North America from Alaska east along arctic tundra and mountain archipelago to n. Man., Southampton I., and s. Baffin I. Isolated population in n. B.C. **HABITAT:** Wet tundra.

DISA ALPINE *Erebia disa*   **PL. 28**

1 ⅝–1 ¾ in. (41–44 mm). Underside: Forewing *reddish* with a submarginal row of 4 to 5 black spots. Hindwing gray-brown with

ROSS'S ALPINE

DISA ALPINE

BANDED ALPINE

RED-DISKED ALPINE

conspicuous *white postmedian spot* beyond end of cell. **SIMILAR SPECIES:** Ross's Alpine has fewer forewing spots, lacks white spot on hindwing underside. **EARLY STAGES:** Not reported. **FLIGHT:** Late May to early July (1 brood), biennial. **RANGE:** Holarctic. In North America, arctic and subarctic spruce and muskeg from Alaska generally east and south across Canada to e.-cen. Ont. and n. Minn. Isolated records in n. Que. and Lab. **HABITAT:** Black Spruce–sphagnum bogs.

BANDED ALPINE *Erebia fasciata*   **PL. 28**
1 ¾–1 ⅞ in. (44–47 mm). *Lacks eyespots.* Underside: *Pale gray* basal and postmedian *bands*. **EARLY STAGES:** Not reported. **FOOD:** Possibly cottongrass. **FLIGHT:** Mid-June to mid-July (1 brood). **RANGE:** Siberia and arctic America from Alaska east to w. edge of Hudson Bay. **HABITAT:** Moist swales on tundra.

RED-DISKED ALPINE *Erebia discoidalis*   **PL. 28**
1 ¹¹⁄₁₆–1 ¹⁵⁄₁₆ in. (43–49 mm). Brown-black. *Lacks eyespots.* Underside: Forewing with *large chestnut red patch*; hindwing plain gray-brown. **EARLY STAGES:** Not reported. **FOOD:** Bluegrasses (*Poa*). Caterpillars have eaten cottongrass in captivity. **FLIGHT:** Early May to mid-June (1 brood). **RANGE:** Holarctic. In North America from Alaska east and south to s. Alta., n. Mont., n. Wis., n. Mich., and s. Que. **HABITAT:** Open sphagnum bogs, grassy areas with acidic soils.

THEANO ALPINE *Erebia theano*   **PL. 28**
1 ¼–1 ³⁄₁₆ in. (37–46 mm). Small and dark brown. Underside: Forewing with postmedian band of *elongated red-orange dashes*; hindwing with 1 blurred cell spot and a *postmedian series*, all *yellow-cream*. **EARLY STAGES:** Caterpillar tan with dark-brown stripes.

FOOD: Not reported, but probably grasses or sedges. **FLIGHT:** July (1 brood), biennial. **RANGE:** Holarctic. In North America as several isolated populations from Alaska and Yukon south to Colo. and along w. edge of Hudson Bay to n. Man. **HABITAT:** Grassy areas in and above wet tundra.

COMMON ALPINE *Erebia episodea*   **PL. 28**

1⅞–2 in. (47–52 mm). A common butterfly in the West and North that barely enters our area in Man. Our only species with eyespots on both wings. Dark brown. Upperside: Black *white-centered* submarginal *eyespot rows* surrounded with *yellow-orange*. Underside: Hindwing with submarginal *black eyespots* on gray background. **SIMILAR SPECIES:** Disa Alpine lacks eyespots on hindwing. **EARLY STAGES:** Caterpillar yellow-green with both darker and yellowish stripes; head yellow-brown. **FOOD:** Not reported, probably grasses. **FLIGHT:** Mid-late June (1 brood). **RANGE:** From Alaska and Yukon south through Rocky Mts. to n. N.M. and west across prairie provinces to sw. Man.; one dubious record from Dist. of Keewatin. **HABITAT:** Virgin high prairie in Man.

RIDINGS' SATYR *Neominois ridingsii*   **PL. 28**

1⅝–2³⁄₁₆ in. (41–56 mm). Unique. May be passed by since its behavior is similar to a grasshopper's: flies low, then quickly lands with closed wings. **EARLY STAGES:** Caterpillar reddish tan with variously colored stripes; head yellow-brown with pale brown vertical stripes. **FOOD:** Blue Grama grass. **FLIGHT:** June–early July (1 brood). **RANGE:** Native prairie and intermountain areas from s. Alta., s. Sask., and sw. Man. south to cen. Ariz. and cen. N.M., west to e. Calif. **HABITAT:** Short-grass prairie or similar grasslands with areas of bare soil.

ARCTICS: GENUS *Oeneis* HÜBNER

The arctics are another Northern Hemisphere group. In North America, most species occur in the West and far North, but we have eight species in the East. Males perch in likely habitats in their quests for receptive mates. Low-growing flowers are visited on rare occasions. Many species require two years to develop from the egg to the adult, and these species may have synchronous flights every other year. In some areas the butterflies fly only during odd-numbered years, and in others they may fly only during even-numbered years. The caterpillars eat grasses and sedges, and are striped longitudinally in somber tans, browns, and yellow-greens. The winter is passed by young caterpillars, which seek shelter at the base of plants or under rocks.

MACOUN'S ARCTIC *Oeneis macounii*　　　　　　　PL. 29

2⅜–2¾ in. (60–72 mm). Large. Upperside: Bright orange-brown. Heavy black marginal band on both wings. Forewing with 2 *submarginal eyespots*; hindwing with eyespot near anal angle. Male forewing lacks specialized scale patch of other arctics. Underside: Hindwing cloudy *gray-brown* with *median band*. SIMILAR SPECIES: Chryxus Arctic is smaller, duller orange above, and has a paler pattern on hindwing underside. EARLY STAGES: Caterpillar is striped pale black, light brown, black-green, and gray-green; head is yellow-green. Caterpillar requires 2 years to complete development, and biennial cycle is synchronized. FLIGHT: Adults fly in odd-numbered years in w. and n. Man. and westward, in even-numbered years eastward from se. Man. Early June to early July (1 brood). RANGE: Resident across s. Canada from n. B.C. and the Caribou Mts. of Alta. across prairie provinces; n. Minn. and n. Mich. (Isle Royale) to cen. Ont. A single record from s. Que. HABITAT: Openings in western Jack or Lodgepole pine forests.

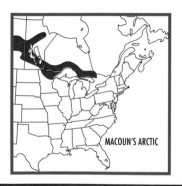

CHRYXUS ARCTIC *Oeneis chryxus*   **PL. 29**

1 ⅞–2⅛ in. (47–53 mm). Upperside: Orange with 2 widely spaced black spots. Forewing of males with darkened patch of specialized sex scales. Underside: Hindwing with fine black and white striations; veins scaled white; a broad, *dark median band*; and never more than *1 black spot* at anal angle. **SIMILAR SPECIES:** Macoun's Arctic is large, has more distinct eyespots, and has underside of hindwing gray-brown. Male lacks specialized sex scaling. **EARLY STAGES:** Caterpillar tan with brown stripes; head capsule dark brown. **FOOD:** *Danthonia spicata*. **FLIGHT:** Late May to early June (1 brood), possibly biennial, flies every year but occurs in greater numbers during even-numbered years in the Great Lakes region. **RANGE:** W. North America mountains to cen. N.M. and east across Canada to Man. Isolated population (*O. c. strigulosa*) in e. Canada and n. Great Lakes states. **HABITAT:** Meadows and open grassy or rocky areas, especially on Canadian Shield (a Precambrian formation).

UHLER'S ARCTIC *Oeneis uhleri*   **PL. 29**

1 ¹¹⁄₁₆–2³⁄₁₆ in. (43–55 mm). Upperside: Dull orange-brown. Underside: Both wings with more than 1, usually *many, small submarginal spots*. Basal half of hindwing dark, outer half lighter. **SIMILAR SPECIES:** (1) Chryxus Arctic has only 1 eyespot on hindwing below, together with a dark median band. (2) Alberta Arctic is smaller, yellow-gray above, and below has forewing with postmedian line bent sharply outward at end of cell. **EARLY STAGES:** Caterpillar green or tan with dark brown stripes; head capsule greenish yellow with pale vertical stripes. **FOOD:** Grasses and sedges. **FLIGHT:** Early June to early July (1 brood). **RANGE:** Yukon and extreme w. N.W. Terr. E. Canadian prairie provinces and Rocky Mt. region south to n. N.M. and east to w. Minn. **HABITAT:** Slopes and summits of hills in dry virgin prairie, tundra.

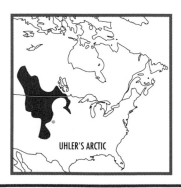

UHLER'S ARCTIC

ALBERTA ARCTIC

WHITE-VEINED ARCTIC

JUTTA ARCTIC

ALBERTA ARCTIC *Oeneis alberta*   PL. 29

1⅛−2¼ in. (48−57 mm). The smallest arctic. Variable. Upperside: Warm yellow-gray. Underside: Forewing with postmedian line *sharply bent outward* at end of cell; hindwing with *sharply outlined dark median band*. **SIMILAR SPECIES:** Uhler's Arctic is orange-brown above and has many small black submarginal spots on underside of hindwing. **EARLY STAGES:** Caterpillar dark brown with various colored stripes; head brown-green. **FOOD:** Bunchgrass, possibly *Festuca*. **FLIGHT:** May (1 brood). **RANGE:** Canadian prairie provinces east to s. Man. and isolated Rocky Mt. populations in Colo., N.M., and Ariz. **HABITAT:** Virgin prairie.

WHITE-VEINED ARCTIC *Oeneis taygete*   PL. 29

1⁷⁄₁₆−1⅞ in. (36−47 mm). Wings translucent. Upperside: Gray-brown, *without eyespots*. Underside: Forewing with faint *brown partial postmedian bar* extending down from costa; hindwing with strong *median dark band outlined with white*. Veins usually *lined with white scales*. **SIMILAR SPECIES:** (1) Melissa Arctic may have faint eyespot on forewing; hindwing below is mottled black and white and lacks white scaling on veins. (2) Polixenes Arctic has more translucent wings and a pronounced medial band on hindwing below, and lacks white scaling along veins. **FOOD:** Sedges or grasses. **FLIGHT:** Late July, rarely late June to late Aug. (1 brood). **RANGE:** Holarctic. In North America, high arctic tundra from Alaska east to Lab., isolated Rocky Mt. alpine populations south to sw. Colo. Isolated population (*O. t. gaspéensis*) on Mt. Albert, Que. **HABITAT:** Grassy alpine slopes, tundra, and subarctic bogs.

JUTTA ARCTIC *Oeneis jutta*   PL. 29

1¹⁵⁄₁₆−2⁵⁄₁₆ in. (49−59 mm). Upperside: Gray-brown. Both wings with *yellow-orange* submarginal *band* (usually interrupted) containing *2 to 4 black spots* on each wing. Underside: Hindwing with

variably contrasting dark median band. **EARLY STAGES:** Caterpillar pale-green with darker stripes and a dorsal brown spot on each segment; head capsule green. **FOOD:** Sedges, including cottongrass. **FLIGHT:** Mid-July to early Aug. (1 brood), biennial. Found in larger numbers during odd-numbered years in the Great Lakes region. **RANGE:** Holarctic. In North America mainly east across Canada and n. Great Lakes in subarctic habitats from Alaska to Me. and the Maritimes. Isolated populations south to Colo. in Rockies. **HABITAT:** Black Spruce–sphagnum bogs often with larch, wet tundra.

MELISSA ARCTIC *Oeneis melissa*   PL. 29
1¾–2 in. (45–51 mm). Wings translucent. Wing fringes often checkered. Upperside: Gray-brown. *Eyespots absent*, or faint if present. Underside: Hindwing mottled black and white, medial band absent or weak and bordered by white. **SIMILAR SPECIES:** (1) White-veined Arctic usually has white scaling on veins of hindwing below. (2) Polixenes Arctic has translucent wings and a strong median band on the hindwing below. These species can be reliably separated only by location or by dissection of male genitalia. **EARLY STAGES:** Caterpillar variable with black and dark green stripes; head capsule yellow-green or green-brown with black bands or spots. **FOOD:** Sedges. **FLIGHT:** Mid-June to early Aug. (1 brood), rarely late Aug. in far North. **RANGE:** Holarctic. Siberia and North American arctic from Alaska east to Baffin I. and Lab., isolated populations in Rockies south to n. N.M. and in N.H.'s White Mts. (*O. m. semidea*). **HABITAT:** Open tundra, rocky summits and saddles, talus slopes, and frost-heaved clear-cut areas.

POLIXENES ARCTIC *Oeneis polixenes*   PL. 29
1¹¹⁄₁₆–2⅛ in. (43–53 mm). Wings relatively translucent. Upperside: Gray-brown. Underside: Medial band on hindwing usually strongly expressed, edged with white. **SIMILAR SPECIES:** (1) Melissa

Arctic has weakly expressed medial band on hindwing below, and wings are not translucent. (2) White-veined Arctic has underside of hindwing with white scaling on veins. All of these species can be reliably separated only by locality or by dissection of the species-distinctive male genitalia. **EARLY STAGES:** Caterpillar light brown with darker stripes; head capsule brown. **FOOD:** Sedges and grasses. **FLIGHT:** Mid-June to early Aug. (1 brood). **RANGE:** North American arctic from Alaska east to Baffin I., Lab., e. Que., and cen. Me. (*O. p. katahdin*). Isolated populations in Rockies south to n. N.M. **HABITAT:** Open moist tundra.

MILKWEED BUTTERFLIES: SUBFAMILY DANAINAE

ROYALTY: GENUS *Danaus* KLUK

This is the most widespread genus of the milkweed butterflies, a group of primarily tropical and subtropical butterflies. In the Americas there are three species, all of which are resident in eastern North America. One species, the Monarch, undergoes dramatic migrations and forms large overwintering colonies in central Mexico and coastal California. The Mexican wintering sites, where our eastern Monarchs are found, number in the millions of butterflies. During the summer, males patrol open fields or similar areas in search of females. The adults store cardiac glycosides, poisonous chemicals derived from their caterpillars' milkweed hosts, and as a result are both distasteful and emetic to most birds who would attempt to eat them. The Viceroy (*Limenitis archip-*

Monarch. Monarch nectaring at Zinnia. Fairfax Co., Va. You can increase the chances of Monarchs visiting your garden by planting attractive nectar sources such as Butterflybush, Zinnia, and Mexican Sunflower.

MONARCH

QUEEN

pus) is a relatively palatable mimic of the Monarch in most of our area, but it mimics the Queen (*Danaus gilippus*) in peninsular Florida and the Southwest. The adults visit flowers for nectar; these are often those of their milkweed hosts, but also include those of many other plants, especially in the Asteraceae family. Eggs are laid singly under host leaves, and the caterpillars are smooth, with fleshy black tubercles at each end, and circular bands of black, yellow, and white. The pupae are green with gold and black markings.

MONARCH *Danaus plexippus*   PLS. 3, 4, 27

3⅜–4⅞ in. (86–125 mm). Our most familiar butterfly. Male is *bright orange* and has *black scent patch* in middle of hindwing above; female is dull orange or brown with more thickly scaled black veins. **SIMILAR SPECIES:** Viceroy has a strong postmedian black line on upperside of both wings, and has only a single marginal row of white spots in the black border. **EARLY STAGES:** Caterpillar transversely ringed with yellow, black, and off-white on each segment; head capsule white and black striped; 3 pairs of black fleshy tubercles on back of segments 2, 5, and 11. **FOOD:** Milkweeds and milkweed vines, rarely dogbane. **FLIGHT:** During warm part of year in e. North America, 1–3 broods in north, 4–6 in south, may breed all year in Fla. and s. Texas. Overwinters in cen. Mexico, sparingly along s. Atlantic Coast or Gulf Coast. **RANGE:** Summer resident in s. Canada and entire continental U.S. In West, individuals overwinter along Calif. coast in large aggregations, and in East adults migrate to and overwinter in cen. Mexico. Resident in most of tropical American lowlands. Colonized and resident on many oceanic islands (including Hawaii) and Australia. **HABITAT:** Open weedy areas, roadsides, pastures, marsh-

Queen. Adult nectaring at lantana flowers. Falcon State Park, Tex. Queens often engage in local migrations, and some fly long distances and appear far north of their normal range. They do not form overwintering colonies as do Monarchs.

es, and similar situations. **REMARKS:** Well known for its long migration to and from cen. Mexico and for its role as a distasteful and emetic model for the edible Viceroy butterfly.

QUEEN *Danaus gilippus*   **PL. 27**

3⅛–3⅞ in. (79–97 mm). Upperside: *Chestnut brown* with marginal black border. Forewing has scattered white spots on apical third. Underside: Hindwing has veins outlined in black; black marginal border has *double row of white spots.* **SIMILAR SPECIES:** (1) Viceroy (Fla. population, *L. a. floridensis*) is smaller, has black postmedian line across hindwing and only a single row of white spots in black border. (2) Soldier is lighter, has black scaling on veins above, and a patch of off-white spots in center of hindwing below. **EARLY STAGES:** Caterpillar brown-white with yellow and brown transverse rings on each segment in addition to a yellow-green lateral stripe on each side; 3 pairs of black fleshy tubercles on back of segments 2, 5, and 11. **FOOD:** Milkweeds and milkweed vines. **FLIGHT:** All year in Fla. and s. Texas, usually July–Aug. to north. **RANGE:** Resident in extreme s. U.S. and throughout tropical American lowlands. Regular stray (and occasional colonist) in plains and more rarely along Atlantic coastal plain, rarely to se. N. D. and Mass. (Nantucket I.). **HABITAT:** Open fields, dry washes, dunes, pastures, river courses, and other open areas. **REMARKS:** A poisonous and emetic model for Viceroys in Fla. and the Southwest. The Monarch is a relatively uncommon breeder in these areas; hence the switch to the Queen as a more advantageous model.

Soldier. Adult perching. Jalisco, Mexico. A recent introduction to Florida and regular in s. Texas, the biology of this more tropical butterfly is not well understood. Adults are more often found in forests than in open fields.

SOLDIER

SOLDIER *Danaus eresimus*   PL. 27

2¾–3¹¹⁄₁₆ in. (71–94 mm). Upperside: Both wings have *veins* marked *thinly with black*. Forewing with fewer white spots. Underside: Hindwing with pale postmedian *band* of *blotchy whitish spots*. **SIMILAR SPECIES:** Queen lacks black scaling on veins above, is darker, and lacks patch of off-white spots in center of hindwing below. **EARLY STAGES:** Caterpillar yellow-green with fine black transverse rings; 8 pairs of black diamonds on upperside; 3 pairs black fleshy tubercles; head capsule black with yellow stripes. **FOOD:** Milkweeds and milkweed vines. **FLIGHT:** All year in s. Fla., especially common Oct.–Dec., s. Texas from Aug–Dec. **RANGE:** Resident from s. Fla. and s. Texas south through lowland American tropics (including West Indies) to Brazil. Rarely strays to s. Ariz. and s. N.M. **HABITAT:** Open pastures and edges of seasonally dry tropical forests.

TIGER MIMIC-QUEEN *Lycorea cleobaea*   PL. 27

3¹¹⁄₁₆–4¼ in. (94–109 mm). Large. Orange with horizontal black stripes. *Black stripes* on hindwing *joined* outwardly to form loop. Male has black hair pencils (scent brushes) at tip of abdomen. **SIMILAR SPECIES:** Isabella's Heliconian is smaller, has more rounded forewing apex, and black stripes on hindwing are unconnected. **EARLY STAGES:** Caterpillar white with narrow black transverse rings; one pair of tubercles behind head. **FOOD:** Papaya, *Jacaratia*, fig, bloodflower. **FLIGHT:** All year in tropics; April, July, Oct. in s. Texas. **RANGE:** Resident throughout tropical American lowlands from West Indies and cen. Mexico south to Peru. **HABITAT:** Tropical forests.

KLUG'S CLEARWING *Dircenna klugii*   **PL. 27**
2⅞–3³⁄₁₆ in. (73–80 mm). Antennae long, orange. Upperside: Wings *translucent pale orange*. Forewing with veins darkened. Inner margin black. Hindwing has outer margin narrowly black-edged. **EARLY STAGES:** Caterpillar green-white, covered with yellow warts and black warts, the latter especially pronounced on back. Head shiny green. **FOOD:** *Solanums*. **FLIGHT:** All year in Cen. America. **RANGE:** Mexico south to Panama. Extremely rare vagrant to s. Texas. **HABITAT:** Wide variety of tropical forests and second-growth habitats. **REMARKS:** Not seen in our area since the last century.

Skippers:
Superfamily Hesperioidea
Skippers: Family Hesperiidae

The skippers are worldwide in distribution. They are poorly represented in the arctic and subarctic, but have many species in the tropics. There are more than 3,500 described species with more than 280 in North America, many of them tropical species found only in south Texas. Most are small to medium, relatively dull-colored with orange, brown, black, white, and gray being frequent wing colors, but a few have iridescent colors. Their antennal clubs are often hooked and have an extension called an apiculus. Males have modified scent scales found in modified forewing patches, called "brands," within folds of the forewing costal margin or on their legs. All three pairs of legs are fully developed. The eyes are large, the antennae are usually short, and the bodies are stout. Flight is often rapid with the wing movement blurred. Males of most species locate mates by perching, but patrolling is used by some in our area. Adults of most species have very long proboscises and feed on floral nectar, but those of some also take up nutrients from bird droppings. Eggs are globular and laid singly.

Within the Family Hesperiidae are three North American skipper subfamilies: the open-winged skippers (Pyrginae), branded skippers (Hesperiinae), and giant-skippers (Megathyminae). Some authorities consider a fourth subfamily, the Heteropterinae, which among our species includes the Arctic Skipper (*Carterocephalus palaemon*).

Open-winged Skippers (Pyrgines):
Subfamily Pyrginae

Primarily tropical American, the open-winged skippers have 112 species in our area. Most genera are mainly tropical, but two, the duskywings (*Erynnis*) and checkered-skippers (*Pyrgus*), also occur in Eurasia. Adults of many species land with their wings open, although some perch with their wings closed or half open. Males of many species imbibe moisture from moist sand or mud. As far as is known, all of our species take nectar from flowers. Some species also feed on bird droppings. Many of our more tropical representatives rest under leaves when not active. Females lay their eggs singly, directly on host plant leaves; some species put their eggs on plants or other objects adjacent to their true host. Almost all species use broad-leafed plants as their caterpillar hosts — oaks, mallows, and legumes are hosts for most of our species. Caterpillars live in rolled leaf or webbed leaf shelters.

GENUS *Phocides* HÜBNER

MANGROVE SKIPPER *Phocides pigmalion*   PL. 30
1 ⁵⁄₁₆−2¾ in. (50−71 mm). *Brown-black.* Hindwing upperside and underside with submarginal row of *iridescent blue streaks.* EARLY STAGES: Caterpillar covered with a powdery white exudate; head capsule brown with 2 large orange or yellow spots in front. FOOD: Red Mangrove. FLIGHT: Nov.−Aug. in s. Fla. RANGE: Coastal peninsular Fla. and Keys (*P. p. okeechobee*) south through West Indies and tropical mainland from Mexico south to Argentina. Has strayed to coastal S.C. HABITAT: Coastal mangrove thickets and nearby openings.

GUAVA SKIPPER *Phocides palemon*   PL. 30
1 ¹⁄₁₆−2½ in. (43−64 mm). Upperside black with *green rays.* Underside black with *white fringes* and *red discal bar* on costa. EARLY STAGES: Caterpillar white; head brown with yellow eyespots. FOOD: Guavas. FLIGHT: Feb., April, June−Dec. in s. Texas. RANGE: S. Texas (lower Rio Grande Valley) south through mainland tropical America to Argentina. HABITAT: Subtropical woods, city flower gardens.

MERCURIAL SKIPPER *Proteides mercurius*   PL. 30
2¼−2¾ in. (57−71 mm). Head and thorax *golden orange above.* Forewing long, extended. Upperside: *Basal portion* of both wings *golden orange.* Underside: Chestnut brown with *white frosting* on outer margins. Hindwing with obscure *white mark* in center. EARLY STAGES: Caterpillar green- or golden yellow mottled with dark brown; red lateral stripes; head red-brown with red eyespots. FOOD: Legume trees and vines. FLIGHT: April−Oct. in s. Texas, April−May in s. Fla. RANGE: American tropics from Mexico and West Indies south to Argentina, strays north to southern U.S. (Fla., La., Texas). HABITAT: Near streams in moist, lowland tropical forests, especially associated edges and openings.

MANGROVE SKIPPER

ZESTOS SKIPPER

SILVER-SPOTTED SKIPPER

SILVER-SPOTTED SKIPPERS: GENUS *Epargyreus* HÜBNER

ZESTOS SKIPPER *Epargyreus zestos*   **PL. 30**

1¾–2⁵⁄₁₆ in. (44–59 mm). Upperside: Brown-black with median golden transparent band across forewing. Underside: *Hindwing red-brown*, often *lacks* any trace of a *silver spot*. **SIMILAR SPECIES:** Silver-spotted Skipper has underside of hindwing brown-black with prominent silver patch. **EARLY STAGES:** Not reported. **FOOD:** *Galactia*. **FLIGHT:** Jan.–Nov. in s. Fla. **RANGE:** Resident in s. Fla. and Keys as well as West Indies.

SILVER-SPOTTED SKIPPER *Epargyreus clarus*   **PLS. 3, 30**

1¹⁵⁄₁₆–2⅝ in. (49–67 mm). The most conspicuous skipper in most of our area. Brown-black. The combination of *transparent gold* forewing spots and the *metallic silver band* on the hindwing beneath make it unmistakable. **SIMILAR SPECIES:** (1) Hoary Edge is smaller; its ventral hindwing has whitish outer margin. (2) Bro-

Silver-spotted Skipper. Adult nectaring on Zinnia. Fairfax Co., Va. The seemingly pugnacious males take up perches about waist-high and fly at most objects that happen by in their effort to find and court females.

ken Silverdrop has smaller, paler forewing spots and ventral hindwing with smaller separated silver spots. (3) Gold-spotted Aguna has more linear blurred silver patch on ventral hindwing and forewing above with median gold spots about equal sized. The two do not occur together. **EARLY STAGES:** Caterpillar yellow with fine black cross lines; head red-brown with 2 large, round red-orange spots low on front. **FOOD:** Black Locust, Wisteria, and many other legumes. **FLIGHT:** May−Sept. (2 broods) in most of East, single brood to north and west, Feb.−Dec. in Deep South. **RANGE:** Resident in extreme s. Canada, most of continental U.S. (except w. Texas and Great Basin), and n. Mexico. **HABITAT:** Many disturbed and open forest situations.

BROKEN SILVERDROP *Epargyreus exadeus*   **NOT SHOWN**
1 ⅚₆−2⅞₆ in. (49−62 mm). One of a confusing complex of tropical skippers. Forewing elongate with small separate pale amber spots. Underside: Hindwing dark brown with separate *small silver median spots* and faint *pale postmedian line*. **EARLY STAGES:** Caterpillar olive green with tiny white dots, transverse rows of black dots, and yellow lateral stripes; prothorax red with a black cervical shield; head black with reddish eyespots. **FOOD:** Legumes. **FLIGHT:** Oct. in s. Texas; May−Nov. in Mexico and Cen. America. **RANGE:** Resident in mainland American tropics from Mexico south to Argentina, rare stray north to s. Texas and s. Calif. **HABITAT:** Tropical woods or scrub and associated edges.

HAMMOCK SKIPPER *Polygonus leo*   **PL. 30**
1 ¹¹⁄₁₆−2⅜₆ in. (43−59 mm). Upperside: Black-brown; forewing with 3 *prominent square white patches.* Underside hindwing with *violet sheen* and small dark, *round basal spot.* **SIMILAR SPECIES:**

Manuel's Skipper is smaller, has bluish gloss at base of forewing and red-brown pale areas on underside of hindwing. **EARLY STAGES:** Caterpillar translucent green with 2 yellow stripes along each side; head green with 2 black spots on upper front. **FOOD:** Jamaican Dogwood and Karum Tree. **FLIGHT:** All year in s. Fla. **RANGE:** S. Fla., West Indies, and Mexico south to Argentina. Strays north to Texas and Southwest. **HABITAT:** Hardwood hammocks in s. Fla. and subtropical woods in s. Texas.

MANUEL'S SKIPPER *Polygonus manueli*   **NOT SHOWN**
1½–1¾ in. (37–44 mm). Extremely rare. *Small.* Upperside: Forewing has bluish gloss at base and brilliantly reflective white spots. Underside of hindwing has *red-brown pale areas.* **SIMILAR SPECIES:** Hammock Skipper is larger. **EARLY STAGES:** Caterpillar half green and half yellow with pale stripes; head light red with black eyespots. **FOOD:** Legume shrub (*Muellera*). **FLIGHT:** Aug.–Sept. in s. Texas; Fla. records old and dubious; Jan.–Oct. in tropics. **RANGE:** West Indies and Mexico south through mainland tropical America to Argentina. Rare stray to s. Texas. Earlier reports of its presence in Fla. are in error. **HABITAT:** Tidal scrub.

GENUS *Chioides* LINDSEY

WHITE-STRIPED LONGTAIL *Chioides catillus*   **PL. 30**
1½–2 in. (37–52 mm). Our only skipper with *exceptionally long tails* and a long *silver band* on hindwing below. **SIMILAR SPECIES:** Zilpa Longtail has a central white trapezoidal patch on hindwing below. **EARLY STAGES:** Caterpillar pale green-yellow with yellow lateral lines and many tiny black dots; prothorax red with a black patch behind head; head red with a black Y on front. **FOOD:** Viny legumes. **FLIGHT:** All year in s. Texas. **RANGE:** Resident from s. Texas and West Indies

south through tropical America to Argentina. Periodic stray to s. Ariz. and sw. N.M. HABITAT: Open areas along trails through tropical and subtropical forests, brush, and associated edges.

ZILPA LONGTAIL *Chioides zilpa* PL. 30

1½–2⅚ in. (37–58 mm). Similar to White-striped Longtail. Underside: Hindwing mottled and has a central *trapezoidal white patch*. EARLY STAGES: Not reported. FLIGHT: March–April, Sept.–Nov. in s. Texas; flies all year in Mexico and Cen. America. RANGE: Resident from Mexico south through tropical America to Ecuador. Strays regularly to s. Texas and se. Ariz., rarely northward. HABITAT: Tropical scrub and associated edges.

GOLD-SPOTTED AGUNA *Aguna asander* PL. 30

1⅞–2⅚ in. (47–56 mm). Upperside: Forewing with median spots pale and approximately equal. Underside: Hindwing with silver patch *linear and blurred*. SIMILAR SPECIES: Silver-spotted Skipper has brighter golden patch on forewing. Silver patch on underside of hindwing is sharper in outline. EARLY STAGES: Not reported. FOOD: Probably legumes. FLIGHT: April, June, Aug.–Nov. in s. Texas; also Dec.–Jan. in Mexico. RANGE: Resident from West Indies and Mexico south through tropical America to Argentina. Strays north to lower Rio Grande Valley, Texas, and se. Ariz. (rarely). HABITAT: Tropical scrub and associated openings and edges.

EMERALD AGUNA *Aguna claxon* NOT SHOWN

1½–1¾ in. (38–45 mm). Hindwings with short lobes instead of tails. Upperside: *Wing bases blue-green*. Underside: Hindwing with sharply defined *silver-white median band*. SIMILAR SPECIES: Tailed Aguna has a long tail and a blurred narrow white median band on each hindwing underside. EARLY STAGES: Not reported. FLIGHT: Oct. in s. Texas; June–Oct. in Mexico. RANGE: Resident from Mexico south through Cen. America to Colombia and Venezuela. Rare stray to lower Rio Grande Valley, Texas.

TAILED AGUNA *Aguna metophis* PL. 30

1⁷⁄₁₆–1⅞ in. (36–47 mm). *Tailed*. Upperside: Wing bases blue-green; Underside: Hindwing with *narrow white median band*, blurred along its outer edge. SIMILAR SPECIES: Emerald Aguna has a short lobe on each hindwing and a sharply defined silver-white band on each hindwing below. EARLY STAGES: Not reported. FOOD: *Bauhinia mexicana* in Mexico. FLIGHT: All year in Mexico; Aug.–Nov. in s. Texas. RANGE: Resident from Mexico south through tropical America to s. Brazil, regular stray to lower Rio Grande Valley, Texas. HABITAT: Thorny tropical scrub.

MOTTLED LONGTAIL *Typhedanus undulatus* **PL. 30**
1 ⅜–1 ⅞ in. (41 –47 mm). Tailed. Forewing apex blunt. Upperside:
Male *lacks costal fold*. Underside: Hindwing dark brown, *striated
with broken black bands*. **SIMILAR SPECIES:** Dorantes Skipper has
rounded forewing, and underside of hindwing has 2 dark brown
bands on a lighter brown background. **EARLY STAGES:** Caterpillar
gray-green with yellow lateral lines; head dark brown with yellow
eyespots enclosed by reddish spots. **FOOD:** *Cassias*. **FLIGHT:** Aug.–
Oct. in s. Texas; Dec.–May in Mexico and Cen. America. **RANGE:**
Resident from Mexico south through tropical mainland to
Argentina. Occasional stray to lower Rio Grande Valley, Texas.
HABITAT: Arid chaparral.

MEXICAN LONGTAIL *Polythrix mexicannus* **NOT SHOWN**
1 ⅜–1 ⅝ in. (34 –40 mm). Tailed. Upperside: Forewing has *two
submarginal spots* near rear part of wing. Male with costal fold.
Underside: forewing with *dark brown postbasal spot*. **SIMILAR SPECIES:**
Eight-spotted Longtail has shorter tails. Forewing upperside has
only 1 submarginal dark spot; below forewing postbasal spot weak
or absent. Male has costal fold, and underside of female's hindwing often has a blurred white central patch. Dissection of genitalia is needed for positive identification. **EARLY STAGES:** Not reported. **FOOD:** *Amerimnon* and *Ichtyomenthia* (legumes). **FLIGHT:** June–
July, Oct. in s. Texas; April–Oct. in Mexico. **RANGE:** Resident in
lowland Mexico, strays north to lower Rio Grande Valley, Texas.
HABITAT: Shaded subtropical woods. **REMARKS:** Polythrixes often perch
upside-down under large leaves in the forest understory.

EIGHT-SPOTTED LONGTAIL *Polythrix octomaculata* **PL. 30**
1 ⅜–1 ¹³⁄₁₆ in. (35 –46 mm). Tailed. Male lacks costal fold and has
short tails. Upperside: Forewing has *only 1 submarginal brown
spot* near rear part of wing. Underside: Forewing *postbasal spot
weak or absent*; female often with blurred white patch on hindwing. **SIMILAR SPECIES:** Mexican Longtail has longer tails. Upperside
of forewing often has two dark submarginal spots near rear part of
wing; underneath the forewing there is a dark brown postbasal
spot. Males lack a costal fold. **EARLY STAGES:** Caterpillar white with
gray lines; head yellow with light red. **FOOD:** Legume trees and
shrubs. **FLIGHT:** March, Aug.–Oct. in s. Texas; March–Nov. in
Mexico. **RANGE:** Resident from Mexico south through tropical
America to Argentina, also on Haiti. Occasional stray to lower Rio
Grande Valley, Texas. **HABITAT:** Streams and shady areas within
tropical seasonal forest or scrub.

WHITE-CRESCENT LONGTAIL NOT SHOWN
Codatractus alcaeus

1 ¹¹⁄₁₆–2¼ in. (43–57 mm). Tailed. Upperside: Dark brown; forewing with *median band of gold spots*. Underside: hindwing with 3 irregular dark bands; *white submarginal patch* on lower part of wing. **SIMILAR SPECIES:** Zilpa Longtail has squared-off forewing apex and differently shaped, more central white patch on hindwing underside. **EARLY STAGES:** Not reported. **FOOD:** Tree legumes. **FLIGHT:** June, Oct. in s. Texas; April–Oct. in Mexico. **RANGE:** Resident from Mexico south to Panama. Rare stray in lower Rio Grande Valley and w. Texas. **HABITAT:** Tropical woods.

LONG-TAILED SKIPPERS: GENUS *Urbanus* HÜBNER

This is the largest of several genera of long-tailed skippers found in the Americas. *Chioldes*, *Aguna*, *Typhedanus*, and *Polythrix* are other genera that have tailed species in our area—mainly in the lower Rio Grande Valley of Texas. There are two common *Urbanus* species, *U. proteus* and *U. dorantes*, in the Southeast and south Texas. The other species of Urbanus included below are found mainly in the lower Rio Grande Valley. The males perch on low vegetation and periodically patrol back and forth. Adults avidly visit flowers such as Lantana and Shepherd's-Needle. The caterpillars live and feed within rolled leaf shelters on various species of legumes, especially those related to the Common Bean. The species cannot survive hard freezes in any stage. Adults spend the winter (or dry season) in reproductive arrest.

LONG-TAILED SKIPPER *Urbanus proteus* PL. 30

1⅞–2⅖₁₆ in. (47–59 mm). Our commonest tailed skipper. This and the two following very similar species have distinct but subtle

LONG-TAILED SKIPPER

pattern characters, as well as distinct genitalia. Upperside dark black-brown with *body* and *basal portion of wings iridescent blue-green*. Male with costal fold. **SIMILAR SPECIES:** (1) Pronus Longtail is likely to be found only in the lower Rio Grande Valley of Texas. It has shorter tails, and the green on the upper surface of the hindwing stops abruptly before the outer margin. Below, the dark spots on the hindwing are clearly separated. (2) Esmeralda Longtail is also a rare stray to the lower Rio Grande Valley. Its male has a costal fold and the central dark band on the hindwing below is broken into well-separated spots. **EARLY STAGES:** Caterpillar yellow-green; a thin black dorsal line; yellow and red stripe and 2 green lines along each side; head black with brown top and 2 large yellow to orange spots low on front. **FOOD:** Many viny legumes, including beans. **FLIGHT:** All year in s. Fla. and s. Texas (2–3 broods), usually late summer to north. **RANGE:** Resident from peninsular Fla. and s. Texas south through West Indies and mainland tropical America to Argentina. Stray and occasional colonist north to Conn., s. Ill., e. Kans., s. Ariz., and s. Calif. **HABITAT:** Open disturbed situations, brushy fields, wood edges, gardens.

PRONUS LONGTAIL   NOT SHOWN
Urbanus pronus

1 5/16–1 3/4 in. (33–44 mm). *Tails short.* Upperside: *Green* on hindwing *stops abruptly*—not diffusely—before outer margin. Male *lacks costal fold.* Underside: central dark spots on hindwing *separated.* **SIMILAR SPECIES:** Long-tailed Skipper has longer tails and the green on the upper surface of the hindwing blends diffusely toward the outer margin; male lacks a costal fold on the forewing. **EARLY STAGES:** Not reported. **FLIGHT:** Oct. in s. Texas; April–Sept. in Mexico. **RANGE:** Resident from Mexico south through tropics to Paraguay and s. Brazil. Rare stray to lower Rio Grande Valley, Texas.

ESMERALDA LONGTAIL *Urbanus esmeraldus*   NOT SHOWN
1 3/8–1 5/8 in. (34–41 mm). Upperside: Male with *costal fold.* Underside: Hindwing with central dark band broken into *well separated spots.* **SIMILAR SPECIES:** Long-tailed Skipper has a solid central dark band, and male lacks a forewing costal fold. **EARLY STAGES:** Not reported. **FOOD:** Beggar's ticks. **FLIGHT:** Aug. in s. Texas; April–Oct. in Mexico. **RANGE:** Resident from Mexico south through American tropics to Paraguay and s. Brazil. Rare stray north to lower Rio Grande Valley, Texas. **HABITAT:** Open woods and wood edges.

Dorantes Skipper. Adult nectaring on orange mallow. Lower Rio Grande Valley, Tex. Less common than the Long-tailed Skipper in the Southeast, it is much more abundant in so. Texas where it predominates amongst the several longtails.

DORANTES SKIPPER *Urbanus dorantes*   **PL. 30**

1 ⁷⁄₁₆ – 2 in. (36 – 52 mm). Tailed. Brown body and wings. *Fringes checkered.* Upperside: Forewing with conspicuous *transparent spots.* **SIMILAR SPECIES:** Long-tailed Skipper has green body and green wing bases above. Several other brown long-tails are encountered only in s. Texas. **EARLY STAGES:** Caterpillar green to pink-orange, brown at rear; dark red-brown dorsal line; head capsule brown to black. **FOOD:** Viny legumes. **FLIGHT:** All year in s. Fla. and s. Texas (3 – 4 broods). **RANGE:** Resident from s. Texas and peninsular Fla. south through West Indies and mainland American tropics to Argentina. Strays north to s. Ga., s. Mo., s. Ariz., and n. Calif. **HABITAT:** Roadsides, overgrown fields, wood edges, trails in hardwood hammocks.

TELEUS LONGTAIL *Urbanus teleus*   **PL. 30**

1 ⅜ – 1 ½ in. (35 – 38 mm). Tailed. Brown. Upperside: Forewing with *thin central transparent band* and male with *4 subapical transparent spots.* Male *lacks costal fold.* **SIMILAR SPECIES:** Tanna Longtail is almost identical to the Teleus, but forewing of the male has 5 tiny subapical transparent spots. Identification is certain only by dissection of the distinctive male genitalia. **EARLY STAGES:** Not reported. **FOOD:** *Paspalum* and other grasses. **FLIGHT:** All year in s. Texas. **RANGE:** Resident from s. Texas south through mainland tropical America to Argentina. **HABITAT:** Tropical scrub and seasonal forest.

TANNA LONGTAIL *Urbanus tanna*   **NOT SHOWN**

1 ⁵⁄₁₆ – 1 ½ in. (33 – 37 mm). Tailed. Brown. Forewing of male has 5 *subapical spots.* **SIMILAR SPECIES:** Teleus Longtail is nearly identical,

DORANTES SKIPPER

but male has 4 tiny subapical transparent spots. Dissection and examination of the distinctive genitalia is necessary for reliable identification. **EARLY STAGES:** Not reported. **FLIGHT:** June in s. Texas; June–Dec. in Mexico. **RANGE:** Resident from Mexico south through Cen. America to French Guiana and Ecuador. Rare stray to lower Rio Grande Valley, Texas.

PLAIN LONGTAIL *Urbanus simplicius*   **NOT SHOWN**
1 ½–1 ⁵⁄₁₆ in. (37–50 mm). Tailed. Brown. Upperside: Forewing *marks obscured or absent*. Male with costal fold. Underside: Hindwing *postbasal band joined to brown spot* near costa. **SIMILAR SPECIES:** Brown Longtail is nearly identical and reliably separated only by dissection of the male genitalia. Postbasal dark brown band on underside of hindwing is separated from brown spot near costa. **EARLY STAGES:** Not reported. **FOOD:** Viny legumes. **FLIGHT:** April in s. Texas; Oct.–July in Mexico and Cen. America. **RANGE:** Resident from Mexico south through tropical America to Argentina. Rare stray to lower Rio Grande Valley, Texas. **HABITAT:** Seasonal lowland tropical forests and nearby openings and edges.

BROWN LONGTAIL *Urbanus procne*   **PL. 30**
1 ⁷⁄₁₆–1 ⅞ in. (36–47 mm). *Tailed. Brown.* Male has forewing costal fold. Underside: Hindwing postbasal *band* is *separated* from *brown spot* near costa. **SIMILAR SPECIES:** Plain Longtail is nearly identical and reliably separated only by examination of male genitalia. Postbasal dark brown band is joined to brown spot near costa. **EARLY STAGES:** Not reported. **FOOD:** Grasses, including Bermuda grass. **FLIGHT:** All year in s. Texas (3 broods). **RANGE:** Resident from s. Texas south through tropical America to Argentina. Rare stray to s. Calif., s. Ariz., and s. N.M. **HABITAT:** Grassy openings in tropical woods.

WHITE-TAILED LONGTAIL *Urbanus doryssus* **PL. 30**
1 ³⁄₁₆–1 ⅞ in. (30–47 mm). Tails broad and short. Upperside: *Tails*
and much of *outer margin white*, contrasting with dark brown on
remainder of wing surfaces. **EARLY STAGES:** Not reported. **FLIGHT:**
March–April, July, Oct.–Nov. in s. Texas. **RANGE:** Resident from
Mexico south through tropical America to Argentina. Strays north
to lower Rio Grande Valley, Texas. **HABITAT:** Subtropical scrub.

FLASHERS: GENUS *Astraptes* HÜBNER

In our territory, the flashers occur regularly only in south Texas.
The Two-barred Flasher is resident, and three others are occasional strays from the tropics. Three of our species have areas of
iridescent blue or blue-green above. Adults spend much of their
time perched upside-down under large leaves in tropical forest
understories or in small clearings. Males perch in sunlit patches
in tropical forests. Adults visit flowers for nectar or feed on bird
droppings.

TWO-BARRED FLASHER *Astraptes fulgerator* **PL. 30**
1 ⅞–2 ⅜ in. (47–60 mm). Large. Tailless. Upperside: Basal portion of wings *iridescent blue*. Male has costal fold on forewing.
Forewing with *transverse white median band* and tiny subapical
white spots. Underside: Head and thorax *yellow-scaled*. Hindwing
costa white at base. **SIMILAR SPECIES:** Gilbert's Flasher lacks tiny
white subapical spots, and male lacks a costal fold. **EARLY STAGES:**
Caterpillar black above, maroon below, with yellow hairs and
transverse yellow rings; maroon patch near head; head black with
white hairs, marked reddish-brown. **FOOD:** Coyotillo in Texas and

*Two-barred Flasher.
Adult nectaring on
Seep-willow. Lower
Rio Grande Valley,
Tex. This tropical
skipper, with its iri-
descent blue and
bright yellow colors,
roosts upside down
under large leaves.
Look for them along
shaded forest streams.*

Vitex in Mexico. **FLIGHT:** All year in s. Texas. **RANGE:** Resident from lower Rio Grande Valley, Texas, south through lowland tropics to Argentina. Strays to cen. Texas and se. N.M. **HABITAT:** Tropical woods near streams or rivers.

SMALL-SPOTTED FLASHER *Astraptes egregius*   **NOT SHOWN**
1½–1¾ in. (37–44 mm). Tailless. Upperside: Wing bases blue-green. Forewing with a few white spots. Males, along with those of Two-barred Flasher, are the only *Astraptes* with a costal fold. Underside: Hindwing with narrow *yellow costal margin.* **EARLY STAGES:** Not reported. **FLIGHT:** Oct. in s. Texas; Feb.–Nov. in Mexico and Cen. America. **RANGE:** Resident from Mexico and tropical America to Venezuela and Ecuador. Rare stray to lower Rio Grande Valley, Texas. **HABITAT:** Seasonal forest or scrub in tropical lowlands.

FROSTED FLASHER *Astraptes alardus*   **NOT SHOWN**
2–2½ in. (51–63 mm). Tailless. Upperside: Wings black with iridescent blue bases. Underside: Hindwing with *white fringe* and diffuse *white outer margin.* **SIMILAR SPECIES:** Gilbert's Flasher, another rare stray to lower Rio Grande Valley, has wing bases above blue-green, not blue, and underside of hindwing has costa edged with white. Lacks white fringe and white outer margin. **EARLY STAGES:** Not reported. **FLIGHT:** June, Sept.–Oct. in s. Texas; June–Dec. in Mexico and Cen. America. **RANGE:** Resident on Cuba and from Mexico south through tropical America to Argentina. Rare stray north to lower Rio Grande Valley, Texas. **HABITAT:** Shady tropical woods.

GILBERT'S FLASHER *Astraptes gilberti*   **NOT SHOWN**
1⅝–1¹⁵⁄₁₆ in. (41–50 mm). Tailless. Upperside: Body and wing bases *iridescent blue-green.* Underside: Hindwing with base of *costa edged with white.* **SIMILAR SPECIES:** Frosted Flasher has wing bases above deep blue, not blue-green, and underside of hindwing has white fringe and white outer margin. **EARLY STAGES:** Not reported. **FOOD:** *Bauhinia.* **FLIGHT:** June–Aug. in Mexico, Oct. in s. Texas. **RANGE:** Resident from n. to cen. Mexico. Rare stray to lower Rio Grande Valley, Texas.

YELLOW-TIPPED FLASHER *Astraptes anaphus*   **NOT SHOWN**
2–2½ in. (51–63 mm). Tailless. Upperside: *Dark brown* with vague black bands; hindwing edged *broadly* with *yellow* on both sides of anal angle. **EARLY STAGES:** Caterpillar yellow; head brown with eyespots. **FOOD:** Viny legumes. **FLIGHT:** April–May, Sept.–Nov. in s. Texas; as early as March in Mexico. **RANGE:** Resident from

Mexico south through West Indies and mainland tropics to Argentina. Strays north to lower Rio Grande Valley, Texas. **HABITAT:** Seasonal forest or scrub in tropical lowlands.

BANDED SKIPPERS: GENUS *Autochton* HÜBNER

GOLD-BANDED SKIPPER *Autochton cellus* **PL. 31**
1½–2 in. (38–52 mm). Upperside: Black with *broad yellow band crossing forewing* from mid-costa to junction of outer and inner margins. Small coalesced white patch near forewing apex. Adults fly in late afternoon. **EARLY STAGES:** Caterpillar bright yellow-green with scattered yellow points and yellow lateral lines; head capsule red-brown with 2 large, round yellow patches on front. **FOOD:** Hog peanut. **FLIGHT:** Late May–Aug. (2 broods) in north, April–Sept. in south. **RANGE:** Resident in U.S. from Md. south to S.C., west to e. Okla. and ne. Texas. Also resident from cen. Ariz., sw. N.M., and w. Tex. south to cen. Mexico. An isolated population in n. Fla. Older records north to N.J. **HABITAT:** Damp, wooded ravines.

HOARY EDGES: GENUS *Achalarus* SCUDDER

HOARY EDGE *Achalarus lyciades* **PL. 31**
1¾–1 ⁵⁄₁₆ in. (45–49 mm). Upperside: Fringes checkered. Both wings dark brown with transparent gold patch in center of forewing. Underside: Hindwing black-brown with fuzzy-edged silver-white marginal patch. **SIMILAR SPECIES:** The much commoner Silver-spotted Skipper is larger, lacks checkered fringes, and has a large metallic silver patch in center of hindwing below. **EARLY STAGES:** Caterpillar dark green with blue-green dorsal line; narrow orange lateral lines; scattered yellow-orange dots; head black. **FOOD:** Beg-

GOLD-BANDED SKIPPER

HOARY EDGE

gar's ticks, occasionally false indigo or bush clover. **FLIGHT:** April–Sept. (2 broods) most of range, June to early Aug. (1 brood) in north. **RANGE:** Resident in e. U.S. from cen. New England south to n. Fla. and west to Iowa, e. Kans., and cen. Texas. Peripheral record in w. Kans. **HABITAT:** Open woods and brushy areas, especially pine or oak woods with sandy soil.

DESERT CLOUDYWING *Achalarus casica*   **NOT SHOWN**
1½–1⁵⁄₁₆ in. (37–50 mm). Upperside: Forewing with small, separated, white transparent spots; hindwing with *white fringe*. Underside: Hindwing with 2 *dark bands* and *mottled white marginal band*. **EARLY STAGES:** Not reported. **FLIGHT:** April–Oct. in Texas and Mexico. **RANGE:** Resident from n. Mexico south to Guatemala. Strays north to se. Ariz., sw. N.M., cen. and w. Texas. **HABITAT:** Desert grassland, pinyon-juniper woodland.

COYOTE CLOUDYWING *Achalarus toxeus*   **PL. 31**
1⅝–1⁵⁄₁₆ in. (40–50 mm). Forewing pointed. Upperside: Dark brown with *darker rectangular spots*. Hindwing usually with *white fringe*. **SIMILAR SPECIES:** Jalapus Cloudywing hindwing has terminal lobe. **EARLY STAGES:** Not reported. **FOOD:** Texas Ebony. **FLIGHT:** Feb.–Nov. (3 broods). **RANGE:** Resident from cen. Texas south through Mexico and Cen. America to Panama. Strays north to s. Ariz. **HABITAT:** City flower gardens, edge of river woods.

JALAPUS CLOUDYWING *Achalarus jalapus*   **NOT SHOWN**
1⅝–1⅞ in. (39–47 mm). Upperside: Dark brown. Forewing with darker rectangular spots. Male has *costal fold*. Hindwing has fringe and is *lobed at anal angle*. Underside: Hindwing with 2 dark bands. **SIMILAR SPECIES:** Coyote Cloudywing is nearly identical but lacks lobe at anal angle of hindwing. **EARLY STAGES:** Not reported. **FLIGHT:** July, Sept.–Oct. **RANGE:** Resident from Mexico south through Cen. America to Colombia. Strays north to lower Rio Grande Valley, Texas. **HABITAT:** Tropical forests, especially near stream courses.

CLOUDYWINGS: GENUS *Thorybes* SCUDDER

The cloudywings are a small group of similar black skippers that is limited to North America and adjacent Mexico. There are three species in the East and three others that occur only in the West. Our three cloudywings are very similar and require care in their identification. Males perch on or close to the ground in woods openings or nearby fields, where they await the appearance of likely mates. Adults readily visit flowers for nectar. The caterpil-

SOUTHERN CLOUDYWING

NORTHERN CLOUDYWING

lars live and feed within folded leaf shelters on legumes, their only hosts. Winter is passed by full-grown caterpillars.

SOUTHERN CLOUDYWING *Thorybes bathyllus*   **PL. 31**

1⁵⁄₁₆–1⅞ in. (33–47 mm). Hindwing elongated. Upperside: Forewing with *transparent spot band broad* and aligned; male *lacks* costal fold. **SIMILAR SPECIES:** (1) Northern Cloudywing male has costal fold, and forewing has small, scattered, triangular transparent spots. (2) Confused Cloudywing has narrow elongated transparent spots on forewing, and underside of hindwing is strongly marked. **EARLY STAGES:** Caterpillar dull red-brown with pale dorsal and lateral lines; head black, deeply cleft with short golden brown hairs. **FOOD:** Beggar's ticks, bush clover, wild bean, milk vetch, and other legumes. **FLIGHT:** Mid-June to mid-July (1 brood) in north, June to early Oct. (2 broods, possibly 3) in most of range. **RANGE:** Resident through most of e. U.S. and extreme s. Ont. Rare stray to N.M. **HABITAT:** Open and scrubby areas—dry meadows, powerline rights of way, prairie hills, upland barrens, etc.

NORTHERN CLOUDYWING *Thorybes pylades*   **PL. 31**

1⅜–1¹³⁄₁₆ in. (35–46 mm). This is the most broadly distributed cloudywing. Upperside: Forewing with transparent spots *triangular, small,* and *not aligned.* Male is our only cloudywing with a *costal fold.* **SIMILAR SPECIES:** (1) Southern Cloudywing has broad, aligned median band of transparent spots across forewing and lacks a forewing costal fold. (2) Confused Cloudywing has narrower median forewing band, and underside of hindwing is boldly marked. **EARLY STAGES:** Caterpillar dark green with brown or maroon dorsal line; 2 pale orange-pink lateral lines on each side; covered with minute bumps bearing short orange hairs; head black to dark

Northern Cloudy-wing. Adult nectaring on mint. Santa Rita Mts., Ariz. Most often found in sunny forest openings or in fields near forests. Adults seem to avoid red, orange, and yellow flowers.

brown. **FOOD:** Beggar's ticks, bush clovers, milk vetches, and other legumes. **FLIGHT:** May–July (1 brood) in north, flying earlier to south. March–Sept. in Texas (2 broods). **RANGE:** Resident through much of temperate North America from Calif. and Alta. east to N.B., south to n. Mexico and s. Fla. **HABITAT:** Open woodland and fields, generally more boreal than other eastern cloudywings.

CONFUSED CLOUDYWING *Thorybes confusis* **PL. 31**

1¼–1⅞ in. (38–48 mm). Forewing apex rounded. Upperside: Forewing *transparent spots elongated*. Male *lacks* a costal fold. Underside: Hindwing *strongly marked*. **SIMILAR SPECIES:** (1) Southern Cloudywing has broad median band of transparent spots across forewing and has less boldly marked hindwing underneath. (2) Northern Cloudywing has triangular nonaligned transparent

CONFUSED CLOUDYWING

spots on forewing, and male has a costal fold on forewing. **EARLY STAGES:** Not reported. **FLIGHT:** April–Aug. (2 broods). **RANGE:** Resident in Deep South, strays north to se. Kans., s. Ill., and N.J. **HABITAT:** Woods in river valleys or near swamps and marshes.

POTRILLO SKIPPER *Cabares potrillo*   PL. 31

1 ⅛–1 ¹¹⁄₁₆ in. (28–42 mm). Similar to cloudywings. Upperside: Forewing with double *U-shaped transparent spot* in cell. Hindwing margin with *shallow lobes.* Underside: hindwing with 2 *dark bands.* **SIMILAR SPECIES:** Mimosa Skipper has only a few small apical transparent spots. Cloudywings are similar but are unlikely to be found in the lower Rio Grande Valley where Potrillo Skipper is resident. **EARLY STAGES:** Caterpillar light brown with black midline and orange lateral lines; head black. **FOOD:** *Priva lappulacea.* **FLIGHT:** All year in s. Texas (3 broods). **RANGE:** Resident from lower Rio Grande Valley, Texas, south through mainland tropical America and West Indies to Venezuela and Colombia. Strays north to cen. Texas. **HABITAT:** Open fields, moist woods, edge of Rio Grande.

FRITZGAERTNER'S FLAT   NOT SHOWN
Celaenorrhinus fritzgaertneri

1 ⅝–1 ¹⁵⁄₁₆ in. (41–50 mm). Partially nocturnal. Rests in caves and under ledges during day. Upperside: Forewing with *white band;* hindwing *mottled;* fringes *checkered.* **SIMILAR SPECIES:** Stallings' Flat is smaller, has uncheckered fringes, and has a broad transparent band across forewing. **EARLY STAGES:** Not reported. **FLIGHT:** Feb., June –July, Sept. in s. Texas; as late as Oct. in Mexico. **RANGE:** Resident from Mexico south to Costa Rica, periodic stray to s. Texas, rarely to s. Ariz.

STALLINGS' FLAT *Celaenorrhinus stallingsi*   PL. 31

1 ⅜–1 ¾ in. (34–44 mm). Upperside: Dark brown. Forewing with *broad transparent spot band.* Fringes brown. **SIMILAR SPECIES:** Fritz-gaertner's Flat is larger, has checkered fringes and a broad white band across the forewing. **EARLY STAGES:** Not reported. **FLIGHT:** May, Aug.–Nov. in s. Texas; flies as early as March in Mexico. **RANGE:** Resident from Mexico south to Costa Rica, periodic stray to lower Rio Grande Valley, Texas.

EURIBATES SKIPPER *Dyscophellus euribates*   NOT SHOWN

1 ¾–2 ¼ in. (45–57 mm). Large. Brown with *heavy orange over-scaling.* Forewing with group of 3 *large translucent gold spots.* Upperside: Hindwing with postmedian row of small black spots. **EARLY STAGES:** Not reported. **FLIGHT:** April–May, Oct.–Nov. in South America. **RANGE:** Costa Rica south to Brazil; rare stray to s. Texas.

FALCATE SKIPPER *Spathilepia clonius* **PL. 31**
1 ⅝–1 ³/₁₆ in. (40–46 mm). Forewing *apex truncated*; outer margins of both wings *scalloped* between vein endings. Upperside: Forewing with *diagonal white band*. **EARLY STAGES:** Caterpillar yellow with X-like marks on back. **FOOD:** Legumes. **FLIGHT:** May–July, Oct. –Nov. in s. Texas; flies all year in Mexico and Cen. America. **RANGE:** Resident from s. Texas and Mexico south through mainland tropical America to Argentina. **HABITAT:** Edge of woods with dense undergrowth along Rio Grande.

GENUS *Cogia* BUTLER

MIMOSA SKIPPER *Cogia calchas* **PL. 31**
1 ³/₁₆–1 ¾ in. (30–44 mm). Forewing apex extended, especially in males. Upperside: Dark brown. Forewing with 3 or 4 tiny white apical spots; sometimes a vague white costal spot halfway from base. Underside: Hindwing brown with *gray anal fold* and *pale wormlike markings*. **EARLY STAGES:** Caterpillar yellow with fine white dots. **FOOD:** *Mimosa pigra*, *Indigofera*. **FLIGHT:** March–Nov. (3 broods); flies all year in Mexico and Cen. America. **RANGE:** Resident from s. Texas and Mexico south through mainland tropical America to Argentina. **HABITAT:** City flower gardens, lakes formed from cut-off river oxbows, canals, fields.

ACACIA SKIPPER *Cogia hippalus* **NOT SHOWN**
1 ⅜–1 ¹¹/₁₆ in. (34–43 mm). Upperside: Forewing with *prominent white spots*. Hindwing *fringe* prominently *white*. Underside: Hindwing with lavender or purplish cast; fringe narrowly white. **SIMILAR SPECIES:** Desert Cloudywing has hindwing underside with more prominent white fringe. **EARLY STAGES:** Not reported. **FLIGHT:** April–Aug. in Texas; as late as Oct. in Mexico. **RANGE:** Resident from cen. Ariz., sw. N.M., and w. Texas south to Brazil. Rare stray to lower Rio Grande Valley, Texas. **HABITAT:** Desert grassland, pinyon-juniper woodland.

OUTIS SKIPPER *Cogia outis* **PL. 31**
1 ³/₁₆–1 ¹¹/₁₆ in. (30–42 mm). Upperside: Forewing with *white transparent spots* reduced in number and size. Hindwing *fringe brown*, sometimes checkered. **SIMILAR SPECIES:** Acacia Skipper is slightly larger, has white fringe on hindwing and more prominent white spots on forewing. **EARLY STAGES:** Not reported. **FOOD:** Acacias. **FLIGHT:** March–Oct. (4 broods). **RANGE:** Resident in cen. Texas; strays north to Okla., sw. Mo., and nw. Ark. as well as south to n. Chihuahua and Coahuila, Mexico. **HABITAT:** Parks, roadsides, hedgerows.

OUTIS SKIPPER

STARRED SKIPPER *Arteurotia tractipennis*　　**NOT SHOWN**
　1⅛–1⅜ in. (28–35 mm). Upperside: *Gray-brown* with *black* sub-apical *patch on costa* associated with 3 *small white dots*. Underside: Orange-brown; hindwing with irregular *white median patches*. **EARLY STAGES:** Not reported. **FOOD:** Crotons. **FLIGHT:** Sept. in s. Texas; May–June in Mexico and Cen. America. **RANGE:** Resident from n. Mexico south through mainland tropical America to Bolivia. Has strayed to lower Rio Grande Valley, Texas.

PURPLISH-BLACK SKIPPER　　　　　　　**NOT SHOWN**
Nisoniades rubescens
　1–1⁷⁄₁₆ in. (25–36 mm). Upperside: Black. *Mottled*, and forewing has *tiny white subapical spots*. The genitalia of both sexes are distinctive. **SIMILAR SPECIES:** Glazed Pellicia lacks white subapical spots and has iridescent purple or violet sheen. **EARLY STAGES:** Not reported. **FOOD:** Wild morning glories. **FLIGHT:** Oct.–Nov. in s. Texas; as early as July in Mexico. **RANGE:** Resident from n. Mexico south through mainland tropical America to Brazil. Occasional stray to lower Rio Grande Valley, Texas.

CONFUSED PELLICIA *Pellicia angra*　　　**NOT SHOWN**
　1⅛–1½ in. (29–37 mm). Primarily black with a pointed forewing. Upperside: Both wings with an iridescent *purple* or *violet sheen*. Vaguely mottled. **SIMILAR SPECIES:** Glazed Pellicia is nearly identical and can be separated only by dissection and examination of the male genitalia. **EARLY STAGES:** Not reported. **FLIGHT:** Oct.–Nov. in s. Texas; from June in Mexico. **RANGE:** Resident from cen. Mexico south through Cen. America to Panama. Rare stray to lower Rio

Grande Valley, Texas. **REMARKS:** Some doubt this skipper has occurred in the U.S.

GLAZED PELLICIA *Pellicia arina* PL. 31

1–1½ in. (25–38 mm). Upperside: Wings black with an iridescent *purple* or *violet sheen*. Vaguely *mottled*. **EARLY STAGES:** Not reported. **FLIGHT:** March–April, June–Dec. in s. Texas; July, Oct.–Feb. in Mexico and Cen. America. **RANGE:** Resident from n. Mexico south through Cen. America to Panama. Periodic stray to lower Rio Grande Valley, Texas. **HABITAT:** Trails and woods edges.

MORNING GLORY PELLICIA *Pellicia dimidiata* NOT SHOWN

⅞–1⅛ in. (23–29 mm). Upperside: Both wings black. *Violet sheen faint or absent.* Underside: Hindwing with *oval glandular patch* over the base of the radial vein. **SIMILAR SPECIES:** Glazed Pellicia has strong violet or purple sheen on upperside and lacks oval glandular patch on underside of hindwing. **EARLY STAGES:** Not reported. **FOOD:** Morning glories. **FLIGHT:** Oct. in s. Texas; April–May, Sept.–Feb. in Mexico and Cen. America. **RANGE:** Resident from n. Mexico south through mainland tropical America to Argentina. Strayed once to lower Rio Grande Valley, Texas.

MOTTLED BOLLA *Bolla clytius* PL. 31

⅞–1⅛ in. (22–29 mm). Upperside: Brown-black with *darker mottling*. Forewing with *tiny white transparent apical spots*. **SIMILAR SPECIES:** (1) Southern Scallopwing is slightly smaller and has scalloped hindwing. (2) Obscure Bolla has scattered orange scales on underside of hindwings. Male lacks tiny white spots on forewing. **EARLY STAGES:** Not reported. **FLIGHT:** June, Oct.–Nov. in s. Texas; as early as March in Mexico. **RANGE:** Resident from n. Mexico south to Honduras. Periodic stray to cen. and s. Texas, s. Ariz. **HABITAT:** Wooded canals.

OBSCURE BOLLA *Bolla brennus* NOT SHOWN

⅞–1³⁄₁₆ in. (23–30 mm). Upperside: Male forewing apex *lacks* tiny white spots. Underside: Hindwing with *scattered orange scales*. **SIMILAR SPECIES:** Reliably separated from Mottled Bolla only by dissection of male reproductive structures. **EARLY STAGES:** Not reported. **FOOD:** *Lycopersicon esculentum.* **FLIGHT:** Oct. in s. Texas; as early as May in Mexico. **RANGE:** Resident from cen. Mexico south through Cen. America to Colombia. Rare stray to lower Rio Grande Valley, Texas.

SCALLOPWINGS: GENUS *Staphylus* GODMAN AND SALVIN

GOLDEN-HEADED SCALLOPWING *Staphylus ceos* **PL. 31**
$^{15}/_{16}$–1 in. (24–26 mm). Wings are less scalloped than other *Staphylus*. Upperside: Head and palpi covered with *golden-orange scales*. Wings black with a few tiny white points on costa near apex. **EARLY STAGES:** Not reported. **FLIGHT:** April–Oct. in Texas. **RANGE:** Resident from s. Ariz., s. N.M., and w. and s. Texas south to Durango, Mexico. **HABITAT:** Valleys, desert canyons, and washes.

SOUTHERN SCALLOPWING **PL. 31**
Staphylus mazans
1–1$^{3}/_{16}$ in. (25–30 mm). Wing margins scalloped. *Fringes* dark brown, *uncheckered*. Upperside: Black with a few small white points on costa near apex. Two darker bands on each wing. **SIMILAR SPECIES:** Hayhurst's Scallopwing has a more northern range, has checkered fringes and more apparent dark bands. **EARLY STAGES:** Not reported. **FOOD:** Lamb's Quarters, amaranths. **FLIGHT:** All year in s. Texas. **RANGE:** Resident from cen. Texas south to Veracruz, Mexico. **HABITAT:** Small clearings in tropical woodlands; weedy areas in parks, wood edges. ·

HAYHURST'S SCALLOPWING **PLS. 3, 31**
Staphylus hayhurstii
1–1$^{1}/_{4}$ in. (25–31 mm). Wing margins scalloped. Upperside: *Black bands* contrast against paler dark brown ground. *Fringe checkered* black and tan. **SIMILAR SPECIES:** Southern Scallopwing more northern and eastern range, has uncheckered fringes and less apparent dark bands on wings. **EARLY STAGES:** Caterpillar deep green, becoming orangish toward rear, covered with fine white

hairs; head capsule purple-brown. **FOOD:** Lamb's Quarters, occasionally Chaff Flower. **FLIGHT:** May—Aug. (2 broods) most of range, April—Sept. in Miss., Feb.—Dec. in Fla. **RANGE:** Resident in s. 2/3 of e. U.S., rarer southward. Strays to s. Ont. **HABITAT:** Vacant weedy lots, suburban gardens, open woods.

VARIEGATED SKIPPER *Gorgythion begga*   **NOT SHOWN**
¹⁵⁄₁₆—1¹⁄₁₆ in. (24—27 mm). Upperside: Dark brown. *Variegated pattern*. Wings overlain with faint iridescent *violet sheen*. Forewing with two tiny transparent subapical spots. **EARLY STAGES:** Not reported. **FLIGHT:** March, Dec. in s. Texas. **RANGE:** Resident from Mexico south through mainland tropical America to Argentina. Rare stray to lower Rio Grande Valley, Texas. **HABITAT:** Small clearings in tropical forests; dry creek beds.

BLUE-STUDDED SKIPPER *Sostrata nordica*   **NOT SHOWN**
¹⁵⁄₁₆—1³⁄₁₆ in. (24—30 mm). Upperside: Dark brown, complexly variegated. Wings covered with *sparse sprinkling of iridescent pale blue scales*. Forewing with 4 small white subapical spots. **EARLY STAGES:** Not reported. **FLIGHT:** Oct. in s. Texas; April—Oct. in Mexico and Central America. **RANGE:** Resident from Mexico south through mainland tropical America to Argentina. Rare stray to lower Rio Grande Valley, Texas. **HABITAT:** Open subtropical scrub.

HOARY SKIPPER *Carrhenes canescens*   **PL. 31**
1—1³⁄₁₆ in. (26—33 mm). Wings *semitranslucent*, especially near body. Upperside: Wings gray-brown with *complex pattern*. Forewing with 8 or 9 small transparent spots. Underside: *Gray-white* with darker thin bands. **EARLY STAGES:** Not reported. **FOOD:** Hibiscus. **FLIGHT:** Feb.—May, Oct.—Dec. in s. Texas. **RANGE:** Periodic resident from s. Texas (lower Rio Grande Valley) south through mainland tropical America to Argentina. **HABITAT:** Tropical scrub; Lemon groves in s. Texas.

GLASSY-WINGED SKIPPER *Xenophanes tryxus*   **PL. 32**
1⅛—1³⁄₁₆ in. (28—33 mm). Forewing with outer margin irregular; hindwing slightly *scalloped*. Upperside: Gray-black with irregular median *transparent patches*. **SIMILAR SPECIES:** White-Patched Skipper has narrower forewings, more extensive white on upperside, lacks transparent areas on wings, and is almost completely white below. Resident in s. Texas and much more likely north of the Mexican border. **EARLY STAGES:** Caterpillar mottled green-white; head brown. **FOOD:** Turk's-cap. **FLIGHT:** Feb.—Dec. in s. Texas (3 broods). **RANGE:** Resident from n. Mexico south through mainland tropical America to Argentina. Periodic resident in lower Rio Grande Valley, Texas, rare stray to sw. N.M.

TEXAS POWDERED-SKIPPER

SICKLE-WINGED SKIPPER

P O W D E R E D - S K I P P E R S : G E N U S *Systasea* E D W A R D S

TEXAS POWDERED-SKIPPER *Systasea pulverulenta* **PL. 31**
¹⁵⁄₁₆−1¹⁄₁₆ in. (24−27 mm). Hindwing outer margin with 2 *lobed projections.* Upperside: Orange-brown with darker olive-brown areas. Forewing with *transparent transverse band.* **EARLY STAGES:** Not reported. **FOOD:** Mallows. **FLIGHT:** Feb.−Dec. in s. Texas. **RANGE:** Resident from s. and w. Texas south through Mexico to Guatemala. **HABITAT:** Open woods, parks, vicinity of rivers.

SICKLE-WINGED SKIPPER *Achlyodes tamenund* **PL. 31**
1³⁄₈−1¹¹⁄₁₆ in. (35−42 mm). Forewing with *shallow notch* below apex. Sexes dimorphic. Upperside: Male dark brown with paler brown spots and *purple sheen;* female brown with *bands* of 4-sided *blue-gray* or *olive-gray* spots. **EARLY STAGES:** Caterpillar light gray-blue above, greenish laterally with a bright yellow stripe; head greenish tan or brown, roughened. **FOOD:** *Zanthoxylum fagara.* **FLIGHT:** All year in s. Texas (most common Aug.−Nov.). **RANGE:** Resident from West Indies and s. Texas south through mainland tropical America to Argentina. Regular stray north to cen. Texas, rarely to Ark. and Kans. **HABITAT:** Openings in tropical thorn forest and scrub; city gardens, wood edges.

HERMIT SKIPPER *Grais stigmaticus* **PL. 32**
1³⁄₁₆−2¹⁄₈ in. (46−53 mm). Rests on the underside of large leaves in the forest understory. Palpi bright yellow-orange below. Underside of abdomen *buff yellow.* Upperside: Dark brown mottled with *darker spots*—sometimes not contrasting with ground. Females with at least a small series of tiny subapical transparent spots. **EARLY STAGES:** Not reported. **FLIGHT:** April, July−Oct. in s. Texas; March−

Dec. in Mexico. **RANGE:** Resident from Mexico south through mainland tropical America to Argentina. Periodic stray to s. Texas, more rarely north to Okla. and Kans. **HABITAT:** Woods and edges, wooded canals.

BROWN-BANDED SKIPPER *Timochares ruptifaciata*   **PL. 32**
1½–1¹¹⁄₁₆ in. (37–42 mm). Upperside: Somewhat similar in size and pattern to a duskywing. Forewing lacks transparent spots and is dark brown with broken bands of darker spots. Hindwing *orange-brown with 3 dark bands*. Underside: Orange-brown with faint mottling. **EARLY STAGES:** Caterpillar with first segment light green; remainder blue-green with many fine yellow dots; orange-yellow lines on each side with orange spots on each segment; head dark brown, ivory, and olive green. **FOOD:** *Malpighia glabra*. **FLIGHT:** March–Nov. in s. Texas and Mexico. **RANGE:** Resident from s. Texas south through Mexico, also occurs on Jamaica. Strays to s. Ariz. and sw. N.M. **HABITAT:** Openings in tropical forests, wood edges, city flower gardens.

WHITE-PATCHED SKIPPER *Chiomara georgina*   **PL. 32**
1¹⁄₁₀–1¼ in. (27–32 mm). Upperside: Brown-black variably invaded by *irregular white patches*. Underside: White except on outer and costal margins. **SIMILAR SPECIES:** Glassy-winged Skipper is much rarer north of the Mexican border, has less white and large transparent areas on both wings. **EARLY STAGES:** Not reported. **FOOD:** *Malpighia glabra* and other malpighia plants. **FLIGHT:** All year in s. Texas (3–4 broods). **RANGE:** Resident in West Indies and from s. Texas south through mainland tropical America to Argentina. Strays north to Kans., Nev., and s. Ariz. **HABITAT:** Small clearings in tropical woodlands, city flower gardens, wood edges.

FALSE DUSKYWING *Gesta invisus*   PL. 32
¹⁵⁄₁₆−1⁵⁄₁₆ in. (24−33 mm). Upperside: *Banded brown-black.*
Forewing with submarginal *blue-gray band* and irregular *brown or
black patch* overlapping discal cell. SIMILAR SPECIES: Funereal Duskywing, the only true duskywing (*Erynnis*) likely in most of south
Texas, is larger and has distinct white fringes on the outer margin
of the hindwing. EARLY STAGES: Caterpillar gray or yellow-green,
whitish toward rear; green dorsal stripe; yellow and orange lateral
bands; head white or orange, spotted red-brown or black. FOOD:
Indigoferas. FLIGHT: April−Nov. in s. Texas (4 broods); all year from
Mexico southward. RANGE: Resident from West Indies and s. Texas
south through mainland tropical America to Argentina. Strays to
e. Texas. HABITAT: Tropical thorn scrub, dry riverbeds, abandoned
fields. REMARKS: This tropical skipper has been previously placed in
the genus *Erynnis* (true duskywings) but is distinctive.

FLORIDA DUSKYWING *Ephyriades brunnea*   PL. 32
1⅝−1⅞ in. (40−48 mm). Forewing apex abruptly angled. Sexes
dimorphic. Upperside: Male black with silky sheen. *Circle* of subapical *white transparent spots.* Female brown with darker outer
margins and mottling; forewing with more, larger subapical and
postmedian transparent spots. SIMILAR SPECIES: True duskywings
(*Erynnis* species) have fewer and smaller transparent white spots
on forewing. All are black, none is as brown as Florida Duskywing
female, and none has the male Florida Duskywing's silky sheen.
All true duskywings have pointed forewings. EARLY STAGES: Caterpillar green with 3 white stripes on each side. FOOD: Key Byrsonima,
Barbados Cherry. FLIGHT: All year in s. Fla. RANGE: Resident in tropical s. Fla. and West Indies. Rare stray to Honduras. HABITAT: Tropical pine-Sabal palm scrub.

TRUE DUSKYWINGS: GENUS *Erynnis* SCHRANK

The somber black duskywings are richest in North America, with
two species (*E. funeralis* and *E. tristis*) ranging through Central
America to South America. Adults are all very similar in a general
way, although many southwestern species often have white hindwing fringes. Our several groups of duskywings have species that
are difficult to separate. Males perch, either in openings or on
promontories, as their method of locating receptive mates. Freshly emerged males are often found visiting moist sand or mud,
where they imbibe moisture. Adults are avid flower visitors.
Caterpillars of most species feed on leaves of woody plants, but
members of the "Persius complex" are exceptional in their choice
of herbaceous legumes.

DREAMY DUSKYWING *Erynnis icelus* PL. 32

1 ³⁄₁₆−1 ½ in. (30−38 mm). Black. Labial palpi *project forward* more than those of other duskywings. Lacks small transparent spots on forewing. Upperside: Forewing grizzled gray with *darker* median and postmedian *bands*. **SIMILAR SPECIES:** Sleepy Duskywing is larger, less gray, has more distinct forewing bands. Other dusky-wings have labial palpi not projected forward, small transparent spots on forewing. **EARLY STAGES:** Caterpillar pale green with small, white, hair-bearing bumps; head strongly angled, depressed, black with reddish and yellowish spots. **FOOD:** Willows, poplars, aspen, occasionally birch. **FLIGHT:** April to early July (1 brood), rare second brood (?) in s. Appalachians. **RANGE:** Widespread in boreal North America from w. N.W. Terr. south through w. mountains south to s. Ariz. and s. N.M., east across s. Canada to N.S., and south in East to Ark., ne. Ala., and n. Ga. **HABITAT:** Open woods or forest edges.

SLEEPY DUSKYWING *Erynnis brizo* PL. 32

1 ⅜−1 ¾ in. (35−45 mm). This duskywing is often found on ridgetops in areas of scrub oak or cut-over oak woods. Upperside: Forewing *bands usually distinct and complete*. **SIMILAR SPECIES:** Dreamy Duskywing is smaller and has long, forward-directed palpi. The upperside of the forewing is grizzled gray, and the two forewing bands are interrupted. **EARLY STAGES:** Caterpillar gray-green with purplish on front and rear; a subdorsal faint white stripe on each side and a dark middorsal stripe. Head is yellowish to dark brown with an orange spot. **FOOD:** Bear Oak, other shrubby oaks. **FLIGHT:** March−June (1 brood), Jan.−May in Fla. and Texas. **RANGE:** Resident from w.-cen. Man., Gaspé Peninsula, and Prince Edward I. south through s. Ont. and e. U.S. to cen. Fla., Gulf

Juvenal's Duskywing. Female nectaring on Winter Cress. Fairfax Co., Va. This is the most abundant eastern duskywing. Its unusual sleeping posture is to roll its wings downward around a small twig.

Coast, and cen. Texas. In West from n. Calif., Utah, and s. Wyo. south through mountains to Baja Calif. Norte and cen. Mexico. **HABITAT:** Oak or oak-pine scrub, barrens, often sandy or shaley soils.

JUVENAL'S DUSKYWING *Erynnis juvenalis* PL. 32

1½–1¹⁵⁄₁₆ in. (38–50 mm). Our most common, widespread spring duskywing. Upperside: Male forewing with *scattered white hairs*. Underside: 2 *round light subapical spots* on the hindwing. **SIMILAR SPECIES:** Horace's Duskywing usually lacks spots on hindwing underside. **EARLY STAGES:** Caterpillar pale to blue-green or dark green; body covered with tiny yellow-white dots, and a yellow subdorsal stripe. Head is tan or green-brown with 4 orange spots. **FOOD:** Oaks. **FLIGHT:** April–June (1 brood), emerges as early as late Jan. in peninsular Fla. **RANGE:** Temperate e. North America from s. Sask. east to N.S. south through most of area to s.-cen. Texas,

Gulf Coast, and s. Fla. (*E. j. juvenalis*). White-fringed populations (*E. j. clitus*) south from w. Texas and cen. Ariz. south to cen.
Mexico. **HABITAT:** Oak woods or scrub and adjacent edges or fields.

MERIDIAN DUSKYWING *Erynnis meridianus* PL. 32

1⅝–1⅞ in. (39–48 mm). Black. Upperside: Forewing with pattern showing *little contrast*. Transparent spots of male small,
those of female large. Hindwing *fringes* are *pale-tipped*. Underside: Hindwing is uniform in color; 2 pale subapical spots are
much reduced in size or absent altogether. **SIMILAR SPECIES:** (1) Juvenal's Duskywing has larger white spots on forewing, dark fringes
on hindwing, and 2 large subapical spots on hindwing below. (2)
Horace's Duskywing has dark fringes on hindwing and usually
lacks the 2 subapical pale spots on hindwing below. These two
species are reliably separated from the Meridian Duskywing only
by dissection and examination of the distinctive male genitalia.
EARLY STAGES: Unreported. **FOOD:** Oaks. **FLIGHT:** March–Sept. (2
broods) in Texas. **RANGE:** Resident from n. and cen. Texas west to s.
Nev. and w. Ariz., south to nw. Mexico. **HABITAT:** Oak thickets in
foothills.

HORACE'S DUSKYWING *Erynnis horatius* PL. 32

1⁷⁄₁₆–1⁵⁄₁₆ in. (36–50 mm). Upperside: Dark brown. Male forewing *lacks white overscaling* and has little pattern contrast.
Female forewing is pale brown with contrasting pattern and large
transparent spots. Underside: Hindwing usually *lacks 2 subapical
spots*. **SIMILAR SPECIES:** Juvenal's Duskywing almost always has 2 pale
subapical spots on hindwing below. Male forewing has white scaling above and more pattern contrast. Female is darker above with
less contrasting pattern. Juvenal's Duskywing is also more common in the spring, and it lacks a second generation. **EARLY STAGES:**

Unreported. **FOOD:** Oaks. **FLIGHT:** April–Sept. (2 broods) in north, Jan.–Nov. (3 broods) in Deep South and Texas. **RANGE:** Resident in extreme s. Ont. and e. U.S. from s. New England west to e. S.D., se. Utah, and ne. Ariz. south to s. Fla., Gulf Coast, and s. Texas. **HABITAT:** Open woods and edges, power-line rights of way, wooded swamps, open fields.

MOURNFUL DUSKYWING *Erynnis tristis*   **NOT SHOWN**
1 ⅝–1 ¹⁵⁄₁₆ in. (39–49 mm). Dark brown-black with *white* hindwing *fringe*. Underside: Hindwing has *marginal row* of *long white spots*. **SIMILAR SPECIES:** Funereal Duskywing has narrower forewings, triangular hindwings, and lacks marginal row of white spots on hindwing below. **EARLY STAGES:** Caterpillar is pale gray-green with minute white points, yellowish subdorsal line, dark dorsal line, and an

Mottled Duskywing. Male perching. Boulder Co., Colo. Males are usually seen perching on hilltops where they await females to court. Females are seen most often near their caterpillar hosts — wild lilacs, most often New Jersey Tea.

orange-brown head showing 3 pale orange spots on each side.
FOOD: Oaks. **FLIGHT:** March–April, June–July, Sept.–Nov. (3
broods) in Texas. **RANGE:** Resident from n. Calif., cen. Ariz., and s.
N.M. south through mountains of Mexico and Cen. America to
Colombia. Strays to s. Texas. **HABITAT:** Oak woodlands.

MOTTLED DUSKYWING *Erynnis martialis*   PL. 32

1 ¼–1 ⅝ in. (31–41 mm). Males are usually found patrolling and
perching on ridgetops. Upperside: Both wings with *strong mot-
tling*. Forewing often with a faint *iridescent violet sheen*. **EARLY
STAGES:** Caterpillar light green with dark red marks on black head.
FOOD: New Jersey Tea, Redroot. **FLIGHT:** March to early Sept. (2
broods). **RANGE:** Resident from s. Que. and s. Ont. west to se.
Man., ne. Wyo., cen. Colo., and cen. Texas, south to S.C. and the
Gulf Coast. **HABITAT:** Open brushy fields, barrens, prairie hills.

ZARUCCO DUSKYWING *Erynnis zarucco*   PL. 32

1 ⅝–1 ¹³⁄₁₆ in. (40–46 mm). Upperside: Dark brown. Forewing is
narrow and pointed with *red-brown patch* at end of cell. Hindwing
lacks white fringe and is relatively triangular. *Note:* Some individuals on Fla. Keys have white hindwing fringes. **EARLY STAGES:** Caterpillar light green with dense white hairs, yellow lateral lines, and
an orange dot on each segment. **FOOD:** Usually Black Locust but
also more herbaceous legumes. **FLIGHT:** March to early Oct. (3
broods) in Deep South, as early as late Jan. in Fla. **RANGE:** Resident
in Southeast from N.C. south to Fla. Keys and west to e. Texas
and cen. Okla. Also on Cuba and Hispaniola. Strays north to e.
Penn. and Conn. **HABITAT:** Open fields, scrub, wood edges. **REMARKS:**
Closely related to the Funereal Duskywing; the ranges of the two
overlap in e. Texas and La. without evidence of their blending.

FUNEREAL DUSKYWING   *Erynnis funeralis*   **PL. 32**

1 5/16 – 1 3/4 in. (33 – 45 mm). Forewing *narrow and pointed*. Hindwing more or less triangular. Upperside: Black. Forewing with
brown patch at end of cell. Hindwing outer margin with *white
fringe*. **EARLY STAGES:** Caterpillar is pale green with yellow subdorsal
stripe, dark middorsal stripe, blue below, and black head. **FOOD:**
Legumes such as vetch, *Sesbania*, *Indigofera*. **FLIGHT:** March – Dec.
(3 broods). **RANGE:** Resident from deep Southwest south through
mainland tropical America to Argentina. Strays north to n. Ill., ne.
Neb., cen. Colo., s. Nev., and cen. Calif. **HABITAT:** Roadsides, wood
edges, trails, etc.

COLUMBINE DUSKYWING   *Erynnis lucilius*   **PL. 32**

1 3/16 – 1 5/8 in. (30 – 40 mm). Upperside: Forewing with *brown patch*
at end of cell relatively *indistinct*. Underside: Hindwing with
marginal and submarginal rows of *pale spots very distinct*. **SIMILAR
SPECIES:** (1) Wild Indigo Duskywing is larger, has distinct orange-
brown spot at end of forewing discal cell, and has basal half of
forewing darker than outer half. (2) Persius Duskywing has patch
at end of forewing discal cell more gray than brown. Forewing of
male has numerous raised white hairs. **EARLY STAGES:** Caterpillar is
pale green with yellow cast; there is a yellowish subdorsal line on
each side and a dark green middorsal line. Head is black with
white or reddish streaks or spots on each side. **FOOD:** Wild
columbine. **FLIGHT:** April – Sept. (2 broods). **RANGE:** Se. Canada and
ne. U.S. from s. Que. and s. New England south to Va. (mountains) and west to Minn., possibly se. Man. **HABITAT:** Ravines or gullies in rich deciduous or mixed woods or their edges. **REMARKS:** The
Columbine, Wild Indigo, and Persius duskywings belong to the
difficult "Persius complex," a group of confusingly similar butterflies.

FUNEREAL DUSKYWING

COLUMBINE
DUSKYWING

WILD INDIGO DUSKYWING *Erynnis baptisiae* PL. 32

1 ⁷⁄₁₆–1 ⁵⁄₈ in. (36–41 mm). Upperside: Forewing with *distinct orange-brown patch* at end of cell. Basal half *dark*; distal half *lighter*. **SIMILAR SPECIES:** (1) Columbine Duskywing is smaller, has indistinct brown patch at end of forewing discal cell. (2) Persius Duskywing is smaller, has indistinct gray patch at end of discal cell on forewing, and has numerous raised white scales on forewing above. **EARLY STAGES:** Not reported. **FOOD:** Wild indigos, lupine, Crown Vetch. **FLIGHT:** April–Sept. (2 broods). **RANGE:** Expanding. Resident from s. New England and extreme s. Ont. west to cen. Neb. and s.-cen. Texas, south to Gulf Coast. **HABITAT:** Barrens and open woods on native hosts, highway shoulders, railroad beds, upland fields on Crown Vetch. **REMARKS:** This butterfly has rapidly expanded its range and abundance by colonizing the plantings of Crown Vetch along highways, interstates, and railroad beds.

PERSIUS DUSKYWING *Erynnis persius* PL. 32

1 ¼–1 ⁵⁄₈ in. (32–40 mm). Upperside: Forewing with patch at end of cell *more gray than brown*. Male forewing with *numerous raised white hairs*. **SIMILAR SPECIES:** (1) Columbine Duskywing and (2) Wild Indigo Duskywing have more distinct patches at end of their forewing cells, and males of the two species lack raised white hairs on their forewings. **EARLY STAGES:** Caterpillar pale green with minute white points, yellowish subdorsal line on each side, a dark green middorsal line, and a dark red-brown to yellow-green head that shows pale vertical streaks. **FOOD:** Lupine; doubtfully willows, poplars, and aspens. **FLIGHT:** April–June (1 brood). **RANGE:** Two population centers. One in ne. U.S. and s. Ont., the other from Alaska and McKenzie R. delta south through w. mountain archipelago to s. Calif., s. Ariz., and se. N.M., east to se. Man. **HABITAT:** Open areas, marshes, seeps, sand plains.

WILD INDIGO DUSKYWING

PERSIUS DUSKYWING

The checkered-skippers occur in both the Old and New worlds. There are four species in eastern North America. One, *Pyrgus centaureae*, also occurs in Eurasia and belongs to a group of small species that feeds mainly on rose family plants. The other three belong to a group of mallow-feeders that is limited to the New World, extending southward to South America. Males of our species perch and patrol in open habitats in their search for receptive females. Our species may wander and can colonize new areas. The Common Checkered-Skipper is an excellent colonizer and each summer invades areas far to the north of the zone where it can survive the winter. The caterpillars live and feed within webbed leaf shelters.

GRIZZLED SKIPPER *Pyrgus centaureae*   **PL. 33**

1 ⅛–1 ⁵⁄₁₆ in. (29–33 mm). *Gray-black* with *white checks*. Fringes checkered. **SIMILAR SPECIES:** Common Checkered-Skipper is larger and has larger white spots. **EARLY STAGES:** Not reported. **FOOD:** Wild strawberry. **FLIGHT:** Biennial in subarctic, annual to south, March–May (1 brood). **RANGE:** Holarctic. In North America, from Alaska south and east to cen. Ont. and n. Mich. Isolated populations in (1) Lab. and arctic Que., (2) cen. Appalachians, and (3) Rocky Mts. from cen. Alta. south to n. N.M. **HABITAT:** Open areas near woods, barrens, taiga(?).

COMMON CHECKERED-SKIPPER *Pyrgus communis* **PL. 33**

1 ¼–1 ½ in. (32–38 mm). The only common black and white checkered-skipper through most of our area. Male has a blue-gray tone, while female appears more plain black and white. Hindwing spots in marginal row are much smaller than those of sub-

GRIZZLED SKIPPER

COMMON CHECKERED-SKIPPER

marginal row. **SIMILAR SPECIES:** (1) Tropical Checkered-Skipper has marginal and submarginal spot rows on hindwing with equal-sized spots, and there is a strong infusion of brown on hindwing below. Male has a mat of long, blue-gray, hairlike scales on upper-side of forewing. (2) Desert Checkered-Skipper is smaller, has minute spots in marginal and submarginal rows on hindwing. **EARLY STAGES:** Caterpillar yellow-white varying to brown with lateral brown and white lines, covered with small white bumps. Head black, covered with yellow-brown hair. **FOOD:** Mallows, Hollyhock. **FLIGHT:** Feb.–Oct. in Deep South, all year in s. Texas. March–Sept. in north. **RANGE:** Resident from cen. U.S. south through Mexico and mainland tropical America to Argentina. Strays and colonizes areas as far north as cen. Alta., s. Ont., and s. New England. **HABITAT:** Open sunny areas with at least some bare soil and low vegetation—open pinewoods, prairies, landfills, highway shoulders, vacant lots, etc.

TROPICAL CHECKERED-SKIPPER *Pyrgus oileus*   **PL. 33**

1¼–1½ in. (32–38 mm). Upperside: Male forewing with *overlying mat* of *long blue-gray hairs*. Hindwing of both sexes has marginal and submarginal rows of equally sized *white spots*. Underside: Hindwing often with a strong *infusion of brown*. Little contrast between bands and pale ground color. **SIMILAR SPECIES:** Common Checkered-Skipper hindwing has marginal spots much smaller than those of submarginal row. **EARLY STAGES:** Caterpillar green with faint dorsal line, small white bumps; head black. **FOOD:** Hollyhock, mallows, *Malva loca, Axocatzin*. **FLIGHT:** All year in Fla. and s. Texas (4–5 broods). **RANGE:** Resident from s. Texas and Fla. south through West Indies and mainland tropical America to Argentina. Strays north to s. Ariz., n. Texas, Ark., and Ga. **HABITAT:** Pastures, brushy fields, roadsides, wooded trails.

TROPICAL
CHECKERED-SKIPPER

DESERT CHECKERED-SKIPPER

DESERT CHECKERED-SKIPPER *Pyrgus philetas*   **PL. 33**
1 – 1 ⅛ in. (25 – 28 mm). Upperside: Forewing with reduced blue-gray hair cover. Hindwing with marginal and submarginal *spots minute*, especially the marginal series. Female with median series highly reduced. Underside: Hindwing pale *gray-white*. **EARLY STAGES:** Not reported. **FOOD:** Mallows. **FLIGHT:** Feb. – Dec. in Texas. **RANGE:** Resident from s. Texas and s. Ariz. south to s. Mexico, strays north to n. Ariz. and n. Texas. **HABITAT:** Open, moist situations amid arid zones.

WHITE-SKIPPERS: GENUS *Heliopetes* BILLBERG

ERICHSON'S WHITE-SKIPPER *Heliopetes domicella*   **PL. 33**
1 ⅛ – 1 ⅜ in. (28 – 34 mm). Fringes checkered. Upperside: Slate gray with a *broad white median band* on each wing. Underside: Whitish and dull yellow-brown. **EARLY STAGES:** Not reported. **FLIGHT:** April – Dec. in s. Texas. All year in tropics. **RANGE:** Resident from n. Mexico south through mainland tropical America to Argentina. Regular stray north to se. Calif., s. Nev., cen. Ariz., and cen. Texas. **HABITAT:** Subtropical scrub and desert.

LAVIANA WHITE-SKIPPER *Heliopetes laviana*   **PL. 33**
1 ⅜ – 1 ⅝ in. (34 – 41 mm). Forewing apex truncated. Upperside: Male largely white; female with more extensive black pattern on margins. Underside: Hindwing with outer third *olive-brown*, sharply *cut off* from paler median area. Basal dark area with pale *triangular patch*. **SIMILAR SPECIES:** Turk's Cap White-Skipper is smaller, has rounder forewing apex, and has more restricted, less patterned black marks on hindwing below. **EARLY STAGES:** Not reported.

Laviana White-Skipper. Male nectaring on yellow mallow. Lower Rio Grande Valley, Tex. Found all year in so. Texas and tropical lowlands, this skipper probably spends the winter as a long-lived adult in reproductive arrest.

FOOD: Mallows. **FLIGHT:** All year in s. Texas. **RANGE:** Resident from s. Texas and n. Mexico south through mainland tropical America to Argentina. Strays regularly to s. Ariz. and cen. Texas—rarely to n. Texas. **HABITAT:** Edge of brushy areas, trails, roadsides.

TURK'S CAP WHITE-SKIPPER *Heliopetes macaira* PL. 33

1¼–1⅜ in. (31–34 mm). Forewing apex rounded. Upperside: Dark markings more restricted. Underside: Hindwing *diffusely patterned*, has *olive-brown band* on outer margin. **SIMILAR SPECIES:** Laviana White-Skipper is larger, has a truncated forewing apex and a strongly patterned hindwing below. **EARLY STAGES:** Not reported. **FOOD:** Turk's-cap. **FLIGHT:** April–Nov. in s. Texas. **RANGE:** Resident from s. Texas south through mainland tropical America to Paraguay. **HABITAT:** Woods or brushy areas.

VEINED WHITE-SKIPPER NOT SHOWN
Heliopetes arsalte

1⁷⁄₁₆–1¹¹⁄₁₆ in. (36–43 mm). Upperside: White with forewing apex black. Underside: Forewing with base of costa margin orange. Hindwing has *principal veins lined with black*. **EARLY STAGES:** Not reported. **FLIGHT:** Oct. in s. Texas; May–Nov. in Mexico and Cen. America. **RANGE:** Resident from cen. Mexico south through mainland tropical America to Argentina. Rare stray to s. Texas. **HABITAT:** Open subtropical scrub.

COMMON STREAKY-SKIPPER *Celotes nessus* PL. 33

⅞–1³⁄₁₆ in. (23–30 mm). Upperside: Both wings orange-brown to dark brown with inward-projecting *dark brown streaks* and irregular median series of *small transparent spots*. Fringes conspicuously

COMMON STREAKY-SKIPPER

COMMON SOOTYWING

SALTBUSH SOOTYWING

checkered. **EARLY STAGES:** Not reported. **FOOD:** Mallows. **FLIGHT:** March
–Nov. in Texas. **RANGE:** Resident in s. Ariz., s. N.M., and the w. ⅔ of
Texas to n. Mexico. Rare stray to s. Okla. and n. La. **HABITAT:** Open
thorn scrub, washes, gulches, flower gardens.

SOOTYWINGS: GENUS *Pholisora* SCUDDER

COMMON SOOTYWING *Pholisora catullus*   PL. 33

1–1 5⁄16 in. (26–33 mm). Our commonest, most widespread small
black skipper. Upperside: *Glossy* black with many *white spots* on
forewing. Female with more white spots, including submarginal
row on hindwing. **SIMILAR SPECIES:** Mexican Sootywing has underside
of hindwing iridescent blue-gray. **EARLY STAGES:** Caterpillar green
with pale dots, black shield behind head, head black. **FOOD:** Lamb's
Quarters, amaranths, Cockscomb, rarely mints. **FLIGHT:** May–Aug.
(2 broods), flies earlier and later in Deep South, March–Nov. in
Texas. **RANGE:** Resident from cen. U.S. south to cen. Mexico, stray
and colonist as far north as s. B.C., n. Mich., s. Que., and s. Me.
Absent from peninsular Fla. **HABITAT:** Landfills, roadsides, rural
areas, vacant lots, gardens.

*Common Sootywing.
Female perching.
Fairfax Co., Va. The
butterfly is almost
always found in close
association with man-
made habitats, where
it flies close to the
ground and nectars
on low flowers.*

MEXICAN SOOTYWING *Pholisora mejicanus* **NOT SHOWN**

$^{15}/_{16}$–1 $^{3}/_{16}$ in. (24–30 mm). Upperside: *Glossy black* with many *white spots* on forewing. Underside: Hindwing *blue-gray* contrasting with *black-lined* veins. **SIMILAR SPECIES:** Common Sootywing has underside of hindwing plain black, without darker veins. **EARLY STAGES:** Caterpillar similar to Common Sootywing but body hairs twice as long. **FOOD:** Amaranths. **FLIGHT:** May–Aug. (2 broods); as late as Sept. in Mexico. **RANGE:** Resident from cen. Colo. south through Mexico to Oaxaca. Rare stray to s. and cen. Texas. **HABITAT:** Gulches and canyons.

SALTBUSH SOOTYWING *Hesperopsis alpheus* **PL. 33**

1–1 $^{1}/_{4}$ in. (26–32 mm). Usually restricted to saltbush flats. Upperside: Black with *mottled gray pattern*. Fringes are *checkered*. **EARLY STAGES:** Caterpillar dark green with many white dots; head blackish with short yellow hairs. **FOOD:** *Atriplex canescens*. **FLIGHT:** May–Sept. (2 broods). **RANGE:** Resident in arid w. U.S. east to lower Rio Grande Valley, Texas, and south to Chihuahua, Mexico. **HABITAT:** Arid canyons, alkali flats.

INTERMEDIATE SKIPPERS: SUBFAMILY HETEROPTERINAE

These small skippers are most closely related to the branded skippers, and they have similar biology. Their antennae lack an apiculus, the extension found at the antennal tips of other skippers. When perched, they hold their wings up at a 45-degree angle. The caterpillars feed on grasses.

ARCTIC SKIPPER *Carterocephalus palaemon*   PL. 33

1 – 1¼ in. (26–31 mm). Upperside: Black with orange spots. Underside: Hindwing *red-orange* with *black-outlined cream spots.* **EARLY STAGES:** Caterpillar cream to blue-green, with a dark green dorsal line and pale yellow lateral stripes enclosed by black spots; head whitish. **FOOD:** Purple Reedgrass, probably other grasses. **FLIGHT:** May–July (1 brood). **RANGE:** Resident in subarctic North America from cen. Alaska south and east across Canada to the Maritime Provinces, south to cen. Calif., nw. Wyo., Great Lakes states, and N.Y. and New England. **HABITAT:** Openings and glades in subarctic woodlands.

SMALL-SPOTTED SKIPPERLING   NOT SHOWN
Piruna microsticta

⅞ – 1 in. (22–25 mm). Upperside: Black with deep chestnut overtones; forewing spotted. Underside: Chestnut brown, with scattered small black-outlined white spots. **EARLY STAGES:** Not reported. **FLIGHT:** Oct. in s. Texas; primarily June–Aug. in Mexico. **RANGE:** Resident from n. to cen. Mexico. Rare stray to s. Texas. **HABITAT:** Arid subtropical chaparral.

BRANDED SKIPPERS: SUBFAMILY HESPERIINAE

The branded skippers, comprising more than 2,000 species, occur worldwide, but most of their species are in the American tropics. The small to medium-sized adults usually have abruptly angled antennae with an apiculus at the tip. Male forewings usually have a brand or stigma with specialized scales. Males never have a forewing costal fold or specialized tufts of modified scales

Arctic Skipper. Male perching. Plumas Co., Calif. Found in sunlit openings in forests or along streams. Adults visit flowers such as irises. This species and the Common Branded Skipper are our only native skippers that range into Eurasia.

ARCTIC SKIPPER

on the tibia as do the open-winged skippers (Subfamily Pyrginae). Many temperate species are predominantly orange, while brown is the most frequent color among tropical species. Adult flight is rapid, and perching posture is unique: the hindwings are opened at a wider angle than the forewings. Males of most species perch as their principal mate-locating behavior. Most species have long proboscises and are avid flower-visitors. The caterpillars feed on monocotyledons (grasses and allied plants) and live in silken leaf nests that sometimes extend underground. Winter is usually passed by caterpillars within their shelters.

MALICIOUS SKIPPER *Synapte pecta*   **PL. 33**
1 −1³⁄₁₆ in. (25−30 mm). Upperside: Dark brown. Forewing with diffuse *dusky yellow or orange band*. Underside: Hindwing light brown with *minute dark striations*. **SIMILAR SPECIES:** Salenus Skipper has only faint band on forewing above and has dark costal and central patch on hindwing below. **EARLY STAGES:** Not reported. **FOOD:** Paspalum. **FLIGHT:** May−Nov. in s. Texas; as early as Feb. in Cen. America. **RANGE:** Resident from lower Rio Grande Valley, Texas, south through mainland tropical America to s. Brazil and Paraguay, also occurs on Cuba. **HABITAT:** Shaded subtropical woods, flower gardens.

SALENUS SKIPPER *Synapte salenus*   **NOT SHOWN**
1 −1¼ in. (25−31 mm). Upperside: Dark brown, *pale bands faint or absent*. Underside: Hindwing brown with fine darker striations and *dark costal and central patches*. **SIMILAR SPECIES:** Malicious Skipper has paler patches on underside of hindwing. Male genitalia also differ. **EARLY STAGES:** Not reported. **FLIGHT:** Aug. in s. Texas; June− Oct. in Mexico. **RANGE:** Resident from n. Mexico south through mainland tropical America to Bolivia, rare stray in Texas.

REDUNDANT SKIPPER *Corticea corticea*   PL. 33

⅞−1 in. (22−26 mm). Upperside: *Pale forewing band*. Underside: Hindwing *orange-brown* without dark striations. Fringe yellow. **EARLY STAGES:** Not reported. **FLIGHT:** Sept.−Dec. in s. Texas. **RANGE:** Resident from Mexico south through mainland tropical America to s. Brazil. Strays north to s. Texas.

PALE-RAYED SKIPPER *Vidius perigenes*   PL. 33

⅞−1⅛ in. (23−29 mm). Upperside: Brown, without markings. Underside: Hindwing *yellow-brown* with *white streak* running from base to apex. **SIMILAR SPECIES:** Julia's Skipper lacks underside hindwing white streak and has 2−5 faint yellow spots on forewing. **EARLY STAGES:** Not reported. **FOOD:** Grasses. **FLIGHT:** March−April, Aug.−Dec. (2 broods?) in s. Texas; as early as Feb. in Mexico. **RANGE:** Resident from lower Rio Grande Valley south through Mexico and Cen. America to Colombia.

VIOLET PATCH SKIPPER *Monca tyrtaeus*   PL. 33

¾−⅞ in. (19−23 mm). Dark brown. Underside: Forewing with white spot on costa. *Hindwing with 2 gray bands*. **EARLY STAGES:** Not reported. **FOOD:** Paspalum. **FLIGHT:** All year in s. Texas. **RANGE:** Resident from lower Rio Grande Valley, Texas, south through Mexico and Cen. America to Colombia. **HABITAT:** Grassy areas in thorn scrub.

SWARTHY SKIPPERS: GENUS *Nastra* EVANS

This is a small genus of about 12 brown tropical American skippers. Three species occur in our area. They are difficult to separate, but their ranges overlap only from central Florida to east Texas. Males perch close to the ground in swales or open weedy areas.

SWARTHY SKIPPER

JULIA'S SKIPPER

SWARTHY SKIPPER *Nastra lherminier* PL. 34

1 −1⅛ in. (26−28 mm). Upperside: Dark brown. Forewing some-times with *trace of 2 light spots*. Underside: Hindwing *yellow-brown with lighter veins*. **SIMILAR SPECIES:** Neamathla Skipper has underside of hindwing yellower without paler scaling on veins. **EARLY STAGES:** Not reported. **FOOD:** Little Bluestem. **FLIGHT:** May−Sept. (2 broods), earlier to south. **RANGE:** Resident in e. U.S. from s. N.Y. west to Kans. and south to s. Fla., the Gulf states, and e. Texas. Strays as far north as n. Minn., s. Mich., and w. Kans. **HABITAT:** Open grassy areas, including meadows, sand barrens, hillsides.

JULIA'S SKIPPER *Nastra julia* PL. 34

¹⁵⁄₁₆−1⅛ in. (24−28 mm). Upperside: Dark brown. Forewing with *2−5 pale spots*. Underside: Hindwing *yellow-brown without paler veins*. **SIMILAR SPECIES:** (1) Pale-rayed Skipper has white streak on underside hindwing. (2) Neamathla Skipper has yellow-brown underside forewing apex more gradually blended into darker brown basal area. **EARLY STAGES:** Not reported. **FOOD:** Bermuda Grass. **FLIGHT:** All year in s. Texas. **RANGE:** S. Texas south to cen. Mexico. **HABITAT:** Open grassy areas in scrub woodland, flower gardens, irri-gation levees.

NEAMATHLA SKIPPER *Nastra neamathla* PL. 34

⅞−1⅛ in. (22−29 mm). Upperside: Brown *without markings*. Underside: Forewing with yellow-brown on more than outer half, black at base. Hindwing is yellow-brown *without pale scaling on veins*. **SIMILAR SPECIES:** Swarthy Skipper has trace of two light spots on forewing above, and has pale scaling on veins of hindwing below. **EARLY STAGES:** Not reported. **FOOD:** Probably grasses. **FLIGHT:** Feb.−Oct. (3 broods). **RANGE:** Resident in se. Texas and peninsular Fla. and the Keys, also south to Costa Rica; strays to s. La. and s.

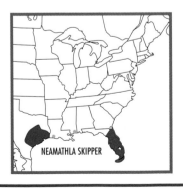

NEAMATHLA SKIPPER

THREE-SPOTTED SKIPPER

CLOUDED SKIPPER

Miss. **HABITAT:** Moist open areas, marsh edges. **REMARKS:** Overlaps the similar Swarthy Skipper in peninsular Fla. and along the Gulf Coast.

THREE-SPOTTED SKIPPER *Cymaenes tripunctus*   **PL. 34**
1 ⅛ – 1 ⁵⁄₁₆ in. (28 – 33 mm). Dull dark brown. Upperside: Forewing with 3 *tiny white transparent spots* on costa near apex and 2 or 3 others at end of cell. Underside: Hindwing *yellow-brown* with faint pale discal spots. **SIMILAR SPECIES:** Eufala Skipper has gray underside hindwing. **EARLY STAGES:** Caterpillar blue-green with gray-green dorsal line; green and gray-green lateral bands; head variable brown and white. **FOOD:** Guinea Grass. **FLIGHT:** March – Oct. **RANGE:** Resident in s. Fla. and the Keys, West Indies, and cen. Mexico south through mainland tropical America to Paraguay.

FAWN-SPOTTED SKIPPER *Cymaenes odilia*   **PL. 34**
¹³⁄₁₆ – 1 ³⁄₁₆ in. (21 – 23 mm). Similar to Clouded Skipper. Dark brown. Upperside: Forewing with tiny white transparent spots. Underside: Hindwing with 2 *pale bands*, the innermost ending on costal margin. **SIMILAR SPECIES:** Clouded Skipper male has prominent stigma. Underside of hindwing has iridescent violet-blue sheen. **EARLY STAGES:** Not reported. **FOOD:** Paspalum. **FLIGHT:** June – Nov. in s. Texas; April – Jan. in Mexico and Central America. **RANGE:** Resident from n. Mexico south through mainland tropical America to Argentina. Rare stray to s. Texas. **HABITAT:** Shaded woods.

CLOUDED SKIPPER *Lerema accius*   **PL. 34**
1 ⅜ – 1 ¾ in. (34 – 44 mm). Upperside: Male with strong black stigma; female forewing with white transparent spots. Underside: Hindwing *variegated* with *violet-blue sheen*. **SIMILAR SPECIES:** Liris Skipper, a rare find in the lower Rio Grande Valley, has the underside of the hindwing yellow-brown and unmarked. Distinctive

features of the male genitalia can also provide identification. **EARLY STAGES:** Caterpillar white, mottled with black; head black-margined with 3 vertical black streaks on front. **FOOD:** Grasses. **FLIGHT:** All year in Fla. and s. Texas. **RANGE:** Resident in se. U.S. south through Texas and mainland tropical America to Venezuela and Colombia. Strays north as far as s. New England, s. Ill., se. Kans., and s. Ariz. **HABITAT:** Woods edges and clearings near swamps and rivers.

LIRIS SKIPPER *Lerema liris* NOT SHOWN
1 – 1 ⅛ in. (26 – 29 mm). Upperside: Brown-black with strong stigma on forewing. Underside: Hindwing *yellow-brown, unmarked*. **EARLY STAGES:** Not reported. **FOOD:** Grasses, including Sugar Cane and bamboo. **FLIGHT:** Aug. – Oct. in s. Texas, all year in Mexico. **RANGE:** Resident from Mexico south through mainland tropical America to Peru. Strays north to lower Rio Grande Valley, Texas. **HABITAT:** Forests adjacent to river courses.

FANTASTIC SKIPPER *Vettius fantasos* NOT SHOWN
1 ¹/₁₆ – 1 ¼ in. (27 – 32 mm). Unique. Underside: Hindwing *ivory white* with *veins outlined with red-brown*. Two discal white spots. **EARLY STAGES:** Not reported. **FOOD:** *Lasiacis*. **FLIGHT:** Oct. in s. Texas; July – Nov. in tropics. **RANGE:** Resident from n. Mexico south through mainland tropical America to Paraguay. Strays north to lower Rio Grande Valley, Texas. **HABITAT:** Tropical forests.

GREEN-BACKED RUBY-EYE *Perichares philetes* NOT SHOWN
1 ½ – 1 ¹¹/₁₆ in. (37 – 42 mm). Upper surface of thorax *iridescent green*. Dark brown, *fringes checkered* black and white. Upperside: Dark brown. Forewing with transparent *pale yellow spots*. Male with curved gray stigma. Underside: Hindwing mottled *purplish, dark brown*, and *violet-gray*. **EARLY STAGES:** Caterpillar green above with poorly defined yellow-green dorsal stripe, yellow-green on sides; head pale green, speckled with black. **FOOD:** Sugar Cane, bamboo, and other rank grasses. **FLIGHT:** Nov. – Dec. in s. Texas; Dec. – Jan. in Mexico. **RANGE:** Resident from n. Mexico south through West Indies and mainland tropical America to Paraguay. Periodic stray to lower Rio Grande Valley, Texas. **HABITAT:** Flower gardens in Texas; fields and wood edges in tropics.

OSCA SKIPPER *Rhinthon osca* NOT SHOWN
1 ⅜ – 1 ⅝ in. (34 – 40 mm). Head and thorax *greenish* above. Upperside: Dark brown. Pointed forewing with *large white spots*. Underside: Hindwing brown with small white discal spot and several small white submarginal spots. **EARLY STAGES:** Not described. **FLIGHT:** Oct. in s. Texas; May – Jan. in Mexico. **RANGE:** Resident from West Indies and n. Mexico south through mainland tropical America to

Ecuador. Periodic stray to lower Rio Grande Valley, Texas. **HABITAT:** Tropical forests.

DOUBLE-SPOTTED SKIPPER *Decinea percosius*   **PL. 34**
⅞–1⅜ in. (25–35 mm). Dark brown. Upperside: Forewing with *angled transparent spot* in discal cell. Hindwing with single small *central transparent spot*. Underside: Hindwing yellow-brown. **EARLY STAGES:** Not reported. **FOOD:** Grasses. **FLIGHT:** March–Nov. in s. Texas and Mexico. **RANGE:** Resident from Mexico south to Belize. Periodically colonizes lower Rio Grande Valley, Texas. **HABITAT:** Flower gardens; tropical scrub and forests.

HIDDEN-RAY SKIPPER *Conga chydaea*   **NOT SHOWN**
¹⁵⁄₁₆–1³⁄₁₆ in. (24–30 mm). Upperside: Dark brown. Forewing with variable number of small transparent spots. Underside: Yellow-brown. Forewing with *short white streak*. **EARLY STAGES:** Not reported. **FLIGHT:** July–Oct. in s. Texas; May–Dec. in Mexico. **RANGE:** Resident from Mexico south to Argentina, rare stray to lower Rio Grande Valley, Texas. **HABITAT:** In Texas found along wooded canal levees.

LEAST SKIPPER *Ancyloxypha numitor*   **PL. 34**
⅞–1⅛ in. (22–28 mm). Weak, fluttering, patrolling flight. May be incredibly abundant in freshwater marshes and ditches. Antennae short. Wings rounded. Upperside: Forewing primarily black (hidden in normal posture) except for *orange apex and costa*. Hindwing yellow-orange with wide black margin. Underside: Forewing black except apex and costa. **EARLY STAGES:** Caterpillar grass green; head dark brown, ringed with a white line on front. **FOOD:** Grasses. **FLIGHT:** May–Oct. (3 broods) in most of range, flies longer in Deep South and Texas (4 broods). **RANGE:** Resident in e. U.S. and s.

LEAST SKIPPER

Poweshiek Skipperling. Male nectaring on Purple Coneflower. Cayler Prairie, Dickinson Co., Iowa. Limited to native tall-grass prairies, often in reserves where it is threatened by overuse of fire by well-meaning conservationists.

Canada from se. Sask. east to N.S., south to s. Fla., Gulf Coast, and s. Texas. Strays to cen. Colo. and s. Alta.(?). **HABITAT:** Wet open areas, ditches, marshes, sluggish streams.

TROPICAL LEAST SKIPPER *Ancyloxypha arene* **NOT SHOWN**
⅞–1 1/16 in. (22–27 mm). Tiny, orange. Male lacks stigma. Upperside: Black border, usually narrow, on both wings. Underside: Hindwing golden orange, with *paler ray* extending from base through cell to outer margin. **SIMILAR SPECIES:** Southern Skipperling has narrower black borders on forewing above, and a white ray (not pale orange) on hindwing below. **EARLY STAGES:** Not reported. **FLIGHT:** April–Aug., as late as Oct. in s. Texas; March–Dec. in Mexico and Cen. America. **RANGE:** Resident from se. Ariz., s. N.M., and w.-cen. Texas south through mainland tropical America to Costa Rica. Strays to s. Texas and ne. N.M. **HABITAT:** Damp grassy areas near streams.

POWESHIEK SKIPPERLING *Oarisma poweshiek* **PL. 34**
1 1/16–1 1/4 in. (27–31 mm). Upperside: Black; forewing costa and veins *lined with orange.* Underside: Hindwings pale brown; *veins lined with white.* **SIMILAR SPECIES:** Garita Skipperling upperside forewing lacks orange veins, and underside hindwing anal fold is

largely orange. **EARLY STAGES:** Caterpillar pale green with dark green dorsal band; many longitudinal cream lines; head pale green. **FOOD:** Spikerush. **FLIGHT:** Late June to early Aug. (1 brood). **RANGE:** Resident from sw. Man. (formerly) south to cen. Iowa and se. Wis., east to s.-cen. Mich. **HABITAT:** Native, tall-grass prairie. This butterfly is in need of protection wherever found.

GARITA SKIPPERLING *Oarisma garita*   PL. 34

1–1³⁄₁₆ in. (25–30 mm). Upperside: Varies from black to orange. Underside: Forewing largely orange; hindwing *light brown*; anal fold largely orange. **EARLY STAGES:** Caterpillar pale green with white lines; head pale green. **FOOD:** Grasses. **FLIGHT:** June–July (1 brood); as early as May in Mexico. **RANGE:** Resident from cen. Alta. east to s. Man. south through Rocky Mt. region to n. Mexico. Strays east to cen. Ont. **HABITAT:** Short-grass prairie knolls, limestone openings, and swales.

ORANGE SKIPPERLING *Copaeodes aurantiacus*   PL. 34

⁷⁄₈–1⅛ in. (24–29 mm). *Orange* above and below. Upperside: Male with *narrow black stigma*; female may have *narrow black border* on forewing. **SIMILAR SPECIES:** Southern Skipperling has white ray running length of underside hindwing. **EARLY STAGES:** Caterpillar green with 2 purplish stripes above converging on a rear hornlike projection; head multicolored, with 2 symmetrical horns. **FOOD:** Bermuda Grass. **FLIGHT:** Feb.–Nov. in Texas. **RANGE:** Resident in sw. U.S. south through mainland tropical America to Panama. Strays to e. Texas and cen. Ark. **HABITAT:** Moist areas along stream courses.

SOUTHERN SKIPPERLING *Copaeodes minimus*   PL. 34

¹¹⁄₁₆–⅞ in. (18–23 mm). The smallest North American skipper. Upperside: Pale orange. Forewing with narrow black border and short narrow black stigma. Underside: Hindwing with *white ray*

GARITA SKIPPERLING

ORANGE SKIPPERLING

extending from base through cell to outer margin. **SIMILAR SPECIES:** Orange Skipperling lacks white ray on hindwing underside. **EARLY STAGES:** Not reported. **FOOD:** Bermuda Grass. **FLIGHT:** March–Oct. (2 broods) in La.; all year in Fla. **RANGE:** Resident in se. U.S. south through mainland tropical America to Costa Rica. **HABITAT:** Open sunny fields, flats.

EUROPEAN SKIPPER *Thymelicus lineola*   PL. 35

1 – 1⅛ in. (25 – 29 mm). Unlike any other skipper in its range. Upperside: Brassy shining *orange*. Both wings with *black borders* and veins *lined with black*. Male has narrow black stigma. A rare albino form occurs in parts of East, notably N.J. **EARLY STAGES:** Caterpillar green with dark dorsal stripe; head light brown with white or yellow stripes on front. **FOOD:** Timothy Grass. **FLIGHT:** Mid-May to mid-July (1 brood). **RANGE:** Holarctic. Introduced accidentally to North America at London, Ont. in 1910. Now found from Nfld. west to e. N.D. and south to s. Ill. and w. S.C. Also established in w. Colo., Idaho, Mont., and B.C. **HABITAT:** Open, grassy fields, pastures, roadsides. May be incredibly abundant.

FIERY SKIPPER *Hylephila phyleus*   PL. 35

1¼ – 1½ in. (32 – 38 mm). Strong sexual dimorphism. Antennae very *short*. Male yellow-orange. Upperside: Both wings with *toothed black margins*; forewing with black stigma. Underside: Hindwing with scattered *small black spots*. Female upperside: Black with irregular orange postmedian band. Underside: Hindwing *pale brown* with *paler checks*. **SIMILAR SPECIES:** (1) Whirlabout male has upperside forewing with more even black margins. Underside hindwing is yellow-orange with fewer and larger dark smudges, not distinct spots. (2) Sachem female has forewing with transparent spot at end of cell; hindwing underside has pale spots or checks instead of black spots. Sachem male is not likely to be

SOUTHERN SKIPPERLING

EUROPEAN SKIPPER

Fiery Skipper. Female nectaring on Sweet Pepperbush. Great Dismal Swamp National Wildlife Refuge, N.C. This skipper of subtropical and tropical habitats often strays northward where it dies out with the arrival of freezing winters.

confused with either sex of the Fiery Skipper. **EARLY STAGES:** Caterpillar gray-brown to yellow-brown with 3 dark longitudinal stripes; head black with red-brown frontal stripes. **FOOD:** Weedy grasses, especially Crabgrass and Bermuda Grass. **FLIGHT:** All year in Fla. and s. Texas. **RANGE:** Resident from s. U.S. south through the West Indies and mainland tropical America to Argentina. Strays north to n. Calif., s. Minn., s. Ont., and s. New England. **HABITAT:** Open, sunny areas including lawns, fields, levees, etc.

GENUS *Hesperia* FABRICIUS

There are 19 species worldwide in this primarily temperate zone genus. One species occurs widely in Eurasia. The adults are predominantly orange, medium-size skippers, often with a pattern of

FIERY SKIPPER

UNCAS SKIPPER

white spots on the underside hindwing. The male stigma is narrow and slightly curved, with a central silver line. The species are difficult to identify, but in most of the East, the location and season can narrow the possibilities to only one or two species. Males perch on hilltops or in glades in their quest for receptive mates. Females lay eggs singly on leaves of perennial grasses, their caterpillar hosts. The caterpillars live in and feed near a silken shelter at the base of their host grass clump, and overwinter in partly underground shelters.

UNCAS SKIPPER *Hesperia uncas* **PL. 34**
1¼–1⅝ in. (32–40 mm). Underside: Hindwing with white postmedian spot band *extended along veins*, contrasting with *black* submarginal *patches*. **EARLY STAGES:** Not well known. **FOOD:** Blue Grama Grass and Needlegrass. **FLIGHT:** May–Sept. (2 broods). **RANGE:** Cen. Alta. east to s. Man., thence south to e.-cen. Calif. (*H. u. macswaini*), se. Ariz., and w. and n. Texas. Strays to sw. Iowa and e. Minn. **HABITAT:** Short-grass prairie.

COMMON BRANDED SKIPPER *Hesperia comma* **PL. 34**
1⅛–1½ in. (29–38 mm). A highly variable species. Many geographic forms with differing appearances. Northern populations (*H. c. laurentina*) *dark* above and below. Western individuals with more extensive *warm orange* above. Upperside: Forewing stigma with *black felt* (use hand lens). Underside: Hindwing *spot band normal*. **EARLY STAGES:** Caterpillar olive green; head black or brown. **FOOD:** Perennial grasses, sedges. **FLIGHT:** Mid-July to early Sept. (1 brood). **RANGE:** Holarctic. From cen. Alaska east to Lab. and south to Baja Calif. Norte, se. Ariz., w. Neb., n. Mich., and Me. **HABITAT:** Open, sunny areas: fields, meadows, open forest.

COMMON
BRANDED SKIPPER

APACHE SKIPPER *Hesperia woodgatei*   **PL. 34**

1 ⁷⁄₁₆–1 ¹¹⁄₁₆ in. (35–42 mm). Large. Upperside: Male forewing stigma with black felt (use hand lens). Underside: Hindwing brown to dark olive green, with *spots* in band *small*, *rounded*, and often *separated*. **SIMILAR SPECIES:** Green Skipper, the only *Hesperia* overlapping with the Apache Skipper in cen. Texas, is smaller, has underside hindwing yellower and with wider, continuous spot band. **EARLY STAGES:** Not reported. **FOOD:** Grasses, sedges. **FLIGHT:** Sept.–Oct. (1 brood). **RANGE:** Separate populations in (1) cen. Texas, (2) w. Texas, and (3) cen. Ariz. and nw. N.M. south to nw. Mexico. **HABITAT:** Open grassy slopes, mountain meadows.

OTTOE SKIPPER *Hesperia ottoe*   **PL. 34**

1 ⁷⁄₁₆–1 ¹¹⁄₁₆ in. (35–43 mm). Upperside: Male forewing stigma with black or gray felt. Underside: Hindwing *yellow-orange, unmarked*

Ottoe Skipper. Male perching on thistle. Larimer Co., Colo. This is a widespread skipper of tall- and midgrass prairies. It is an excellent indicator of undisturbed prairie conditions.

in males, occasionally with faint spot band in females. SIMILAR SPECIES: Pawnee Skipper upperside forewing stigma has yellow interior felt, and it flies at end of summer. EARLY STAGES: Caterpillar green-brown; head dark brown. FOOD: Little Bluestem, Fall Witchgrass, and other grasses. FLIGHT: Late June to early Aug. (1 brood). RANGE: S. Man. south along high plains to n. Texas, east across Neb. and Kans. to cen. Ill. and sw. Mich. HABITAT: Tall-grass prairie. Populations of this skipper should be conserved wherever found.

LEONARD'S SKIPPER *Hesperia leonardus*   PL. 34

1½–1¾ in. (37–45 mm). Includes two very different-looking subspecies, both with male forewing stigma with yellow interior felt (use hand lens). LEONARD'S SKIPPER (*H. l. leonardus*): Upperside red-orange with broad black borders. Underside: Hindwing *brick red* with band of distinct *white, cream,* or *yellow spots*. PAWNEE SKIPPER (*H. l. pawnee*): Black on upperside more limited in extent. Underside: Hindwing *yellow-orange*, may have *faint spot band*. Intermediate individuals are found in Wis. and Minn. EARLY STAGES: Not reported. FOOD: Various perennial grasses, including Little Bluestem and Blue Grama grass. FLIGHT: Aug. to early Oct. (1 brood). RANGE: W. Mont. and se. Sask. east to s. Que. and N.S., south to cen. Colo., n. Ark., and n. Ga. Strays to cen. Mont. and cen. Ala. HABITAT: Open, grassy areas: fields, barrens, native prairies.

PAHASKA SKIPPER *Hesperia pahaska*   PL. 35

1⅜–1⅝ in. (34–41 mm). Upperside: Yellow-orange with broad black borders. Male has black forewing stigma with *yellow interior felt* (use hand lens). Underside: Hindwing orange-brown with

Leonard's Skipper. Male nectaring on New York Ironweed. Fairfax Co., Va. This is one of the only single-brooded eastern butterflies that fly in late summer and early fall. The adults visit pink, blue, or purple flowers almost without exception.

complete spot band. **SIMILAR SPECIES:** Green Skipper is nearly identi-cal. Males can be best separated by habitat and the presence of black felt in the forewing stigma. Females cannot be separated where the two species reside in the same area except by dissection and examination of their genitalia. These two butterflies fly at the same time. Males of Pahaska Skipper perch on hilltops, whereas those of the Green Skipper are found along gullies and stream courses. **EARLY STAGES:** Caterpillar light brown; head dark brown with cream marks. **FOOD:** Blue Grama Grass, *Erioneuron.* **FLIGHT:** Late May–July (1 brood) in North, April–Oct. (2 broods) in Texas. **RANGE:** Rocky Mt. range from cen. Mont. and nw. N.D. south to cen. Mexico, west to se. Calif., and east to nw. Minn. (stray). **HABITAT:** Foothills with short-grass prairie, open pine forest.

COBWEB SKIPPER *Hesperia metea*   **PL. 34**
1 ⅛–1 ⅜ in. (29–35 mm). Upperside: Dark brown or blackish with light areas restricted. Underside: Hindwing with white scaling

from spots extended along veins, giving *cobweb* effect. Individuals from Texas (*H. m. licinus*) are extremely dark on both surfaces. **EARLY STAGES:** Not reported. **FOOD:** Big Bluestem and Little Bluestem grasses. **FLIGHT:** Late March to early June (1 brood)—the earliest "branded skipper" in the Northeast. **RANGE:** E. U.S. from s. Me. south to cen. Ga., west to cen. Kans., cen. Okla., and cen. Texas. **HABITAT:** Pine barrens, oak savannah, open sandy scrub.

GREEN SKIPPER *Hesperia viridis*   **PL. 35**

1–1 5⁄16 in. (25–33 mm). Upperside: Bright golden-orange; stigma of male with black interior felt. Underside: Hindwing bright green-orange to yellow-orange with *well-developed white spot pattern*. Spot band *concave* from outer margin. **SIMILAR SPECIES:** Pahaska Skipper, rare in our area, is nearly identical and can best be separated by behavior. Male Pahaska Skippers perch on hilltops or knolls and have yellow interior felt in the male forewing stigma (use hand lens). Females cannot be separated without dissection in areas where the two species overlap. **EARLY STAGES:** Not reported. **FOOD:** *Erioneuron pilosum*. **FLIGHT:** April–Oct. (2 broods). **RANGE:** E. Wyo. and w. Neb. south in a broad band through high plains and foothills to cen. Texas and cen. Mexico. **HABITAT:** Canyons, ravines, roadsides, dunes.

DOTTED SKIPPER *Hesperia attalus*   **PL. 35**

1 3⁄8–1 5⁄8 in. (34–40 mm). This skipper is variable and difficult to characterize, but is rarely encountered. Forewing *strongly pointed*, especially in male. Upperside: Male dull tawny to dark with broad borders. Female dark with few light spots. Underside: Dull orange to green-brown with or without *small pale spots*. **EARLY STAGES:** Not reported. **FOOD:** Switchgrass, Fall Witchgrass. **FLIGHT:** May–Sept. (2

broods); flies earlier and later in Fla. **RANGE:** Atlantic seaboard from from e. Mass. (rarely) south to peninsular Fla. and Gulf Coast. Separate population from cen. Kans. south to e.-cen. Texas. Stray to e. Neb. **HABITAT:** Pine barrens, short-grass prairies.

MESKE'S SKIPPER *Hesperia meskei*   **PL. 35**
1¼–1½ in. (31–37 mm). Upperside: *Dark* markings *extensive*, but restricted light areas are *bright orange*. Underside: Hindwing *bright yellow-orange* with *faint spot band* of paler spots. **SIMILAR SPECIES:** Dotted Skipper has forewings more pointed; orange colors duller, muted. **EARLY STAGES:** Not reported. **FLIGHT:** April–Oct. (2 broods), May–Dec. in s. Fla. **RANGE:** Southeast from s. N.C. south to Fla. Keys. Isolated populations in cen. Ark. and e. Texas. Stray to s. Texas. **HABITAT:** Sparse, open woods.

DAKOTA SKIPPER *Hesperia dacotae*   **PL. 35**
1¼–1⅜ in. (31–35 mm). An endangered prairie relative of the Indian Skipper. Forewings *stubby*, not noticeably pointed. Upperside: Golden-orange; dark markings blurred; male forewing stigma with *black interior felt*. Female forewing with white transparent spot below end of cell. Underside: Male hindwing *yellow-orange* with or without faint macular band. Female hindwing *brown-gray* with or without faint macular band. **SIMILAR SPECIES:** Ottoe Skipper is larger; forewings pointed. Male upperside hindwing usually immaculate; female hindwing yellow-orange, not gray. **EARLY STAGES:** Caterpillar light brown, cervical shield black; head dark brown. **FOOD:** Native grasses. **FLIGHT:** Mid-June to early Aug. (1 brood). **RANGE:** S. Man. and w. N.D. to w. Minn. south to nw. Iowa, formerly e. Iowa and possibly ne. Ill. **HABITAT:** Native tall-grass prairies. All populations should be protected.

Indian Skipper. Male perching. Pendleton Co., W. Va. Adult Indian Skippers nectar at flowers such as Henbit, hawkweed, blackberry, lithospermum, and phlox.

INDIAN SKIPPER *Hesperia sassacus* **PL. 35**

1 ¼ – 1 ⅜ in. (31 – 35 mm). The only orange early-summer *Hesperia* in the Northeast. Upperside: Yellow-orange with clear-cut black markings. Hindwing *black border often toothed*. Underside: Hindwing *yellow-orange* with spot band yellow, not contrasting with ground. **SIMILAR SPECIES:** Sometimes occurs with Long Dash, which has more rounded forewing apex, broader black borders, and black on underside of forewing not extending beyond base. Black stigma on male forewing is longer. **FOOD:** Grasses, especially *Andropogon*. **FLIGHT:** May – July (1 brood). **RANGE:** S. Canada and ne. U.S. from se. Man. east to s. Que. and cen. Me. south to n. Ind., s. Ohio, and w. N.C. **HABITAT:** Brushy old fields, clearings, pastures, headlands.

INDIAN SKIPPER

NEVADA SKIPPER *Hesperia nevada* **NOT SHOWN**

1 ³/₁₆–1 ⁷/₁₆ in. (30–36 mm). Rarely enters our area. Upperside: Tawny orange. Male forewing stigma with black interior felt (use hand lens). Underside: Hindwing *gray-green* to *golden-green* with irregular white spot band—most basal spot often *offset* inward. **SIMILAR SPECIES:** (1) Pahaska Skipper does not occur with this species in our area. (2) Common Branded Skipper flies later in summer. **EARLY STAGES:** Not reported. **FOOD:** Perennial grasses. **FLIGHT:** Late May to early July (1 brood). **RANGE:** W. mountains from s. B.C. south to cen. Calif., cen. Ariz., and n. N.M. Extends east across prairie provinces to s. Man. **HABITAT:** Sagebrush flats, prairies, mountain summits.

GENUS *Polites* SCUDDER

This is a small genus of 10 species, all of which are North American. Six occur in the East, and only two have ranges that extend south of the United States. Most are small, orange species with short, stout-clubbed antennae. Males have a prominent sinuous

NEVADA SKIPPER

PECK'S SKIPPER

BARACOA SKIPPER

(almost S-shaped) stigma. Two of our species (*Polites origenes* and *P. themistocles*) are difficult to separate without close inspection, but the other eastern species are distinctive. Grasses, including those found in lawns such as bluegrasses, are the hosts.

PECK'S SKIPPER *Polites peckius*   **PL. 35**

1–1¼ in. (25–31 mm). Small. Underside: Hindwing with *central patch of yellow spots* surrounded by dark border. **EARLY STAGES:** Caterpillar dark maroon mottled light brown; head black with white streaks and patches. **FOOD:** Grasses. **FLIGHT:** May–Oct. (2–3 broods). **RANGE:** Temperate North America from B.C. east across s. Canada to Nfld. and N.S., south to ne. Ore., s. Colo., nw. Ark., and n. Ga. **HABITAT:** Open, grassy areas: lawns, landfills, marshes, power-line rights of way.

BARACOA SKIPPER *Polites baracoa*   **PL. 36**

⅞–1⅛ in. (22–28 mm). A small Antillean skipper. Upperside: Male forewing with *very short stigma*. Underside: Hindwing usually with *postmedian spot row*. **SIMILAR SPECIES:** Tawny-edged Skipper is paler and lacks spot band on underside of hindwing. Male has a longer, more distinct stigma on the forewing. **EARLY STAGES:** Caterpillar brown with a dark brown dorsal stripe and 2 lateral lines; head dull yellow-brown with white stripes and patches. **FOOD:** Grasses. **FLIGHT:** March–Nov. **RANGE:** Fla., adjacent parts of s. Ala. and s. Ga.; West Indies. **HABITAT:** Grassy areas near streams and marshes.

TAWNY-EDGED SKIPPER *Polites themistocles*   **PL. 35**

⅞–1⁷⁄₁₆ in. (23–36 mm). Upperside: Forewing of both sexes with *orange along costa* invading end of cell. Male stigma *sinuous*. Underside: Hindwing usually *brassy*, without spots. **SIMILAR SPECIES:**

Tawny-edged Skipper. Male nectaring on Purple Prairie-clover. Dickinson Co., Iowa. This skipper is much more likely to be found in native grasslands and prairies than its close relative, the Crossline Skipper.

TAWNY-EDGED SKIPPER

CROSSLINE SKIPPER

LONG DASH

WHIRLABOUT

Crossline Skipper is larger; male with forewing more pointed, stigma straighter; female upperside forewing usually without orange along costa. **EARLY STAGES:** Caterpillar similar to that of the Crossline Skipper; head with 2 white vertical stripes on front. **FOOD:** Panic grasses. **FLIGHT:** April–Sept. from N.Y. south (2 broods), only 1 brood in north, all year in Fla. **RANGE:** S. Canada and e. 3/4 of U.S; se. B.C. east to N.S., south to s. Ariz., s. N.M., se. Texas, Gulf Coast, and cen. Fla. **HABITAT:** Lawns, pastures, vacant lots, prairie swales.

CROSSLINE SKIPPER *Polites origenes*   **PL. 35**

1 3/16–1 1/2 in. (30–38 mm). Upperside: Male forewing with stigma *long* and relatively *straight*. Female forewing usually without orange along costa. Large, squarish spot below end of cell. Underside: Hindwing usually orangish with *faint postmedian spot band*. **SIMILAR SPECIES:** Tawny-edged Skipper is smaller and is brassy tan or gray on hindwing underside, without a spot row. Male stigma on upperside of forewing is sinuous; female has orange invad-

ing front area of forewing upperside. **EARLY STAGES:** Caterpillar dark brown with dirty white mottling; head dull black. **FOOD:** Purpletop and other grasses. **FLIGHT:** May–Sept. (2 broods), June to early Aug. (1 brood) in north. **RANGE:** Se. Canada and e. U.S.; w. N.D., cen. Minn., s. Ont., s. Que., and cen. Me. south to ne. Texas, Gulf Coast, and n. Fla. Separate population (*P. o. rhena*) along Rocky Mts. from n. Colo. to ne. N.M. **HABITAT:** Open grassy areas, including old fields, openings, prairie hills, barrens, and power-line rights of way.

LONG DASH *Polites mystic*   PL. 35

1 ³/₁₆–1 ½ in. (30–38 mm). Upperside: Forewing with male stigma long, slightly curved—may or may not be connected to dash running to apex. Hindwing orange-brown with contrasting curved *postmedian band* of equal-sized *yellow spots*. Female has broad black basal patch on upperside of forewing, and underside of hindwing has distinct pattern. **EARLY STAGES:** Caterpillar dark brown mottled dull white; head dull black. **FOOD:** Bluegrasses. **FLIGHT:** Late May to early Aug. (1 brood). **RANGE:** S. Canada and n. U.S. from s. B.C. to N.S., south to sw. Colo., s. Iowa, s. Ohio, and s. Va. (mountains). **HABITAT:** Moist, open areas: prairie swales, streams, marshes, woods edges.

WHIRLABOUT *Polites vibex*   PL. 35

1 ³/₁₆–1 ½ in. (30–38 mm). Sexes dissimilar. Male yellow-orange. Female dark brown. Upperside: Male forewing with black stigma and associated modified scales forming large 4-sided patch. Hindwing with black margins smooth inwardly. Underside: Male hindwing with *large dark spots*. Female hindwing gray or sooty yellow with *pale central patch* outlined with *dark scaling*. **SIMILAR SPECIES:** Male Fiery Skipper has narrower toothed outer margins on both wings above, and more, smaller black dots on hindwing below. Females are not similar. **EARLY STAGES:** Caterpillar pale with faint lateral stripes; head black with yellow-white stripes and patches. **FOOD:** Grasses including Bermuda Grass and St. Augustine Grass. **FLIGHT:** April–Sept. (2 broods) at northern limits of residence; all year in Fla. and s. Texas. **RANGE:** Se. U.S. and West Indies south through e. Mexico and mainland tropical America to Argentina. Periodic strays north as far as ne. Iowa, n. Ohio, and Conn. **HABITAT:** Open areas: fields, dunes, pinewoods, roadsides.

SOUTHERN BROKEN-DASH *Wallengrenia otho*   PL. 36

1–1 ³/₈ in. (25–35 mm). Upperside: Male forewing with orange or red-orange areas along costa and beyond end of cell. Female forewing with spots pale orange. Underside: Hindwing *orange or*

red-orange with *faint postmedian spot band.* **SIMILAR SPECIES:** Northern Broken-Dash has similar pattern, but underside of hindwing is dark brown or purple-brown with a distinct paler spot band. On the upperside, the male has a cream or yellow spot at the end of the forewing discal cell. **EARLY STAGES:** Caterpillar green, mottled with white and red-brown; orange lateral spots; head purple-brown or black marked with white. **FOOD:** *Paspalum,* other weedy grasses. **FLIGHT:** April–Oct. (2 broods, sometimes a partial 3rd); all year in peninsular Fla. and s. Texas. **RANGE:** Se. U.S. and e. Texas south through West Indies and mainland tropical America to Argentina. Strays north as far as cen. Mo., n. Ky., and Del. **HABITAT:** Open areas near wooded swamps or rivers.

NORTHERN BROKEN-DASH   *Wallengrenia egeremet*   **PL. 36**
1–1½ in. (25–37 mm). Upperside: Dark brown. Male forewing with *cream or yellow spot* at end of cell; female forewing with a few (usually 2) elongated *cream or yellow spots.* Underside: *Dark brown* or *purple-brown* with distinctive paler *spot band,* usually with reflective highlights when freshly emerged. **SIMILAR SPECIES:** Southern Broken-Dash has underside of the hindwing orange or red-orange with only a faint postmedian spot band. On the upperside, the male has orange or red-orange areas along the costa and the outer end of the forewing discal cell. **EARLY STAGES:** Caterpillar pale, mottled green; green and yellow side stripes; head dark brown with dark central and pale vertical stripes on front. **FOOD:** Panic grasses. **FLIGHT:** June–Aug. (1 brood), May to early Oct. (2 broods) in Deep South and e. Texas. **RANGE:** Se. Canada and e. U.S. from se. N.D. east across Great Lakes states, s. Ont. to s. Me., south to se. Texas, Gulf Coast, and cen. Fla. **HABITAT:** Open areas near woods or scrub. Most likely to be found in city parks in Northeast.

LITTLE GLASSYWING *Pompeius verna*   **PL. 36**

1 ¹⁄₁₆ – 1 ½ in. (27 – 37 mm). Black or black-brown. Upperside: Male forewing with *black stigma* with several *transparent white spots* above and below, including a large one below end of stigma. Female with *square transparent spot* at end of cell. Underside: Hindwing black often with a few faint pale postmedian spots. **SIMILAR SPECIES:** (1) Northern Broken-Dash female forewing has elongated yellow spot at end of cell. (2) Dun Skipper female forewing has a few pale diffuse irregular spots. To be reliably identified, these females and some males must be captured for close examination. **EARLY STAGES:** Caterpillar yellow-green to yellow-brown, covered with dark brown bumps; dark midline and 3 dark lines on each side; head dark red-brown rimmed with black. **FOOD:** Purpletop, possibly other grasses. **FLIGHT:** Mid-June to early Aug. (1 brood) in North, April – Sept. (2 broods) in South. **RANGE:** Se.

Northern Broken-Dash. Male nectaring on Red Clover. Fairfax Co., Va. The caterpillars are unusual in that they cut out circular pieces of plants which they carry over themselves. A distinct but close relative of the Southern Broken-dash.

Sachem. Female nectaring on Zinnia. Fairfax Co., Va. This is the most widespread colonizing eastern skipper. Most years the Sachem can be found throughout much of the U.S., often in gardens and fields.

Canada and e. U.S.; cen. Neb. east across s. Ont. and s. Que. to s. New England, south to s. Texas, Gulf Coast, and n. Fla. **HABITAT:** Moist areas near shaded wood edges.

SACHEM *Atalopedes campestris*   **PL. 37**
1 ⅜–1 ⅝ in. (35–41 mm). Upperside: Male forewing with large 4-sided *black stigma*. Females variable, light to very dark, but can always be identified by *square white transparent spot* at end of forewing cell. Underside: Female hindwing brown with *squarish white or cream spots*—similar to a *Hesperia*. **SIMILAR SPECIES:** Fiery Skipper females lack square transparent spot on forewing. Underside: Hindwing with black spots instead of pale spots. **EARLY STAGES:** Caterpillar dark olive green with dark bumps; head black. **FOOD:** Grasses, including Bermuda Grass. **FLIGHT:** May–Nov. (3 broods) at northern limit, March–Dec. (4–5 broods) in Deep South. **RANGE:** S. U.S. south through Mexico and mainland tropical America to Brazil. Regular stray and colonist north as far as cen. N.D., s. Mich., and n. Pa. **HABITAT:** Open, disturbed areas: landfills, lawns, pastures, roadsides.

AROGOS SKIPPER *Atrytone arogos*   **PL. 36**
1 ⅛–1 ⁷⁄₁₆ in. (28-36 mm). Bright yellow-orange. Upperside: Wings with *broad black borders*. Underside: Hindwing *veins with pale scaling*. **SIMILAR SPECIES:** (1) Delaware Skipper is brighter orange, lacks broad black borders. (2) Male Byssus Skipper has extensive black areas at bases of both wings above. **EARLY STAGES:** Caterpillar pale yellow-green with yellow intersegmental folds; head gray-white with 4 vertical orange-brown stripes. **FOOD:** Big Bluestem, probably other native grasses. **FLIGHT:** Late June to July (1 brood) in

Delaware Skipper. Male perching. Pendleton Co., W. Va. Find this species in wet or moist areas where the males can be seen perching prominently within 3 feet of the ground.

North and West, April–Sept. (2 broods) in South. **RANGE:** Atlantic Coast and Gulf Coast; also separate prairie populations: (1) N.J. (formerly N.Y. and Staten I.) south to ne. Ga., (2) peninsular Fla., (3) Gulf Coast, (4) se. N.D. and cen. Minn. south to s. Texas, and (5) Colo. front range. Strays to Ill., n. Ark., and w. Va. **HABITAT:** Undisturbed prairies, serpentine barrens.

DELAWARE SKIPPER *Anatrytone logan* **PL. 36**
1–1 ¹¹/₁₆ in. (25–42 mm). Bright yellow-orange. Upperside: Outer margins black; *veins with black* in submarginal area; forewing with *black bar* at end of cell. Underside: Hindwing *unmarked*. **SIMILAR SPECIES:** Arogos Skipper is limited to native prairies or coastal marshes; has broader black borders on both wings above and lacks any black markings inside the borders. **EARLY STAGES:** Caterpillar blue-white with minute black bumps; head white with black

AROGOS SKIPPER

DELAWARE SKIPPER

frontal stripes. **FOOD:** Grasses. **FLIGHT:** July–Aug. (1 brood) in north; May–Sept. (2 broods) in south; Feb.–Oct. in Fla. **RANGE:** Se. Sask. east across n. U.S. and extreme s. Ont. to s. New England, south through most of U.S., and Mexican highlands to El Salvador. **HABITAT:** Damp or wet fields, marshes, prairies.

BYSSUS SKIPPER *Problema byssus*   PL. 36

1 7/16–1 13/16 in. (36–46 mm). Upperside: Black borders, females dark basally. Forewing with *black bar* at end of cell. Underside: Hindwing dull yellow (males), rusty or orange (females) with postmedian *band of paler spots*. **SIMILAR SPECIES:** Rare Skipper only overlaps the Byssus Skipper from N.C. to Ga., is much larger, and is clear yellow on the underside of the hindwings. **EARLY STAGES:** Caterpillar blue-green, covered with fine white hairs; head pale red-brown with vertical yellow-white lines and streaks. **FOOD:** Eastern Grama grass. **FLIGHT:** June–July (1 brood) in Midwest, April–Oct. (2 broods) along Atlantic Coast. **RANGE:** S. Atlantic Coast from N.C. south to peninsular Fla., Gulf states, and prairies from cen. Kans. east to n. Ind. **HABITAT:** Tall-grass prairie in Midwest, edges of coastal marshes along Atlantic Coast.

RARE SKIPPER *Problema bulenta*   PL. 36

1 1/2–2 1/8 in. (38–54 mm). Large. Upperside: Yellow-orange with black borders, especially in female. Underside: Forewing with *black* extending from termen (corner) halfway up outer margin. Hindwing clear yellow. **SIMILAR SPECIES:** (1) Byssus Skipper, not likely to be found in same habitat, is smaller, lacks black on corner of forewing underneath, and has faint submarginal spot band. (2) Delaware Skipper is much smaller and has much narrower black borders on both wings above. **EARLY STAGES:** Not reported.

MULBERRY WING

FLIGHT: May, July–Sept. (2 broods), possibly only 1 in north. **RANGE:** Sporadic along Atlantic Coast from s. N.J. and Md. south to coastal Ga. During the late 1980s, the species seems to have extended its range northward to N.J., where it was formerly absent. **HABITAT:** Brackish river marshes, abandoned rice paddies.

GOLDEN SKIPPERS: GENUS *Poanes* SCUDDER

This American genus has about 12 species. Seven occur in eastern North America; the others occur in the tropics. Adults of most species are predominantly yellow-orange, but those of the Mulberry Wing, as well as the female of *Poanes zabulon* and the dark female of *P. hobomok*, are primarily dark. Although the males of all species have similar genitalia, males of some species have a

Hobomok Skipper. Male nectaring on Dame's-rocket. Mallette Co., S.D. This is the only eastern skipper with two distinct female forms. The origin of the two forms is not understood.

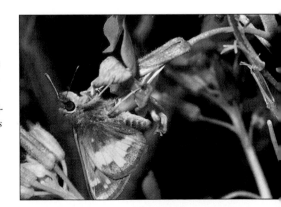

Zabulon Skipper. Female nectaring at French Marigold. Fairfax Co., Va. This skipper has only one female form. Females are found most frequently in shady woods.

forewing stigma and others don't. Perching is the principal mate-locating strategy of four species (*hobomok, taxiles, yehl,* and *zabulon*), while patrolling is the chief method for the other three (*aaroni, massasoit,* and *viator*). Several species are found primarily in wetlands (marshes, swamps, river forests) or similar moist situations. Grasses are the principal caterpillar hosts.

MULBERRY WING *Poanes massasoit*   **PL. 37**

1 ⅛–1 ⁷⁄₁₆ in. (29–36 mm). Wings rounded. Upperside: *Black* with tiny (male) or slightly larger (female) spots. Underside: Hindwing with large *irregular yellow central patch*. In rare individuals, underside hindwing is rusty, lacks yellow patch. **EARLY STAGES:** Not fully reported. **FOOD:** Sedges. **FLIGHT:** Late June to mid-Aug. (1 brood). **RANGE:** Se. N.D. and s. Minn. east to s. Ont. Coastal population from s. N.H. south to Md. **HABITAT:** Freshwater marshes or bogs.

HOBOMOK SKIPPER

ZABULON SKIPPER

Zabulon Skipper. Male perching. Fairfax Co., Va. Males are seen most often in sunlit forest openings or forest edges. There they await females with whom they court.

HOBOMOK SKIPPER *Poanes hobomok*   PL. 36

1 ⅜–1 ¹¹⁄₁₆ in. (34–42 mm). Wings *rounded*. Upperside: Male yellow-orange with *irregular black borders*; *lacks stigma*. Female with 2 *forms*: (1) normal form is similar to male, but orange is less extensive and duller. (2) "Pocahontas" form is purple-black with a few clouded white spots on forewing. Underside: Hindwing with yellow-orange (male) or orange (normal female) outer postmedian area and inner margin purple-gray. Pocahontas form purple-black, pattern obscured. **SIMILAR SPECIES:** Zabulon Skipper has somewhat more pointed forewings. Male is similar but has underside of hindwing with more extensive yellow-orange and base dark brown. Female is most similar to Pocahontas form of Hobomok Skipper, but underside of hindwing is 2-toned brown and purple-gray, and costal margin is white-edged. **EARLY STAGES:** Not fully reported. **FOOD:** Panic grasses, bluegrasses. **FLIGHT:** April–July (1 brood). **RANGE:** Temperate e. North America from e.-cen. Alta. across s. Canada to N.S. south to cen. Kans., e. Okla., and n. Ga. Isolated population from cen. Colo. to n. N.M. **HABITAT:** Edges of damp woods or bogs, light gaps along streams, city parks.

ZABULON SKIPPER *Poanes zabulon*   PL. 36

1 ⅜–1 ⅝ in. (34–39 mm). Sexes dissimilar. Forewings more *pointed* than those of the Hobomok Skipper. Upperside: Male bright yellow-orange. Female purple-brown. Underside: Male hindwing mainly yellow; *base* and *outer margin dark brown*. Female hindwing two-toned brown and purple-gray; costal margin *white-edged*. **EARLY STAGES:** Not reported. **FOOD:** Grasses. **FLIGHT:** May–Sept. (2 broods) in North, all year in tropics. **RANGE:** E. U.S. from cen. Kans. east through s. Mich. to Mass., south to ne. Texas, s. La.,

and cen. Fla. Strays to N.M., S.D., and s. Que. Also cen. Mexico
south to Panama. **HABITAT:** Brushy areas and openings near moist
woods or streams, city parks.

TAXILES SKIPPER *Poanes taxiles*   PL. 36

1 ⁷⁄₁₆–1 ¹¹⁄₁₆ in. (36–43 mm). Upperside: Male is yellow-orange with
very *narrow black borders*; female is unlike male, dark orange-
brown with patches of pale orange in forewing and central hindwing. Underside: Forewing of male has *slightly darkened* apex and
outer margin. Hindwing yellow-orange with darkened base and
outer margin. Anal margin orange-brown. Hindwing of female
violet-brown with patch of gray scales near outer margin and
paler postmedian spot band. **SIMILAR SPECIES:** Zabulon Skipper has
wings less rounded, orange less extensive. **EARLY STAGES:** Caterpillar
orange-tan with several brown lateral lines; head red-brown,
orange on front. **FOOD:** Grasses. **FLIGHT:** Mid-June to Aug. (1 brood).
RANGE: W. S.D. and n.-cen. Neb., south through s. Rocky Mt. complex and foothills south to cen. Mexico. **HABITAT:** Openings in river
forests, stream valleys.

AARON'S SKIPPER *Poanes aaroni*   PL. 36

1 ⁵⁄₁₆–1 ¹¹⁄₁₆ in. (33–42 mm). Upperside: Both sexes have broad,
sharply defined *black borders* on both wings. Forewing of the male
has *faint black stigma*. Underside: Hindwing is orange-tan with a
pale *central streak* from the base to the outer margin. **SIMILAR
SPECIES:** Broad-winged Skipper is larger, has more complicated pattern above, and more extensive pale area in center of hindwing
beneath. **EARLY STAGES:** Not reported. **FLIGHT:** May–Sept. (2 broods)
in north, progressively earlier southward. **RANGE:** Atlantic seaboard
from N.J. south to s. peninsular Fla. **HABITAT:** Coastal salt marshes.

YEHL SKIPPER *Poanes yehl*   **PL. 37**
  1⁵⁄₁₆–1¾ in. (33–44 mm). Upperside: Male forewing has *strong linear stigma*. Underside: Female hindwing dark brown, that of male orange; both with 3–5 *pale postmedian dots*. **SIMILAR SPECIES:** (1) Male Black Dash has heavier stigma; underside hindwing spots clumped as curved postmedian patch. (2) Female Broad-winged Skipper lacks the 3 dots on underside hindwing. **EARLY STAGES:** Not reported. **FOOD:** Probably cane (*Arundinaria*). **FLIGHT:** May–Nov. (2 broods). **RANGE:** Se. U.S. from sw. Mo. east to se. Va., south to n. Fla., Gulf Coast, and e. Texas. **HABITAT:** Clearings or edges in wet or swampy woods.

BROAD-WINGED SKIPPER *Poanes viator*   **PL. 37**
  1¼–2³⁄₁₆ in. (32–56 mm). Forewings rounded. Upperside: Dark brown. Forewing primarily dark with *small cream spots* and small yellow-orange area. Hindwing primarily orange with black border. *Veins black-lined*. Underside: Hindwing orange-brown with *yellow-orange streak* running outward from base and *postmedian band* of yellow-orange *squarish spots*. **EARLY STAGES:** Not reported. **FOOD:** Common Reed (*Phragmites australis*), Wild Rice, Marsh Millet. **FLIGHT:** Late June to early Aug. (1 brood) inland, July–Aug. (2 broods) along mid-Atlantic Coast, May–Aug. (4 broods?) in Texas. **RANGE:** Inland areas (*P. v. viator*) from e. Dakotas east to s. Que. and cen. N.Y. Coastal population (*P. v. zizaniae*) from Mass. south to n. Fla. and west along Gulf Coast to cen. Texas. Strays elsewhere. **HABITAT:** Freshwater and brackish marshes. Locally abundant on coast.

MEXICANA MELLANA *Quasimellana eulogius*   **PL. 37**
  1¹⁄₁₆–1¼ in. (27–31 mm). Sexually dimorphic. Male yellow-orange. Upperside: Male forewing with brown-black border. *Dark*

YEHL SKIPPER

BROAD-WINGED SKIPPER

brown streak extending from cell to border. Hindwing with *veins lined dark brown*. Underside: Tan-orange with ill-defined pale postmedian spot band. **EARLY STAGES:** Not reported. **FLIGHT:** April–Nov. in s. Texas; all year in Mexico and Cen. America. **RANGE:** N. Mexico south through mainland tropical America to Paraguay. Periodic stray to lower Rio Grande Valley, Texas. **HABITAT:** Open areas in subtropical thorn forest.

GENUS *Euphyes* SCUDDER

There are almost two dozen *Euphyes*; all are limited to the New World, primarily in the tropics. Nine species occur in the East; six of these are restricted to the Southeast, and only two (*E. bimacula* and *E. vestris*) extend to the West. Males have a conspicuous stigma composed of two more or less equal oval patches that form a short, black broken dash. Wetlands are the primary or sole habitat for most species, and males perch in swales or other low spots, where they await likely mates. Caterpillars of our eastern species feed on sedges or rushes.

PALMETTO SKIPPER *Euphyes arpa*   PL. 37
1⅝–1⁵⁄₁₆ in. (39–49 mm). Head and thoracic collar *bright orange*. Upperside: Male forewing with *restricted tawny yellow areas*. Underside: Hindwing unmarked, bright *yellow-orange*. **EARLY STAGES:** Caterpillar streaked yellow and green; cervical shield black; head black with white streaks and edging. **FOOD:** Saw Palmetto. **FLIGHT:** March–Nov. (probably 3 broods). **RANGE:** Peninsular Fla., rare on Keys; se. Ga., immediate Gulf Coast including s. Ala. and s. Miss. **HABITAT:** Lowland palmetto scrub.

PALMETTO SKIPPER

PALATKA SKIPPER

DION SKIPPER

DUKE'S SKIPPER

PALATKA SKIPPER *Euphyes pilatka*   **PL. 37**

1 ¹³⁄₁₆–2 ⅛ in. (46–53 mm). Large. Upperside: Wings extensively orange with *black borders*. Underside: Hindwing *dull brown*. **EARLY STAGES:** Caterpillar yellow-green with minute dark bumps; head brown with white upper front with 3 vertical black stripes. **FOOD:** Sawgrass. **FLIGHT:** May–Sept. (2 broods) along Atlantic Coast; Jan. –Nov. (probably 3 broods) in Fla. **RANGE:** Immediate coastlines from se. Va. south to Fla. Keys (regular inland in peninsular Fla.) and west along Gulf Coast to s. Miss. Strays to n. Md. and sw. La. **HABITAT:** Coastal brackish and freshwater marshes.

DION SKIPPER *Euphyes dion*   **PL. 37**

1 ⁷⁄₁₆–1 ¾ in. (36–45 mm). Variable. Upperside: Male forewing with restricted orange. Hindwing: Dark brown with *broad orange streak*. Underside: Hindwing red-brown or orange-brown with 2 *yellow-orange rays*—one through cell and the second above anal fold. **SIMILAR SPECIES:** (1) Black Dash is smaller, and there is a curved yellow patch in center of hindwing below. (2) Bay Skipper, found only in a limited area along the Gulf Coast, has males with more extensive orange above and a narrower forewing stigma. Females cannot be easily distinguished. **EARLY STAGES:** Not fully reported. **FOOD:** Sedges. **FLIGHT:** July to early Aug. (1 brood) in north, May– Sept. (2 broods) in south. **RANGE:** An incomplete ring of coastal and inland populations. South along Atlantic Coast from w. Mass. and se. N.Y. to ne. Fla., west to ne. Texas, then north in an increasingly broad belt to se. N.D., n. Wis., s. Ont., and extreme s. Que. **HABITAT:** Open marshes, bogs, and swamps.

BAY SKIPPER *Euphyes bayensis*   **PL. 37**

1 ½–1 ¾ in. (37–44 mm). Upperside: Both wings of male with broad black borders. Forewing with basal ⅔ *orange* and a *narrow*

BLACK DASH

BERRY'S SKIPPER

black stigma extending from near inner margin. Female is brown-black above with several small yellow spots on forewing. Underside: Hindwing is orange-brown with 2 yellow-orange rays, one through cell and one above anal fold. **SIMILAR SPECIES:** Dion Skipper is found in freshwater marshes. Its males have less extensive orange and a broader black stigma on the forewing above. **EARLY STAGES:** Not reported. **FLIGHT:** May, Sept. **RANGE:** Known only from coastal Miss. **HABITAT:** Brackish Sawgrass marsh.

DUKE'S SKIPPER *Euphyes dukesi*   PL. 37
1½–1¾ in. (37–45 mm). *Sooty black* (dark brown after death). Underside: Hindwing pale brown with *yellow streak* from base through cell. **EARLY STAGES:** Not reported. **FOOD:** Sedges. **FLIGHT:** June–Sept. (2 broods) in mid-South, May–Nov. (3 broods) in Deep South. **RANGE:** Three population centers in e. U.S.: (1) Atlantic Coast from se. Va. to n. peninsular Fla., (2) lower Mississippi Valley from cen. Mo. and s. Ill. south to Gulf Coast, and (3) extreme s. Ont., se. Mich., ne. Ind., and n. Ohio. **HABITAT:** Shaded tupelo swamps in south, partially shaded marshes and ditches in Midwest.

BLACK DASH *Euphyes conspicuus*   PL. 37
1¼–1⅝ in. (32–40 mm). A medium-sized, dark marsh skipper. Upperside: Male forewing with heavy stigma. Underside: Hindwing of both sexes *red-brown* with central *curved yellow patch*. **SIMILAR SPECIES:** Dion Skipper is larger and has 2 yellow-orange rays on hindwing below. **EARLY STAGES:** Not reported. **FOOD:** Sedges. **FLIGHT:** June–Aug. (1 brood). **RANGE:** Two population centers: (1) upper Midwest from e. Neb. east to s. Ont.; (2) central Atlantic Coast from Mass. south to se. Va. **HABITAT:** Boggy marshes, wet meadows.

BERRY'S SKIPPER *Euphyes berryi*   PL. 37

1⅜–1¾ in. (35–45 mm). A very rare, local butterfly. Upperside: Limited light areas. Underside: Hindwing pale *brown* with *veins white-scaled*. **EARLY STAGES:** Not reported. **FLIGHT:** March–Oct. (2 broods). **RANGE:** Deep Southeast from coastal S.C. south to peninsular Fla. and w. panhandle. **HABITAT:** Wet areas near ponds and swamps.

TWO-SPOTTED SKIPPER *Euphyes bimacula*   PL. 38

1⅜–1⅝ in. (35–41 mm). Forewings pointed. *Fringe white*. Upperside: Male forewing with limited *tawny patch*; female dark, forewing with 2 pale spots. Underside: Hindwing orange-brown. *Veins paler*. Anal fold and underside of *head and body white*. **SIMILAR SPECIES:** Dion Skipper has red-brown or orange-brown hindwing below with 2 paler yellow-orange rays. Fringes are dark and body is orange-brown below. **EARLY STAGES:** Not reported. **FOOD:** Sedges. **FLIGHT:** June–July (1 brood) in north, May–Aug. (2 broods) in south. **RANGE:** Two populations: (1) a western one in ne. Colo. and w. Neb., and (2) an eastern one from e. Neb. east in an expanding band to s. Que., and from N.B., and s. Me. south to cen. Va. Also resident on coastal plain south to Ga. and on Gulf Coast. **HABITAT:** Wet sedge meadows, marshes, bogs.

DUN SKIPPER *Euphyes vestris*   PL. 38

1⅛–1⅜ in. (28–35 mm). One of three common blackish skippers (with Northern Broken-Dash and Little Glassywing), the females of which are known as the "three black witches." Upperside: Male brown-black with black stigma. Female forewing with up to 2 *tiny diffuse white spots*. **SIMILAR SPECIES:** (1) Female Little Glassywing's forewing has relatively large transparent white spot; (2) Female

Northern Broken-Dash has one or two elongate yellow or cream forewing spots. **EARLY STAGES:** Caterpillar pale green with a white overcast and many white dashes; head tricolored black, caramel brown, and cream. **FOOD:** Sedges. **FLIGHT:** June to early Aug. (1 brood) in north, May–Sept. (2 broods) in mid-South, broader flight in Deep South and Texas. **RANGE:** Temperate North America including s. Canada from s. Alta. east to N.S. west to se. Ariz. and Nueva Leon, Mexico. Separate populations on Pacific Coast. **HABITAT:** Wet areas near deciduous woods or streams.

MONK SKIPPER *Asbolis capucinus* **PL. 38**

1 $^{15}\!/_{16}$–2 $^3\!/_8$ in. (50–61 mm). Introduced to s. Fla. from West Indies about 1947–1948. Upperside: Black; male with gray stigma; female forewing with small diffuse pale patch. Underside: Hindwing *dull brick red* and *black*. **EARLY STAGES:** Not reported. **FOOD:** Palms. **FLIGHT:** All year in Fla. (3–4 broods). **RANGE:** West Indies and peninsular Fla., including the Keys. **HABITAT:** Disturbed or natural areas near palms.

DUSTED SKIPPER *Atrytonopsis hianna* **PL. 38**

1 $^3\!/_8$–1 $^{11}\!/_{16}$ in. (35–42 mm). An uncommon, highly localized skipper. Gray-black wings with white facial area. Upperside: Fringes brown; a few white spots. Male with a tiny stigma. Underside: Hindwing *gray, lighter outwardly.* Usually at least a *single white spot* at base. Populations in Fla. and the south Atlantic coastal plain have white-spotted underside hindwings (*A. h. loammi*), while on the southern Great Plains the skippers are paler gray (*A. h. turneri*). **SIMILAR SPECIES:** Cloudywings (Genus *Thorybes*) have broader wings and usually hold their wings open instead of closed. **EARLY STAGES:** Caterpillar pale lavender above with prothorax and sides pale gray; cervical shield dark brown; head deep red-

BRONZE ROADSIDE-SKIPPER

LINDA'S ROADSIDE-SKIPPER

purple. **FOOD:** Big Bluestem and Little Bluestem. **FLIGHT:** May–June (1 brood) in North; March–Oct. (2 broods) in Fla. **RANGE:** U.S. from cen. Texas, n. N.M., cen. Colo., e. Wyo. east to N.H. and Mass. south to peninsular Fla. and Gulf Coast. **HABITAT:** Prairies, barrens, old fields.

ROADSIDE-SKIPPERS: GENUS *Amblyscirtes* SCUDDER

The roadside-skippers are another entirely American group. Most of the two dozen or more species occur in the Southwest and Mexico. These are small, darkish butterflies with small white spots and distinctive patterns on the hindwings below. The males perch on the ground or on large rocks where they await the appearance of receptive females. Most species have not been observed at flowers — the Common Roadside-Skipper (*A. vialis*) is an exception. Grasses are the caterpillar hosts for most species. Much remains to be discovered about the life histories of many species.

BRONZE ROADSIDE-SKIPPER *Amblyscirtes aenus*   **PL. 38**
1 1/16–1 1/4 in. (27–32 mm). Upperside: Brown with slight orange sheen. Few indistinct obscure *pale spots* on forewing. Male *stigma indistinct*. Underside: Forewing *red-brown* basally. Form "erna," formerly considered a separate species, is an unspotted variety. **SIMILAR SPECIES:** Linda's Roadside-Skipper lacks bronze tones on underside of forewing and has smaller dots on hindwing below. **EARLY STAGES:** Caterpillar pale blue-white; cervical shield gray-white; head black. **FOOD:** Grasses. **FLIGHT:** April–July (1 brood) in Colo., April–Sept. (2 broods) in southern part of range. **RANGE:** Southwest from e. Ariz., N.M., and w. Texas south to cen. Mexico, north

to n. cen. Colo., and east to w. Okla. and cen. Texas. **HABITAT:** Gullies, stream bottoms, foothills.

LINDA'S ROADSIDE-SKIPPER *Amblyscirtes linda* **PL. 38**
1 ⅛ – 1 5⁄16 in. (28 – 33 mm). Upperside: Dark brown, without sheen. Stigma on male forewing indistinct. Underside: Forewing with apex darker black, rest of wing chocolate brown. Hindwing black-brown with dusting of gray scales and postmedian band of pale gray spots. **SIMILAR SPECIES:** The more western Bronze Roadside-Skipper has underside forewing red-brown and usually has larger white marks on underside forewing. These two butterflies may be conspecific. **EARLY STAGES:** Caterpillar pale blue-white; head white with black bands on front. **FOOD:** Broadleaf Uniola. **FLIGHT:** April – July (2 broods). **RANGE:** S. Midwest from sw. Ill. and w. Tenn. west to sw. Mo. and e. Okla. **HABITAT:** Near woodland streams.

OSLAR'S ROADSIDE-SKIPPER *Amblyscirtes oslari* **PL. 38**
1 ⅛ – 1 ⅜ in. (29 – 34 mm). Forewings pointed. Upperside: Orange-brown, *unspotted.* Underside: Hindwing *light gray* with paler postmedian band. **EARLY STAGES:** Not reported. **FOOD:** Probably Blue Grama grass. **FLIGHT:** May – July in North, April – Sept. in N.M. and Texas. **RANGE:** S. Sask. south along high plains and Rocky Mts. to n. Texas. Isolated populations in Ariz., N.M., and s. Texas. **HABITAT:** Prairie ravines, canyon bottoms.

PEPPER AND SALT SKIPPER *Amblyscirtes hegon* **PL. 38**
1 – 1 3⁄16 in. (25 – 30 mm). This local skipper and the Common Roadside-Skipper are both widespread in temperate e. North America. Upperside: Forewing *lightly spotted,* including discal cell. Underside: Hindwing light gray-green with *paler postmedian band.* **SIMILAR SPECIES:** Bell's Roadside-Skipper has smaller spots on

OSLAR'S
ROADSIDE-SKIPPER

PEPPER AND SALT
SKIPPER

upper forewing and a darker hindwing below with indistinct spots. **EARLY STAGES:** Caterpillar pale green-white with 3 dark green dorsal stripes and 2 white lateral stripes; head dark brown with pale brown vertical stripes and bands. **FOOD:** Grasses. **FLIGHT:** April– July, rarely early Aug. (1 brood), earliest in south. **RANGE:** E. North America from s. Man. east to N.S., south to se. Texas and n. Fla. —largely absent from coastal plain. **HABITAT:** Glades, wood edges, or by streams.

LACE-WINGED ROADSIDE-SKIPPER   PL. 38
Amblyscirtes aesculapius

1 3/16–1 1/2 in. (30–37 mm). Unique. Fringes strongly checkered black and white. Underside: Hindwing black with bold pale yellow or white *cobweb pattern*. **EARLY STAGES:** Not reported. **FOOD:** Probably cane (*Arundinaria*). **FLIGHT:** March–Sept. (2 broods). **RANGE:** Se. U.S. from e. Okla. and e. Texas east to Atlantic Coast from Del. (rare) and se. Va. south to n. Fla. **HABITAT:** Dense woods with cane growth.

CAROLINA ROADSIDE-SKIPPER   PL. 38
Amblyscirtes carolina

1 1/8–1 7/16 in. (28–36 mm). Upperside: Forewing dark brown with small yellow spots. Underside: Forewing apex dull yellow, basal 2/3 black. Hindwing: Dull *yellow* with postmedian band of *dark spots*. **SIMILAR SPECIES:** Reversed Roadside-Skipper has underside of hindwing rust brown with a postmedian row of yellow spots and a discal cell spot. **EARLY STAGES:** Not reported. **FLIGHT:** April–Sept. (3 broods). **RANGE:** A band from se. Va. south to S.C., then extending west to n. Miss. Apparently has isolated populations in Del., s. Ill., and nw. Ark. **HABITAT:** Wet woods, usually near streams or swamps.

LACE-WINGED
ROADSIDE-SKIPPER

CAROLINA
ROADSIDE-SKIPPER

REVERSED ROADSIDE-SKIPPER

Amblyscirtes reversa

1 ⅛–1 ⅜ in. (28–34 mm). Underside: Hindwing *rust brown* with postmedian row of *yellow spots* and *discal cell spot*. **SIMILAR SPECIES:** Carolina Roadside-Skipper has underside of hindwing dull yellow with a postmedian band of dark spots. **EARLY STAGES:** Not reported. **FOOD:** Switch Cane. **FLIGHT:** April–Aug. (2–3 broods). **RANGE:** Patchily distributed from se. Va. south to n. Ga., also s. Miss. and s. Ill. **HABITAT:** Swamp woods or wet woods near sluggish streams. Cane stands must be present.

NYSA ROADSIDE-SKIPPER *Amblyscirtes nysa*   PL. 38

¹⁵⁄₁₆–1 ³⁄₁₆ in. (24–30 mm). Fringes checkered black and white. Upperside: Black with 3–5 tiny white spots on forewing apex. Underside: Hindwing *variegated* with irregular *black*, *gray*, and *brown* patches. **EARLY STAGES:** Caterpillar pale green with dark green

dorsal stripe; head cream-white with vertical orange-brown streaks and bands. **FOOD:** Grasses. **FLIGHT:** March–Oct. (3 broods) in Mo.; all year in s. Texas. **RANGE:** Se. Neb., Kans., and w. Mo. south to n. Mexico, west to s. Ariz. **HABITAT:** Dry rocky ravines, wood edges, yards, gardens.

DOTTED ROADSIDE-SKIPPER *Amblyscirtes eos* **PL. 38**
1 1/16–1 1/4 in. (27–32 mm). Distinctive. Fringes primarily white. Upperside: Black with tiny white spots. Underside: Hindwing gray-brown with basal and postmedian *round white spots* narrowly edged with black. **EARLY STAGES:** Not reported. **FLIGHT:** March–Sept. **RANGE:** Southwest from sw. Colo., s. Kans., and ne. Texas south to cen. Ariz., s. Texas, and nw. Mexico. **HABITAT:** Ravines, canyons, roadsides.

COMMON ROADSIDE-SKIPPER *Amblyscirtes vialis* **PL. 38**
1–1 3/16 in. (25–30 mm). Our most common, most widespread roadside-skipper. Fringes checkered buff and black. Upperside: Black with tiny white spots on forewing apex. Underside: Forewing apex and outer half of hindwing *dusted with violet-gray.* **SIMILAR SPECIES:** Pepper and Salt Skipper has light spots in center of forewing above and gray-green-dusted hindwing with postmedian row of paler spots. **EARLY STAGES:** Caterpillar pale green, covered with small green bumps; head dull white with vertical red-brown stripes on front. **FOOD:** Grasses. **FLIGHT:** March–July (1 brood), partial second brood to Sept. in South. **RANGE:** Much of temperate North America from B.C. east across Canada to the Gaspé Peninsula and N.S., south to cen. Calif., n. N.M., ne. Texas, and peninsular Fla. **HABITAT:** Open areas in or near woods, often near streams.

CELIA'S ROADSIDE-SKIPPER *Amblyscirtes celia*　**PL. 38**
⅞–1 1/16 in. (23–27 mm). Upperside: Dark brown. Forewing usually with light spot at end of cell. Underside: Hindwing gray with
white basal and postmedian *spot series*. **SIMILAR SPECIES:** Bell's Roadside-Skipper is darker above and has white basal spot and postmedian spot row on underside of hindwing. **EARLY STAGES:** Not
reported. **FOOD:** Paspalum. **FLIGHT:** May–Sept. in cen. Texas; all year
in s. Texas. **RANGE:** Texas south to ne. Mexico, stray to sw. La. **HABI-
TAT:** Openings in woods.

BELL'S ROADSIDE-SKIPPER *Amblyscirtes belli*　**PL. 38**
1 3/16–1 1/4 in. (30–32 mm). An obscurely marked skipper. Upperside: Dark brown. Forewing with pale spots, but always lacking
spot in cell. Underside: Hindwing *gray-black* with *pale gray* basal
and postmedian *spot series*. **EARLY STAGES:** Caterpillar pale green with
white overcast; covered with black setae on back; orange setae on
sides; head cream white with vertical orange-brown bands. **FOOD:**
Broadleaf Uniola. **FLIGHT:** April–Sept. (3 broods). **RANGE:** S. Midwest from e. Kans., cen. Okla., and cen. Texas east to sw. Ohio,
cen. Ky., e. Tenn., and w. S.C. **HABITAT:** Grassy areas in open woods,
by creeks, woods edges, city gardens.

DUSKY ROADSIDE-SKIPPER *Amblyscirtes alternata*　**PL. 38**
⅞–1 in. (23–25 mm). Small. Forewing pointed. Fringes white
with small black checks. Upperside: Forewing with faint series of
pale spots. Underside: Hindwing dusted *dull gray*. **SIMILAR SPECIES:**
Common Roadside-Skipper lacks pale spots in center of forewing
above, and below has violet-gray dusting on forewing apex and
outer half of hindwing. **EARLY STAGES:** Not reported. **FLIGHT:** March–
Aug. (2 broods) in most of range; as late as Nov. in Fla., Gulf
states, and Texas. **RANGE:** Southeast from se. Va. south to Fla. and
west to e. Texas. **HABITAT:** Open pine woods.

EUFALA SKIPPER *Lerodea eufala*   **PL. 39**
1 ⅟₁₆ – 1 ⅜ in. (27 – 34 mm). This small skipper occasionally
expands its range northward in the summer but dies out during
the succeeding cold winter. Upperside: Gray-brown. Forewing
with 3 – 5 *small transparent spots*. Stigma lacking. Underside:
Hindwing brown with *gray overscaling*, rarely with faint spots. **SIM-**
ILAR SPECIES: Swarthy Skipper has underside hindwing yellow-
brown with paler veins. **EARLY STAGES:** Caterpillar bright green with
dark dorsal stripe and faint white lateral lines; head dull white
with orange-brown blotches. **FOOD:** Grasses. **FLIGHT:** Feb.–Oct. (2
broods) in Deep South; all year in Fla. and s. Texas. **RANGE:** Resident in Cuba and s. U.S. south through mainland tropical America to Patagonia. Vagrant and occasional colonist north to cen.
Calif., N.D., Wis., n. Mich., and Wash., D.C. **HABITAT:** Open, sunny
areas: road edges, vacant lots, agricultural areas.

OLIVE-CLOUDED SKIPPER *Lerodea arabus*   **PL. 39**
1 –1 ¼ in. (25 –31 mm). Upperside: Dark brown with translucent
white spots on forewing. Underside: Hindwing has *central dark*
patch often edged outwardly with tiny white spots. **SIMILAR SPECIES:**
Eufala Skipper has smaller white spots on forewing and lacks
central dark patch on underside of hindwing. **EARLY STAGES:** Not
reported. **FOOD:** Grasses. **FLIGHT:** June, Oct.–Nov. in s. Texas; Jan.–
Nov. in Mexico. **RANGE:** Resident from s. Texas south to Guerrero,
Mexico. **HABITAT:** Subtropical thorn forest.

TWIN-SPOT SKIPPER *Oligoria maculata*   **PL. 39**
1 ⅜ –1 ⅝ in. (35 –41 mm). Wings rounded. Underside: Hindwing
with pale red-brown overlay and 3 distinct oval *white spots*—one
separate and two together. **EARLY STAGES:** Caterpillar pale green with
dark posterior; light brown shield behind head; head light brown.
FOOD: Probably grasses. **FLIGHT:** April–Sept. (2 broods), possibly 3

TWIN-SPOT SKIPPER

broods in Fla. **RANGE:** Southeast from coastal N.C. south through Fla. and west to e. Texas. Rare stray as far north as N.J. **HABITAT:** Pinewoods, coastal swamps.

BRAZILIAN SKIPPER *Calpodes ethlius*   **PL. 39**

1 ¹⁵⁄₁₆–2⅜ in. (50–61 mm). Also known as the Canna Leafroller. Large and robust. Upperside: Brown-black with *large translucent spots*, forewing pointed. Underside: Red-brown. **EARLY STAGES:** Caterpillar pale green with white subdorsal lines; head dark orange with black spots. **FOOD:** Cannas. **FLIGHT:** April–Dec. in s. Texas; all year in Fla. and tropics. Late summer to north. **RANGE:** S. Fla. and s. Texas south through the West Indies and mainland tropical America to Argentina. Strays and occasionally colonizes north to s. Nev., n. Texas, Ill., and Mass. **HABITAT:** Residential areas and gardens.

GENUS *Panoquina* HEMMING

Panoquina is a moderate-sized tropical American genus with six species in eastern North America, primarily in the Southeast and south Texas. The adults are small to medium-sized with brown wing surfaces above. Their elongated forewings have two to eight transparent white spots. The males have a perching mate-location strategy, and both sexes are avid flower visitors. The life histories of most species are unknown or poorly understood, but caterpillars of several species feed on grasses, including Sugar Cane.

SALT MARSH SKIPPER *Panoquina panoquin*   **PL. 39**

1 ³⁄₁₆–1½ in. (30–38 mm). May be abundant in its proper habitat. Dark brown; forewing pointed. Underside: Hindwing dark-brown with *veins yellow*; short *white dash* at end of cell. **SIMILAR SPECIES:**

Obscure Skipper lacks pale veins and has 3 pale postmedian spots on underside of hindwing. **EARLY STAGES:** Not reported. **FOOD:** Seashore Saltgrass. **FLIGHT:** May–Aug. (2 broods) in North; April–Oct. (3 broods) in South; Feb.–Dec. in Fla. **RANGE:** Immediate Atlantic Coast from N.Y. (Long I.) south to Fla. Keys and west to s. Texas. **HABITAT:** Coastal salt and brackish marshes.

OBSCURE SKIPPER *Panoquina panoquinoides*   **PL. 39**
1⅛–1¼ in. (28–32 mm). Small. Upperside: *Spots on forewing small or lacking.* Underside: Hindwing plain brown with 3 *pale postmedian spots.* **SIMILAR SPECIES:** Salt Marsh Skipper is larger, has larger spots on forewing, and has veins on underside of hindwing lined with pale scales. **EARLY STAGES:** Caterpillar green with 4 green-white dorsal lines and a pale yellow dorsal line along each side; head brown. **FOOD:** Grasses, including Bermuda Grass. **FLIGHT:** Feb.–Dec. in Fla., 2 major flights. **RANGE:** Immediate coast from Fla. west along Gulf Coast to s. Texas, south through West Indies and South America to Peru. **HABITAT:** Salt marshes, open fields, dunes.

OCOLA SKIPPER *Panoquina ocola*   **PL. 39**
1⅜–1¹¹⁄₁₆ in. (34–42 mm). One of the few skippers known to partake in mass emigrations. Also wanders north of its permanent range. Forewings *elongated*, projecting far beyond hindwings when butterfly is at rest. Underside: *Unmarked.* Female hindwing with blue-purple iridescent sheen. **SIMILAR SPECIES:** (1) Hecebolus Skipper has rounded spot in cell; underside of hindwing has veins lightened. Forewings do not project beyond hindwings when the butterfly is at rest. (2) Purple-washed Skipper has an elongated spot in cell and a straight line of white or blue spots on the underside of the hindwing. Hecebolus and Purple-washed skippers likely to be found only in s. Texas. **EARLY STAGES:** Caterpillar gray-green

with first 2 segments blue-green; dark dorsal line and green-white stripe along each side; head light green. **FOOD:** Grasses. **FLIGHT:** All year in Fla. and s. Texas; in warm summer months to north. **RANGE:** Resident from Deep South west to s. Texas, south through West Indies and mainland tropical America to Paraguay. Strays north to cen. Mo., Ohio, cen. Pa., and s. N.Y. (Long I.). **HABITAT:** Low damp fields and pastures.

HECEBOLUS SKIPPER *Panoquina hecebola* **PL. 39**

1 ³⁄₁₆−1 ½ in. (30−37 mm). Upperside: Forewing of males with rounded spot in cell. Underside: Hindwing with *veins lightened*, rarely with spot band or purple wash. **EARLY STAGES:** Not reported. **FLIGHT:** Oct.−Nov. in s. Texas; all year in Mexico. **RANGE:** N. Mexico south through mainland tropical America to Paraguay. Regular stray to lower Rio Grande Valley, Texas; rarely to Fla. Keys. **HABITAT:** Open subtropical scrub and woods edges.

PURPLE-WASHED SKIPPER *Panoquina sylvicola* **PL. 39**

1 ³⁄₁₆−1 ½ in. (30−37 mm). Upperside: Forewing of males with elongated spot in cell. Underside: Hindwing with straight line of *white or blue spots*. Female with blue or purple wash. **SIMILAR SPECIES:** Hecebolus Skipper has a round spot in cell of forewing and lacks the straight line of spots on the underside of the hindwing. **EARLY STAGES:** Caterpillar gray-green with dorsal lines and a white lateral stripe on each side; head green with black marks on front. **FOOD:** Coarse grasses, including Sugar Cane. **FLIGHT:** Aug.−Dec. in s. Texas; all year in Mexico. **RANGE:** N. Mexico south through West Indies and mainland tropical America to Argentina. Regular stray

Evans' Skipper. Adult nectaring at lantana. Sinaloa, Mexico. This is the species described in the text. The butterfly shown on Plate 39 is the Fusina Skipper, a South American skipper.

north to lower Rio Grande Valley, rarely to cen. Texas. **HABITAT:** Openings in subtropical scrub, forest edges, and adjacent fields.

EVANS' SKIPPER *Panoquina evansi*   **P. 402**
   1⅝−1¾ in. (40−45 mm). Large. Upperside: Forewing with large amber translucent spots. Underside: Hindwing with blue-violet sheen; males with vague irregular *white* postmedian *band*— almost absent on females. South American Fusina Skipper with bold white hindwing band is illustrated on plate 39. **SIMILAR SPECIES:** Brazilian Skipper is larger and has translucent spots on hindwing. **EARLY STAGES:** Caterpillar gray-green; 2 yellow stripes along each side; head gray with black vertical stripes and edging. **FOOD:** Adults have been found near Sugar Cane. **FLIGHT:** Oct.−Nov. in s. Texas; May−Nov. in Mexico. **RANGE:** Jamaica and cen. Mexico south through mainland tropical America to Paraguay. Periodic stray to lower Rio Grande Valley, Texas.

VIOLET-BANDED SKIPPER *Nyctelius nyctelius*   **PL. 39**
   1¹⁄₁₆−1½ in. (27−37 mm). Upperside: Black-brown with white double spot in discal cell of forewing. Underside: Hindwing pale brown with violet cast and 2 *darker bands* and a small, round *dark subcostal spot*. **EARLY STAGES:** Caterpillar blue-gray with faint pale gray bands; black shield behind head; head yellowish with vertical black stripes. **FOOD:** Sugar Cane and other coarse grasses. **FLIGHT:** May−Dec. in s. Texas; all year in tropics. **RANGE:** West Indies and Mexico south through mainland tropical America to Argentina. Periodic stray to lower Rio Grande Valley and cen. Texas. **HABITAT:** Subtropical thorn forest.

CHESTNUT-MARKED SKIPPER *Thespieus macareus*   **PL. 39**
   1⁵⁄₁₆−1½ in. (33−37 mm). Upperside: Both wings with transparent white spots. Underside: Hindwing *variegated* white, gray, red, and brown. **EARLY STAGES:** Not reported. **FLIGHT:** July−Nov. in s. Texas; as early as Feb. in Mexico and Cen. America. **RANGE:** Cen. Mexico south through Cen. America to Colombia and Venezuela. Occasional stray to lower Rio Grande Valley, Texas. **HABITAT:** Subtropical thorn scrub.

GIANT-SKIPPERS: SUBFAMILY MEGATHYMINAE

The giant-skippers comprise four genera. These large, robust insects are limited to the United States and Mexico. Most species occur in the Southwest and adjacent desert portions of Mexico. Outside of south Texas, where *Stallingsia* occurs, the reader will encounter only species of *Megathymus*. The antennae are not

hooked, and some species have a short apiculus—others none at all. The males have long hairlike scales on the upper surface of the hindwings, and they lack brands or costal folds. Males visit wet sand where they imbibe moisture. Giant-skippers rarely feed as adults. The hosts for all species are various Agave family plants, primarily agaves, manfreda, and yuccas. Eggs are glued to host leaves (*Megathymus* and *Stallingsia*) or dropped into host plant clumps (*Agathymus*). Caterpillars burrow into host leaves and stems and feed within their silk-lined tunnels. The pupae, which are flexible, are formed in the larval tunnels and are capable of moving up and down.

YUCCA GIANT-SKIPPER *Megathymus yuccae* **PL. 39**
1⅞–3⅛ in. (48–79 mm). Black. Upperside: Forewing with small white spots near apex and costa; *yellow submarginal band* on outer margin. Hindwing with *yellow band on outer margin*. Females with additional spots on hindwing. Underside: Hindwing gray with *white marks on costa*. **SIMILAR SPECIES:** (1) Cofaqui Giant-Skipper is often smaller, has a broader yellow submarginal band on forewing, and has a series of white postmedian spots on the underside of the hindwing. (2) Strecker's Giant-Skipper is usually larger, flies later where the two species are found together, and has a series of larger postmedian white spots on the hindwing below. **EARLY STAGES:** Caterpillar white with black shield behind head and black head. **FOOD:** Yuccas. **FLIGHT:** Mid-Feb. to mid.-May (1 brood). **RANGE:** Southeast from se. Va. south to s. peninsular Fla., west to Ark. and La. In West from s. Calif. and cen. Nev. east to Neb. and e. Texas, south to n. Mexico. **HABITAT:** Coastal dunes, pinewoods, old fields. **REMARKS:** The populations west of the Mississippi are sometimes called a separate species, the Southwest-

ern Giant-Skipper (*Megathymus coloradensis*). I consider the complex to be one species.

COFAQUI GIANT-SKIPPER *Megathymus cofaqui*   PL. 39

1 ⁵⁄₁₆–2 ⁷⁄₁₆ in. (49–62 mm). Forewing relatively short and blunt. Upperside: Forewing *yellow submarginal band broad*, blurred and arching inwardly to mid-costa. Hindwing with long erect hairlike scales. Underside: Hindwing gray with *small white* postmedian spots. **SIMILAR SPECIES:** Yucca Giant-Skipper is usually larger and lacks the postmedian white spots on the underside of the hindwing. **EARLY STAGES:** Caterpillar cream white; shield behind head and plate on rear are off-white; head brown-black. **FOOD:** Yuccas. **FLIGHT:** July–Sept. (1 main brood) in Ga.; March–Nov. (2 broods) in Fla. **RANGE:** Southeast, in two isolated populations: (1) Ga. and w. Fla. panhandle (*M. c. harrisi*) and (2) peninsular Fla. (*M. c. cofaqui*). **HABITAT:** Coastal dunes, pinewoods.

STRECKER'S GIANT-SKIPPER   PL. 39
Megathymus streckeri

2½–3 ¹⁄₁₆ in. (64–78 mm). A large western plains relative of the southeastern Cofaqui Giant-Skipper. Upperside: Hindwing with long erect hairlike scales. Underside: Hindwing with several *large white postmedian spots*. **SIMILAR SPECIES:** Yucca Giant-Skipper is usually smaller, flies earlier, has more pointed forewings, and lacks postmedian white spots on underside of hindwing. **EARLY STAGES:** Caterpillar yellow-white with brown hairs; shield behind head and plate on rear are both yellow-white; head dark red-brown. **FOOD:** Small Soapweed (*Yucca glauca*). **FLIGHT:** May–July (1 brood). **RANGE:** Se. Mont. and sw. N.D. south to s. Texas and west to nw. Ariz. and sw. Utah. **HABITAT:** Short-grass prairie, sand hills, rocky bluffs.

STRECKER'S GIANT-SKIPPER

MANFREDA GIANT-SKIPPER

MANFREDA GIANT-SKIPPER *Stallingsia maculosa* PL. 39

1 ¾ – 1 ¹⁵⁄₁₆ in. (47 – 50 mm). Brown-black. Upperside: Forewing has postmedian series of *small oval cream spots*. Underside: Hindwing brown-black with gray dusting outwardly. **EARLY STAGES:** Caterpillar white with tan hairs; shield behind head brown; plate on rear whitish; head pale tan. **FOOD:** *Polianthes*. **FLIGHT:** April – May, Sept. – Oct. (2 broods). **RANGE:** S. Texas and ne. Mexico. **HABITAT:** Subtropical thorn forest and pine forest. This species is now very rare because of the destruction of most of its habitat.

LIFE LIST
BUTTERFLIES OF EASTERN NORTH AMERICA AND GREENLAND

Keep a "life list," checking the butterflies you have seen. Or keep a check list of the butterflies in your collection.

This list covers those species and subspecies that have been found in eastern North America, including Greenland, east of the 100th meridian on the Great Plains. It includes all of the species mentioned in the text, but does not include undocumented species; these are included in a list of hypothetical species following the life list.

This list follows the order found in the Miller and Brown 1981 Catalogue/Checklist of the Butterflies of North America and the supplement to the list by Ferris (1989), both published as Memoirs of the Lepidopterists' Society. Generic name usage is conservative and based on the author's decisions and advice of colleagues. The English (common) names follow with a few exceptions the common names list edited by J. Miller (1991) and Glassberg (1995).

The list that follows lists superfamily, family, and subfamily categories. Species within genera are numbered, and those names representing taxa not found in eastern North America are indicated by an asterisk. For those who are interested in subspecies names, all of those reliably reported for the area are listed, even though relatively few subspecies are mentioned in the text.

SUPERFAMILY PAPILIONOIDEA: THE TRUE BUTTERFLIES

FAMILY PAPILIONIDAE: SWALLOWTAILS

SUBFAMILY PAPILIONINAE: TRUE SWALLOWTAILS
Parides Hübner

____ *1. eurimedes* (Stoll), Cattle Heart
____   a. *mylotes* (Bates)

Battus Scopoli

_____ 1. *philenor* (Linnaeus), Pipevine Swallowtail
_____ 2. *polydamas* (Linnaeus), Polydamas Swallowtail
_____   a. *polydamas* (Linnaeus)
_____   b. *lucayus* (Rothschild and Jordan)

Eurytides Hübner

_____ 1. *marcellus* (Cramer), Zebra Swallowtail
_____ 2. *philolaus* (Boisduval), Dark Kite-Swallowtail
_____ 3. **celadon* (Lucas), Cuban Kite-Swallowtail

Papilio Linnaeus

     1. **polyxenes Fabricius,* Black Swallowtail
_____   a. *asterius* Stoll
_____ 2. *joanae* J.R. Heitzman, Ozark Swallowtail
     3. *brevicauda* Saunders, Short-tailed Swallowtail
_____   a. *brevicauda* Saunders
_____   b. *gaspeensis* McDunnough
_____   c. *bretonensis* McDunnough
_____ 4. *bairdii* W.H. Edwards, Baird's Swallowtail
     5. **machaon Linnaeus,* Old World Swallowtail
_____   a. *hudsonianus* A.H. Clark
     6. *zelicaon* Lucas, Anise Swallowtail
_____   a. *nitra* W.H. Edwards
     7. **thoas* (Linnaeus), Thoas Swallowtail
_____   a. *autocles* (Rothschild and Jordan)
_____ 8. *cresphontes* (Cramer), Giant Swallowtail
     9. **aristodemus* (Esper)
_____   a. *ponceanus* (Schaus), Schaus' Swallowtail
    10. **andraemon* Hübner
_____   a. *bonhotei* (E.M.Sharpe), Bahaman Swallowtail
_____ 11. *ornythion* (Boisduval), Ornythion Swallowtail
_____ 12. **astyalus* (Godart), Broad-banded Swallowtail
_____   a. *pallas* (G.R. Gray)
    13. **androgeus* (Cramer), Androgeus Swallowtail
_____   a. *epidaurus* (Godman and Salvin)
_____ 14. *glaucus* (Linnaeus), Eastern Tiger Swallowtail
_____ 15. *canadensis* (Rothschild and Jordan), Canadian Tiger Swallowtail
_____ 16. *rutulus* Lucas, Western Tiger Swallowtail
_____ 17. *multicaudatus* W.F. Kirby, Two-tailed Swallowtail
_____ 18. *pilumnus* (Boisduval), Three-tailed Swallowtail
    19. *troilus* (Linnaeus), Spicebush Swallowtail
_____   a. *troilus* (Linnaeus)
_____   b. *ilioneus* (J.E. Smith)

____ 20. *palamedes* (Drury), Palamedes Swallowtail
____ 21. *victorinus* (Doubleday), Victorine Swallowtail
____ 22. *pharnaces* Doubleday, Pink-spotted Swallowtail
____ 23. **anchisiades* Esper, Ruby-spotted Swallowtail
____   a. *idaeus* Fabricius

FAMILY PIERIDAE: WHITES AND SULPHURS

SUBFAMILY DISMORPHIINAE: MIMIC WHITES
Enantia Hübner

____ 1. *albania* (Bates), Costa-spotted Mimic White

SUBFAMILY PIERINAE: WHITES
Neophasia Behr

____ 1. *menapia* (C. and R. Felder), Pine White

Appias Hübner

____ 1. **drusilla* (Cramer), Tropical White
____   a. *poeyi* Butler
____   b. *neumoegeni* (Skinner)

Pontia Fabricius

____ 1. *protodice* (Boisduval and Leconte), Checkered White
____ 2. *occidentalis* (Reakirt), Western White

Pieris Schrank

____ 1. **napi* (Linnaeus), Mustard White
____   a. *frigida* (Scudder)
____   b. *oleracea* (Harris)
____ 2. *virginiensis* (W.H. Edwards), West Virginia White
____ 3. *rapae* (Linnaeus), Cabbage White

Ascia Scopoli

____ 1. *monuste* (Linnaeus), Great Southern White
____   a. *monuste* (Linnaeus)
____   b. *phileta* (Fabricius)

Ganyra Billberg

____ 1. **josephina* (Godart), Giant White
____   a. *josepha* (Salvin and Godman)

Euchloe Hübner

____ 1. *ausonides* (Lucas), Large Marble
____   a. *ausonides* (Lucas)

_____   b. *mayi* F. and R. Chermock
_____   c. *palaeoreis* K. Johnson
_____   2. *olympia* (W.H. Edwards), Olympia Marble

Anthocharis Boisduval, Rambur, and Graslin

    1. *midea* (Hübner), Falcate Orangetip
_____   a. *midea* (Hübner)
_____   b. *annickae* dos Passos and Klots

SUBFAMILY COLIADINAE: SULPHURS AND YELLOWS

Colias Fabricius

_____   1. *philodice* Godart, Clouded Sulphur
_____   2. *eurytheme* Boisduval, Orange Sulphur
    3. **occidentalis,* Western Sulphur
_____   a. *christina* W.H. Edwards
_____   b. *krauthii* Klots
    4. *hecla* Lefèbvre, Hecla Sulphur
_____   a. *hecla* Lefèbvre
_____   b. *hecla* Strecker
    5. *nastes* Boisduval, Labrador Sulphur
_____   a. *nastes* Boisduval
_____   b. *rossii* Guenée
_____   c. *moina* Strecker
_____   d. *subarctica* (McDunnough)
    6. *gigantea* Strecker, Giant Sulphur
_____   a. *gigantea* Strecker
_____   b. *mayi* F. and R. Chermock
_____   7. *pelidne* Boisduval and Leconte, Pelidne Sulphur
    8. *interior* Scudder, Pink-edged Sulphur
_____   a. *interior* Scudder
_____   b. *laurentina* (Scudder)
_____   c. *vividior* Berger
    9. **palaeno* (Linnaeus), Palaeno Sulphur
_____   a. *chippewa* W.H. Edwards
_____   b. *baffinensis* Ebner and Ferris
_____ 10. *cesonia* (Stoll), Southern Dogface

Anteos Hübner

    1. **clorinde* (Godart), White-angled Sulphur
_____   a. *nivifera* (Fruhstorfer)
    2. **maerula* (Fabricius), Yellow-angled Sulphur
_____   a. *lacordairei* (Boisduval)

Phoebis Hübner

      1. *sennae (Linnaeus), Cloudless Sulphur
____   a. *eubule* (Linnaeus)
____   b. *marcellina* (Cramer)
____ 2. *philea* Johansson, Orange-barred Sulphur
      3. *agarithe* (Boisduval), Large Orange Sulphur
____   a. *agarithe* (Boisduval)
____   b. *maxima* (Neumoegen)
____ 4. *argante* Fabricius, Apricot Sulphur
____ 5. *neocypris* (Hübner), Tailed Sulphur
      6. *statira (Cramer), Statira Sulphur
____   a. *jada* (Butler)
____   b. *floridensis* (Neumoegen)
____ 7. *orbis* (Poey), Orbed Sulphur

Kricogonia Reakirt

____ 1. *lyside* (Godart), Lyside Sulphur

Eurema Hübner

      1. *daira* (Godart), Barred Yellow
____   a. *daira* (Godart)
____   b. *palmira* (Poey)
____   c. *lydia* (C. and R. Felder)
____ 2. *boisduvalianum* (C. and R. Felder), Boisduval's Yellow
____ 3. *mexicanum* (Boisduval), Mexican Yellow
      4. *salome (C. and R. Felder), Salome Yellow
____   a. *limoneum* (C. and R. Felder)
____ 5. *proterpia* (Fabricius), Tailed Orange
____ 6. *lisa* (Boisduval and Leconte), Little Yellow
      7. *nise* (Cramer), Mimosa Yellow
____   a. *nise* (Cramer)
____   b. *nelphe* (R. Felder)
      8. *messalina (Fabricius)
____   a. *blakei* (Maynard), Shy Yellow
      9. *dina (Poey), Dina Yellow
____   a. *westwoodi* (Boisduval)
____   b. *helios* M. Bates
____ 10. *nicippe* (Cramer), Sleepy Orange

Nathalis Boisduval

____ 1. *iole* Boisduval, Dainty Sulphur

FAMILY LYCAENIDAE: HARVESTERS, COPPERS, HAIRSTREAKS, AND BLUES

SUBFAMILY MILETINAE: HARVESTERS
Feniseca Grote

____ 1. *tarquinius* (Fabricius), Harvester

SUBFAMILY LYCAENINAE: COPPERS
Lycaena Fabricius

1. *phlaeas (Linnaeus)
____   a. *americana* Harris, American Copper
____   b. *feildeni* (M'Lachlan)
____ 2. *dione* (Scudder), Gray Copper
____ 3. *hyllus* (Cramer), Bronze Copper
    4. *rubidus (Behr), Ruddy Copper
____   a. *longi* K. Johnson and Balogh
    5. *epixanthe* (Boisduval and Leconte), Bog Copper
____   a. *epixanthe* (Boisduval and Leconte)
____   b. *phaedrus* (G.C. Hall)
____   c. *michiganensis* (Rawson)
    6. *dorcas* (W. Kirby), Dorcas Copper
____   a. *dorcas* (W. Kirby)
____   b. *dospassosi* McDunnough
____   c. *claytoni* Brower
____ 7. *helloides* (Boisduval), Purplish Copper

SUBFAMILY THECLINAE: HAIRSTREAKS
Eumaeus Hübner

    1. *atala (Poey), Atala
____   a. *florida* Röber
____ 2. *toxea* (Godart), Mexican Cycadian

Allosmaitia Clench

____ 1. *strophius* (Godart), Strophius Hairstreak

Atlides Hübner

____ 1. *halesus* (Cramer), Great Purple Hairstreak

Rekoa Kaye

____ 1. *marius* (Lucas), Marius Hairstreak
____ 2. *palegon* (Stoll), Gold-bordered Hairstreak

Chlorostrymon Clench

____ 1. *maesites* (Herrich-Schäffer), Amethyst Hairstreak
____ 2. *telea* (Hewitson), Telea Hairstreak
____ 3. *simaethis* (Drury), Silver-banded Hairstreak
____   a. *simaethis* (Drury)
____   b. *sarita* (Skinner)

Ocaria Clench

____ 1. *ocrisia* (Hewitson), Black Hairstreak

Phaeostrymon Clench

____ 1. *alcestis* (W.H. Edwards), Soapberry Hairstreak

Satyrium Scudder

   1. *titus* (Fabricius), Coral Hairstreak
____   a. *titus* (Fabricius)
____   b. *mopsus* (Hübner)
____   c. *watsoni* (Barnes and Benjamin)
____ 2. *acadicum* (W.H. Edwards), Acadian Hairstreak
____ 3. *edwardsii* (Grote and Robinson), Edwards' Hairstreak
   4. *calanus* (Hübner), Banded Hairstreak
____   a. *calanus* (Hübner)
____   b. *falacer* (Godart)
____ 5. *caryaevorum* (McDunnough), Hickory Hairstreak
____ 6. *kingi* (Klots and Clench), King's Hairstreak
   7. *liparops* (Leconte), Striped Hairstreak
____   a. *liparops* (Leconte)
____   b. *strigosum* (Harris)
____   c. *fletcheri* (Michener and dos Passos)
   8. *favonius* J.E. Smith, Southern Hairstreak
____   a. *favonius* J.E. Smith
____   b. *ontario* (W.H. Edwards)
____   c. *autolycus* (W.H. Edwards)

Cyanophrys Clench

____ 1. *miserabilis* (Clench), Clench's Greenstreak
____ 2. *goodsoni* (Clench), Goodson's Greenstreak
____ 3. *herodotus* (Fabricius), Tropical Greenstreak

Callophrys Billberg

   1. *gryneus* (Hübner), Juniper Hairstreak
____   a. *gryneus* (Hübner)

_____ b. *smilacis* (Boisduval and Leconte)
_____ c. *sweadneri* (F.H. Chermock)
_____ d. *castalis* (W.H. Edwards)
_____ e. *siva* (W.H. Edwards), Juniper Hairstreak
_____ 2. *hesseli* (Rawson and Ziegler), Hessel's Hairstreak
_____ 3. *xami* (Reakirt), Xami Hairstreak
_____ a. *texami* (Clench)
_____ 4. *augustinus* (W. Kirby), Brown Elfin
_____ a. *augustinus* (W. Kirby)
_____ b. *helenae* (dos Passos)
_____ c. *croesoides* (Scudder)
_____ 5. *polios* Cook and Watson, Hoary Elfin
_____ 6. *irus* (Godart), Frosted Elfin
_____ a. *irus* (Godart)
_____ b. *arsace* (Boisduval and Leconte)
_____ c. *hadros* Cook and Watson
_____ 7. *henrici* (Grote and Robinson), Henry's Elfin
_____ a. *henrici* (Grote and Robinson)
_____ b. *margaretae* dos Passos
_____ c. *solatus* Cook and Watson
_____ d. *turneri* Clench
_____ 8. *lanoraieensis* Sheppard, Bog Elfin
_____ 9. *niphon* (Hübner), Eastern Pine Elfin
_____ a. *niphon* (Hübner)
_____ b. *clarki* T.N. Freeman
_____ 10. *eryphon* (Boisduval), Western Pine Elfin

Parrhasius Hübner

_____ 1. *m-album* (Boisduval and Leconte), White M Hairstreak

Oenomaus Hübner

_____ 1. *ortygnus* (Cramer), Aquamarine Hairstreak

Tmolus Hübner

_____ 1. *echion* (Linnaeus), Echion Hairstreak

Ministrymon Clench

_____ 1. *azia* (Hewitson), Azia Hairstreak
_____ 2. *clytie* (W.H. Edwards), Clytie Hairstreak

Siderus Kaye

_____ 1. *tephraeus* (Geyer), Tephraeus Hairstreak

Erora Scudder

_____ 1. *laetus* (W.H. Edwards), Early Hairstreak

Calycopis Scudder

____ 1. *cecrops* (Fabricius), Red-banded Hairstreak
____ 2. *isobeon* (Butler and H. Druce), Dusky-blue Groundstreak

Electrostrymon Clench

____ 1. *sangala* (Hewitson), Ruddy Hairstreak
____ 2. *angelia* (Hewitson), Fulvous Hairstreak
____ 3. *canus* (Druce), Muted Hairstreak

Strymon Hübner

____ 1. *melinus* Hübner, Gray Hairstreak
____   a. *melinus* Hübner
____   b. *humuli* (Harris)
____   c. *franki* Field
____ 2. *rufofusca* (Hewitson), Red-crescent Scrub-Hairstreak
____ 3. *bebrycia* (Hewitson), Red-lined Scrub-Hairstreak
____ 4. *martialis* (Herrich-Schäffer), Martial Scrub-Hairstreak
____ 5. *yojoa* (Reakirt), Yojoa Scrub-Hairstreak
____ 6. *albata* (C. and R. Felder), White Scrub-Hairstreak
      7. **acis* (Drury)
____   a. *bartrami* (W.P. Comstock and Huntington), Bartram's Scrub-Hairstreak
____ 8. *alea* (Godman and Salvin), Lacey's Scrub-Hairstreak
      9. *istapa* (Reakirt), Mallow Scrub-Hairstreak
____   a. *modesta* (Maynard)
____   b. *istapa* (Reakirt)
____ 10. *limenia* (Hewitson), Disguised Scrub-Hairstreak
____ 11. *cestri* (Reakirt), Tailless Scrub-Hairstreak
____ 12. *bazochii* (Godart), Lantana Scrub-Hairstreak

SUBFAMILY POLYOMMATINAE: BLUES

Brephidium Scudder

____ 1. *exile* (Boisduval), Western Pygmy-Blue
      2. **isophthalma* (Herrich-Schäffer), Eastern Pygmy-Blue
____   a. *pseudofea* (Morrison)

Leptotes Scudder

      1. **cassius* (Cramer), Cassius Blue
____   a. *theonus* (Lucas)
____   b. *striata* (W.H. Edwards)
____ 2. *marina* (Reakirt), Marine Blue

Zizula Chapman

_____ 1. *cyna* (W.H. Edwards), Cyna Blue

Hemiargus Hübner

1. **thomasi* Clench
_____ a. *bethunebakeri* W.P. Comstock and Huntington, Miami Blue
2. **ceraunus* (Fabricius), Ceraunus Blue
_____ a. *antibubastus* Hübner
_____ b. *zachaeina* (Butler and Druce)
3. **isola* (Reakirt), Reakirt's Blue
_____ a. *alce* (W.H. Edwards)

Everes Hübner

1. *comyntas* (Godart), Eastern Tailed-Blue
_____ a. *comyntas* (Godart)
_____ b. *texanus* R. Chermock
2. *amyntula* (Boisduval), Western Tailed-Blue
_____ a. *valeriae* Clench

Celastrina Tutt

1. **argiolus* (Cramer), Spring Azure
_____ a. *ladon* (Cramer)
_____ b. *lucia* (W. Kirby)
_____ c. *argentata* (Fletcher)
_____ 2. *neglectamajor* Opler and Krizek, Appalachian Azure
_____ 3. *ebenina* (W.H. Edwards), Dusky Azure

Glaucopsyche Scudder

1. *lygdamus* (Doubleday), Silvery Blue
_____ a. *lygdamus* (Doubleday)
_____ b. *mildredi* F.H. Chermock
_____ c. *couperi* Grote
_____ d. *afra* (W.H. Edwards)
_____ e. *jacki* Stallings and Turner

Lycaeides Hübner

1. **idas* (Linnaeus), Northern Blue
_____ a. *scudderii* (W.H. Edwards)
_____ b. *aster* (W.H. Edwards)
_____ c. *empetri* (T.N. Freeman)
_____ d. *nabokovi* Masters
2. *melissa* (W.H. Edwards), Melissa Blue
_____ a. *melissa* (W.H. Edwards)
_____ b. *samuelis* Nabokov, Karner Blue

Plebejus Kluk

    1. *saepiolus (Boisduval), Greenish Blue
____   a. *amica* (W.H. Edwards)
    2. *acmon (Westwood and Hewitson), Acmon Blue
____   a. *texanus* Goodpasture

Vacciniina Tutt

    1. *optilete (Knoch), Cranberry Blue
____   a. *yukona* (Holland)

Agriades Hübner

    1. *glandon (de Prunner), Arctic Blue
____   a. *franklinii* (Curtis)
____   b. *lacustris* (T.N. Freeman)
____   c. *bryanti* (Leussler)

FAMILY RIODINIDAE: METALMARKS

Calephelis Grote and Robinson

____   1. *virginiensis* (Guérin-Méneville), Little Metalmark
____   2. *borealis* (Grote and Robinson), Northern Metalmark
     3. *nemesis (W.H. Edwards), Fatal Metalmark
____   a. *australis* (W.H. Edwards)
____   4. *nilus* (C. and R. Felder), Rounded Metalmark
____   5. *mutica* McAlpine, Swamp Metalmark
____   6. *rawsoni* McAlpine, Rawson's Metalmark

Caria Hübner

    1. *ino Godman and Salvin, Red-bordered Metalmark
____   a. *melicerta* Schaus

Lasaia H.W. Bates

    1. *sula Staudinger
____   a. *peninsularis* Clench, Blue Metalmark

Melanis Hübner

____   1. *pixe* (Boisduval), Red-bordered Pixie

Emesis Fabricius

____   1. *emesia* (Hewitson), Curve-winged Metalmark
____   2. *tenedia* (Felder), Falcate Metalmark

Apodemia C. and R. Felder

____   1. *multiplaga* Schaus, Narrow-winged Metalmark

_____ 2. *walkeri* Godman and Salvin, Walker's Metalmark

FAMILY NYMPHALIDAE: BRUSHFOOTS

SUBFAMILY LIBYTHEINAE: SNOUTS
Libytheana Michener

1. *carinenta* (Cramer), American Snout
_____ a. *bachmanii* (Kirtland)
_____ b. *larvata* (Strecker)
_____ c. *motya* (Boisduval and Leconte)

SUBFAMILY HELICONIINAE: HELICONIANS
Agraulis Boisduval & Leconte

1. **vanillae* (Linnaeus), Gulf Fritillary
_____ a. *nigrior* (Michener)
_____ b. *incarnata* (Riley)

Dione Hübner

1. **moneta* Hübner, Mexican Silverspot
_____ a. *poeyi* Butler

Dryadula Michener

_____ 1. *phaetusa* (Linnaeus), Banded Orange Heliconian

Dryas Hübner

1. **iulia* (Fabricius), Julia
_____ a. *largo* Clench
_____ b. *moderata* (Riley)

Eueides Hübner

1. **isabella* (Stoll), Isabella's Heliconian
_____ a. *zorcaon* Reakirt

Heliconius Kluk

1. **charithonius* (Linnaeus), Zebra
_____ a. *tuckeri* W.P. Comstock and F.M. Brown
_____ b. *vazquezae* W.P. Comstock and F.M. Brown
2. **erato* (Linnaeus),
_____ a. *petiveranus* Doubleday, Erato Heliconian

Euptoieta Doubleday

_____ 1. *claudia* (Cramer), Variegated Fritillary
2. **hegesia* (Cramer)
_____ a. *hoffmanni* W.P. Comstock, Mexican Fritillary

Speyeria Scudder

_____ 1. *diana* (Cramer), Diana
     2. *cybele* (Fabricius), Great Spangled Fritillary
_____   a. *cybele* (Fabricius)
_____   b. *novascotiae* (McDunnough)
_____   c. *krautwurmi* (Holland)
_____   d. *pseudocarpenteri* (F. and R. Chermock)
     3. *aphrodite* (Fabricius), Aphrodite Fritillary
_____   a. *aphrodite* (Fabricius)
_____   b. *winni* (Gunder)
_____   c. *alcestis* (W.H. Edwards)
_____   d. *manitoba* (F. and R. Chermock)
_____ 4. *idalia* (Drury), Regal Fritillary
_____ 5. *edwardsii* (Reakirt), Edwards' Fritillary
     6. **coronis* (Behr)
_____   a. *halcyone* (W.H. Edwards), Coronis Fritillary
     7. **callippe* (Boisduval), Callippe Fritillary
_____   a. *calgariana* (McDunnough)
     8. *atlantis* (W.H. Edwards), Atlantis Fritillary
_____   a. *atlantis* (W.H. Edwards)
_____   b. *canadensis* (dos Passos)
_____   c. *hollandi* (F. and R. Chermock)
_____   d. *dennisi* dos Passos and Grey
     9. **mormonia* (Boisduval), Mormon Fritillary
_____   a. *eurynome* (W.H. Edwards)

Boloria Moore

     1. **napaea* (Hoffmansegg), Mountain Fritillary
_____   a. *nearctica* Verity
     2. **eunomia* (Esper), Bog Fritillary
_____   a. *triclaris* (Hübner)
_____   b. *dawsoni* (Barnes and McDunnough)
     3. **selene* (Denis and Schiffermüller), Silver-bordered Fritillary
_____   a. *myrina* (Cramer)
_____   b. *nebraskensis* (Holland)
_____   c. *sabulocollis* Kohler
_____   d. *atrocostalis* (Huard)
_____   e. *terraenovae* (Holland)
     4. *bellona* (Fabricius), Meadow Fritillary
_____   a. *bellona* (Fabricius)
_____   b. *toddi* (Holland)
_____   c. *jenistai* (Stallings and Turner)
     5. **frigga* (Thunberg), Frigga Fritillary
_____   a. *saga* (Staudinger)
_____ 6. *improba* (Butler), Dingy Fritillary

7. *polaris* (Boisduval), Polaris Fritillary
____ a. *polaris* (Boisduval)
____ b. *stellata* Masters
____ 8. *freija* Thunberg, Freija Fritillary
9. **titania* (Esper), Titania Fritillary
____ a. *boisduvalii* (Duponchel)
____ b. *grandis* (Barnes and McDunnough)
____ c. *montina* (Scudder)
10. **chariclea* (Schneider), Arctic Fritillary
____ a. *arctica* (Zetterstedt)
____ b. *butleri* (W.H. Edwards)

SUBFAMILY NYMPHALINAE: BRUSHFOOTS

Poladryas Bauer

____ 1. *minuta* (W.H. Edwards), Dotted Checkerspot

Thessalia Scudder

1. **theona* (Ménétriés), Theona Checkerspot
____ a. *bollii* (W.H. Edwards)
____ 2. *fulvia* (W.H. Edwards), Fulvia Checkerspot

Chlosyne Butler

1. **lacinia* (Geyer), Bordered Patch
____ a. *adjutrix* Scudder
____ 2. *definita* (E.M. Aaron), Definite Patch
____ 3. *endeis* (Godman and Salvin), Banded Patch
____ 4. *janais* (Drury), Crimson Patch
5. **rosita* Hall, Rosita Patch
____ a. *browni* Bauer
____ 6. *marina* (Hübner), Red-spotted Patch
7. *gorgone* (Hübner), Gorgone Checkerspot
____ a. *gorgone* (Hübner)
____ b. *carlota* (Reakirt)
8. *nycteis* (Doubleday and Hewitson), Silvery Checkerspot
____ a. *nycteis* (Doubleday and Hewitson)
____ b. *reversa* (F. and R. Chermock)
9. *harrisii* (Scudder), Harris' Checkerspot
____ a. *harrisii* (Scudder)
____ b. *liggetti* (Avinoff)
____ c. *hanhami* (Fletcher)
____ 10. *acastus* (W.H. Edwards), Sagebrush Checkerspot

Microtia H.W. Bates

____ 1. *elva* H.W. Bates, Elf

Dymasia Higgins

____ 1. *dymas* (W.H. Edwards), Tiny Checkerspot

Texola Higgins

1. **elada* (Hewitson), Elada Checkerspot
____ a. *ulrica* (W.H. Edwards)

Phyciodes Hübner

1. *texana* (W.H. Edwards), Texan Crescent
____ a. *texana* (W.H. Edwards)
____ b. *seminole* (Skinner), Seminole Crescent
2. *frisia* (Poey), Cuban Crescent
____ a. *frisia* (Poey), Cuban Crescent
____ b. *tulcis* (H.W. Bates), Tulcis Crescent
____ 3. *ptolyca* (H.W. Bates), Black Crescent
____ 4. *vesta* (W.H. Edwards), Vesta Crescent
____ 5. *phaon* (W.H. Edwards), Phaon Crescent
____ 6. *tharos* (Drury), Pearl Crescent
7. *cocyta* (Cramer), Northern Crescent
____ a. *cocyta* (Cramer)
____ b. *arcticus* dos Passos
____ 8. *batesii* (Reakirt), Tawny Crescent
9. **pratensis* (Behr), Field Crescent
____ a. *camillus* W.H. Edwards
____ 10. *pictus* W.H. Edwards, Painted Crescent

Euphydryas Scudder

1. *phaeton* (Drury), Baltimore Checkerspot
____ a. *phaeton* (Drury)
____ b. *ozarkae* Masters
2. *chalcedona* (Boisduval), Variable Checkerspot
____ a. *hutchinsi* McDunnough

Polygonia Hübner

____ 1. *interrogationis* (Fabricius), Question Mark
____ 2. *comma* (Harris), Eastern Comma
____ 3. *satyrus* (W.H. Edwards), Satyr Comma
4. *faunus* (W.H. Edwards), Green Comma
____ a. *faunus* (W.H. Edwards)
____ b. *smythi* A.H. Clark
5. *gracilis* (Grote and Robinson), Hoary Comma
____ a. *gracilis* (Grote and Robinson)
____ b. *zephyrus* (W.H. Edwards)
____ 6. *progne* (Cramer), Gray Comma

Nymphalis Kluk

  1. *vau-album (Denis and Schiffermüller), Compton Tortoise-shell
    ____ a. *j-album* (Boisduval and Leconte)
    ____ 2. *californica* (Boisduval), California Tortoiseshell
    3. *antiopa* (Linnaeus), Mourning Cloak
    ____ a. *antiopa* (Linnaeus), Mourning Cloak
    ____ b. *hyperborea* (Seitz)
    4. *milberti* (Godart), Milbert's Tortoiseshell
    ____ a. *milberti* (Godart), Milbert's Tortoiseshell
    ____ b. *viola* dos Passos
    ____ 5. *urticae* (Linnaeus), Small Tortoiseshell

Vanessa Fabricius

  1. *atalanta (Linnaeus)
  ____ a. *rubria* (Fruhstorfer), Red Admiral
  ____ 2. *virginiensis* (Drury), American Lady
  ____ 3. *cardui* (Linnaeus), Painted Lady
  ____ 4. *annabella* (Field), West Coast Lady

Hypolimnas Hübner

  ____ 1. *misippus* (Linnaeus), Mimic

Junonia Hübner

  ____ 1. *coenia* (Hübner), Common Buckeye
  ____ 2. *evarete* (Cramer), Mangrove Buckeye
    3. *genoveva (Stoll),
  ____ a. *zonalis* C. and R. Felder, Tropical Buckeye
  ____ b. *nigrosuffusa* Barnes and McDunnough, Dark Buckeye

Anartia Hübner

  1. *jatrophae (Johansson), White Peacock
  ____ a. *guantanamo* Munroe
  ____ b. *luteipicta* Fruhstorfer
  ____ 2. *chrysopelea* (Godart), Caribbean Peacock
  ____ 3. *fatima* (Fabricius), Banded Peacock

Siproeta Hübner

  1. *stelenes (Linnaeus), Malachite
  ____ a. *biplagiata* (Fruhstorfer)

SUBFAMILY LIMENITIDINAE

Epiphile Doubleday

  ____ 1. *adrasta* Hewitson, Common Banner

Limenitis Fabricius

1. *arthemis* (Drury), Red-spotted Purple
____ a. *arthemis* (Drury), White Admiral
____ b. *rubrofasciata* (Barnes and McDunnough), White Admiral
____ c. *astyanax* (Fabricius), Red-spotted Purple
2. *archippus* (Cramer), Viceroy
____ a. *archippus* (Cramer)
____ b. *floridensis* Strecker
____ c. *watsoni* (dos Passos)
3. *weidemeyerii W.H. Edwards, Weidemeyer's Admiral
____ a. *oberfoelli* F.M. Brown

Adelpha Hübner

____ 4. *fessonia* (Hewitson), Band-celled Sister
____ 5. *basiloides* (Bates), Spot-celled Sister
6. *bredowii Geyer, California Sister
____ a. *eulalia* (Doubleday and Hewitson)

Myscelia Doubleday

____ 1. *ethusa* (Boisduval), Mexican Bluewing

Eunica Hübner

____ 1. *monima* (Stoll), Dingy Purplewing
2. *tatila* (Herrich-Schäffer), Large Purplewing
____ a. *tatila* (Herrich-Schäffer)
____ b. *tatilista* Kaye

Dynamine Hübner

____ 1. *dyonis* Geyer, Blue-eyed Sailor

Diaethria Billberg

____ 1. *clymena* (Cramer), Cramer's Eighty-eight
____ 2. *asteria* (Godman and Salvin), Mexican Eighty-eight

Mestra Hübner

____ 1. *amymone* (Ménétriés), Common Mestra

Biblis Fabricius

1. *hyperia (Cramer), Red Rim
____ a. *aganisa* Boisduval

Hamadryas Hübner

1. *feronia (Linnaeus), Variable Cracker
____ a. *farinulenta* (Fruhstorfer)
2. *februa (Hübner), Gray Cracker

_____   a. *gudula* (Fruhstorfer)
_____ 3. **amphinome* (Linnaeus), Red Cracker
_____   a. *mexicana* (Lucas)
_____ 4. *iphthime* (Bates), Brownish Cracker
_____ 5. *guatemalena* (Bates), Guatemalan Cracker
_____ 6. *amphichloe* (Boisduval), Pale Cracker

Historis Hübner

_____ 1. *odius* (Fabricius), Orion

Smyrna Hübner

_____ 1. *blomfildia* (Hübner), Blomfild's Beauty

Marpesia Hübner

_____ 1. *zerynthia* Hübner, Waiter Daggerwing
_____ 2. *chiron* (Fabricius), Many-banded Daggerwing
_____ 3. *petreus* (Cramer), Ruddy Daggerwing
_____ 4. *eleuchea* Hübner, Antillean Daggerwing

SUBFAMILY CHARAXINAE: LEAF BUTTERFLIES

Anaea Hübner, Leafwings

_____ 1. *aidea* (Guérin-Méneville), Tropical Leafwing
_____ 2. *floridalis* F. Johnson and W.P. Comstock, Florida Leafwing
_____ 3. *andria* Scudder, Goatweed Leafwing
_____ 4. *glycerium* (Doubleday), Angled Leafwing
_____ 5. *pithyusa* (R. Felder), Pale-spotted Leafwing
_____ 6. *echemus* Doubleday and Hewitson, Chestnut Leafwing

SUBFAMILY APATURINAE: HACKBERRY BUTTERFLIES

Asterocampa Röber

   1. *celtis* (Boisduval and Leconte), Hackberry Emperor
_____   a. *celtis* (Boisduval and Leconte)
_____   b. *antonia* (W.H. Edwards)
_____   c. *alicia* (W.H. Edwards)
   2. **leilia* (W.H. Edwards), Empress Leilia
_____   a. *cocles* (Lintner)
   3. *clyton* (Boisduval and Leconte), Tawny Emperor
_____   a. *clyton* (Boisduval and Leconte)
_____   b. *flora* (W.H. Edwards)
_____   c. *texana* (Skinner)
_____   d. *louisa* Stallings and Turner

Doxocapa Hübner

____ 1. *pavon* (Latreille), Pavon Emperor
____ 2. *laure* (Drury), Silver Emperor

SUBFAMILY SATYRINAE: SATYRS AND WOOD-NYMPHS

Enodia Hübner

____ 1. *portlandia* (Fabricius), Southern Pearly-Eye
____   a. *portlandia* (Fabricius)
____   b. *floralae* (J.R. Heitzman and dos Passos)
____   c. *missarkae* (J.R. Heitzman and dos Passos)
____ 2. *anthedon* A.H. Clark, Northern Pearly-Eye
____ 3. *creola* (Skinner), Creole Pearly-Eye

Satyrodes Scudder: Browns

____ 1. *eurydice* (Johansson), Eyed Brown
____   a. *eurydice* (Johansson)
____   b. *fumosa* Leussler, Smoky Eyed Brown
____ 2. *appalachia* (R.L. Chermock), Appalachian Brown
____   a. *appalachia* (R.L. Chermock)
____   b. *leeuwi* (Gatrelle and Arbogast)

Cyllopsis R. Felder

____ 1. *gemma* (Hübner), Gemmed Satyr
____   a. *gemma* (Hübner)
____   b. *freemani* (D. Stallings and Turner)

Hermeuptychia Forster

____ 1. *sosybius* (Fabricius), Carolina Satyr

Neonympha Hübner

____ 1. *areolata* (J.E. Smith), Georgia Satyr
____   a. *areolata* (J.E. Smith)
____   b. *septentrionalis* Davis
____ 2. *mitchellii* French, Mitchell's Satyr
____   a. *mitchellii* French
____   b. *francisci* Parshall and Kral

Megisto Hübner

____ 1. *cymela* (Cramer), Little Wood-Satyr
____ 2. *viola* (Maynard), Viola's Wood-Satyr
____ 3. *rubricata* (W.H. Edwards), Red Satyr

Coenonympha Hübner

1. *tullia,* Common Ringlet
   ____ a. *inornata* W.H. Edwards
   ____ b. *mcisaaci* dos Passos
   ____ c. *nipisquit* McDunnough
   ____ d. *heinemani* F.M. Brown

Cercyonis Scudder

1. *pegala* (Fabricius), Common Wood-Nymph
   ____ a. *pegala* (Fabricius)
   ____ b. *alope* (Fabricius)
   ____ c. *nephele* (W. Kirby)
   ____ d. *olympus* (W.H. Edwards)
   ____ e. *texana* (W.H. Edwards)

Erebia Dalman

1. *rossii* (Curtis), Ross's Alpine
   ____ a. *rossii* (Curtis)
   ____ b. *ornata* Leussler
2. *disa* (Thunberg), Disa Alpine
   ____ a. *mancinus* Doubleday and Hewitson
   ____ 3. *fasciata* Butler, Banded Alpine
   ____ 4. *discoidalis* W. Kirby, Red-disked Alpine
5. *theano* (Tauscher), Theano Alpine
   ____ a. *sofia* Strecker
6. *epipsodea* Butler, Common Alpine
   ____ a. *freemani* Ehrlich

Neominois Scudder

____ 1. *ridingsii* (W.H. Edwards), Ridings' Satyr

Oeneis Hübner

____ 1. *macounii* (W.H. Edwards), Macoun's Arctic
2. *chryxus* (Doubleday and Hewitson), Chryxus Arctic
   ____ a. *strigulosa* McDunnough
   ____ b. *calais* (Scudder)
3. *uhleri* (Reakirt), Uhler's Arctic
   ____ a. *varuna* (W.H. Edwards)
   ____ 4. *alberta* Elwes, Alberta Arctic
5. *taygete* Geyer, White-veined Arctic
   ____ a. *taygete* Geyer
   ____ b. *gaspeensis* dos Passos
   ____ c. *hanburyi* Watkins
6. *jutta* (Hübner), Jutta Arctic
   ____ a. *terraenovae* dos Passos

_____ b. *ascerta* Masters and Sorenson
_____ c. *ridingiana* F. and R. Chermock
_____ d. *harperi* F.H. Chermock
_____ e. *leussleri* Bryant
7. *melissa* (Fabricius), Melissa Arctic
_____ a. *melissa* (Fabricius)
_____ b. *semidea* (Say)
_____ c. *semplei* Holland
_____ d. *assimilis* Butler
8. *polixenes* (Fabricius), Polixenes Arctic
_____ a. *polixenes* (Fabricius)
_____ b. *katahdin* (Newcomb)
_____ c. *subhyalina* (Curtis)
_____ d. *luteus* Troubridge and Parshall

SUBFAMILY DANAINAE: MILKWEED BUTTERFLIES
Danaus Kluk

_____ 1. *plexippus* (Linnaeus), Monarch
2. **gilippus* (Cramer), Queen
_____ a. *berenice* (Cramer)
_____ b. *strigosus* (Bates)
3. **eresimus* (Cramer), Soldier
_____ a. *montezuma* Talbot
_____ b. *tethys* Forbes

Lycorea Doubleday and Hewitson

1. **cleobaea* (Godart), Tiger Mimic-Queen
_____ a. *atergatis* Doubleday and Hewitson
b. **demeter* (C. and R. Felder)

Dircenna Doubleday

1. **klugii* Geyer, Klug's Clearwing

SUPERFAMILY HESPERIOIDEA: THE SKIPPERS

FAMILY HESPERIIDAE: THE SKIPPERS

SUBFAMILY PYRGINAE: THE OPEN-WINGED SKIPPERS, PYRGINES
Phocides Hübner

1. **pigmalion* (Cramer)
_____ a. *okeechobee* (Worthington), Mangrove Skipper
2. **palemon* (Cramer), Guava Skipper
_____ a. *lilea* (Reakirt)

Proteides Hübner

1. *mercurius* (Fabricius), Mercurial Skipper
   - ___ a. *mercurius* (Fabricius)
   - ___ b. *sanantonio* (Lucas)

Epargyreus Hübner

- ___ 1. *zestos* (Geyer), Zestos Skipper
- ___ 2. *clarus* (Cramer), Silver-spotted Skipper
- 3. **exadeus* (Cramer), Broken Silverdrop
  - ___ a. *cruza* Evans

Polygonus Hübner

1. **leo* (Gmelin), Hammock Skipper
   - ___ a. *arizonensis* (Skinner)
- ___ 2. *manueli* Bell and W.P. Comstock, Manuel's Skipper

Chioides Lindsey

1. **catillus* (Cramer), White-striped Longtail
   - ___ a. *albofasciatus* (Hewitson)
- ___ 2. *zilpa* (Butler), Zilpa Longtail

Aguna R.C. Williams

- ___ 1. *asander* (Hewitson), Gold-spotted Aguna
- ___ 2. *claxon* Evans, Emerald Aguna
- ___ 3. *metophis* (Latreille), Tailed Aguna

Typhedanus Butler

- ___ 1. *undulatus* (Hewitson), Mottled Longtail

Polythrix E.Y. Watson

- ___ 1. *mexicannus* H.A. Freeman, Mexican Longtail
- ___ 2. *octomaculata* (Sepp), Eight-spotted Longtail

Codatractus Lindsey

- ___ 1. *alcaeus* (Hewitson), White-crescent Longtail

Urbanus Hübner

- ___ 1. *proteus* (Linnaeus), Long-tailed Skipper
- ___ 2. *pronus* Evans, Pronus Longtail
- ___ 3. *esmeraldus* (Butler), Esmeralda Longtail
- ___ 4. *dorantes* (Stoll), Dorantes Skipper
- ___ 5. *teleus* (Hübner), Teleus Longtail
- ___ 6. *tanna* Evans, Tanna Longtail
- ___ 7. *simplicius* (Stoll), Plain Longtail

_____ 8. *procne* (Plötz), Brown Longtail
_____ 9. *doryssus* (Swainson), White-tailed Longtail

Astraptes Hübner

_____ 1. **fulgerator* (Walch), Two-barred Flasher
_____   a. *azul* (Reakirt)
_____ 2. *egregius* (Butler), Small-spotted Flasher
_____ 3. **alardus* (Stoll), Frosted Flasher
_____   a. *latia* Evans
_____ 4. *gilberti* H.A. Freeman, Gilbert's Flasher
_____ 5. **anaphus* (Cramer), Yellow-tipped Flasher
_____   a. *annetta* Evans

Autochton Hübner

_____ 1. *cellus* (Boisduval and Leconte), Gold-banded Skipper

Achalarus Scudder

_____ 1. *lyciades* (Geyer), Hoary Edge
_____ 2. *casica* (Herrich-Schäffer), Desert Cloudywing
_____ 3. *toxeus* (Plötz), Coyote Cloudywing
_____ 4. *jalapus* (Plötz), Jalapus Cloudywing

Thorybes Scudder

_____ 1. *bathyllus* (J.E. Smith), Southern Cloudywing
_____ 2. *pylades* (Scudder), Northern Cloudywing
_____ 3. *confusis* Bell, Confused Cloudywing

Cabares Godman and Salvin

_____ 1. *potrillo* (Lucas), Potrillo Skipper

Celaenorrhinus Hübner

_____ 1. *fritzgaertneri* (Bailey), Fritzgaertner's Flat
_____ 2. *stallingsi* H.A. Freeman, Stallings' Flat

Dyscophellus Godman and Salvin

_____ 1. *euribates* (Stoll), Euribates Skipper

Spathilepia Butler

_____ 1. *clonius* (Cramer), Falcate Skipper

Cogia Butler

_____ 1. *calchas* (Herrich-Schäffer), Mimosa Skipper
_____ 2. *hippalus* (W.H. Edwards), Acacia Skipper
_____ 3. *outis* (Skinner), Outis Skipper

Arteurotia Butler and Druce

____ 1. *tractipennis* Butler and Druce, Starred Skipper

Nisoniades Hübner

____ 1. *rubescens* (Möschler), Purplish-black Skipper

Pellicia Herrich-Schäffer

____ 1. *angra* Evans, Confused Pellicia
____ 2. *arina* Evans, Glazed Pellicia
____ 3. *dimidiata* Herrich-Schäffer, Morning Glory Pellicia

Bolla Mabille

____ 1. *clytius* (Godman and Salvin), Mottled Bolla
____ 2. *brennus* (Godman and Salvin), Obscure Bolla

Staphylus Godman and Salvin

____ 1. *ceos* (W.H. Edwards), Golden-headed Scallopwing
____ 2. *mazans* (Reakirt), Southern Scallopwing
____ 3. *hayhurstii* (W.H. Edwards), Hayhurst's Scallopwing

Gorgythion Godman and Salvin

____ 1. **begga* (Prittwitz), Variegated Skipper
            a. *pyralina* (Möschler)

Sostrata Godman and Salvin

____ 1. *nordica,* Blue-studded Skipper

Carrhenes Godman and Salvin

____ 1. *canescens* (R. Felder), Hoary Skipper

Xenophanes Godman and Salvin

____ 1. *tryxus* (Stoll), Glassy-winged Skipper

Systasea W.H. Edwards

____ 1. *pulverulenta* (R. Felder), Texas Powdered-Skipper

Achlyodes Hübner

____ 1. *tamenund* (W.H. Edwards), Sickle-winged Skipper

Grais Godman and Salvin

____ 1. *stigmaticus* (Mabille), Hermit Skipper

Timochares Godman and Salvin

____ 1. *ruptifaciata* (Plötz), Brown-banded Skipper

Chiomara Godman and Salvin
_____ 1. *georgina* (Reakirt), White-patched Skipper

Gesta Evans
_____ 1. *invisus* (Butler and H. Druce), False Duskywing

Ephyriades Hübner
1. **brunnea* (Herrich-Schäffer)
_____   a. *floridensis* Bell and W.P. Comstock, Florida Duskywing

Erynnis Schrank: Duskywings
_____ 1. *icelus* (Scudder and Burgess), Dreamy Duskywing
     2. *brizo* (Boisduval and Leconte), Sleepy Duskywing
_____   a. *brizo* (Boisduval and Leconte)
_____   b. *somnus* (Lintner)
_____ 3. *juvenalis* (Fabricius), Juvenal's Duskywing
_____ 4. *meridianus* Bell, Meridian Duskywing
_____ 5. *horatius* (Scudder and Burgess), Horace's Duskywing
     6. **tristis* (Boisduval), Mournful Duskywing
_____   a. *tatius* (W.H. Edwards)
_____ 7. *martialis* (Scudder), Mottled Duskywing
_____ 8. *zarucco* (Lucas), Zarucco Duskywing
_____ 9. *funeralis* (Scudder and Burgess), Funereal Duskywing
_____ 10. *lucilius* (Scudder and Burgess), Columbine Duskywing
_____ 11. *baptisiae* (Forbes), Wild Indigo Duskywing
     12. *persius* (Scudder), Persius Duskywing
_____   a. *persius* (Scudder)
_____   b. *fredericki* H.A. Freeman

Pyrgus Hübner
     1. **centaureae* (Rambur), Grizzled Skipper
_____   a. *freija* (Warren)
_____   b. *wyandot* (W.H. Edwards)
     2. *communis* (Grote), Common Checkered-Skipper
_____   a. *communis* (Grote)
_____   b. *albescens* Plötz
_____ 3. *oileus* (Linnaeus), Tropical Checkered-Skipper
_____ 4. *philetas* W.H. Edwards, Desert Checker-Skipper

Heliopetes Billberg
_____ 1. *domicella* (Erichson), Erichson's White-Skipper
_____ 2. *laviana* (Hewitson), Laviana White-Skipper
_____ 3. *macaira* (Reakirt), Turk's Cap White-Skipper
_____ 4. *arsalte* (Linnaeus), Veined White-Skipper

Celotes Godman and Salvin: Streaky Skippers

____ 1. *nessus* (W.H. Edwards): Common Streaky-Skipper

Pholisora Scudder

____ 1. *catullus* (Fabricius), Common Sootywing
____ 2. *mejicanus* (Reakirt), Mexican Sootywing

Hesperopsis Dyar

1. **alpheus* (W.H. Edwards), Saltbush Sootywing
____ a. *texanus* Scott

SUBFAMILY HETEROPTERINAE: INTERMEDIATE SKIPPERS

Carterocephalus Lederer

1. **palaemon* (Pallas)
____ a. *mandan* (W.H. Edwards), Arctic Skipper

Piruna Evans

____ 1. *microsticta* (Godman), Small-spotted Skipperling

SUBFAMILY HESPERIINAE: BRANDED SKIPPERS

Synapte Mabille

____ 1. *pecta* Evans, Malicious Skipper
____ 2. *salenus* (Mabille), Salenus Skipper

Corticea Evans

____ 1. *corticea* (Plötz), Redundant Skipper

Vidius Evans

____ 1. *perigenes* (Godman), Pale-rayed Skipper

Monca Evans

____ 1. *tyrtaeus* (Plötz), Violet Patch Skipper

Nastra Evans

____ 1. *lherminier* (Latreille), Swarthy Skipper
____ 2. *julia* (H.A. Freeman), Julia's Skipper
____ 3. *neamathla* (Skinner and R.C. Williams), Neamathla Skipper

Cymaenes Scudder

____ 1. *tripunctus* (Herrich-Schäffer), Three-spotted Skipper
____ 2. **odilia* (Burmeister), Fawn-spotted Skipper
____ a. *trebius* (Mabille)

Lerema Scudder

____ 1. *accius* (J.E. Smith), Clouded Skipper
____ 2. *liris* Evans, Liris Skipper

Vettius Godman

____ 1. *fantasos* Stoll, Fantastic Skipper

Perichares Scudder

____ 1. **philetes* (Gmelin), Green-backed Ruby-Eye
  a. *adela* (Hewitson)

Rhinthon Godman

____ 1. *osca* (Plötz), Osca Skipper

Decinea Evans

____ 1. *percosius* (Godman), Double-spotted Skipper

Conga Evans

____ 1. *chydaea* (Butler), Hidden-ray Skipper

Ancyloxypha C. Felder

____ 1. *numitor* (Fabricius), Least Skipper
____ 2. *arene* (W.H. Edwards), Tropical Least Skipper

Oarisma Scudder

____ 1. *poweshiek* (Parker), Poweshiek Skipperling
____ 2. *garita* (Reakirt), Garita Skipperling

Copaeodes Speyer

____ 1. *aurantiacus* (Hewitson), Orange Skipperling
____ 2. *minimus* (W.H. Edwards), Southern Skipperling

Thymelicus Hübner

____ 1. *lineola* (Ochsenheimer), European Skipper

Hylephila Billberg

____ 1. *phyleus* (Drury), Fiery Skipper

Hesperia Fabricius

____ 1. *uncas* W.H. Edwards, Uncas Skipper
  2. **comma* (Linnaeus), Common Branded Skipper
____ a. *manitoba* (Scudder)
____ b. *assiniboia* (Lyman)
____ c. *laurentina* (Lyman)
____ d. *borealis* (Lindsey)

_____ 3. *woodgatei* (R.C. Williams), Apache Skipper
_____ 4. *ottoe* W.H. Edwards, Ottoe Skipper
_____ 5. *leonardus* Harris, Leonard's Skipper
_____   a. *leonardus* Harris
_____   b. *pawnee* Dodge, Pawnee Skipper
_____ 6. *pahaska* (Leussler), Pahaska Skipper
       7. *metea* Scudder, Cobweb Skipper
_____   a. *metea* Scudder
_____   b. *licinus* (W.H. Edwards)
_____ 8. *viridis* (W.H. Edwards), Green Skipper
       9. *attalus* (W.H. Edwards), Dotted Skipper
_____   a. *attalus* (W.H. Edwards)
_____   b. *slossonae* (Skinner)
    10. *meskei* (W.H. Edwards), Meske's Skipper
_____   a. *meskei* (W.H. Edwards)
_____   b. *straton* (W.H. Edwards)
_____ 11. *dacotae* (Skinner), Dakota Skipper
    12. *sassacus* Harris, Indian Skipper
_____   a. *sassacus* Harris
_____   b. *manitoboides* (Fletcher)
_____ 13. *nevada* (Scudder), Nevada Skipper

Polites Scudder

_____ 1. *peckius* (Kirby), Peck's Skipper
_____ 2. *baracoa* (Lucas), Baracoa Skipper
_____ 3. *themistocles* (Latreille), Tawny-edged Skipper
_____ 4. *origenes* (Fabricius), Crossline Skipper
       5. *mystic* (W.H. Edwards), Long Dash
_____   a. *mystic* (W.H. Edwards)
_____   b. *dacotah* (W.H. Edwards)
       6. *vibex* (Geyer), Whirlabout
_____   a. *vibex* (Geyer)
_____   b. *praeceps* (Scudder)
_____   c. *brettoides* (W.H. Edwards)

Wallengrenia Berg

       1. *otho* (J.E. Smith), Southern Broken-Dash
_____   a. *otho* (J.E. Smith)
_____   b. *curassavica* (Snellen)
_____ 2. *egeremet* (Scudder), Northern Broken-Dash

Pompeius Evans

       1. *verna* (W.H. Edwards), Little Glassywing
_____   a. *verna* (W.H. Edwards)
_____   b. *sequoyah* (H.A. Freeman)

Atalopedes Scudder

    1. **campestris* (Boisduval), Sachem
_____   a. *huron* (W.H. Edwards)

Atrytone Scudder

    1. *arogos* (Boisduval and Leconte), Arogos Skipper
_____   a. *arogos* (Boisduval and Leconte)
_____   b. *iowa* (Scudder)

Anatrytone Dyar

    1. *logan* (W.H. Edwards), Delaware Skipper
_____   a. *logan* (W.H. Edwards)
_____   b. *mazai* Freeman

Problema Skinner and R.C. Williams

    1. *byssus* (W.H. Edwards), Byssus Skipper
_____   a. *byssus* (W.H. Edwards)
_____   b. *kumskaka* (Scudder)
_____   2. *bulenta* (Boisduval and Leconte), Rare Skipper

Poanes Scudder

    1. *massasoit* (Scudder), Mulberry Wing
_____   a. *massasoit* (Scudder)
_____   b. *chermocki* Andersen and Simmons
_____   2. *hobomok* (Harris), Hobomok Skipper
_____   3. *zabulon* (Boisduval and Leconte), Zabulon Skipper
_____   4. *taxiles* (W.H. Edwards), Taxiles Skipper
    5. *aaroni* (Skinner), Aaron's Skipper
_____   a. *aaroni* (Skinner)
_____   b. *howardi* (Skinner)
_____   6. *yehl* (Skinner), Yehl Skipper
    7. *viator* (W.H. Edwards), Broad-winged Skipper
_____   a. *viator* (W.H. Edwards)
_____   b. *zizaniae* Shapiro

Quasimellana Burns

_____   1. *eulogius* (Plötz), Mexicana Mellana

Euphyes Scudder

_____   1. *arpa* (Boisduval and Leconte), Palmetto Skipper
_____   2. *pilatka* (W.H. Edwards), Palatka Skipper
    3. *dion* (W.H. Edwards), Dion Skipper
_____   a. *dion* (W.H. Edwards)
_____   b. *alabamae* (Lindsey)

_____ 4. *bayensis* Shuey, Bay Skipper
_____ 5. *dukesi* (Lindsey), Duke's Skipper
6. *conspicuus* (W.H. Edwards), Black Dash
_____ a. *conspicuus* (W.H. Edwards)
_____ b. *buchholzi* (Ehrlich and Gillham)
_____ 7. *berryi* (Bell), Berry's Skipper
_____ 8. *bimacula* (Grote and Robinson), Two-spotted Skipper
9. **vestris* (Boisduval), Dun Skipper
_____ a. *metacomet* (Harris)

Asbolis Mabille

_____ 1. *capucinus* (Lucas), Monk Skipper

Atrytonopsis Godman

1. *hianna* (Scudder), Dusted Skipper
_____ a. *hianna* (Scudder)
_____ b. *turneri* H.A. Freeman
_____ c. *loammi* (Whitney), Loammi Skipper

Amblyscirtes Scudder: Roadside-Skippers

_____ 1. *aenus* W.H. Edwards, Bronze Roadside-Skipper
_____ 2. *linda* H.A. Freeman, Linda's Roadside-Skipper
_____ 3. *oslari* (Skinner), Oslar's Roadside-Skipper
_____ 4. *hegon* (Scudder), Pepper and Salt Skipper
_____ 5. *aesculapius* (Fabricius), Lace-winged Roadside-Skipper
_____ 6. *carolina* (Skinner), Carolina Roadside-Skipper
_____ 7. *reversa* Jones, Reversed Roadside-Skipper
_____ 8. *nysa* W.H. Edwards, Nysa Roadside-Skipper
_____ 9. *eos* (W.H. Edwards), Dotted Roadside-Skipper
_____ 10. *vialis* (W.H. Edwards), Common Roadside-Skipper
_____ 11. *celia* Skinner, Celia's Roadside-Skipper
_____ 12. *belli* H.A. Freeman, Bell's Roadside-Skipper
_____ 13. *alternata* (Grote and Robinson), Dusky Roadside-Skipper

Lerodea Scudder

_____ 1. *eufala* (W.H. Edwards), Eufala Skipper
_____ 2. *arabus* (W.H. Edwards), Olive-clouded Skipper

Oligoria Scudder

_____ 1. *maculata* (W.H. Edwards), Twin-spot Skipper

Calpodes Hübner

_____ 1. *ethlius* (Stoll), Brazilian Skipper

Panoquina Hemming

_____ 1. *panoquin* (Scudder), Salt Marsh Skipper

_____ 2. *panoquinoides* (Skinner), Obscure Skipper
_____ 3. *ocola* (W.H. Edwards), Ocola Skipper
_____ 4. *hecebola* (Scudder), Hecebolus Skipper
_____ 5. *sylvicola* (Herrich-Schäffer), Purple-washed Skipper
_____ 6. *evansi* (H.A. Freeman), Evans' Skipper

Nyctelius Hayward

_____ 1. *nyctelius* (Latreille), Violet-banded Skipper

Thespieus Godman

_____ 1. *macareus* (Herrich-Schäffer), Chestnut-marked Skipper

SUBFAMILY MEGATHYMINAE: GIANT-SKIPPERS

Megathymus Scudder

    1. *yuccae* (Boisduval and Leconte), Yucca Giant-Skipper
_____ a. *yuccae* (Boisduval and Leconte)
_____ b. *buchholzi* H.A. Freeman
_____ c. *coloradensis* C.V. Riley
_____ d. *stallingsi* H.A. Freeman
_____ e. *reinthali* H.A. Freeman
_____ f. *kendalli* H.A. Freeman
    2. *cofaqui* (Strecker), Cofaqui Giant-Skipper
_____ a. *cofaqui* (Strecker)
_____ b. *harrisi* H.A. Freeman
    3. **streckeri* (Skinner), Strecker's Giant-Skipper
_____ a. *texanus* Barnes and McDunnough
_____ b. *leussleri* Holland

Stallingsia H.A. Freeman

_____ 1. *maculosa* (H.A. Freeman), Manfreda Giant-Skipper

HYPOTHETICAL SPECIES IN
EASTERN NORTH AMERICA

    Battus devilliers (Godart), Devilliers Swallowtail
    Papilio alexiares (Hopffer), Mexican Tiger Swallowtail
    Papilio eurymedon Lucas, Pale Swallowtail
    Euchloe creusa (Doubleday), Northern Marble
    Colias eurydice Boisduval, California Dogface
    Eurema chamberlaini (Butler), Chamberlain's Yellow
    Eumaeus minijas (Hübner)
    Pseudolycaena marsyas (Linnaeus)
    Philaethria dido (Linnaeus), Bamboo Page
    Apodemia mormo (C. and R. Felder), Mormon Metalmark
    Chlosyne erodyle (H.W. Bates)

Tegosa anieta luka Higgins
Hypanartia lethe (Fabricius), Small Brown Shoemaker
Myscelia cyananthe C. and R. Felder, Dark Wave
Mestra cana floridana (Strecker)
Hamadryas ferox (Staudinger)
Historis acheronta (Fabricius), Cadmus
Smyrna karwinskii (Geyer), Karwinski's Beauty
Morpho sp., Morpho
Greta polissena umbrana (Haensch)
Phocides urania (Westwood)
Polythrix procera (Plötz)
Urbanus albimargo (Mabille)
Astraptes galesus (Mabille)
Callimormus saturnus (Herrich-Schäffer)
Choranthus radians (Lucas), Radiant Skipper
Choranthus haitensis (Skinner), Haitian Skipper
Agathymus gilberti (H.A. Freeman), Gilbert's Agave Skipper

GLOSSARY

ABDOMEN. The terminal (third) body region of an adult insect.

ALKALINE. Basic, not acidic — as of habitats with soils dominated by alkaline salts.

ALPINE. The area above timberline in mountainous regions.

ANAL. The vein along the inner margin of a butterfly's hindwing (see Figure 3, p. 7).

ANGLE. The angle of a butterfly's wing where 2 margins are joined.

ANDROCONIA. Specialized wing scales, usually of males, believed to produce odors involved in courtship.

ANTENNA(E). One of two long, clubbed filamentous sensory structures on the insect head.

APEX. The tip, referring here to the outer tip of a butterfly's forewing (see Figure 2, p. 6).

APICAL. The area near the apex (see Figure 2, p. 6).

APICULUS. An extension of the antennal club in skippers.

ARCHIPELAGO. A group of islands.

ARCTIC. Found above the Arctic Circle or in arcticlike habitats.

BASAL. The wing area closest to the thorax (see Figure 2, p. 6).

BASKER. A butterfly that exposes its wings to sunlight in order to attain flight temperature.

BIOGEOGRAPHER. A person who studies the distribution of animals, plants, and their habitats.

BIOSPHERE. The thin layer of the Earth where life abounds.

BIOTIC PROVINCE. A geographic region within which similar habitats are likely to be occupied by the same sets of animal and plant species.

BOREAL. Pertaining to cooler environments, especially the Canadian, Hudsonian, and Arctic life zones.

BRACKISH. The slightly salty transitional area between saltwater and freshwater environments.

BROAD-LEAF. Non-coniferous woody trees, shrubs, or vines.

CELL. An area of a butterfly wing bounded on all sides by veins.

CHITINOUS. Characteristic of the hard exoskeleton of an insect; made with chitin.

CHRYSALIS (CHRYSALID). The resting stage of development during which a caterpillar, enclosed in a firm, hard case, transforms to an adult.

COLONIST. A butterfly that establishes a temporary or permanent population in a new area.

CONIFER. A needle-bearing tree or shrub, usually but not always evergreen.

CONIFEROUS. A habitat dominated or characterized by conifers.

COSTA. The front or forward edge of a butterfly's wing (see Figure 2, p. 6).

COSTAL MARGIN. The wing area adjacent to the costa (see Figure 2, p. 6).

COXA. The segment of an insect's leg closest to the body.

CREMASTER. The hooklike structures at the terminal end of a chrysalis.

CUBITAL. Pertaining to wing veins.

DECIDUOUS. Capable of detaching; descriptive of trees that lose their leaves and remain bare for at least a brief period.

DIAPAUSE. A state of developmental arrest in insects in which they may pass seasons unfavorable for growth or activity.

DIMORPHIC. Having different forms for the two sexes, or two forms of one sex, as in the yellow and white female forms of most sulphurs.

DIPHENIC. Having two seasonal forms, e.g., summer and winter or dry-season and wet-season forms.

DISCAL CELL. A cell in the center of a butterfly's wing.

DISTAL. That portion which is furthest away from the origin or point of attachment.

DIURNAL. Active during daylight.

DORSAL. The upper portion or surface.

ECOLOGY. The study of animals, plants, and their environments.

ECOREGION. A geographic region characterized by similar ecological features.

EMBRYO. The dividing mass of cells inside the egg destined to become a caterpillar.

EMIGRANT. A butterfly that leaves an area, usually embarking on a long-distance flight.

ESTIVATE. To spend the summer in an inactive state.

ETHYL ACETATE. A chemical used to kill butterflies.

EVAPOTRANSPIRATION. The loss of moisture to the atmosphere due to evaporation.

EVERGREEN. A tree or shrub that keeps its leaves year-round, often a conifer.

EXCRETORY. Pertaining to structures that rid a caterpillar's body of waste products.

EXOSKELETON. The hard outer covering of an insect's body, composed of chitin.

EXTRALIMITAL. Outside of a species' usual distribution.

FAT BODY. Globular structures in an insect's abdomen used to store energy-rich fats and oils.

FEMUR. The second segment of an insect's leg. (Plural: *femora*).

FOLD (as in costal fold or anal fold). A folded-over portion of a butterfly's wing, thought to house scales or hairs that emit chemicals employed during courtship.

FOREWING. The forward wing of each pair.

FRASS. The solid excretory product of caterpillars.

FRENULUM. A series of hooks that holds a moth's forewing and hindwing together in flight.

FUMIGANT. A chemical, usually napthalene or paradichlorbenzene, used to protect insect collections from "museum pests."

GENITALIA. The structures used in mating.

GLASSINE. A translucent material used to store unmounted butterfly specimens.

GRAVID. Pertaining to female butterflies when carrying eggs.

HABITAT. The place where a butterfly may find all of its necessary resources — its home.

HAMMOCK. Groves of trees, usually evergreen, surrounded by brush or marsh habitat.

HEMIMETABOLA. Insects that have an incomplete life cycle, i.e., egg, nymph, adult. See **HOLOMETABOLA**.

HEMOLYMPH. The circulatory fluid of insects.

HERBACEOUS. Plants that lack woody stems, often but not always annual.

HERBICIDE. A chemical used to kill plants.

HIBERNATION. The process of overwintering in an inactive or torpid condition.

HINDWING. The rear wing of each pair.

HOLOMETABOLA. Insects that have a complete life cycle; i.e., egg, larva, pupa, adult. See **HEMIMETABOLA**.

HOLARCTIC. Native to both North America and Eurasia.

IMMIGRANT. A butterfly that enters an area, often after a long-distance flight.

INNER MARGIN. The trailing, or hind, edge of the forewing (see Figure 2, p. 6).

INSECTICIDE. A chemical used to kill insects.

INSTAR. A caterpillar stage between molts.

INVERTEBRATE. An animal that lacks a backbone.

LABIAL PALPUS. The mouth part that lies outside the coiled proboscis of adult butterflies. (Plural: *palpi*.)

LARVA. The eating and growth stage of butterflies, i.e., the caterpillar. (Plural: *larvae*.)

MARGINAL. Pertaining to the outer margin of the wing (see Figure 2, p. 6).

MEDIAL. Pertaining to the fourth wing vein and its three branches (see Figure 3, p. 7).

MEDIAN. The area of a butterfly's wing halfway between the base and apex.

MESOTHORAX. The central portion of the thorax, with which the forewings and middle pair of legs articulate.

METATHORAX. The rear portion of the thorax with which the hindwings and rear pair of legs move.

MIGRANT. An insect that makes regular two-way long-distance flights.

MOLTING. The process by which a caterpillar sheds its exoskeleton; also termed *ecdysis*.

NAPTHALENE. A chemical fumigant.

NECTAR. The sugary fluid secreted by flowers of many plants. The principal food of many kinds of adult butterflies.

NOCTURNAL. Active at night.

NUDUM. The inner part of the antennal club, bare or sparsely covered with scales.

OMMATIDIUM. One of the visual elements that make up an insect's compound eye. (Plural: *ommatidia*.)

OUTER MARGIN. The outer edge of a butterfly's wing (see Figure 2, p. 6).

OVIPOSIT. To deposit one or more eggs.

OVIPOSITION. The process of depositing eggs.

PALPUS. An insect mouthpart; herein usually a labial palp.

PARADICHLORBENZENE (PDB). A chemical fumigant.

PARASITE. A small animal that lives on and feeds on a larger animal.

PARASITOIDISM. Feeding by insect parasites on another insect's immature stages.

PATROLLING. A mate-locating behavior of butterflies characterized by males flying through likely habitat in search of receptive females.

PERCHING. A mate-locating behavior of butterflies characterized by males perching on objects or spaces by which receptive females are likely to pass.

PERENNIAL. Plants that live two or more years.

PESTICIDE. A chemical agent used to kill pest organisms.

POSTBASAL. That part of the wing that lies just beyond the base (see Figure 2, p. 6).

POSTMEDIAN. That part of the wing that lies just beyond the central, or median, portion (see Figure 2, p. 6).

PROBOSCIS. The coiled tube through which adult butterflies imbibe nectar and other fluids.

PROLEG. One of the front pair of legs.

PROTEINACEOUS. Composed of proteins.

PULVILLUS. The pad between the tarsal claws of an adult butterfly's leg.

PUPA. The resting stage within which a caterpillar transforms to an adult. (Plural: *pupae*.)

PUPATE. To form a pupa or chrysalis; to pass through a pupal stage.

RADIAL VEINS. Butterfly wing veins that terminate in the apical area (see Figure 3, p. 7).

REHYDRATE. To restore the former moisture content.

SEGMENT. One of the ringlike units of a caterpillar or an adult butterfly's abdomen.

SETA. The hair or scale of a caterpillar or adult butterfly. (Plural: *setae*.)

SPIRACLE. A circular or oval breathing hole along the side of a caterpillar or adult butterfly.

STIGMA. A group of specialized scales on the forewing of most male branded skippers.

SUBAPICAL. Just inward from the apical part of the wing (see Figure 2, p. 6).

SUBARCTIC. Those habitats or environments that lie just below the Arctic Circle.

SUBCOSTAL VEIN. The second wing vein, unbranched (see Figure 3, p. 7).

SUBDORSAL. Referring to marks or stripes on a caterpillar just below the dorsal area.

SUBMARGINAL. That part of the wing that lies between the median and postbasal areas (see Figure 2, p. 6).

SUCTORIAL. Capable of sucking.

TAIGA. A broad zone of stunted trees, lakes, and bogs lying south of the tundra.

TARSAL CLAW. The claw at the end of an insect's leg.

TARSUS. The last portion of an insect's leg, composed of several segments.

TERRITORIALITY. A behavior by which a male protects and occupies a specific piece of landscape.

THERMOREGULATION. The process of regulating body temperature.

THORAX. The central portion of an insect's body.

TIBIA. That part of an insect's leg lying between the femur and tarsus. (Plural: *tibiae*.)

TIMBERLINE. The line above which trees cannot grow.

TORNUS. The wing angle between the outer and inner margins (see Figure 2, p. 6).

TRANSLUCENT. Capable of transmitting light, but not a clear image.

TROPICAL. Occurring between the Tropic of Cancer and Tropic of Capricorn; occurring in tropical environments.

TUBERCLE. A small, rounded projection on the body surface.

TUNDRA. An arctic or alpine environment with dense growths of short herbaceous vegetation.

ULTRAVIOLET. Light characterized by short wavelengths, some of which are beyond the visible range.

References

General

Brewer, Jo, and Winter, Dave. 1986. *Butterflies and Moths—a Companion to Your Field Guide*. New York: Phalarope Books.

Douglas, M. M. 1986. *The Lives of Butterflies*. Ann Arbor: University of Michigan Press.

Edwards, William Henry. 1868–1897. *The Butterflies of North America*. 3 vols. Philadelphia: American Entomological Society, Vol. 1; Boston: Houghton Mifflin Co., Vols. 2 & 3.

Ferris, C. D., ed. 1989. *Supplement to: A Catalogue/Checklist of the Butterflies of America North of Mexico*. Lepidopterists' Memoir No. 3.

Glassberg, J. (ed.) 1995. *The North American Butterfly Association Checklist and English Names of North American Butterflies*. North American Butterfly Association.

Howe, W. H. 1975. *The Butterflies of North America*. Garden City, N.Y.: Doubleday and Co.

Klots, A. B. 1951. *A Field Guide to the Butterflies of Eastern North America*. Boston: Houghton Mifflin Co.

Miller, J. Y. (ed.) 1991. *The Common Names of North American Butterflies*. Washington, D.C.: Smithsonian Institution Press.

Miller, L. D., and Brown, F. M. 1981. *Catalog/Checklist of the Butterflies of North America*. Lepidopterists' Society Memoir No. 2.

Mitchell, Robert T., and Zim, Herbert S. 1962. *Butterflies and Moths*. New York: Golden Press.

Opler, P. A., and Krizek, G. O. 1984. *Butterflies East of the Plains*. Baltimore: Johns Hopkins University Press.

Pyle, R. M. 1981. *The Audubon Society Field Guide to North American Butterflies*. New York: Chanticleer Press.

Scott, J. A. 1986. *The Butterflies of North America.* Stanford, Calif.: Stanford University Press.

Scudder, Samuel H. 1889. *The Butterflies of the Eastern United States and Canada with Special Reference to New England.* Cambridge, Mass.: Samuel Scudder.

STATE AND REGIONAL

Allen, T. J. 1997. *A Field Guide to the Butterflies of West Virginia.* Division of Natural Resources, Morgantown, W. Va.

Bethune, C. J. S. 1894. "Butterflies of the Eastern Provinces of Canada." *25th Annual Report, Entomological Society of Ontario.* 1894: 29–44.

Brower, A. E. 1974. *A List of the Lepidoptera of Maine. Part 1: The Macrolepidoptera.* Life Sciences and Agricultural Station Technical Bulletin No. 66. Orono, Me.: University of Maine.

Clark, Austin H. 1932. *The Butterflies of the District of Columbia and Vicinity.* United States National Museum Bulletin No. 157.

———, and Clark, Leila F. 1951. *The Butterflies of Virginia.* Smithsonian Miscellaneous Collection No. 116.

Comstock, W. P. 1940. "Butterflies of New Jersey." *Journal of the New York Entomological Society* 48:47–84.

Covell, Charles V., Jr., and Straley, Gerald B. 1973. "Notes on Virginia Butterflies, with two new state records." *Journal of the Lepidopterists' Society* 27:144–154.

Drees, Bastian M., and Butler, L. 1978. "Rhopalocera of West Virginia." *Journal of the Lepidopterists' Society* 32:198–206.

Ebner, James A. 1970. *Butterflies of Wisconsin.* Milwaukee Public Museum Popular Science Handbook No. 12.

Ely, Charles A., Marvin D. Schwilling, and Marvin E. Rolfs. 1986. *An Annotated List of the Butterflies of Kansas.* Fort Hays Studies; Third Series (Science) No. 7. Hays, Kansas: Fort Hays Studies Committee.

Fales, John H. 1974. "Check-list of the skippers and butterflies of Maryland." *Chesapeake Science* 15(4):222–229.

Ferguson, Douglas C. 1955. *The Lepidoptera of Nova Scotia. Part 1: Macrolepidoptera.* Nova Scotia Museum of Science Bulletin No. 1.

Fiske, W. F. 1901. *An Annotated Catalogue of the Butterflies of New Hampshire.* New Hampshire College Agricultural Experiment Station, Technical Bulletin No. 1.

Harris, Lucien, Jr. 1972. *Butterflies of Georgia.* Norman, Okla.: University of Oklahoma Press.

Heitzman, J. Richard, and Heitzman, Joan E. 1987. *Butterflies and Moths of Missouri*. Jefferson City, Mo.: Conservation Commission of the State of Missouri.

Holmes, Anthony M. 1983. *The Occurrence and Distribution of Ontario Butterflies*. Toronto: published by the author.

Iftner, D.; Shuey, J.; and Calhoun, J. 1992. *Butterflies and Skippers of Ohio*. Ohio Biological Survey.

Irwin, Roderick R., and Downey, John C. 1973. *Annotated Checklist of the Butterflies of Illinois*. Illinois Natural History Survey Biological Notes No. 81.

Jones, Frank Morton, and Kimball, Charles P. 1943. *The Lepidoptera of Nantucket and Martha's Vineyard Islands, Massachusetts*. Nantucket Maria Mitchell Association publication No. 4.

Kimball, Charles P. 1965. *The Lepidoptera of Florida*. Gainesville: Florida Department of Agriculture.

Klassen, P.; Westwood, A. R.; Preston, W. B.; and McKillop, W. B. 1989. *The Butterflies of Manitoba*. Winnipeg: Manitoba Museum of Man and Nature.

Lambremont, E. N. 1954. "The Butterflies and Skippers of Louisiana." *Tulane Studies in Zoology* 1:127–164.

Layberry, Ross A.; LaFontaine, J. D.; and Hall, P.W. 1982. "Butterflies of the Ottawa District." *Trail and Landscape* 16:3–59.

McGuire, William C., and Rickard, M. 1974. *An Annotated Checklist of the Butterflies of Bentsen-Rio Grande Valley State Park and Vicinity*. Mission, Texas: Texas Parks and Wildlife Dept.

Majka, C. 1972. *A Checklist of New Brunswick Rhopalocera*. Sackville, New Brunswick: Mt. Allison University.

Mather, Bryant, and Mather, K. 1958. "The Butterflies of Mississippi." *Tulane Studies in Zoology* 6:63–109.

Moore, Sherman. 1960. *A Revised Annotated List of the Butterflies of Michigan*. Occasional paper of the Museum of Zoology, University of Michigan 617:1–39.

Morris, Ray F. 1980. *Butterflies and Moths of Newfoundland and Labrador*. Agriculture Canada, Research Branch, Publication No. 1691.

Nelson, John. 1979. "A Preliminary Checklist of the Skippers and Butterflies of Oklahoma." *Proceedings of the Oklahoma Academy of Sciences* 59:41–46.

Nielsen, Mogens C. 1970. "Distributional Maps for Michigan Butterflies, Part 1." *Mid-Continent Lepidoptera Series* 1:1–10.

Pavulaan, Harry. 1985. "Field Survey of the True Butterflies (Papilionoidea) of Rhode Island." *Journal of the Lepidopterists Society* 39:19–25.

————. 1990. "The Skippers (Hesperioidea) of Rhode Island with recent records of the True Butterflies (Papilionoidea)." *Atala* 16:6–13.

Riotte, J. C. E. 1971. "Butterflies and Skippers of Northern Ontario." *Mid-Continent Lepidoptera Series* 2(21):1–21.

Rosche, Richard C. 1986. *Nebraska Butterfly Distribution Maps.* Chadron, Neb.: Published by the author.

Royer, Ronald Alan. 1988. *Butterflies of North Dakota.* Science Monograph No. 1. Minot, N.D.: Minot State University.

Sedman, Yale, and Hess, David F. 1985. *The Butterflies of West Central Illinois.* Series in the Biological Sciences No. 11. Macomb, Ill.: Western Illinois University.

Shapiro, Arthur M. 1966. *Butterflies of the Delaware Valley.* Philadelphia, Pa.: American Entomological Society Special Publication.

Shapiro, Arthur M. 1974. "Butterflies and Skippers of New York State." *Search* 4:1–60.

Shull, Ernest M. 1987. *The Butterflies of Indiana.* Indianapolis: Indiana Academy of Science.

Tietz, H. M. 1952. *The Lepidoptera of Pennsylvania.* University Park, Pa.: Pennsylvania Agricultural Experiment Station.

DIRECTORY OF BUTTERFLY SOCIETIES AND DEALERS

BUTTERFLY HOUSES AND INSECT ZOOS

Butterfly Place, Papillion Park, 120 Tyngsboro Road, Westford, MA 01886

Butterfly World, Tradewinds Park, 3600 W. Sample Road, Coconut Creek, FL 33037

Day Butterfly Center, Callaway Gardens, Pine Mountain, GA 31822

Houston Museum of Natural Science, One Hermann Circle Drive, Houston, TX 77030

Metro Toronto Zoo, P.O. Box 280, West Hill, ONT M1 E 4R5

Smithsonian Institution, Washington, DC 20560. Live insect zoos and interpretation are located in Natural History Museum and National Zoo.

Wings of Wonder, Cypress Gardens, P.O. Box 1, Cypress Gardens, FL 33884

World of Insects Exhibit, Cincinnati Zoo, 3400 Vine Street, Cincinnati, OH 45220

SUPPLY HOUSES

BioQuip Products, 17803 LaSalle Avenue, Gardena, CA 90248. Extensive line of equipment, supplies, and books; insect labels printed to order.

Carolina Biological Supply Co., Burlington, NC 27215. Wide range of equipment, supplies, and books.

Clo Wind Company, 827 Congress Avenue, Pacific Grove, CA 93950. Aerial butterfly nets, sweep nets, and insect pins.

Combined Scientific Supplies, P.O. Box 1446, Fort Davis, TX 79734. Limited to insect boxes, glassine envelopes, spreading boards, pins, vials, and specimens.

Complete Scientific Supplies, P.O. Box 307, Round Lake, IL 60073. Insect cases, boxes, envelopes, Riker mounts, insect pins, and specimens.

E.W. Classey, Ltd., P.O. Box 93, Faringdon, Oxon. SN7 7DR, England. Limited to publications. Excellent inventory of new used books and pamphlets, many on butterflies.

Entomological Reprint Specialists, P.O. Box 77224, Dockweiler Station, Los Angeles, CA 90007. Wide range of entomological publications.

Flora & Fauna Books, P.O. Box 3004, Seattle, WA 98114. New and used books in all fields of natural history.

Flora and Fauna Publications, 4300 NW 23rd Avenue, Suite 100, Gainesville, FL 32606. Publishes books on many aspects of natural history, especially insects.

Ianni Butterfly Enterprises, P.O. Box 81171, Cleveland, OH 44181. Limited to insect pins, envelopes, insect cases, Riker mounts, fumigant boxes, books, and specimens.

Insect Museum Supply, 1021 8th Avenue South, Moorhead, MN 56560. Insect labels and insect pins.

Lane Science Equipment Corp., 225 West 34th Street, Suite 1412, New York, NY 10122. Insect drawers and cases.

Nasco, 901 Janesville Avenue, Ft. Atkinson, WI 53538; Nasco West, 1524 Princeton Avenue, Modesto, CA 93552. A variety of entomological supplies and equipment.

Student Science Service, 622 W Colorado Street, Glendale, CA 91204. Chemicals, dissection instruments, forceps, fumigants, killing jars, pinning blocks, spreading boards, vials, etc.

Ward's Natural Science Establishment, 5100 West Henrietta Road, P.O. Box 92912, Rochester, NY 14692. Wide range of equipment, supplies, and books.

Wedge Entomological Research Foundation, c/o Ronald H. Hodges, MRC 127, National Museum of Natural History, Washington, DC 20560. Publishes *Moths of North America*.

Wildlife Publications, Inc., 1014 NW 14th Avenue, Gainesville, FL 32601. Devoted to natural history publications, including butterflies.

ORGANIZATIONS DEVOTED TO LEPIDOPTERA:

High Country Lepidopterists, c/o Paul A. Opler, P. O. Box 2662, Loveland, CO 80539. Devoted to the study and conservation of Lepidoptera of the high plains and Rocky Mountain states. Annual meeting.

Holarctic Lepidoptera Society, c/o John B. Heppner, P.O. Box

141210, Gainesville, FL 32614. Publishes *Holarctic Lepidoptera*.

Idalia Society of Mid-American Lepidopterists, c/o Suzette Slocomb, 219 W 68th Street, Kansas City, MO 64113. Publishes a newsletter.

Nebraska Lepidopterist Newsletter, c/o Steve Spomer, 1235 N 50th Street, Lincoln, NE 68504.

New York City Butterfly Club, c/o Guy Tudor, 111-14 76th Avenue, #107, Forest Hills, NY 11375. Devoted to butterfly watching and photography. Publishes *The Mulberry Wing*.

North American Butterfly Association, 4 Delaware Road, Morristown, NJ 07960. Publishes *American Butterflies* and *The Anglewing*.

Society of Kentucky Lepidopterists, c/o Charles V. Covell, Jr., Department of Biology, University of Louisville, Louisville, KY 40292. Publishes *Kentucky Lepidopterist*.

The Lepidoptera Research Foundation, c/o Santa Barbara Museum of Natural History, 2559 Puesta Del Sol Road, Santa Barbara, CA 93105. Publishes *Journal of Research on the Lepidoptera*.

The Lepidopterists' Society, c/o Robert J. Borth, Treasurer, 6926 North Belmont Lane, Fox Point, WI 53217. Publishes *Journal of the Lepidopterists' Society*, *News of the Lepidopterists' Society*, and *Memoirs*.

The Ohio Lepidopterists, c/o Eric Metzler, 1241 Kildale Square North, Columbus, OH 43229. Publishes The *Ohio Lepidopterist* and sells a wide variety of publications and equipment.

The Southern Lepidopterists' Society, c/o Jeff Slotten, 5421 N.W. 69th Lane, Gainesville, FL 32653. Publishes *Southern Lepidopterists' News*.

ORGANIZATIONS DEVOTED TO INSECTS, INCLUDING LEPIDOPTERA:

Entomological Society of America, 9301 Annapolis Road, Suite 300, Lanham, MD 20706. Publishes many entomological journals and monographs, including *American Entomologist* and *Annals of the Entomological Society of America*.

Entomological Society of Canada, 1320 Carling Avenue, Ottawa, Ontario, Canada K1Z 7K9. Publishes *Canadian Entomologist* and *Memoirs*.

Entomological Society of Ontario, Department of Environmental Biology, University of Guelph, Guelph, Ont., Canada

N1 G 2W1 . Publishes *Proceedings of the Entomological Society of Ontario.*

Entomological Society of Washington, Department of Entomology, NHB 168, Smithsonian Institution, Washington, DC 20560. Publishes *Proceedings of the Entomological Society of Washington.*

Kansas Entomological Society, P.O. Box 368, Lawrence, KS 66044. Publishes *Journal of the Kansas Entomological Society.*

Maryland Entomological Society, c/o Edgar A. Cohen, 5454 Marsh Hawk Way, Columbia, MD 21045. Publishes *Maryland Entomologist* and *Phaeton.*

Société Entomologique du Québec, a/s Claude Bouchard, Complex Scientifique, D.I. 300.6, 2700, rue Einstein, Sainte Foy, Québec, Canada G1 P 3W8. Publishes *Revue d'Entomologie du Québec.*

Sonoran Arthropod Studies, Inc. (SASI), P.O. Box 5624, Tucson, AZ 85703. Publishes *Backyard Bugwatching.*

The American Entomological Society, 1900 Race Street, Philadelphia, PA 19103. Publishes *Entomological News* and *Memoirs.*

The Florida Entomological Society, P.O. Box 7326, Winter Haven, FL 33883. Publishes *The Florida Entomologist.*

The Xerces Society, 4828 Southeast Hawthorne Boulevard, Portland, OR 97215. Devoted to conservation of invertebrates on an international basis. Publishes *Atala, Fourth of July Butterfly Count* reports, and *Wings.*

Young Entomologists' Society, 1915 Peggy Place, Lansing, MI 48910. Publications and other educational items for young persons.

4-H Clubs. For teenagers and younger children. University Agricultural Extension offices sponsor local 4-H Clubs. Entomology study projects can be organized if there is interest and a leader can be found. Ask your county farm adviser for information.

COLLECTING GUIDELINES

The authors' suggestions on proper conduct and procedures in collecting butterflies appear on p. 14.

Because of environmental concerns and implications of the Federal Endangered Species Act, and following a poll of the membership, The Lepidopterists' Society appointed a committee in 1980 to establish guidelines for collecting of butterflies and moths, and related activities. The report prepared by this Committee under the chairmanship of Dave Winter was approved by the Executive Council and published in 1982.

THE LEPIDOPTERISTS' SOCIETY STATEMENT OF THE COMMITTEE ON COLLECTING POLICY

PREAMBLE

Our ethical responsibility to assess and preserve natural resources, for the maintenance of biological diversity in perpetuity, and for the increase of knowledge, requires that lepidopterists examine the rationale and practices of collecting Lepidoptera, for the purpose of governing their own activities.

To this end, the following guidelines are outlined, based on these premises:

Lepidoptera are a renewable natural resource.

Any interaction with a natural resource should be in a manner not harmful to the perpetuation of that resource.

The collection of Lepidoptera:
- is a means of introducing children and adults to awareness and study of their natural environment;
- has an essential role in the elucidation of scientific information, both for its own sake and as a basis from which to develop rational means for protecting the environment, its

resources, human health and the world food supply;
- is a recreational activity which can generally be pursued in a manner not detrimental to the resource involved.

GUIDELINES

Purposes of Collecting (consistent with the above):
- To create a reference collection for study and appreciation.
- To document regional diversity, frequency, and a variability of species, and as voucher material for published records.
- To document faunal representation in environments undergoing or threatened with alteration by man or natural forces.
- To complement a planned research endeavor.
- To aid in dissemination of educational information.
- To augment understanding of taxonomic and ecologic relationships for medical and economic purposes.

RESTRAINTS AS TO NUMBERS

- Collection (of adults or of immature states) should be limited to sampling, not depleting, the population concerned; numbers collected should be consistent with, and not excessive for, the purpose of the collecting.
- When collecting where the extent and/or the fragility of the population is unknown, caution and restraint should be exercised.

COLLECTING METHODS

- Field collecting should be selective. When consistent with the reasons for the particular collecting, males should be taken in preference to females.
- Bait or light traps should be live-traps and should be visited regularly; released material should be dispersed to reduce predation by birds.
- The use of Malaise or other killing traps should be limited to planned studies.

LIVE MATERIAL

- Rearing to elucidate life histories and to obtain series of immature stages and adults is to be encouraged, provided that collection of the rearing stock is in keeping with these guidelines.
- Reared material in excess of need should be released, but only in the region where it originated, and in suitable habitat.

ENVIRONMENTAL AND LEGAL CONSIDERATIONS

- Protection of the supporting habitat must be recognized as the sine qua non of protection of a species.

- Collecting should be performed in a manner such as to minimize trampling or other damage to the habitat or to specific food plants.
- Property rights and sensibilities of others must be respected (including those of photographers and butterfly-watchers).
- Regulations relating to publicly controlled areas and to individual species and habitats must be complied with.
- Compliance with agricultural, customs, medical and other regulations should be attained prior to importing live material.

RESPONSIBILITY FOR COLLECTED MATERIAL
- All material should be preserved with full data attached, including parentage of immatures when known.
- All material should be protected from physical damage and deterioration, as by light, molds, and museum pests.
- Collections or specimens, and their associated written and photographic records, should be willed or offered to the care of an appropriate scientific institution, if the collector lacks space or loses interest, or in anticipation of death.
- Type specimens, especially holotype or allotype, should be deposited in appropriate scientific institutions.

RELATED ACTIVITIES OF COLLECTORS
- Collecting should include permanently recorded field notes regarding habitat, conditions, and other pertinent information.
- Recording of observations of behavior and of biological interactions should receive as high priority as collecting.
- Photographic records, with full data, are to be encouraged.
- Education of the public regarding collecting and conservation, as reciprocally beneficial activities, should be undertaken whenever possible.

TRAFFIC IN LEPIDOPTERAN SPECIMENS
- Collection of specimens for exchange or sale should be performed in accordance with these guidelines.
- Rearing of specimens for exchange or sale should be from stock obtained in a manner consistent with these guidelines and so documented.
- Mass collecting of Lepidoptera for commercial purposes, and collection or use of specimens for creation of saleable artifacts, are not included among the purposes of the Society.

From the NEWS of the Lepidopterists' Society, No. 5, Sept./Oct. 1982. Reproduced with permission.

INDEX TO HOST AND
NECTAR PLANTS

INDEX TO BUTTERFLIES

THE PETERSON SERIES®

PETERSON FIELD GUIDES®

PLANTS

EDIBLE WILD PLANTS (23) Eastern and central North America 31870-X
EASTERN TREES (11) North America east of 100th meridian 90455-2
FERNS (10) Northeastern and central North America, British Isles and
Western Europe 19431-8
MEDICINAL PLANTS (40) Eastern and central North America 92066-3
MUSHROOMS (34) North America 91090-0
PACIFIC STATES WILDFLOWERS (22) Washington, Oregon, California, and
adjacent areas 91095-1
ROCKY MOUNTAIN WILDFLOWERS (14) Northern Arizona and New Mexico to
British Columbia 18324-3
TREES AND SHRUBS (11A) Northeastern and north-central U.S. and south-
eastern and south-central Canada 35370-X
WESTERN TREES (44) Western U.S. and Canada 90454-4
**WILDFLOWERS OF NORTHEASTERN AND NORTH-
CENTRAL NORTH AMERICA** (17) 91172-9
SOUTHWEST AND TEXAS WILDFLOWERS (31) 36640-2

EARTH AND SKY

GEOLOGY (48) Eastern North America 66326-1
ROCKS AND MINERALS (7) North America 91096-X
STARS AND PLANETS (15) 91099-4
ATMOSPHERE (26) 33033-5

REPTILES AND AMPHIBIANS

EASTERN REPTILES AND AMPHIBIANS (12) Eastern and
central North America 90452-8

WESTERN REPTILES AND AMPHIBIANS (16) Western North America, including
Baja California 38253-X

SEASHORE

SHELLS OF THE ATLANTIC (3) Atlantic and Gulf coasts
and the West Indies 69779-4
PACIFIC COAST SHELLS (6) North American Pacific coast, including Hawaii
and the Gulf of California 18322-7
ATLANTIC SEASHORE (24) Bay of Fundy to Cape Hatteras 31828-9
CORAL REEFS (27) Caribbean and Florida 46939-2
SOUTHEAST AND CARIBBEAN SEASHORES (36) Cape Hatteras to the Gulf Coast,
Florida, and the Caribbean 46811-6

AUDIO AND VIDEO

EASTERN BIRDING BY EAR
cassettes 50087-7
CD 71258-0

WESTERN BIRDING BY EAR
cassettes 52811-9
CD 71257-2

EASTERN BIRD SONGS, Revised
cassettes 53150-0
CD 50257-8

WESTERN BIRD SONGS, Revised
cassettes 51746-X
CD 51745-1

BACKYARD BIRDSONG
cassettes 58416-7
CD 71256-4

MORE BIRDING BY EAR
cassettes 71260-2
CD 71259-9

WATCHING BIRDS
Beta 34418-2
VHS 34417-4

PETERSON'S MULTIMEDIA GUIDES: NORTH AMERICAN BIRDS
(CD-ROM for Windows) 73056-2

PETERSON FLASHGUIDES™

ATLANTIC COASTAL BIRDS	79286-X
PACIFIC COASTAL BIRDS	79287-8
EASTERN TRAILSIDE BIRDS	79288-6
WESTERN TRAILSIDE BIRDS	79289-4
HAWKS	79291-6
BACKYARD BIRDS	79290-8
TREES	82998-4
MUSHROOMS	82999-2
ANIMAL TRACKS	82997-6
BUTTERFLIES	82996-8
ROADSIDE WILDFLOWERS	82995-X
BIRDS OF THE MIDWEST	86733-9
WATERFOWL	86734-7
FRESHWATER FISHES	86713-4

WORLD WIDE WEB: http://www.petersononline.com

PETERSON FIELD GUIDES can be purchased at your local
bookstore or by calling our toll-free number, (800) 225-3362.

When referring to title by corresponding ISBN number,
preface with 0-395.